July 1, 2024

For Jerry & Anne,

Love, Susan

& Thanks to Jerry for sponsoring conference

Public Administration and Expertise in Democratic Governments

This collection deals with challenges confronting public law and public administration in twenty-first century democracies across the world. It draws together contributions from leading scholars, examining cutting-edge topics, and projecting the scholarship forward. It emphasizes the importance both of justifying executive policymaking to citizens and of drawing on bureaucratic expertise and professional competence. Contributors examine the role of courts and argue for new forms of public participation that can incorporate democratic values into executive-branch policymaking. Finally, the work confronts problems in the administration of the criminal law that are generating increased public concern. Building on Rose-Ackerman's scholarship, writers compare the American experience with contemporary developments in other leading democracies—in particular, Germany, France, the EU, Canada, and Latin America. The work will be an invaluable resource for academics, researchers and policymakers working in the area of Administrative Law, Public Law, and Political Science.

Susan Rose-Ackerman is Henry R. Luce Professor Emeritus of Law and Political Science, Yale University. She has published widely on comparative administrative law and the political economy of corruption.

Routledge Research in Public Law

Available titles in this series include:

Rule of Law in Crisis
Constitutionalism in a State of Flux
Edited by Martin Belov

Lawfare and Judicial Legitimacy
The Judicialisation of Politics in the case of South Africa
Kate Dent

Public Administration and Expertise in Democratic Governments
Comparative Public Law in the Twenty-First Century
Edited by Susan Rose-Ackerman

Public Sector Performance, Corruption and State Capture in a Globalized World
Edited by Susan Rose-Ackerman

For more information about this series, please visit: https://www.routledge.com/Routledge-Research-in-Public-Law/book-series/RRIPL

Public Administration and Expertise in Democratic Governments

Comparative Public Law in the Twenty-First Century

Edited by Susan Rose-Ackerman

Routledge
Taylor & Francis Group
LONDON AND NEW YORK

First published 2024
by Routledge
4 Park Square, Milton Park, Abingdon, Oxon OX14 4RN

and by Routledge
605 Third Avenue, New York, NY 10158

Routledge is an imprint of the Taylor & Francis Group, an informa business

British Library Cataloguing-in-Publication Data
A catalogue record for this book is available from the British Library

Library of Congress Cataloging-in-Publication Data
Names: Rose-Ackerman, Susan, editor.
Title: Public administration and expertise in democratic governments : comparative public law in the twenty-first century/edited by Susan Rose-Ackerman.
Description: Abingdon, Oxon [UK] ; New York, NY : Routledge, 2024. | Series: Routledge research in public law | Includes bibliographical references and index. | Summary: — Provided by publisher.
Identifiers: LCCN 2023049458 | ISBN 9781032524283 (hardback) | ISBN 9781032542676 (paperback) | ISBN 9781003416036 (ebook)
Subjects: LCSH: Public law. | Public administration. | Administrative law.| Democracy. | Economic and Monetary Union.
Classification: LCC K3150 .P825 2024 | DDC 342—dc23/eng/20231023
LC record available at https://lccn.loc.gov/2023049458

ISBN: 978-1-032-52428-3 (hbk)
ISBN: 978-1-032-54267-6 (pbk)
ISBN: 978-1-003-41603-6 (ebk)

DOI: 10.4324/9781003416036

Typeset in Galliard
by Apex CoVantage, LLC

Contents

Contributors

Editor

Susan Rose-Ackerman is Henry R. Luce Professor Emeritus of Law and Political Science, Yale University. She has published widely on comparative administrative law, and the political economy of corruption.

Contributors

Blake Emerson is Professor of Law at UCLA. He is the author of a book and numerous articles on US public law. He served as a Research Fellow at the Administrative Conference of the United States, and he holds a JD and a Ph.D. in political science from Yale University.

Stefanie Egidy is a Professor of Law at the University of Mannheim, where she teaches constitutional and administrative law. She holds an LL.M. from Yale Law School and a doctorate from the University of Würzburg. She completed her Habilitation at the University of Bonn in 2023 while a Senior Research Fellow at the Max Planck Institute for Research on Collective Goods.

Maciej Kisilowski is Associate Professor of Law and Strategy at Central European University in Vienna. He co-founded the Social Contract Incubator (*Inkubator Umowy Społecznej* or *IUS*) – a non-partisan forum proposing a new democratic settlement for Poland. He holds a J.S.D. and an LL.M. He hold an LLM from Yale Law School, an M.P.A. from Princeton University and an M.B.A. from Insead.

Peter Lindseth is the Olimpiad S. Ioffe Professor of International and Comparative Law at the University of Connecticut, School of Law. He has published widely, both individually and with Susan Rose-Ackerman, on comparative administrative law.

Jud Mathews is Professor of Law and Political Science at Penn State University and Associate Dean for Academic Affairs at Penn State Law. He researches and teaches principally in the areas of administrative law, constitutional law, and comparative law. He holds a JD and a Ph.D. in Political Science from Yale University.

Edgar Andrés Melgar is a doctoral candidate in Near Eastern Studies at Princeton and a graduate of Yale Law School. His work explores the relationship between bureaucracy and public accountability in hyper-presidential regimes and in those with weak democratic norms. His dissertation traces the origins of technocracy, stressing expertise over popular participation, in the Middle East and Latin America.

Joana Mendes is Professor of Comparative and Administrative Law at the University of Luxembourg, specializing in Comparative Administrative Law and EU Law. She holds a doctorate from the European University Institute (Italy) and was a Fulbright Visiting Scholar at Yale Law School (2014). She is co-founder of *European Law Open* and was previously co-editor of the *European Law Journal.*

Anne Joseph O'Connell is the Adelbert H. Sweet Professor of Law at Stanford University. She is a presidentially appointed member of the Council of the Administrative Conference of the United States and an elected fellow of the American Academy of Arts and Sciences and the National Academy of Public Administration.

Thomas Perroud is Professor of Public Law at Panthéon-Assas University (CERSA) and a Humboldt Fellow (Experienced Researcher) at Humboldt University (Walter Hallstein Institute).

Athanasios (Akis) Psygkas is Associate Professor at the Faculty of Law at Western University in Canada, where he directs the Public Law Research Group. His research interests include comparative public law, law of democracy, regulation and governance, and he has advised international NGOs on these issues.

Matthias Rossbach is Head of the Representation of the German State of North Rhine-Westphalia in Berlin. He studied law at the Universities of Muenster and Cambridge, earned an LL.M. from Yale Law School (2012) and a doctorate in law from Humboldt University, Berlin (2018). His research focuses on German and US constitutional law, administrative law, constitutional history and theory, and comparative law.

Hans-Bernd Schäfer is Affiliate Professor of Law and Economics at Bucerius Law School and Professor Emeritus of Economics at the University of Hamburg, where he directed the Institute of Law and Economics. He has published widely on the economic analysis of law and on law and economic development. He was president of the European Association of Law and Economics, which awarded him the Scholar Prize.

Joshua Spannaus completed his first state examination in law at Justus-Liebig-University in Gießen in June 2023. Currently, he is a research assistant and doctoral candidate at the Chair of Public Law under Professor Gabriele Britz.

Peter Strauss is the Betts Professor of Law Emeritus at Columbia Law School. He is a noted scholar of administrative law and the editor of leading teaching materials on the subject. Many of his writings explicate American public law for those familiar with parliamentary democracies, reflecting a lifetime of teaching and lecturing about the subject abroad.

Editor's Preface

This volume is one of two that resulted from a 2022 conference in my honor, proposed by my Yale Law School colleague Jerry Mashaw and by two graduate students Ximena Benavides and Eugenio Garcia-Huidobro. The event was funded by a generous grant from the Law School's Oscar M. Ruebhausen Fund. It brought together many of my former students, several co-authors, and a fellow pioneer in the field of law and economics. This volume concentrates on contemporary issues in public law from a comparative perspective and reflects my own long-standing interest in the intersection between the law on the books and the institutional and political context in which it operates. A companion volume brings together authors writing on public sector performance and its links to corruption and state capture.

I am very pleased with the high quality of the contributions to both volumes. Especially meaningful to me was the chance for colleagues and students from different times and places in my career to meet and find common scholarly interests. The resulting discussions in the sessions and over breaks and meals were lively and fascinating. Needless to say, I am very proud and happy to have helped support the careers of such a wonderful collection of creative and committed scholars.

The conference was originally planned for the summer of 2020 and was delayed twice by the coronavirus pandemic. Jerry and I discussed holding a virtual conference online in 2021, but rejected that option as inconsistent with the goal of bringing people together whose main connection was a shared link to me and my scholarship. Renee DeMatteo stayed with the project from the beginning, and she was absolutely essential in keeping the project on track through the pandemic delays. My long-time administrative assistant, Cathy Orcutt, provided her usual high level of excellent and patient support for the organization of the event and management of the flows of draft papers. At present, Quiana Atkinson has very competently taken her place and has helped me to bring the book projects to fruition with grace and skill.

Peter Strauss generously welcomed me to Columbia Law School in the 1980s and supported my transition from law and economics to administrative law. Thus, he was the obvious choice to give a keynote address at the conference dinner. He stressed the contributions of my 2021 book: *Democracy and*

Executive Power: Policymaking Accountability the US, the UK, Germany, and France. The essence of those remarks has been incorporated into his introductory chapter along with snapshots of the subsequent chapters. At the end of the volume, Peter Lindseth, who organized two conferences with me on comparative administrative law, provides a chapter tying together many of the volume's contributions.

1 Introduction

Peter L. Strauss

These collected chapters on public law, written by Susan Rose-Ackerman's former students and colleagues, originated with a Festschrift given in her honor in August 2022. Each chapter both reflects and goes beyond aspects of Susan's own writing on public law and public policy. (A second volume, also resulting from that conference, builds on her research on corruption and public sector performance in a globalized world.) Crediting me with her introduction to public law at Columbia Law School,[1] she honored me with an invitation to deliver the keynote remarks for this remarkable conference, so appropriately celebrating her deep and wide-ranging scholarship. Converting those remarks into a Preface entailed what those remarks had not attempted: providing a guide to its many fine papers. Susan herself has provided those summaries and integrated them into my remarks, and for this I am deeply grateful.

As America's intellectual leader in comparative administrative law, Susan has spent decades asking what contemporary democracies can learn from one another about the development and implementation of policies that seek to protect the environment, promote public health and safety, suppress corruption, or redress the failures of the markets on which democracies generally depend for their day-to-day functioning.

In her recent book: *Democracy and Executive Power: Policymaking Accountability in the US, the UK, Germany, and France*, Susan thanks me and her Yale colleague, Jerry Mashaw, for accepting her as "an interloper from economics and public policy, as a colleague and friend in administrative law."[2] During her time at Colombia Law School in the 1980s, Susan, in turn, enriched my own work in public law through her deeply informed understandings of economics and political institutions, as well as law. In this introductory essay, I highlight the contributions of her recent book and show how this edited volume complements and extends themes prominent in *Democracy and Executive Power* and in other aspects of her research and teaching over the years.

To begin, her 2021 book concentrates on the way ordinary policymaking across the globe is carried out by executive-branch agencies and departments staffed by both political officials and career bureaucrats. She celebrates the

DOI: 10.4324/9781003416036-1

democratic potential of what we in America call "rulemaking" as a technique for the executive's generation of secondary legislation.

Reading Susan's book, I was struck by how well it parallels Jerry's splendid analysis in *Bureaucratic Justice* of the adjudications through which federal administrators resolve disputes over individual entitlements to certain welfare benefits.[3] Jerry identified three models by which those adjudications might be evaluated. The first is bureaucratic rationality in which costs are contained and errors in granting and denying claims are evenly distributed and tightly bunched. The second is reliance on the judgment and service commitments of professionals associated with these decisions—doctors, in his study—taking care to avoid the possible costs of disrespecting the profession's integrity. Finally, there is moral judgment, stressing fairness to the claimant and respect for her perspectives and dignity. As he wrote:

> If these hypotheses are correct, then it may also follow that the best system of administrative adjudication may be the one most open to criticism. A compromise that seeks to preserve the values and to respond at once to the insights of all of these conceptions of justice will, from the perspective of each separate conception, appear incoherent and unjust. The best system of administrative adjudication that can be devised may fall tragically short of our inconsistent ideals.[4]

I have long found these words a powerful evocation of the dilemmas of administrative adjudication.

Democracy and Executive Power brings similar wisdom to bear on the executive development of regulations to implement statutory directives. Susan analyzes this process in each of four contrasting Western democracies, reflecting her deep understanding of their political structures and prevailing ethos. For her, the central issue is reconciling democratic values with the claims of unelected bureaucrats to make policy, including those operating under politically appointed superiors. Part of her argument is that the so-called "chain of legitimacy" back to the voters is insufficient to assure the democratic legitimacy of policy.[5]

The development of regulations within the executive branch is a universal necessity of governance in this complex and interdependent world. In Western democracies, the subjects of her deep personal knowledge and study, that reconciliation depends on the relationship of the rulemaker, conceived as technocratic expert or bureaucrat, to the public directly and to democratic institutions overseeing their actions, legislative or executive. But this linkage is imperiled by the practical limits on legislative decision-making and oversight, and the consequences of these limits can be dramatic. On her analysis, then, I would put it this way:

> If her hypotheses are correct, then it may also follow that the best system of administrative rulemaking may be the one most open to criticism.

> A compromise that seeks to preserve the values and to respond at once to the insights of all of these conceptions will appear incoherent and unjust from the perspective of each separate conception. The best system of administrative rulemaking that can be devised may fall tragically short of our inconsistent ideals.

Like William Novak in his important recent book, *New Democracy: The Creation of the Modern American State*,[6] Susan finds fundamental elements of democracy in the public, interactive procedures that characterize American agencies' processes for rulemaking. They establish a relatively independent process for the development of secondary legislation (that is, regulations with legal force). The process begins with public notice of proposals, an opportunity for comment, followed by a statement of reasons and an opportunity for meaningful judicial review. Taken together, these provide an alternative democratic element to whatever electoral controls may constrain a powerful chief executive.

The Supreme Court term that ended in June 2022 denied the validity of two important federal regulations, regulations developed to protect workers and the environment, respectively, from the risks of the Covid-19 pandemic and of global warming.[7] The Court did this by invoking what has come to be called "the major questions doctrine," which requires clearly demonstrable authorization in the statutory language for the most consequential regulatory actions.[8] Fortunately, at least from my perspective, the decisions went no further. The Court invoked the doctrine again in the term ending in June 2023, to strike down President Biden's student-loan-forgiveness program, arguing that the wide-ranging action had not been authorized by the language of the relevant statute; Justice Barrett's concurrence suggested understanding the doctrine as the kind of "clear statement" constraint on delegations that has long characterized decisions of other national courts, notably in Germany.[9]

Of course, achieving statutory clarity presents its own challenges. The highly polarized US Congress is at best imperfectly representative of public wishes on important political issues—abortion, for example. The connection between democratic values and legislation, then, is at best imperfect. Legislatures may find it difficult to identify what level of instruction a future court will find sufficient to authorize a future regulatory response to an imperfectly anticipated need.

Are these recent Supreme Court decisions responsive to the threats that an overly powerful executive, even an elected one, presents to democracy? As America's recent experience has well illustrated, reliance on a political executive in itself can imperil democracy. And the courts, too, may be politicized, particularly if, as in the US, they are selected in a highly political way. Because Supreme Court Justices have life tenure once appointed, Presidents who nominate judges in their forties can project their political preferences decades into the future—and those preferences may not even reflect the democratic values prevailing at the time of nomination.

Nowhere does the success of Susan's intellectual marriage of economics and law shine more brightly than in the chapters of *Democracy and Executive Power* that discuss the values and limits of cost-benefit analysis and impact assessment, review public participation options for generating executive regulations, and assess the impact of judicial review.[10] Her discussion of the executive generation of policymaking norms is sensitive to the limits of cost-benefit analysis and impact assessment without rejecting them altogether. She points to their inattention to distributional consequences, to the ways in which past injustices can skew calculations, and to the interests of future generations so fundamental to debates over responses to the crisis of climate change. It is very refreshing, and a reflection of Susan's balance and wisdom, to find a trained economist underscoring the risks of reliance on analyses reflecting today's preferences. Her deep knowledge of administrative law as well as economics informs her understanding, as well, of the ways the governmental structures of the four countries influence the use of public participation in the regulatory process, as an element of democratic control, as well as the possible contributions and hazards of judicial review.

But what about the risks of an over-powerful political executive—hyper-presidentialism, as Susan describes it in a recent paper written with Edgar Andrés Melgar about executive policymaking in Latin America?[11] Presidential actions taken over decades have considerably undercut the impact of American rulemaking procedures, steadily moving outcome control from public agency processes to White House interventions—both explicit and unpublicized. Furthermore, one can see autocratic tendencies even in parliamentary and semi-presidential middle-European countries, such as Hungary and Poland, and in the pretensions of the Trump administration, as developed by Daniel Ziblatt and Steven Levitsky in *How Democracies Die*.[12]

The chapters that follow add nuance to the challenges facing all democracies, even those that are well established. They examine the tensions between professional bureaucratic administration and efforts to justify executive policymaking through concerted exercises in democratic accountability.

The contributions begin with **Blake Emerson**'s "What's Democratic about Administration?" which engages with the fundamental issue of enhancing the democratic pedigree of public administration in representative democracies. He argues that agencies should not merely be neutral sites for discussion within the government but should also actively engage in political deliberation in the public sphere. Officials ought to be not merely makers of policy but also guardians of collective rights, such as rights to public health and safety and to social equality. Next, **Jud Mathews and Joshua Spannaus** consider "The Lawfulness of Public Law in Germany and the United States." They defend German public law against the claim in *Democracy and Executive Power* that German rulemaking processes lack public accountability. The principal target of their chapter, however, is Philip Hamburger's assault on the American administrative state and his claim that it is an alien import from Bismarck's Germany.[13] Mathews and Spannaus back up their own claims through a careful analysis of administrative law in Germany after the restoration of democracy post-World War II. **Stefanie Egidy**'s "Administrative Resilience" assesses the importance of administrative resilience, a key requirement in the face of rapid real-world developments, such as the Covid-19 pandemic, the climate crisis, and the economic and social impact of military conflict, such as the war in the Ukraine. In stressing the importance of competent leadership, she echoes the concerns expressed by **Anne Joseph O'Connell**'s chapter on "Bureaucrats as Temporary Leaders" based on the US experience. Her well-documented paper demonstrates the widespread use of temporary leaders, their connection to the time-consuming and contested process of Senate approval for political appointees, and the large number of positions that turn over when the administration changes. Returning to the comparison between the US and Germany, **Matthias Rossbach**'s "The Creation of the Modern American Civil Service and the (Constitutional) Limits of German Influence" argues that the US civil service tradition, although influenced by UK and Germany models, has remained true to the distinctive US constitutional framework.

Administrative law intersects with the political imperatives of incumbents, some of whom may have little understanding or sympathy with the challenges of making policy and of administering public programs. In the US, the tension between presidential priorities and delegated policy obligations was manifestly evident during the Donald Trump administration, but **Thomas Perroud** in "The Neoliberal Turn of Contemporary French Administrative Law" points to related neoliberal tendencies in present-day French administrative law. He argues that these trends threaten to undermine the ability of the French state to perform the tasks assigned to it by constitutional and statutory law. He is particularly concerned that cost-benefit analysis and economic impact assessment will be counterproductive.

Joana Mendes shifts the focus from agency policymaking to the role of courts. In "Law and Monetary Policy: From Limited Judicial Review to Parliamentary Scrutiny in the European Monetary Union", she emphasizes that judges typically lack the professional background required to assess administrative policy decisions—particularly when those decisions require the application of sophisticated economic analysis. She argues that recent calls by US scholars to revisit the exceptional character of monetary policy in relation to public law could find some answers in the monetary policy judgments of the EMU. Mendes argues for heightened parliamentary scrutiny that could overcome the limitations of the current monetary dialogue. The goal is not to democratize monetary policy, but, rather, to expand the voices that influence policy decisions. Her conclusion supports the call in *Democracy and Executive Power* for new forms of public participation as a way to incorporate democratic values into expert administrative law decision-making.

Akis Psygkas in "Administrative Democracy and Federalism: The US, the EU, and Canada" connects participation to federalism. He posits a system in which the component entities face a minimum standard but are free to move beyond it to enhance public accountability. Some good practices may be subsequently "uploaded" onto the center and generalized. He explores these possibilities through the cases of the European Union (EU), the United States, and Canada.

Maciej Kisilowki faces a more specific problem in "From Election to Autocracy: Can Strategic Decentralization Bring Us Back?" He asks how a deeply divided polity can govern itself. His chapter examines the Polish case where the electoral system has given national power to conservative forces in spite of considerable public support for more progressive policies. His response is to reform the government to give more power to local or regional governments, essentially recognizing the diversity by building it into the structure of the state.

Next, extending beyond their prior work on Latin America, **Edgar Andrés Melgar and Susan Rose-Ackerman** assess "Judicial Review of the Executive in Hyper-Presidential Regimes" by considering the role of the judiciary in such systems. They argue that judicial independence and concern for democratic accountability are necessary but not sufficient to confront the authoritarian tendencies of hyper-presidential systems.

Hans-Bernd Schäfer, who pioneered the field of law and economics in Europe, considers "Equal versus Efficient Security against Crime: Differences and Unintended Consequences." Constitutional lawyers have proposed that crime fighting by public police should aim to provide equal security for all residents of a state. Schäfer shows that equal security can violate other important policy goals. It usually fails to reduce crime rates to the lowest possible level, given the police budget. It can lead to severe indirect discrimination against immigrants and minorities if it requires concentration of police forces in hot spots. Or it might require unreasonably high police budgets. Thus the chapter points to the inherent tension in efforts to balance equity and efficiency in criminal law enforcement.

Finally, **Peter Lindseth** in "Administration and Democracy" links the volume's contributions to his own deep engagement with the role of the judiciary as achieving "a reconciliation between, on the one hand, the inevitability of technocracy and juristocracy in administrative governance and, on the other, our deeply held commitments, inherited from the past, to democratic self-government through the mechanisms of political representation, whether legislative or executive." His focus on the essential role of the legislature reminds us that administrative law is embedded in each state's overall constitutional framework.

Susan's book and the fascinating chapters generated by the conference in her honor present a challenge to those who seek to build further on Susan's remarkable book and the additional issues raised here. Susan deals *only* with the four developed democracies of England, France, Germany and the United States. With civilian as well as common-law grounded systems in her sights, she was able to consider the ways in which government structure can influence the important questions of democracy and executive power, much more persuasively than a contemporary analysis limited to the US and the UK. However, the global variation in democratic forms and public law practices is much wider. Might others follow her more recent turn to the Latin American context of hyper-presidentialism? Can contemporary scholars bring the same questions to bear on other democracies with distinct characteristics and histories? Are democracies deeply threatened by a claimed worldwide trend of substituting autocracy for democracy? The executives in autocracies also have bureaucrats who draft regulations to implement statutory instructions. Are there important differences in the controls available to autocratic executives, as distinct from democratic ones? Might awareness of those difficulties help arrest the slide toward autocracy? What might contribute to the challenging trend toward the elevation of executive power and against democracy? Clearly, there is much work to be done to illuminate these developments. The body of Susan's work can help encourage that work in ways that assess and evaluate global developments. Political systems and historical legacies differ widely, but the relationship of citizens to the state is a global concern that requires sustained interdisciplinary study across borders.

Notes

1 Although my scholarship directed to readers outside the United States has generally been concerned with explaining American public law to those acquainted with parliamentary systems, Peter L. Strauss, *Administrative Justice in the United States* (Durham NH: Carolina Academic Press, 1998, 2002, 2016), Susan has done much to bring me into the comparative administrative law community, e.g. Peter L. Strauss, Politics and Agencies in the Administrative State: The U.S. Case (in Rose-Ackerman & Lindseth, eds., *Comparative Administrative Law* (London UK, Elgar 2017)).

2 Susan Rose-Ackerman, *Democracy and Executive Power: Policymaking Accountability in the US, the UK, Germany, and France* (New Haven CT: Yale University Press, 2021), p. x.

3 Jerry L. Mashaw, *Bureaucratic Justice: Managing Social Security Disability Claims* (New Haven CT: Yale University Press, 1983).

4 *Id.*, at 23.

5 Rose-Ackerman, *Democracy and Executive Power*, 3–4, 96–99.

6 William J. Novak, *New Democracy: The Creation of the Modern American State* (Cambridge MA: Harvard University Press, 2022).

7 National Federation of Independent Businesses v. OSHA, 597 U.S.__, 142 S. Ct. 661(vaccine case); West Virginia v. EPA, 597 U.S.__ (2022) (climate change case).

8 Nathan Richardson, "Anti-Deference: Covid, Climate and the Rise of the Major Questions Canon," *Virginia Law Review Online* 108: 174–206 (2022), https://virginialawreview.org/articles/antideference-covid-climate-and-the-rise-of-the-major-questions-canon/.

9 Biden v. Nebraska, 600 U.S.__ (2023). In dissent, Justice Kagan outlines reasons that Congress decides to delegate policy choices, including the executive's expertise and its ability to accommodate changing circumstances over time. She points as well to the practical reality that Congress cannot "do everything" when faced with a full agenda of pressing issues (id., Kagen, J. dissent).
10 Rose-Ackerman, *Democracy and Executive Power*, chapters 5 and 6, pp.122–183.
11 Susan Rose-Ackerman & Edgar Andrés Melgar, "Hyper-Presidential Administration: Executive Policymaking in Latin America," *Arizona Law Review* 64: 1097–1184 (2022).
12 Daniel Ziblatt & Steven Levitsky, *How Democracies Die* (New York: Crown, 2018).
13 Philip Hamburger, *Is Administrative Law Unlawful?* (Chicago: University of Chicago Press, 2014).

2 What's Democratic about Administration?

Blake Emerson

"The owl of Minerva takes flight only when the shades of night are gathering." So wrote the German philosopher G.W.F. Hegel in the preface to his 1821 lectures on law and the modern state, *Elements of the Philosophy of Right*. Hegel meant that we could only truly understand a political order when its time had come to an end. Some aspects of the regime-type Hegel described in Prussia have survived to the present day. Germany, the United States, and many other nations continue to rely on professional civil servants—what Hegel called "the universal estate"—to regulate economy and society under broad statutory authorities. But the great difference between nineteenth-century Prussia, on the one hand, and present-day Germany and the United States, on the other, has been the advent of democracy.[1] Popular sovereignty has worked a fundamental reorientation in the norms and practices not only of constitutional but also of administrative law. Bureaucracies are governed not by constitutional monarchs but rather by the people.

Two hundred years after Hegel's Berlin lectures, in the unstable and conflictual environment of contemporary Europe and the United States, one might wonder if Susan Rose-Ackerman's landmark, *Democracy and Executive Power*,[2] comes at another moment when "the shades of night are gathering"—this time on the project of democratic administration she describes and endorses. A leading scholar of comparative administrative law, policy reasoning, and democratic process, Rose-Ackerman shows deliberative-democratic administration expanding from the United States, where it has long had purchase to the United Kingdom, Germany, and France.

While participatory forms of administration policymaking may be gaining steam in Europe, the United States itself seems to be losing its grip on democratic norms. That is not because agencies have given up on reason-giving or because there is no hope of engaging the public effectively in rulemaking. Rather, as Rose-Ackerman notes, presidential administration threatens to displace deliberative democracy. During the Trump Administration, the very constitutional foundations of democracy were at risk. Less extreme but still serious problems have filtered down into the administrative process as well, as civil servants lose their independence and White House political dictates come to dominate administration policymaking.[3] Meanwhile, the Supreme Court,

DOI: 10.4324/9781003416036-2

enthralled by an anti-administrative ideology, is keen to squelch out agencies' authority to make important policy decisions.[4]

In this hostile environment, some scholars have lost faith in the project of democratic reason-giving. They have argued either for conflictual "agonism"[5] or have railed against administrative law's "procedure fetish" in favor of maximizing administrative discretion.[6] Some have sought to recenter administrative expertise or "competence," reinvigorating the model advanced by James Landis during the New Deal.[7]

While these critics have identified significant weak spots in contemporary administrative law and propose some promising avenues for reform, they abandon the project of participatory administration too quickly. Deliberative-democratic administration is more deeply rooted, well justified, and resilient than they suggest. But its form and content need to adapt in response to the inhospitable institutional landscape. As a procedural matter, we should begin to think of agencies not merely as neutral sites for democratic deliberation within the government but as *engaged participants* in political deliberation out in the public sphere. As a matter of substance, administrative officials ought to be not merely makers of policy but rather guardians of *collective rights*, such as rights of public health and safety and of social equality. We should both elevate the normative claims of agency action and shift their loci from the dreary halls of bureaus into the open spaces of the public square.

Part I of this chapter describes democratic proceduralism in US administrative law in its instrumental and deliberative variants. It explains the limits of each of these conceptions of democratic legitimacy in the present political landscape. Part II argues for a reconceptualization of democratic administration, in which agencies enter directly into political discourse to articulate and protect collective rights. Part III offers some procedural suggestions for how agencies might carry out this task in the face of an inimical Supreme Court.

Democratic Procedure in US Administrative Law

Administrative law in the United States has long been a procedural subject. Scholars and students focus on the Administrative Procedure Act of 1946 (APA), which categorizes administrative action in terms of rulemaking and adjudication and sets out the standards for judicial review. Such review has traditionally focused on how the agency reached its decision, not whether the decision was right or wrong. The scholarly reflex has been to analyze, either at a broad constitutional level or within the detailed bureaucratic latticework of agencies, the forms of policymaking and the allocation of authority amongst offices and institutions.

This procedural approach has been particularly prominent in analyzing the democratic legitimacy of administrative action. The specter of "unelected bureaucrats" making policy has inspired vociferous criticism of agencies as well as efforts to justify or reform such authority on democratic grounds. Focusing either on political control by elected officials, or on public participation in the administrative process, scholars and judges have examined whether and how bureaucracies may remain accountable to the public they regulate.

Democratic Instrumentalism

The first form of democratic procedure—call it democratic instrumentalism—treats administrative agencies as the literal "agents" of one or another representative body. Agencies are generally created and authorized by Congress, which is accountable to the people by way of elections. They are then generally supervised by an elected president who has power to appoint their leadership as well as to conduct regulatory review over agency outputs and agenda. Agencies are democratic insofar as they carry out the directives of these elected principals. This view tends to rely on a Weberian conception of administration, in which civil servants make technocratic rather than value-based decisions within a strict hierarchy controlled by elected officials and statutory law.[8]

This instrumental conception has merit but is vulnerable to significant objections. First, neither of the elected branches is capable of tight control over agencies. One reason administrative power is important is that Congress cannot, and perhaps as a matter of policy ought not, to make all of the policy decisions with regard to economic and social regulation.[9] There is simply too much on the agenda, compromise on many issues proves elusive, social facts change rapidly, and Congress, even with its staff, lacks the expertise to solve all problems in statutory text. Moreover, Congress is not unimpeachably democratic by either majoritarian or deliberative standards. The Senate heavily overcounts the votes and values of residents of small-population states.[10]

The President, meanwhile, cannot personally direct all of the policy decisions agencies make. Again, there is simply too much to do. As Cristina Rodríguez has recently argued, the President can use his appointment power and other levers to create a "regime" that aligns with his party's political preferences.[11] But in an era where presidents regularly do not win the popular vote, and where the very integrity of the electoral process is at risk,[12] there is an increasingly tenuous connection between popular will and presidential policymaking.

Even if the President and the Congress had perfect majoritarian credentials, moreover, that alone would not satisfy democratic requirements. Pure majoritarianism could lead to administrative practices that undermine the political freedom and equality of all persons, on which modern democracy rests.[13] For these reasons, *deliberative* democratic theory requires that majoritarian decision-making be subject to reasoned argument amongst affected persons.[14] Reason-giving places constraints of generality, transparency, and mutual acceptability on government action. Neither Congress nor the President can provide for such deliberation on its own. The presidency poses a particularly acute threat to deliberation because of the often unilateral and hierarchical nature of White House control, which runs contrary to a horizontal exchange of arguments among those affected.

Deliberative Democracy

Deliberative-democratic approaches to administrative law accordingly seeks to legitimate agencies based on their participatory processes and reasoned argumentation. Although scholarship has long focused on the expansive use of public participation in the 1960s and '70s, such deliberative forms administrative decision-making can be found at least as far back as the Progressive Era.[15] In one remarkable example described by John Preston Comer, the Forest Service in 1923 held weeks-long deliberative hearings with ranchers over grazing rights on public lands.[16] The Federal Trade Commission (FTC) in that era also adopted "trade practice submittals," in which firms could allege unfair trade practices and the Commission would assemble firms in the market to evaluate the practice.[17] Such broad-based participatory practices persisted through the New Deal, when government agencies engaged in extensive deliberative hearings with farmers to implement land use reforms.[18]

The benefits of public participation in administrative rulemaking were a central concern in debates leading up to the enactment of the APA in 1946.[19] The influential minority report of the Attorney General's Committee on Administrative Procedure, for instance, presented the notice-and-comment process as a "democratization" of agency rulemaking that was "designed to extend the legislative process" into the formulation of administration policy.[20] This vision came to fruition with fresh grants of rulemaking authority during the 1960s and '70s, and judicial interpretations that likewise strongly encouraged agencies to engage in and take seriously the participatory process of public comment.[21]

This era brought into existence a brand of administrative policymaking particularly suitable to deliberative-democratic legitimacy. Notice-and-comment rulemaking is open to any and all who wish to comment, thus recognizing deliberative democracy's requirement that all parties affected by a policy have a say in its formulation. Rose Ackerman thus argues that, among the national administrative-law regimes she examines, "notice-and-comment rulemaking under the APA comes closest to the democratic ideal of public involvement in delegated policymaking."[22] Jerry Mashaw likewise argues that the strong reason-giving requirements that emerged from judicial embellishment of the APA have required agencies to exercise a form of "public reason" when they respond to comments and finalize their policies.[23]

Empirical studies of the public comment process show that, under some circumstances, comments from the public can shape agency decision-making.[24] This is particularly so where regulated parties are internally divided, and so unable to control the process, and agencies engage in an "iterative" process of policy formulation that allows for a genuine back and forth with the affected public.[25] Many agencies today—such as the Forest Service, Consumer Financial Protection Bureau, the Fish and Wildlife Service, and the Nuclear Regulatory Commission—also deploy extensive public participation and deliberation when developing proposed rules.[26]

The Limits of Deliberative Democracy

But can deliberative-democratic ideals thrive amidst the current realities of administrative politics? Regulated entities often dominate both the notice-and-comment process and the formulation of proposed rules.[27] Agencies have strong legal incentives not to substantially change their rules between proposal and finalization, so they are unlikely to treat the comment process as a genuine opportunity for policy development. As Rose-Ackerman suggests, in cases that are particularly high profile, presidential policy preferences are likely to predetermine the outcome whatever the internal agency recommendations may be.[28] Committed deliberative democrats insists that these real problems aren't fatal to the normative goal of democratic administration; they can be addressed through feasible procedural reforms. These include "regulatory public defenders" as Mariano-Florentino Cuellar suggests,[29] or supplementing public comment with "mini-publics" in which more fulsome deliberation takes place, as Rose-Ackerman argues.[30]

Critics of deliberation nonetheless argue that the problem goes deeper. In the present politically polarized landscape, it is hopeless for agencies to engage in anything like reasoned deliberation that will convince people in ideologically opposed camps. Daniel Walters goes so far as to claim that there is an "ontological impossibility of reconciling" political conflicts in administrative policymaking.[31] He therefore proposes changes that would facilitate swift administrative policy change while also opening the regulatory agenda to more extensive (but less reasoned) public participation. In a different vein, Nicholas Bagley argues that public deliberation is a costly exercise that is not constitutionally required and does not enhance the sociological acceptance of administrative decision-making.[32] Better to focus on substantive outcomes and recognize administrative law for what it has become: "blood sport."[33]

These critiques identify profound ideological conflict and the related costs of participatory procedures as obstacles to deliberative administration. Administrative policymaking is, as Walters suggests, "agonistic" today, in the sense that profoundly divided partisan regimes implement their preferred preferences so long as they retain control of the presidency. It is also true that reason-giving requirements are costly and may delay or impede the implementation of policy. But these concerns do not obviate the need for deliberative and participatory administration in a democratic state. Enhancing contestation and facilitating policy change *without* robust reason-giving is likely over the long haul to benefit the groups with the greatest social power because they have the greatest wherewithal for such contestation. As the Progressive Era theorist of public administration Mary Follett once observed, a political theory that abandons the effort to identify the common interest must trust that a "balance of power" can be found.[34] But in a highly unequal and fragmented society such as our own, the struggle for power will not end in parity, but rather in "antagonistic interest, then jealous interest, then competing interest, then dominating interests—a fatal climax."[35]

The decline of public reason and the intensification of political conflict make deliberative administration harder, but also that much more necessary. We desperately need what John Rawls called an "exemplar of public reason"—a governmental institution that can demonstrate what reasoned, inclusive, and fair decision-making looks like.[36] If power is not justified in these terms, it is likely to be arbitrary. Without requirements of transparency, justification, and responsiveness, officials may either abuse their power or else misunderstand the needs and values of those their actions affect.

This is the risk posed by presidential administration in a landscape of deep disagreement, political conflict, and economic inequality.[37] Some scholars have been tempted to turn to the plebiscitary theory of administration advocated by Carl Schmitt, and maintain hope that political rather than legal control will constrain executive power.[38] Even if the Schmittian approach may resonate in an American context that looks increasingly like the Weimar Republic, there are extraordinary dangers in unfettered presidential control over the immense bureaucratic competencies of the federal government. Elections cannot systemically or granularly control the exercise of power within the executive branch, and recent experience has shown us the abuses of which presidents are capable.

All that said, there is no doubt that deliberative democracy of the traditional form has reduced space to maneuver. Though Rawls thought that public reason would be safeguarded by the "exemplar" of the Supreme Court, that assessment has not withstood the test of time. To the contrary, the Supreme Court today is one of the primary threats to deliberative democracy within the administrative state and beyond, arrogating power to itself while threatening the foundations of electoral democracy.[39] Its administrative law jurisprudence deprives agencies of their democracy-enhancing potential. In a pair of shadow docket rulings on the COVID-19 pandemic,[40] followed by its decision in *West Virginia v. EPA*,[41] the Court has held that agencies cannot decide "major questions" without express congressional authorization. The major questions doctrine was once milder, merely requiring courts not to defer to agencies' interpretations if they raised issues of "deep economic and political significance."[42] But this new doctrine goes further and bars agencies from exercising powers the court deems "major" if the statutory text does not specify those powers in excruciating detail.

These rulings imperil deliberative democratic administration—as well as congressional power more broadly—because they prevent agencies from serving as sites for the resolution of serious political issues. If major questions generally aren't for agencies to solve, then agencies will not be able to engage in forthright deliberation about public needs and values. They will have strong incentives to present the substantial value choices as narrow technical matters so as not to draw judicial ire. As a result, agencies either won't address major policy problems, or they will do so in a way that conceals the major questions at issue. This is a recipe for paternalistic, opaque, and disingenuous policymaking.

Turning Administrative Democracy Inside Out

If deliberative democracy remains core to administrative legitimacy but that process has been imperiled by deep political cleavages, White House control, and a hostile of the Supreme Court, what is there left for agencies to do? It's time for us to rethink both what administrative deliberation means and how it ought to operate. Administrative deliberation should concern the collective rights of the democratic public. Agencies should shift their discourse from policymaking to public rights protection. This shift has legal and rhetorical advantages over current thinking, which makes the goals of agency action subservient to private rights, market efficiency, and judicial supremacy. Administrative deliberation should supplement notice-and-comment with direct, political engagement with the public, where agencies can model reasoned argument in an environment where it is currently in short supply. These steps will not cure judicial hostility to administrative action. But they may help to resist the Court's arbitrary restrictions on governmental power by way of public-facing arguments for regulatory initiatives.

From Making Policy to Protecting Public Rights

Agencies are generally conceived as policymakers and policy implementers. While the term "policy" is ubiquitous in administrative case law and scholarship, it is rarely defined. Political scientists Karren Orren and Stephen Skowronek offer a helpful definition: "policy is a commitment to a designated goal or course of action, made authoritatively on behalf of a given entity or collectivity, and accompanied by guidelines for its accomplishment."[43] On their account, the modern American state as a whole is a "policy state" in which administrative agencies play a central role. Agencies set out to accomplish goals enunciated by Congress or by the President, such as promotion of health and safety or maintenance of efficient markets. As compared to traditional rights claims, policy choices tend to be more discretionary, politically sensitive, and responsive to social and scientific facts.

The presence of such policy matters has long justified administrative rulemaking as well as judicial deference to such rules. The APA defines rules, in part, as agency statements that "implement, interpret, or prescribe law or policy."[44] *Chevron* justifies judicial deference in part on the grounds that the interpretation of ambiguous statutory terms involves "policy choices."[45] Given that agencies have greater institutional competence to make policy judgments than courts do, courts ought to respect agency interpretations that involve policy judgments.

The legitimation of administrative power on the basis of policy prowess doesn't work as smoothly as it used to. *Chevron* itself hasn't been relied on by the Supreme Court in years and agencies increasingly seem to avoid *Chevron* arguments. Justice Gorsuch would hold that Congress cannot constitutionally delegate to agencies the authority to make "policy decisions."[46] That rule is likely to be difficult to administer because of the ubiquity of programmatic goal-setting in administrative action. If the Court adopts Gorsuch's approach, it would either have to strike down large swaths of the administrative state or apply the rule arbitrarily. Nonetheless, the Court's increasing hostility to *Chevron*, the possible revival of the nondelegation doctrine, as well as the souped-up major questions doctrine already discussed, all suggest that agencies cannot safely rely on claims to special competency to make policy.

The time is therefore ripe to shift agencies' self-conception from policy-makers to the guardians of collective rights. The concept of collective or public rights protected by government is not new. The common law has long recognized public rights against unreasonable interference with public health and safety or access to public ways and vital resources.[47] Agencies have come to displace or complement such common-law rights against public nuisance with governmental enforcement mechanisms that are more efficient and politically accountable.[48] In administrative case law, the term public right has been deployed to described those matters that administrative tribunals rather than article III courts may adjudicate, such as rights to collective bargaining or to workplace safety.[49] It also refers, in the context of public utility law, to the people's right to the use of private property that is "affected with a public interest," such as common carriers and monopolistic enterprises.[50]

The tradition of public rights is a rich one that I cannot possibly do full justice to here.[51] For present purposes, the concept of public rights provides us with a different and more robust language for understanding what administrative agencies ought to do. Public rights were traditionally associated with the prerogatives of the kingship and of common law courts. Within a democratic scheme of government, however, public rights are held by the people in their collective capacity, and are grounded in their shared interest in self-governance. The shared interests that public rights protect aren't fully determined ex ante, but are rather the subject of legislative and administrative deliberation. Through such deliberation, the public has expressed interests in the enjoyment of healthy and safe living and workplace conditions; the creation and preservation of fair and stable marketplaces; the maintenance of the physical and institutional infrastructure that makes economic, social, and political exchanges feasible; and the provision of basic needs and services to those who cannot obtain them on their own initiative.

One of agencies' fundamental purposes is to protect such collective rights. They play a central role in regulating economic and social life to protect democratic fundamentals. Consider, for instance, the role of the Centers for Medicaid and Medicare Services in providing healthcare to the elderly and to those in severe economic need.[52] These programs provide direct benefits to individuals, and they may carry ancillary benefits for economic efficiency. But beyond these impacts, they play a more fundamental, constitutive role. They help to underwrite an egalitarian society in which illness or the cost of medical care does not place debilitating restrictions on people's ability to participate in social and political life.

What does it add to describe such collective interests as "rights" rather than as "policies"? Rights are normatively binding to an extent that policies are not. A right demands respect and protection, whereas a policy may be pursued or abandoned at the government's discretion. Given the superior normative weight of rights, it biases public law to describe the collective interests as "policy" but affected private interests as "rights." The judiciary in particular increasingly privileges the protection of private rights of property against government interference. This bias can be seen in the law of standing, which permits parties to challenge government action where their property is at risk, but looks with increasing skepticism at claims to represent shared interests, such as those in environmental protection or against economic exploitation.[53] It is also evident in decisions holding administrative action unlawful because of its profound effects on property relations and private lives, while upholding similarly broad actions that involve the provision of government benefits.[54]

Once we conceptualize agencies not just as policymakers but as the trustees for public rights, the current legal and political constellation takes on a new valence. The anti-administrative reaction against the regulatory state doesn't merely hamstring the government's power to promote efficiency or to increase overall welfare. More than this, it threatens to injure the collective rights of the public to a healthy, safe, and egalitarian society. Because these rights are at issue, the agencies empowered to vindicate these rights should change the tenor and the targets for their reasoned deliberation.

Reasoning about Public Rights

Understood as the law of public rights, administrative law would need to shift from a centralized concern with efficiency to discrete concern with rights to public health, safety, and equality. Agencies and scholars ought to develop a pluralistic mode of regulatory review that not only analyzes costs and benefits but acknowledges the independent value of multiple collective rights. Agencies have a duty to protect these rights even if their monetizable cost exceeds their benefits. Efficiency should matter, but it ought not play the central role it often does.

One of the contributions of Rose-Ackerman's work has been her sensitive critique of cost-benefit analysis (CBA). Although she acknowledges that CBA is well suited to correct market failures, especially where sound data on revealed preferences are available, she argues that it is not well suited for evaluating non-economic values as well as large-scale problems of long duration, such as climate change.[55] Thoughtful advocates for cost-benefit analysis don't dispute these points. Richard Revesz and Michael Livermore, for instance, acknowledge that "[t]reating cost benefit analysis as a master procedure is actually an abuse of the technique."[56] A tailored role for CBA is salutary, however. Insistence on rigorous consideration of social benefits as well as costs certainly provides an important lens to critique and in some cases to stop unjustified deregulatory as well as regulatory efforts.[57] But once we consider values other than net welfare maximization, CBA simply cannot answer many of the important questions. The appeal of quantification, the broadly agreed upon importance of economic welfare, and the related power of economists in the political arena have nonetheless crowned CBA as the hegemon in bureaucratic reasoning.[58]

The Biden Administration appears to have heard the critiques of undue emphasis on efficiency. Biden's executive order on "Modernizing Regulatory Review" instructs the Director of the Office of Management and Budget to "provide concrete suggestions on how the regulatory review process can promote public health and safety, economic growth, social welfare, racial justice, environmental stewardship, human dignity, equity, and the interests of future generations" and to "propose procedures that take into account the distributional consequences of regulations, including as part of any quantitative or qualitative analysis of the costs and benefits of regulations, to ensure that regulatory initiatives appropriately benefit and do not inappropriately burden disadvantaged, vulnerable, or marginalized communities."[59] In pursuit of that mandate, the Office for Information and Regulatory Affairs is revising Circular A-4, which instructs agencies how to perform the "regulatory impact analyses" that must accompany significant regulations.

The concept of public rights may provide some useful guidance in fleshing out values other than efficiency in regulatory impact analysis. These rights are discrete entitlements at issue in regulatory programs, which must be independently characterized and weighted rather than melted down into coins. Under a pure efficiency approach, all interests become fungible and comparable into the medium of price. The drawback, of course, is that this conversion distorts the underlying value at stake. The collective right to public health or racial equality is irreducible to its exchange value. They are, instead, legal interests with their own logics and their own related fields of disciplinary study that need to be understood and consulted. We must think about the content of these rights independently and then determine how to do justice to each of them when government action implicates them. Determining the content of these rights is hard and controversial, and measuring them may be yet more challenging. The concept of public rights nonetheless provides a starting point for giving interests other than efficiency their proper legal standing as distinct, shared entitlements commanding official respect.

Agencies as Public Deliberators

Rose-Ackerman's comparative study has made a strong case that the United States' notice-and-comment process, combined with more fine-grained, in-person participatory procedures, provides the best forum for public participation in administrative policymaking.[60] As I've suggested, however, the political and judicial headwinds against this effort are strong. The pressure from the Supreme Court encourages agencies not to explicitly wrestle with the value choices implicated in their decisions. Agencies will not have strong incentives, in terms of litigation risk, to engage in more extensive public participation, because the Supreme Court seems more focused on limiting agency action than scrutinizing the quality of the agency's decision-making record. If major policy decisions are likely to get struck down regardless, there is little self-interested reason for an agency to engage in more than the legal bare minimum of public participation. At the same time, White House control often privileges implementation of the policy preferences of the President and his party, even though some aspects of the Biden administration's emerging practice suggests more broad-based participation. Between the Scylla of presidential supervision and the Charybdis of judicial review, there appears to be little room for deliberative democracy to maneuver *within* administrative proceedings.

I emphasize "within" because there is another way in which agencies can contribute to democratic deliberation: out in the public sphere. This approach can be highly political and even agonistic. But if agencies can remain true to their institutional competencies for evidence-based and well-reasoned decision-making, they can make positive contributions to political discourse. They can model values-based but nonetheless empirically supported argument and inspire more such conduct in public life.

It is often contended that the Constitution is at best silent about and at worst hostile to administrative power. I've shown in other work, however, that the administrative state has always been in the Constitution, hiding in plain sight.[61] The Constitution refers to executive branch "Departments" to be created by Congress.[62] These departments serve the rule of law by ensuring that executive power is regularized and distributed amongst multiple officers who can check and guide one another's discretion. The internal deliberative norms that have developed within the executive branch are anchored in the Constitution's Opinion Clause, which provides that the President may "require the opinion in writing from the Principal Officers in each of the Executive Departments concerning the Duties of their respective Offices."[63] As Peter Shane has argued, the structure of Article II of the Constitution contemplates not unilateral dictates from the Oval but rather collaborative processes of consultation and justification in the execution of law.[64]

Considered as constitutional actors, executive departments can play a role analogous to the "interbranch dialogue" that occurs amongst the three branches or "principal departments" of government.[65] As Jon D. Michaels and others have argued, agencies are not unitary actors, but rather are composites made up of political leadership, civil servants, and public participants, who contest and check one another's reasoning.[66] The relatively moderate political makeup of the civil service can also serve to temper political decision-making and serve as a "ballast" between major swings from left to right.[67]

These features position agencies to contribute to political deliberation in the public sphere. When we think about the democratic qualities of agencies, we therefore ought not to look only at how agencies justify their decisions ex ante, in terms of the quality of public participation and reason-giving in notice-and-comment and other processes. We should look at how these agencies contribute to public discourse. For instance, the FTC's effort to strengthen antitrust enforcement has heightened political debate around the purposes of competition law—should it focus merely on consumer prices or should it also consider a wider set of republican values?[68] Even if the Commission's antitrust regulations are ultimately struck down by the courts, that contribution to the political debate may have lasting implications even after the agency's leadership changes. Of course, agencies do not always make a positive or healthy contribution to democratic discourse. There are arguably grounds to criticize CDC's inconsistent guidance during the COVID-19 pandemic, for instance. But such controversies are the stuff of politics. At its best, agency deliberation can provide the public with both value judgments and empirical data relevant to political debate, electoral decisions, and legislation.

Agency officials might go one step further and use their bully pulpit not only to advance particular policy positions but also to underscore to the public the deliberative credentials of their decision-making, thus connecting ex ante with ex post administrative democracy. For instance, when Ann Carlson, Chief Counsel to the National Highway Traffic and Safety Administration, announced new fuel economy standards, she recognized the "members of the public" who contributed to their decision-making process, including over six thousand comments and a virtual public hearing. She emphasized the importance of participants who "spoke with a unified voice" that "we need to do what is right to protect not just ourselves, but our children . . . and our grandchildren, and all the future generations to come."[69] This kind of messaging, which unites the substance and procedure of administrative decision-making, has a chance of resetting our policy conversation. Agencies can speak as agents, not just of Congress, but of the people—both in terms of the substantive democratic rights to goods like clean air, but also as representatives of those who participate in administrative proceedings.[70] Greater resort to rhetorical administration, like the "rhetorical presidency,"[71] could reorient American democracy around the multiple and distinct executive departments that represent plural public rights.

Forms of Agency Action to Promote Public Rights

If we evaluate agencies' deliberative credentials ex post, rather than merely ex ante, we might shift focus from notice-and-comment rulemaking to other forms of agency action. Below I outline four of these: guidance documents, interim final rules, enforcement actions, and procedural rules. These often lack rulemaking's participatory credentials but may have greater capacity to make material contributions to political discourse.

Guidance

Guidance documents like "policy statements" and "enforcement memoranda" need not be issued through notice-and-comment rulemaking requirements.

They nonetheless can have significant impact on regulated parties, as they communicate how the agency intends to use its binding and otherwise coercive powers.[72] Guidance at the same time provides agencies with a relatively low-cost way to take a public stance on policy. Guidance documents can "start a conversation" to advance new policy positions or advise the public on how to comply with their legal and perhaps even moral obligations.[73] Agencies could extend this policy further and use guidance to advance political arguments in the public sphere concerning issues ranging from abortion access to climate change to medical billing to workplace safety. If such documents are framed in accessible and vivid terms, they may garner media attention and political discussion, even if they do not carry significant legal consequences on their own terms.

There are certainly downsides to guidance, for both the agency and public beneficiaries. Because guidance is generally not legally binding, it does not pack the same punch as legislative rules. The policies advanced in guidance will usually not earn judicial deference, and the agency cannot prove a private party's violation merely by demonstrating their non-compliance with guidance. As Nina Mendelsohn has pointed out, guidance is also harder for public interest groups to challenge where it arguably under-enforces the law, because it is harder to influence and obtain judicial review of such documents.[74]

In the shifting landscape of administrative law, however, both of these concerns are comparatively less significant. The Court seems less willing to defer to *any* agency pronouncement, regardless of its procedural provenance. The courts appear more willing to entertain pre-enforcement challenges to significant guidance and standing for public interest groups has become harder across the board. In a world where courts treat even rules carrying the force of law as more advisory than binding, guidance documents that are easier to issue may prove a relatively powerful way to contribute to democratic discourse and shift public understanding.[75]

Enforcement Actions

Enforcement actions are the least statutorily and judicially regulated form of administrative action. They fall through the cracks of the APA with its focus on rulemaking and adjudication. Courts are reluctant to review enforcement decisions prior to an adjudicatory order. Yet, enforcement actions can be politically salient and convey messages about the administration's value choice and its conception of collective rights. Consider, in this regard, the role of state attorneys general in bringing public nuisance actions against opioid producers.[76] By singling out bad actors, the government can convey a broader message about common rights to health and safety and the private wrongs committed against them.

One could imagine federal administrative agencies dedicating increased resources to such enforcement actions as their rulemaking and adjudicatory prerogatives become more costly and less attractive. Agencies might use existing authorities, for instance, to investigate and even cut off funding for educational institutions that discriminate against women in their efforts to obtain abortions. They might pursue high-profile claims against nursing homes or long-term care facilities receiving federal funds who commit fraud or provide substandard care. These efforts could be accompanied by public announcements that invoke public rights to gender equality and to reasonable access to healthcare, rather than hewing to a legalistic account of statutory violations. By shining a light on bad actors, and articulating the nature of their wrongs against the public, agencies can contribute to political deliberation about how to better protect these rights and redress these injuries in the future.

There is certainly a risk of abuse here, which rises in proportion to the penalties imposed upon the private parties and the extent to which the judiciary provides an external check. And, of course, there is likely to be intense political disagreement about which actors are "bad" and what the public interest requires. But agencies already are engaged in these political debates, and they ought to be self-conscious, thoughtful, and strategic about their role within them. They should focus more attention on taking public actions that articulate relevant value commitments so as to contribute to vibrant and transparent democratic debate.

Interim Final Rules

The APA exempts rules from notice-and-comment procedures "when the agency for good cause finds . . . that notice and public procedure thereon are impracticable, unnecessary, or contrary to the public interest."[77] Agencies already rely on this provision to issue what are often called "interim final rules."[78] Recently, the Supreme Court has suggested a greater willingness to entertain their use.[79] There is reason to doubt the justices will remain open if interim rules advance progressive causes. The opinion nonetheless gives grounds for agency counsel to condone more expansive use of such rules under the right circumstances.

Agencies might use such rules as deliberative mechanisms. They might provide a "good cause" explanation which states that public deliberation will be most useful and effective *after* the rule is in place and the public has had some experience with how it works in practice. The agency might then provide for more expansive public deliberation after promulgation than it would have provided through the ordinary notice-and-comment process, with a deadline for the agency to revise the rule in light of such feedback. Public hearings, listening sessions, and online convenings might focus deliberation on the felt effects of the rule and how it might be improved. This could be more useful than abstract speculation, before a rule is put into effect, about how well it will work in practice and comport with public values.

This approach will be particularly attractive in areas of high political salience requiring a rapid response, such as the use of emergency authorities to address climate change, to protect abortion access, to reduce gun violence, or to prevent future pandemics. It is likely a high-risk strategy before a court skeptical of administrative power. Again, however, when the baseline of anti-administrative hostility is already so high, how much higher can the risk get?

Even if these actions get struck down, legislative and executive acquiescence in judicial aggrandizement is unwise. At a minimum the elected branches must fulfill their duty to protect public rights and force the Court to own up to and publicly explain its obstructionism. Losing before a hostile court is its own form of democratic deliberation. Because of the visibility of Court rulings, agencies can use these interim rules as opportunities to showcase the justifications for their actions and to turn the Court's resistance into a question for broader public deliberation.

Procedural Rules

Guidance, enforcement, and interim rules all provide efficient and potentially high visibility means for agencies to contribute to political discourse. A final route for deliberative agency action—procedural rules—takes a different tack. Whereas the previous forms of action increase agency discretion in the public sphere, procedural rules may serve as precommitment mechanisms that constrain agency conduct going forward.[80] Procedural rules need not go through notice-and-comment rulemaking, but they do have the force of law.[81] Such rules can be used to support democratic values in the face of the particularly acute risks, raised by the Trump presidency, that some administrations may abuse their power and undermine the rule of law.

The Trump Administration itself, ironically, made use of such procedural rules to require executive agencies to engage in extensive public participation on significant guidance documents.[82] Present and future administrations could build on this strategy to commit agencies to good governance principles in administrative decision-making, such as considering social reliance interests and registering the advice of career staff. Because such rules have the force of law, they would provide a significant guardrail against future authoritarian presidents who attempt to undermine lawful and well-reasoned decision-making. If attended by appropriate public fanfare, they could enhance the people's understanding of the ingredients of thoughtful government conduct and alert them to incursions against it.

Conclusion

In the preface to Frank Goodnow's foundational 1893 text, *Comparative Administrative Law*, he observed that "the great problems of modern public law are almost exclusively administrative in character. While the age that has passed was one of constitutional, the present age is one of administrative reform."[83] Borrowing from the Hegelian tradition of public law, Goodnow understood the executive branch to be the central locus for social change.

Today, it no longer seems credible that constitutional issues are resolved and only administrative matters remain. Rather, administrative law has become a site for constitutional politics. Rose-Ackerman has shown that agencies can participate actively in democratic decision-making, not merely by carrying out legislative will, but also by developing and adopting new policies by democratic means. Her latest work adapts Goodnow's project to the present, and draws our attention to the democratic competencies of the administrative state. She invites scholars to think creatively about what democracy can mean in a context of political fragmentation, presidentialism, and increasingly intensive judicial government. In the present regime of public law that she has canvassed, administrative reform *is* constitutional reform.

Notes

1 Blake Emerson, The Public's Law: Origins and Architecture of Progressive Democracy 23–112 (2019).
2 Susan Rose-Ackerman, Democracy and Executive Power: Policymaking and Accountability in the US, the UK, Germany, and France (2021).
3 Blake Emerson & Jon Michaels, *Abandoning Presidential Administration: A Civic Governance Agenda to Promote Democratic Equality and Prevent Creeping Authoritarianism*, 68 UCLA L. Rev. 104 (2021).
4 Gillian Metzger, *The Supreme Court 2016 Term—Foreword: 1930s Redux: The Administrative State Under Siege*, 131 Harv. L. Rev. 1 (2017).
5 Daniel E. Walters, *The Administrative Agon: A Democratic Theory for a Conflictual Regulatory State*, 132 Yale L. J. 1 (2022).
6 Nicholas Bagley, *The Procedure Fetish*, 118 Mich. L. Rev. 345 (2019).
7 Elizabeth Fisher & Sidney A. Shapiro, Administrative Competence: Reimagining Administrative Law (2020).
8 Max Weber, Economy and Society: An Outline of Interpretive Sociology 217–26 (Guenther Roth & Clauss Wittich eds., 1978).
9 *See, e.g.*, Jerry L. Mashaw, *Prodelegation: Why Administrators Should Make Political Decisions*, 1 J. L. & Econ. Org. 81 (1985).
10 Jerry L. Mashaw, Reasoned Administration and Democratic Legitimacy: How Administrative Law Supports Democratic Government 163–79 (2018).
11 Cristina M. Rodríguez, *The Supreme Court 2020 Term—Foreword: Regime Change*, 135 HARV. L. REV. 1 (2021).
12 *See* Jennifer Nou, *Constraining Executive Entrenchment*, 135 Harv. L. Rev. F. 20 (2021).
13 Blake Emerson, *The Value of Official Equality: Structuring the Execution of Democratic Law*, 13 Jurisprudence 73 (2021).
14 *See, e.g.*, Jürgen Habermas, *Three Normative Models of Democracy*, *in* Democracy and Difference: Contesting the Boundaries of the Political 21 (Seyla Benhabib ed., 1996); Hélène Landemore, Open Democracy: Reinventing Popular Rule for the Twenty-First Century 6–7 (2020)
15 Emerson, *supra* note 1, at 61–112 (2019).
16 John Preston Comer, Legislative Functions of National Administrative Authorities 208–11 (1927).
17 Gerald C. Henderson, The Federal Trade Commission: A Study in Administrative Procedure 79 (1925).

18 Jess Gilbert, Planning Democracy: Agrarian Intellectuals and the Intended New Deal (2015).
19 Blake Emerson, *"Policy" in the Administrative Procedure Act: Implications for Delegation, Deference, and Democracy*, 97 Chi.-Kent L. Rev. 113 (2022); Emily Bremer, *The Undemocratic Roots of Agency Rulemaking*, 108 Cornell L. Rev. 69 (2022).
20 U.S. Attorney General's Committee on Administrative Procedure, Final Report 225 (1941).
21 Reuel Schiller, *Rulemaking's Promise: Administrative Law and Legal Culture in the 1960s and 1970s*, 53 Admin. L. Rev. 1139 (2001).
22 Rose-Ackerman, Democracy and Executive Power, *supra* note 2, at 9.
23 Mashaw, Reasoned Administration, *supra* note 10, at 167–79.
24 Wendy Wagner, William West, Thomas McGarity, and Lisa Peter, *Deliberative Rulemaking: An Empirical Study of Participation in Three Agency Programs*, 73 Admin. L. Rev. 609 (2021).
25 *Id.* at 651.
26 Michael Sant'Ambrogio & Glen Staszewski, *Democratizing Rule Development*, 98 Wash U. L. Rev. 793 (2021)
27 For example, Jason Webb Yackee and Susan Webb Yackee, *A Bias in Favor of Business? Assessing Interest Group Influence on the U.S. Bureaucracy*, 68 J. Pol. 128 (2006).
28 Rose-Ackerman, Democracy and Executive Power, *supra* note 2, at 79.
29 Mariano-Florentino Cuéllar, *Rethinking Regulatory Democracy*, 57 Admin. L. Rev. 411 (2005).
30 Rose Ackerman, Democracy and Executive Power, *supra* note 2, at 182.
31 Walters, *Administrative Agon*, *supra* note 5, at 53.
32 Bagley, *Procedure Fetish*, *supra* note 6.
33 Thomas McGarity, *Administrative Law as Blood Sport: Policy Erosion in a Highly Partisan Age*, 61 Duke L. J. 1671 (2012).
34 Mary Parker Follett, The New State: Group Organization the Solution of Popular Government 306 (1918).
35 *Id.* at 308.
36 John Rawls, Political Liberalism 231 (2005).
37 Elena Kagan, *Presidential Administration*, 114 Harv. L. Rev. 2245 (2001).
38 Eric Posner & Adrian Vermeule, The Executive Unbound: After the Madisonian Republic (2010).
39 For example, Michael J. Klarman, *The Supreme Court 2019 Term—Foreword: The Degradation of American Democracy—and the Court*, 134 Harv. L. Rev. 1, 178–230 (2020). Leah Litman, *Hey, Stephen*, 120 Mich. L. Rev. 1109, 1121 (2022) (book review of Stephen Breyer, The Authority of the Court and the Peril of Politics (Harvard Univ. Press 2021)).
40 Alabama Ass'n of Realtors v. HHS, 141 S. Ct. 2320 (2021); Nat'l Fed'n of Indep. Bus. v. DOL, 142 S. Ct. 661 (2022).
41 142 S. Ct. 2587 (2022).
42 For example, King v. Burwell, 576 U.S. 473 (2015). *See* Blake Emerson, *Administrative Answers to Major Questions: On the Democratic Legitimacy of Agency Statutory Interpretation*, 102 Minn. L. Rev. 2019 (2018).
43 Karen Orren & Stephen Skowronek, The Policy State: An American Predicament 27 (2017).
44 5 U.S.C. § 551(4).
45 467 U.S. 837, 865 (1984).
46 Gundy v. United States, 139 S. Ct. 2116, 2142 (2019) (Gorsuch, J., dissenting).
47 William Blackstone, 4 Commentaries on the Laws of England 4, 161–67 (1769).

48 American Elec. Power Co. v. Connecticut, 564 U.S. 410 (2011); Thomas W. Merrill, *Is Public Nuisance a Tort?* 4 J. Tort L. 1, 36 (2011).
49 Atlas Roofing Co. v. Occupational Safety & Health Rev. Comm'n, 430 U.S. 442, 456 (1977).
50 Munn v. Illinois, 94 U.S. 113, 126 (1876).
51 For broader discussion, *see* Blake Emerson, *Vindicating Public Rights*, 26 U. Pa. J. Const. L. __ (forthcoming 2024) (on file with author).
52 *See* 42 U.S.C. § 1396–91; Gresham v. Azar, 950 F.3d 93, 104 (D.C. Cir. 2020); for discussion, *see* Blake Emerson, *Public Care in Public Law: Structure, Procedure, and Purpose*, 16 Harv. L. & Pol'y Rev. 101, 114 (2021).
53 For example, Transunion LLC v. Ramirez, 141 S.Ct. 2190 (2020).
54 Compare NFIB v. DOL 142 S. Ct. 661 (2022) (vaccine or testing mandate for private employers unlawful) with Biden v. Missouri, 142 S. Ct. 746 (2022) (vaccine mandate for hospitals participating in Medicaid or Medicare lawful).
55 Susan Rose-Ackerman, *Putting Cost-Benefit Analysis in Its Place: Rethinking Regulatory Review*, 65 U. Miami L. Rev. 335 (2011).
56 Richard L. Revesz & Michael A. Livermore, Retaking Rationality: How Cost-Benefit Analysis Can Better Protect the Environment and Our Health 15 (2008).
57 Caroline Cecot, *Deregulatory Cost-Benefit Analysis and Regulatory Flexibility*, 68 Duke L. J. 1519 (2019).
58 *See* Elizabeth Popp Berman, Thinking Like an Economist: How Efficiency Replaced Equality in U.S. Public Policy (2022).
59 The White House, Memorandum for the Heads of Executive Departments and Agencies (Jan. 20, 2021), available at: https://perma.cc/433L-464J.
60 Rose-Ackerman, Democracy and Executive Power, *supra* note 2, at 181–83.
61 Blake Emerson, *The Departmental Structure of Executive Power: Subordinate Checks from Madison to Mueller*, 38 Yale J. Regul. 90 (2021).
62 U.S. Const. art II, § 2, cls. 1, 2.
63 U.S. Const. art. II, § 2, cl. 1.
64 Peter M. Shane, Madison's Nightmare: How Executive Power Threatens American Democracy 11 (2009).
65 For example, James J. Brudey & Ethan J. Leib, *Statutory Interpretation as "Interbranch Dialogue"?* 66 UCLA L. Rev. 346 (2019).
66 Jon D. Michaels, Constitutional Coup: Privatization's Threat to the American Republic 56–75 (2017).
67 Brian D. Feinstein & Abby K. Wood, *Divided Agencies*, 95 So. Cal. L. Rev. 731 (2022).
68 *See* Lina Khan, *The Separation of Platforms and Commerce*, 119 Colum. L. Rev. 973 (2019).
69 Remarks by Ann Carlson at the Department of Transportation's announcement of New Fuel Economy (CAFE) Standards (Apr. 1, 2022), available at: https://www.youtube.com/watch?v=bJQNsKP1z4Q&t=1348s.
70 Kathryn Jackson, *All the Sovereign's Agents: The Constitutional Credentials of Administration*, 30 William & Mary Bill of Rights J. 777 (2022).
71 Jeffrey K. Tulis, The Rhetorical Presidency (1988).
72 For example, Nicholas R. Parrillo, *Federal Agency Guidance and the Power to Bind*, 36 Yale J. Regul. 165 (2019).
73 Blake Emerson & Ronald M. Levin, Agency Guidance Through Interpretive Rules: Research and Analysis, Report to the Administrative Conference of the United States 8 (March 8, 2019), *available at*: https://perma.cc/FM5Y-EG9B.
74 Nina Mendelsohn, *Regulatory Beneficiaries and Informal Agency Policymaking*, 92 Cornell L. Rev. 937 (2007).

75 I am grateful to Jodi Short for this insight.
76 *See* Leslie Kendrick, *The Perils and Promise of Public Nuisance*, 132 YALE L. J. 702 (2023).
77 5 U.S.C. §553(b)(B).
78 Abbe R. Gluck, Anne Joseph O'Connell & Rosa Po, *Unorthodox Lawmaking, Unorthodox Rulemaking*, 115 COLUM. L. REV. 1789, 1800–01 (2015).
79 Little Sisters of the Poor Saints Peter and Paul Home v. Pennsylvania, 140 S. Ct. 2367, 2384–86 (2020).
80 Elizabeth Magill, *Agency Self-Regulation*, 77 GEO. WASH. L. REV. 859, 870–76 (2009).
81 5 U.S.C. 553(b)(A); U.S. v. Nixon, 418 U.S. 683 (1974).
82 Executive Order 13,891, 84 Fed. Reg. 13,891 (2019).
83 FRANK J. GOODNOW, COMPARATIVE ADMINISTRATIVE LAW iv (1897).

Selected Sources

SUSAN ROSE-ACKERMAN, DEMOCRACY AND EXECUTIVE POWER: POLICYMAKING AND ACCOUNTABILITY IN THE US, THE UK, GERMANY, AND FRANCE (2021).

BLAKE EMERSON, THE PUBLIC'S LAW: ORIGINS AND ARCHITECTURE OF PROGRESSIVE DEMOCRACY (2019).

ELIZABETH FISHER & SIDNEY A. SHAPIRO, ADMINISTRATIVE COMPETENCE: REIMAGINING ADMINISTRATIVE LAW (2020).

JERRY L. MASHAW, REASONED ADMINISTRATION AND DEMOCRATIC LEGITIMACY: HOW ADMINISTRATIVE LAW SUPPORTS DEMOCRATIC GOVERNMENT (2018).

Gillian Metzger, *The Supreme Court 2016 Term—Foreword: 1930s Redux: The Administrative State Under Siege*, 131 Harv. L. Rev. 1 (2017).

JON D. MICHAELS, CONSTITUTIONAL COUP: PRIVATIZATION'S THREAT TO THE AMERICAN REPUBLIC (2017).

KAREN ORREN & STEPHEN SKOWRONEK, THE POLICY STATE: AN AMERICAN PREDICAMENT (2017).

Nicholas R. Parrillo, *Federal Agency Guidance and the Power to Bind*, 36 Yale J. Regul. 165 (2019).

Cristina M. Rodríguez, *The Supreme Court 2020 Term—Foreword: Regime Change*, 135 Harv. L. Rev. 1 (2021).

PETER M. SHANE, MADISON'S NIGHTMARE: HOW EXECUTIVE POWER THREATENS AMERICAN DEMOCRACY 11 (2009).

Wendy Wagner, William West, Thomas McGarity, and Lisa Peter, *Deliberative Rulemaking: An Empirical Study of Participation in Three Agency Programs*, 73 Admin. L. Rev. 609 (2021).

Daniel E. Walters, *The Administrative Agon: A Democratic Theory for a Conflictual Regulatory State*, 132 Yale L. J. 1 (2022).

3 The Lawfulness of Public Law in Germany and the United States

Jud Mathews and Joshua Spannaus

Introduction

Susan Rose-Ackerman is a key figure in the revival of comparative administrative law in the United States.[1] The conferences that she, Peter Lindseth, and later Blake Emerson convened in the past two decades, and the resulting volumes published by Edward Elgar, helped shape the identity of the field and its research agenda through the present day. But of course, her contributions date back earlier. Her 1995 book *Controlling Environmental Policy: The Limits of Public Law in Germany and the United States* was something new: a comparative analysis that explored a single field of regulatory law in depth while at the same time tackling big questions about how administrative institutions and practices embody or belie democratic commitments.[2] The book illustrated how comparative administrative law scholarship could contribute to important public policy debates even as it drew attention to the German-American comparison in particular as a vivid study in contrasts. *Controlling Environmental Policy* also developed arguments that Rose-Ackerman would extend to countries besides Germany and contexts besides environmental law a quarter century later, in her ambitious and wide-ranging *Democracy and Executive Power: Policymaking Accountability in the US, the UK, Germany, and France*.[3]

Although *Controlling Environmental Policy*'s depiction of German regulatory processes was sophisticated, the perspective, in Rose-Ackerman's words, was deliberately that of an "innocent abroad."[4] The book asks what is notable about the German approach to environmental policymaking, for good or ill, from the perspective of American regulatory law. There are important similarities: most significantly, in both countries, many consequential environmental policy decisions are made not by legislatures, through statutes, but by administrators, through regulations (in Germany, *Rechtsverordnungen*). But in contrast to the United States, where the regulatory process requires administrators to solicit and engage with comments from the public, general administrative law in Germany has precious little to say about how administrators set norms.[5] Rather, German administrative law, which is built largely on conceptual foundations laid in the late nineteenth and early twentieth centuries,

DOI: 10.4324/9781003416036-3

focuses much more on the one-on-one legal interaction between an individual citizen and the regulating state, crystalized in doctrine in the concept of the "administrative act" (*Verwaltungsakt*).[6]

This orientation toward retail acts of execution may have made sense a century or more ago, when most legal rules were set by statute and the expectation of public participation in governance was weaker. But, Rose-Ackerman argues, the failure to mandate a more public and participatory process for making regulations today is hard to square with our contemporary commitment to democratic governance. Nearly thirty years after the book appeared, German scholarship on the regulatory process continues to engage with Rose-Ackerman's arguments, even if most German scholars tend to defend existing practices against aspects of the critique.[7]

Many years after Rose-Ackerman's book appeared, German administrative law again found itself the object of transatlantic attention, this time in the service of a root-and-branch critique of American administrative law. In his book *Is Administrative Law Unlawful?*, Professor Philip Hamburger argues that administrative law is not really worthy of the name "law" at all, because it violates fundamental precepts of legality. On his account, administrative law emerged as a tool of absolutist rule in continental Europe and still bears features of that heritage. These features, and the ideas about government encoded in them, make administrative law incompatible with the understanding of law forged in the constitutional struggles of the Anglo-American legal tradition. Germany, in particular, is at fault. German legal scholars are responsible for the mature conception of administrative law that influenced turn-of-the-century American legal innovators, who duly introduced elements into our law. Administrative law, in Hamburger's phrase, amounts to the "Prussification of society."[8]

To be clear, Hamburger's argument is by no means an extension or continuation of Rose-Ackerman's. Indeed, the two arguments point in opposite directions. Roughly speaking, if Rose-Ackerman faults German administrative law for not being more American, Hamburger faults American administrative law for being too German. What is more, Hamburger's critique is far more radical and far less thorough in its engagement with the substance of German administrative law.[9] What they have in common is that both engage critically with German administrative law from self-consciously American perspectives. Both find that German administrative law falls short with respect to principles of governance that are important to us today. Simplifying somewhat, Rose-Ackerman finds German administrative law to short-change the democratic principle, and Hamburger, the rule of law.[10]

This contribution takes stock of this episodic transatlantic engagement with German administrative law. With respect to Rose-Ackerman, we survey the original argument in *Controlling Environmental Policy* and consider subsequent developments both in German administrative law and in her perspective, as reflected in *Democracy and Executive Power*. With respect to Hamburger, we focus on his assertion that administrative law is not really or fully law. We argue that a closer look at contemporary German law shows something quite different. German administrative law doctrine today is practically a proof of concept for how administrative governance can be subordinated to law and rigorously conceptualized in terms of coherent legal categories. We do not argue that German administrative law is perfect. But we do argue that it provides robust and effective protection of individuals' interests plus conceptual machinery that facilitates the clear legal analysis of administrative law issues. Far from being Exhibit Number 1 in the case against administrative law's lawfulness, Germany demonstrates in exemplary fashion how administrative power can be effectively domesticated by law.

Controlling Environmental Policy Revisited

Drawing on extensive interviews with stakeholders and experts as well as primary and secondary written sources, *Controlling Environmental Policy* offered a synoptic account of German environmental policymaking from an outsider's perspective. The book's normative lodestar is the proposition that "[m]odern states should develop principles of administrative practice that match substance with procedure."[11] By these lights, Rose-Ackerman concludes, Germany does a poor job.

Administrators make decisions with very different dimensions: some are technical; some affect rights; and some are irreducibly political, whether involving zero-sum games or the possibility of net benefits.[12] The decision-making process should be tailored to the character of the decision to be reached. In particular, when the decision involves balancing competing interests, Rose-Ackerman argues that the decision-makers should engage with the perspectives of those affected. German law, however, largely leaves it up to administrators to decide what the regulatory process entails. She finds it regrettable that interest groups and the public at large often have no right to a seat at the table, or even in the audience, as administrators consider the options.

The book concludes with a series of recommendations that would leave the German administrative process more closely resembling its American counterpart. When administrators must strike trade-offs between affected interests, Rose-Ackerman argues, they should provide broad notice, opportunities for public input, and reasoned explanations for the choices they make. And crucially, these requirements should be enforceable through judicial review.

Years have passed since Rose-Ackerman's critique first appeared, and German administrative law is not the same as it was in the mid-1990s. In fact, the intervening decades have seen developments in German administrative law that move it some distance closer to Rose-Ackerman's ideal. Writing in the 1990s, Rose-Ackerman noted that there were some legally mandated opportunities for participation in norm-setting: for instance, in the planning process.[13] There are now more such opportunities, thanks in part to the influence of European Union (EU) law. The Aarhus Convention, which took effect in 2001, requires EU member states to establish participation rights for civil society groups in public decisions with environmental impacts.[14] EU and international influences have also helped to direct more attention to issues of procedure and public participation in German environmental law scholarship.[15]

At the same time, legislative efforts to speed up infrastructure projects—efforts that began around the time of German Reunification—have continued. For instance, a 2020 statute establishes that certain infrastructure plans can be issued by means of statute, rather than through a planning process, which includes more stakeholder involvement and is typically quite time-consuming.[16] The drumbeat to further accelerate infrastructure projects has grown louder under pressures to accelerate the energy transition and to adapt to the loss of Russian oil following Russia's invasion of Ukraine.

Rose-Ackerman acknowledges these further developments in *Democracy and Executive Power*. As in *Controlling Environmental Policymaking*, public participation in the administrative process occupies a central place in her account of democratic legitimacy.[17] Accordingly, developments in German administrative law are welcome insofar as they promote meaningful public consultation and unwelcome to the extent they threaten it. She notes that the public consultation requirements are triggered by concrete projects, rather than norm-setting processes, but that accepting civil society input on regulations has become more common in the environmental area.[18] She also notes with approval how some administrative processes outside of the environmental area have become more open and transparent over time.[19] With respect to the public consultations involved in implementing the energy transition, she voices the criticism that they come too late in the process to shape the key policy choices, but she has a more positive view about other efforts to engage citizens in discussion about energy policy.[20]

On the whole, then, German administrative processes today measure somewhat better along Rose-Ackerman's yardstick for democratic legitimacy than they did in the 1990s but still fall short. Defenders of Germany's arrangements do have arguments they can make in response.[21] The first is that institutional differences between Germany and the United States blunt the force of Rose-Ackerman's democratic critique. A key concept in German public law is the chain of legitimation (*Legitimationskette*), whereby all exercises of state power are traceable back, through an unbroken chain, to electoral choices made by the people.[22] There are at least three ways in which the link between regulatory outputs and the electoral process may be tighter in Germany than in the United States, making this account more plausible in the former. First, as a parliamentary democracy, the legislative majority and the executive branch in principle work hand in glove, limiting the loss of traction that divided government can introduce between elected representatives and regulatory policy.[23] Second, Germany has a stricter nondelegation doctrine than the United

States, pursuant to which it is the legislature and not the administrators that must make the critical policy choices.[24] Third, under some circumstances, Germany's federal parliament, the *Bundestag*, may participate in the promulgation of regulations, adding an additional layer of democratic involvement to the regulatory process.[25]

What is more, there is more than one conception of what democracy should look like in practice. The German regulatory process may not look very democratic when viewed from the United States, with a perspective on democracy shaped by interest group pluralism and a long tradition of adversarial legalism.[26] We expect to see competing interests clashing, often noisily, in pursuit of their goals, and then ultimately repairing to courts when dissatisfied with the outcome of the policy process. If German regulation does not conform to this picture, it fits better with a different account of what self-government looks like. The standard account in Germany accepts that the formal institutions of administration operate pursuant to a democratic mandate thanks to the chain of legitimation and expects them to engage informally with relevant stakeholders in formulating rules. As Rose-Ackerman notes, this mode of consensus-seeking, deliberative engagement is characteristic of German labor management relations, but it is also of a piece with German postwar policy processes more broadly.[27]

Further, it is also important to bear in mind the distinction drawn in German doctrine between general administrative law (*allgemeines Verwaltungsrecht*) and particular administrative law (*besonderes Verwaltungsrecht*)—that is, special rules applicable to particular areas of law. While there are no participation requirements for administrative law generally, there are some such requirements in particular contexts, such as planning, as noted.[28] Rose-Ackerman argues that administrative law should adopt procedures that match the substance. German administrative lawyers could argue that their system does precisely that, adopting a differentiated instrumentarium of processes for different subject matters, including public participation where it is most appropriate.[29] Further, even if consultation with stakeholders is not generally required by law in the regulatory process, it is in fact typical for administrators to undertake such consultation on their own initiative, as Rose-Ackerman also acknowledges.[30]

These rebuttals to Rose-Ackerman's critique have force. Even so, Rose-Ackerman identifies what for German administrative law is an uncomfortable truth: administrators as a practical matter enjoy substantial policymaking latitude when they decide how to apply statutes in the form of regulations. As Eberhard Schmidt-Aßmann notes, German doctrine has never grappled with how executive norm-setting might call for a different way of thinking about statutory interpretation.[31] And statutory provisions, even when approached with a maximum of lawyerly skill, are typically too abstract to steer administrators towards a determinate outcome.[32] Perhaps German administrative lawyers would be less sanguine about the absence of procedural constraints on administrative norm-setting if they recognized the extent to which policy choice inheres in the formulation of administrative norms. And indeed, the scholarly literature is increasingly open to public participation as a mode of legitimation.[33]

Administrative Unlawfulness?

Philip Hamburger's *Is Administrative Law Unlawful?* is unsparing in its critique of administrative law and clear about where the root of the problem ultimately lies: in American administrative law's German heritage. "American administrative law," he writes, "revives absolute power."[34] On Hamburger's account, early modern England fought off absolutist modes of rule pioneered in continental Europe. In the years that followed, European thinkers, and especially Germans, developed a science of administration that presupposed a consolidated state power not meaningfully constrained by courts or legislatures. Around the turn of the twentieth century, American legal reformers adopted elements of German administrative law thinking, and, in so doing, transplanted seeds of absolutist statecraft into American soil.

Hamburger's book is full of extraordinary claims, and it is worthwhile at the outset to make clear that our engagement with his arguments is limited in its scope.[35] We do not contest the assertion that German ideas about law and administration were influential on Progressive-era scholars and reformers in the United States.[36] Nor are we responding to his characterization of late nineteenth-century German administrative law as an embodiment of absolute power—not because he has made a compelling case,[37] but because the core of his challenge to administrative law reaches beyond this historical claim.

His argument, as we understand it, is not about problems with administrative law at a given point in time, but that administrative governance is *inherently* incompatible with fundamental requirements of legality. The features of administrative governance that Hamburger finds "unlawful" are characteristic of both historical and contemporary administrative law systems.[38] We aim to demonstrate, contrary to Hamburger's claim, that administrative law can be fully lawful in every sense that matters. The subject of our demonstration is the jurisdiction that Hamburger identified as the root of the trouble, Germany, in its contemporary incarnation.

We start, though, by trying to get a better fix on the charge Hamburger levels. What are the features of administrative law that are objectionable, and why?

Hamburger never precisely explains what he means when he claims administrative law is "unlawful,"[39] but he does define other terms that help fill out the contours of his complaint. Instead of the "rule of law" ideal, which Hamburger rejects as "so vague as to be a distraction from the real problems with administrative law," he substitutes a pair of desiderata: rule *through* law and rule *under* law.[40] Rule through law, on Hamburger's account, means that only legislatures and courts can issue binding legal commands to subjects.[41] Rule under law for Hamburger means not only that no authority above the law is recognized, but also that courts' independent interpretations of laws' meaning are always controlling.[42] The term "absolute power" also recurs frequently in Hamburger's argument, but he downplays the conventional understanding of absolute power as unlimited power. Instead, absolute power is the negation of rule through and under law: it is extralegal and supralegal. The third feature of absolute power that Hamburger highlights is that it is "consolidated," by which he means that it blends legislative, judicial, and executive elements.[43]

If "unlawfulness" simply cashed out into these stipulative definitions, then Hamburger would be right about American administrative law. No one denies that agencies issue binding rules; that courts offer deference of different forms to agency interpretations of statutes; or that some agencies perform a mix of executive, adjudicative, and legislative functions. But these features do not, without more, justify the dramatic conclusion that administrative law is unlawful. The idea must be—or so we suppose here[44]—that administrative modes of governance somehow short-change important values associated with law and lawful governance. For the charge to stick, it must be that administrative law revives absolute power in a meaningful sense, not only in the idiosyncratic and technical sense described above.[45] Conversely, a demonstration that administrative law effectively subordinates the power of the state to a coherent normative system that provides robust and consistent protection for persons' important interests would take the air out of Hamburger's critique.

The remainder of this contribution aims to offer such a demonstration, or at least the outlines of one; space limitations prevent anything comprehensive. Our point of reference is German administrative law, not U.S. administrative law. Our contribution is still relevant to the thrust of Hamburger's critique, which we understand to impugn administrative modes of governance in general, and not just administrative law in the United States.[46] To the extent German administrative law beats the charge of unlawfulness, any inherent connection posited between administrative law and lawful governance dissolves.

Thinking Compartmentally

By reputation, German legal thinking tends towards a certain formalism, with analysis heavily structured by a dense framework of finely wrought distinctions.[47] The charge of compartment-based thinking, or *Schubladendenken*, is by no means taken as a reproach by German public lawyers.[48] Rather, a well-stocked inventory of concepts is appreciated as an aid to clear analysis and, ultimately, consistent outcomes.[49]

The emphasis in administrative law on legal forms (*Rechtsformen*) is characteristic of this approach.[50] The legal forms are predefined modes of legal activity in administrative law. They function as containers filled with specific doctrinal contents.[51] As soon as an agency has taken the decision in favor of one legal form, the most crucial legal consequences are locked in. Although there is not a *numerus clausus* of legal forms, the legal features of the important forms—*Rechtsverordnung* (regulation), *Satzung* (bylaw), *Verwaltungsakt* (administrative act), *Verwaltungsvertrag* (administrative contract), *Verwaltungsvorschrift* (internal prescription), and *Realakt* (real act)—are well established.[52] The legal forms facilitate the conceptual compartmentalization of administrative activity that promotes consistency and predictability within German administrative law.[53]

Each legal form has its own set of procedural and/or substantive requirements as well as its own rules for how and where it can be challenged.[54] Each also has a well-defined legal character, such that knowing the legal form of an agency action gives us important information about how it functions legally.[55] The focal point in the discussion that follows is the *Verwaltungsakt*, the legal form traditionally at the heart of German administrative law doctrine, and the one that brings the individual most directly into contact with administrative power.[56]

The Administration in Action

In its classic form, the *Verwaltungsakt* (plural *Verwaltungsakte*) is an authoritative measure issued by the administration to govern a concrete, individual case in a legally binding way.[57] Without having the character of legal norms, which in German law are typically abstract and general,[58] *Verwaltungsakte* mandate binding legal consequences.[59] *Verwaltungsakte* can implicate citizens' fundamental rights very directly, inasmuch as they target a specific individual and subject matter.[60]

The legal "bite" of a *Verwaltungsakt* is regulated by statute. Doctrine draws a distinction between *Wirksamkeit* (in adjective form, *wirksam*) and *Bestandskraft* (in adjective form, *bestandskräftig*).[61] A *Verwaltungsakt* is *wirksam* from the time it is made public, and as such, legally binding for both the issuing authority and the addressee.[62] It is subject to challenge, however, until it has become *bestandskräftig*.[63] German doctrine distinguishes between two kinds of *Bestandskraft*: "*materiell*" and "*formell*."[64] "*Materiell*" in this connection refers to the substantive legal effect of the *Verwaltungsakt*, and "*formell*" concerns the procedural formalities and their consequences. A *Verwaltungsakt* is *formell bestandskräftig* once the time allowed for an appeal, typically one month, has expired. Once an administrative act is *formell bestandskräftig*, it becomes legally uncontestable.[65] The consequence is that the act also becomes *materiell bestandskräftig*: its substantive legal effect is now permanent, and with *erga omnes* impact.[66]

One can see how the *Verwaltungsakt* might raise some rule-of-law concerns. The administration can change individuals' rights and duties in a legally binding way that may be irreversible. The legal force of *Verwaltungsakte* is comparable to the legal force of judgments. In civil procedure, a court judgment is usually required before a party seeks execution.[67] In administrative law, however, the *Verwaltungsakt* is a legally sufficient basis for administrative agencies to create their own deeds of execution.[68] German doctrine recognizes this administrative prerogative as the *Recht der Verwaltung zur*

Selbsttitulierung—the administration's right to issue its own legally binding titles.[69] What is more, even a *Verwaltungsakt* that is contrary to law (*rechtswidrig*), either substantively or procedurally, becomes legally effective if the addressee does not appeal before the deadline.[70]

Other concerns arise when we compare how the administration and the legislature shape the legal environment. A *Rechtsverordnung* and a *Satzung* function substantively like legislative acts. Yet they tend to be far easier to put into place than statutes, as their procedural requirements tend to be minimal in comparison to the rules governing parliamentary lawmaking.[71] Because the *Rechtsverordnung* and the *Satzung* are more flexible and adaptable tools than the statute, they typically regulate matters more minutely than statutes, which are harder to change.[72] The chain of democratic legitimation is of course longer for the administration than the (directly elected) parliament[73]—and yet it is the administration that regulates the lives of individuals more intensively, and with fewer required procedures.[74]

How is it reconcilable with rule-of-law values for the administration to alter legal rights and duties so freely, seemingly acting as a law unto itself? Let us bracket for a moment the issue of *Verwaltungsakte* that are contrary to law and nonetheless legally binding, which we take up below, and focus first on the fact that the administration can unilaterally alter legal rights and duties.

The Law-Limited Leviathan

The first point to make is that the administration can only alter legal rights and duties pursuant to specific and explicit authorization from the legislature.[75] The doctrine of reservation of law (*Vorbehalt des Gesetzes*) provides that the administration may only take measures that burden individuals if the legislature, by statute, has explicitly authorized the administration to reach into individuals' private sphere in that manner.[76] Relatedly, according to the abstraction doctrine, German law strictly separates the tasks given to the administration and the powers it has to fulfill those tasks.[77] Specifically, one cannot extrapolate any administrative powers from a task entrusted to an agency, even those powers necessary to complete the task effectively.[78] Accordingly, when interpreting statutory provisions, it is important to distinguish between norms that set tasks and those that confer powers, as only the latter can legitimate the interference with individuals' rights.[79]

The reservation of law is essentially a binary: it answers the question of whether or not a legislative act is necessary before the administration can act.[80] Other legal principles address the character of the legislation necessary to authorize administrative infringements. Article 80, paragraph 1, sentence 2 of the German Basic Law embodies a nondelegation principle, pursuant to which the legislature is required to lay down the content, purpose, and extent of all statutes it enacts, including those delegating regulatory power to other bodies.[81] Relatedly, the essentiality doctrine (*Wesentlichkeitstheorie*) demands that in matters implicating the relationship between citizen and state, the legislature has to make the key decisions itself.[82] Moreover, most fundamental right provisions in the Basic Law include a statutory reservation (*Gesetzesvorbehalt*), meaning that a statute is required if the content of the right is to be affected.[83] Together, these mechanisms ensure that those interactions between individuals and the administration where much is at stake are closely regulated by the legislature itself.[84] Along with the reservation of law and the abstraction doctrine, these requirements have the effect of tying administrative activity that affects individuals' legal interests back to the legislative process, both procedurally and substantively, such that the administration by no means functions as a law unto itself.[85]

But to return to the problem bracketed earlier, what about the *Verwaltungsakt* that is contrary to law yet nonetheless legally binding? This would surely be irreconcilable with rule of law values if those affected had no meaningful opportunity to challenge such acts. But in fact, German administrative law provides robust opportunities to seek review of adverse administrative actions, including *Verwaltungsakte*.

Legal protections against administrative action play out against a sweeping constitutional guarantee. Article 19, paragraph 4, sentence 1 of the Basic Law provides that "[s]hould any person's rights be violated by public authority, he may have recourse to the courts."[86] Given this guarantee, the executive power to intervene in the citizens' rights has as a necessary correlate the provision of legal supervision by competent courts. Statutory provisions define the contours of this constitutional promise, regulating the process by which individuals can challenge adverse administrative actions, including *Verwaltungsakte*.[87] Following (in most cases) a required appeal to the administration, a challenger can seek review in a specialized, independent administrative court.[88] To bring a challenge, litigants must point to a legal norm that grounds the relief they seek.[89] In the case of *Verwaltungsakte* that are contrary to law, this is easily done. The *Elfes*-doctrine, named after a 1957 decision of Germany's Federal Constitutional Court,[90] recognizes in the Basic Law a fundamental right to a general freedom of action.[91] A *Verwaltungsakt* that is contrary to law threatens to permanently infringe the recipient's general freedom of action, providing a basis for suit.[92, 93]

If the availability of judicial review addresses the problem of the administrative act that is contrary to law, what about situations where meaningful legal standards to judge an action against are missing? Discretion plays an important role in German administrative law, in the form of *Ermessensspielraum*.[94] *Ermessensspielraum* presupposes a conditional norm, which is very common in German administrative law.[95] Conditional norms have an "if, then" structure: if condition *x* obtains, then consequence *y*.[96] *Ermessensspielraum* exists in the form of decisional discretion (*Entschließungsermessen*) when it is up to the administration to decide *whether* to impose a consequence, as when a norm provides that the administration *can* do *y*, if *x*.[97] *Ermessensspielraum* exists in the form of selection discretion (*Auswahlermessen*) when it is up to the administration to decide *which* consequence to impose, as when a norm provides that the administration shall do *y* or *z*, if *x*.[98] Where the administration acts with discretion, the scope for judicial review contracts considerably, leaving individuals more at the mercy of the administration.[99]

It does not fully resolve concerns about administrative discretion to observe that, in those areas where the administration enjoys discretion, no one is entitled to a particular legal outcome. A better response is that even when the administration uses discretion, it remains subject to legal standards that can form a basis for judicial review. Even where the administration has exercised discretion, judges may still examine whether it identified the facts correctly, whether it took extraneous considerations into account, and whether it acted arbitrarily.[100]

Discretionary actions are also defective if they violate the principle of proportionality.[101] The principle of proportionality offers a wide-reaching protection against government overreach, operationalized through a series of legal tests: a chosen measure must be suitable to achieve its chosen purpose, must restrict freedoms no more than necessary, and must not stand out of proportion to its intended goal.[102] The proportionality principle was originally developed in police law, a subfield of administrative law,[103] but now is regarded as following from the rule of law.[104] There are no law-free spaces in German administrative law.

It is true that, if the addressee of a *Vewaltungsakt* does not bring a timely challenge, the act becomes permanently binding, regardless of any errors it may contain.[105] But clear rules governing the legal status of official actions, including deadlines for filing challenges, also serve the end of legal certainty. And if the gravity of the defect is truly extreme, the act is void *ab initio* and therefore never binding.[106]

The focus to this point has been on the *Verwaltungsakt*, but the controls on administrative power apply to other legal forms as well. And if, as noted, the externally valid, abstract-general norms created by the administration—the *Rechtsverordnung* and *Satzung*—are easier to put into place than a statute, they are also easier to set out of force, as a procedural matter. Pursuant to Article 100, paragraph 1, sentence 1 of the Basic Law, only the Federal Constitutional Court can invalidate a statute.[107] By contrast, the Higher Administrative Courts, which exist at the state level, are in general competent to dismiss executive norms such as *Rechtsverordnungen* and *Satzungen*.[108] What is more, every court is authorized to disapply any norm issued by the executive.[109] In contrast to the *Verwaltungsakt*, a *Rechtsverordnung* that is contrary to law is void and therefore not binding.[110]

Conclusion

There is much that separates how Susan Rose-Ackerman and Philip Hamburger engage with German administrative law, but both self-consciously regard it from the outside, from a perspective external to the German legal system.

Encounters such as these can be productive, vividly highlighting the contrasts between different legal systems. They can potentially generate insights both about the object of study and about one's own perspective.

Susan Rose-Ackerman's work on Germany makes an important contribution by highlighting the limited role public participation plays in administrative norm-setting. This feature of German public law stands out especially when contrasted with American expectations for policymaking, shaped by presidentialism and an interest group pluralist conception of democracy. But even if Germany's approach is more readily reconcilable with its own model of democracy than the American, Rose-Ackerman's perspective helps to spotlight the degree to which norm-setting amounts to naked policy choice, an inconvenient truth that German doctrine is reluctant to confront.

The lesson from Hamburger's work is different. This chapter has aimed to show that, in fact, German administrative law takes high marks for conformity with rule-of-law values. The claim is not that German administrative law is perfect, or a model for every legal system, but that Germany's is an administrative law system that takes law and lawfulness seriously.[111] Hamburger's engagement with the foundations of German administrative law does not tell us much about Germany, but instead highlights the emptiness of his critique of administrative governance.

Notes

1 The most notable landmark of comparative administrative law's first flowering in the United States was Frank Goodnow's massive study. Frank J. Goodnow, Comparative Administrative Law: An Analysis of the Administrative Systems, National and Local, of the United States, England, France and Germany (1893).

2 Susan Rose-Ackerman, Controlling Environmental Policy: The Limits of Public Law in Germany and the United States (1995). The year before the book appeared, Rose-Ackerman published a piece in the *Harvard Law Review* that previewed the book's main arguments. *See* Susan Rose-Ackerman, *American Administration Law Under Siege: Is Germany a Model?*, 107 Harv. L. Rev. 1279 (1994).

3 Susan Rose-Ackerman, Democracy and Executive Power: Policymaking Accountability in the US, the UK, Germany, and France (2021).

4 Rose-Ackerman, *supra* note 2, at vii.

5 As discussed further below, some particular areas of administrative law—*besonderes Verwaltungsrecht*, in German—do regulate the process by which administrators set norms.

6 The *Verwaltungsakt*, discussed further below, is an official measure with direct, outward-facing legal effect taken by an administrative authority to govern an individual case. *See* Verwaltungsverfahrensgesetz [VwVfG] [Administrative Procedure Act] § 35, sentence 1 (providing a legal definition).

7 *See* Eberhard Schmidt-Assmann, Das Verwaltungsrecht der Vereinigten Staaten von Amerika 183–86 (2021). *Controlling Environmental Policy* also appeared in Germany in translation. Susan Rose-Ackerman, Umweltrecht und Politik in den Vereinigten Staaten und der Bundesrepublik Deutschland (1995).

8 Philip Hamburger, Is Administrative Law Unlawful? 505 (2014).
9 The bulk of Hamburger's book is focused on formative developments in the constitutional history of England, rather than Germany. Hamburger's claims about English legal history have also not gone unchallenged. *See* Paul Craig, *The Legitimacy of US Administrative Law and the Foundations of English Administrative Law: Setting the Historical Record Straight*, Oxford Legal. Stud. Rsch. Paper No. 44/2016 (2016); *see also* Philip Hamburger, *Early Prerogative and Administrative Power: A Response to Paul Craig*, 81 Mo. L. Rev. 939 (2016); Paul Craig, *English Foundations of US Administrative Law: Four Central Errors*, Oxford Legal Stud., Rsch. Paper No. 3/2017, 2016.
10 As discussed further below, Hamburger himself rejects the term "rule of law" as too vague.
11 Rose-Ackerman, *supra* note 2, at 120.
12 *Id.* at 122. With respect to political decisions where net benefits are possible, she further distinguishes between settings where all interests are and are not well represented.
13 Rose-Ackerman, *supra* note 2, at 82; Baugesetzbuch [BauGB] [Building Code], § 3.
14 1998 Aarhus Convention on Access to Information, Public Participation in Decision-Making and Access to Justice in Environmental Matters, 2161 U.N.T.S. 447, 38 I.L.M. 517 (1999).
15 *See* Eberhard Schmidt-Aßmann & Ann-Katrin Kaufhold, *Der Verfahrensgedanke im deutschen und europäischen Verwaltungsrecht* (§ 27), *in* 2 Grundlagen des Verwaltungsrechts rn. 73 ff. (Andreas Voßkuhle, Martin Eifert & Christoph Möllers eds., 3d ed. 2022) (referring to the concept of an informed public).
16 Gesetz zur Vorbereitung der Schaffung von Baurecht durch Maßnahmengesetz im Verkehrsbereich [Maßnahmengesetzvorbereitungsgesetz - MgvG] [Act to Prepare for the Establishment of Construction Law Through Legal Measures Legislation in the Area of Transportation], Bundesgesetzblatt [BGBl.] I, p. 640 (March 20, 2020).
17 *See, e.g.*, Rose-Ackerman, *supra* note 3, at 16 ("[E]xecutive branch agencies ought to engage in public consultation in their efforts to fill the constitutional and statutory gaps that are a precondition for effective policymaking.").
18 *Id.* at 56.
19 *See, e.g.*, *id.* at 109 (describing the increased accountability of the Standardization Institute (*Deutsches Institut für Normung*, DIN).
20 *Id.* at 58–59.
21 Peter Lindseth's review of *Controlling Environmental Policy* lays out versions of these arguments. Peter L. Lindseth, *Comparing Administrative States: Susan Rose-Ackerman and the Limits of Public Law in Germany and the United States*, 2 Colum. J. Eur. L. 589 (1996).
22 Ernst-Wolfgang Böckenförde, *Demokratie als Verfassungsprinzip* (§ 24), *in* 1 Handbuch des Staatsrechts der Bundesrepublik Deutschland rn. 11–25 (Josef Isensee & Paul Kirchhof eds., 3d ed. 2004).
23 *See, e.g.*, Horst Dreier, Hierarchische Verwaltung im Demokratischen Staat 131–32 (1991).
24 It should be noted that the case law applying this requirement is often faulted for its less than lapidary precision, *see, e.g.*, Eberhard Schmidt-Assmann, *supra* note 7 at 84, and as Rose-Ackerman notes of environmental law, in certain contexts very broad delegations have been sustained. Rose-Ackerman, *supra* note 2, at 58.
25 Grundgesetz [GG] [Basic Law], art. 80, para. 2. *See also* Arnd Uhle, *Die Rechtsverordnung* (§ 24), in Gesetzgebung: Rechtsetzung durch Parlamente und Verwaltungen sowie ihre gerichtliche Kontrolle [hereinafter Gesetzgebung] rn. 74–95 (Winfried Kluth & Günter Krings eds., 1st ed. 2014). For a critical perspective on the Constitutional Court's jurisprudence on participation

rights, *see* Mario Martini, *Normsetzung und andere Formen exekutivischer Selbstprogrammierung* (§ 33), *in* 2 Grundlagen des Verwaltungsrechts, *supra* note 15, rn. 39 ff. (criticizing the jurisprudence of the Constitutional Court on this issue). In addition, the Bundesrat, which represents the states in the German legislative process, also sometimes participates in the promulgation of regulations. *See, e.g.*, Kreislaufwirtschaftsgesetz [KrWG] [Circular Economy Act] § 63.

26 *See* Jud Mathews, *Minimally Democratic Administrative Law*, 68 Admin. L. Rev. 613–22 (2016) (on interest group pluralism and administrative law); Robert A. Kagan, Adversarial Legalism (2019) (on adversarial legalism generally).

27 Writing in the decade before reunification, Peter Katzenstein argued that the dispersal of decisional power across institutions and actors in Germany's postwar political order gives policy change in Germany a distinctive signature. Because no institution is in a position to undertake significant change unilaterally, cooperative processes are a necessity, and the changes coming out of these processes are generally incremental. Peter J. Katzenstein, Policy and Politics in West Germany: The Growth of a Semisovereign State (1987).

28 For additional examples of participation rights, *see* Bundesimmissionsschutzgesetz [BImSchG] [Federal Emission Control Law] § 10; Bundesnaturschutzgesetz [BNatSchG] [Federal Natural Protection Act] § 63, para. 2, sentence 1 and para. 3, sentence 1.

29 *See* Schmidt-Assmann, *supra* note 24, at 185–86 (describing complex, participatory procedures in planning and social security law, and suggesting that the existence of processes such as these may be a reason the demand for participation opportunities more generally has been limited).

30 Rose-Ackerman, *supra* note 2, at 68.

31 *See* Schmidt-Assmann, *supra* note 24, at 374. Schmidt-Aßmann observes that the basic techniques of statutory interpretation are adapted from the private law context, where executive norm-setting is not an issue. It should be added that constitutional considerations do shape the use of interpretive techniques in the public law context. *See* Bernd Rüthers, *Wer schafft Recht? – Methodenfragen als Macht- und Verfassungsfragen*, 58 JuristenZeitung 995, 996 (2003).

32 For a detailed discussion of the reasons why the steering power of statutes is limited, *see* Dreier, *supra* note 23, at 160–74.

33 *See, e.g.*, Jens Kersten, *Beteiligung—Partizipation—Öffentlichkeit* (§ 29), *in* 2 Grundlagen des Verwaltungsrechts, *supra* note 15, rn. 56 ff.; Hans-Heinrich Trute, *Die demokratische Legitimation der Verwaltung* (§ 9), *in* 2 Grundlagen des Verwaltungsrechts, *supra* note 15, rn. 69 ff.

34 *See* Hamburger, *supra* note 8, at 441.

35 For a wider ranging critique of Hamburger's claims, *see* Emad Atiq & Jud Mathews, *The Uncertain Foundations of Public Law Theory*, 31 Cornell J. Law & Pub. Pol. 389 (2023).

36 For an argument that Hegelian thought in particular was influential for *fin de siècle* U.S. public administration thinkers, *see* Blake Emerson, The Public's Law: Origins and Architecture of Progressive Democracy (2019).

37 For a measured appraisal of the Prussian Administrative Court, which powerfully shaped the administrative law of the period, *see* Kenneth F. Ledford, *Formalizing the Rule of Law in Prussia: The Supreme Administrative Law Court, 1876–1914*, 37 Cent. Europ. Hist. 203–224 (2004).

38 There are, of course, variations in time as well as by jurisdiction. Judicial deference to administrative interpretations of law, which Hamburger identifies as "supralegality," is much more characteristic of American administrative law than its German counterpart.

39 It is also worth pausing to consider what, exactly, the term "administrative law" refers to. Administrative law can mean the law *of* administration—that is, the legal

norms produced by the administration—as well as the law *for* administration—the legal benchmarks for administrative agencies. In our view, administrative law encompasses both.

40 Hamburger, *supra* note 8, at 7.

41 *Id.* at 22–24.

42 *Id.* at 24–25; 313–15.

43 *Id.* at 25–26.

44 In a previous paper, one of us and a co-author analyze the argument in jurisprudential terms, as a claim about the nature of law and identify both positivist and anti-positivist versions of the claim that the text supports. Ultimately, we conclude that both versions rest on controversial or implausible assumptions that are never fleshed out or defended. *See* Atiq & Mathews, *supra* note 35.

45 Hamburger plays up the dramatic associations of the term "absolute power." Hamburger's identification of administrative law with absolute power—whose essence he distils into the Roman maxim "What pleases the prince has the force of law" — suggests that administrative law is dangerous, in his view, precisely in that it leaves people vulnerable to the will of those in positions of authority.

46 More specifically, Hamburger's charges of extralegality, supralegality, and consolidation of powers could also be applied to German administrative law, even though the specific legal mechanisms in the two systems differ.

47 *See, e.g.*, Robin Hofmann, *Formalism Versus Pragmatism—A Comparative Legal and Empirical Analysis of the German and Dutch Criminal Justice Systems with Regard to Effectiveness and Efficiency*, 28 Maastricht J. Eur. & Comp. Law 452–78 (2021).

48 Wolfgang Hoffmann-Riem & Matthias Bäcker, *Rechtsformen, Handlungsformen, Bewirkungsformen* (§ 33), *in* 2 Grundlagen des Verwaltungsrechts, *supra* note 15, rn. 11.

49 *Id.*, rn. 10.

50 Eberhard Schmidt-Assmann, Das allgemeine Verwaltungsrecht als Ordnungsidee 297, rn. 34 (2d ed. 2006).

51 *Id.* The complementary concept "form of action" (*Handlungsform*) focuses on the content of administrative activity, rather than how it is instantiated legally. *See* Schmidt-Assmann, *supra* note 50, at 297, rn. 34. For instance, during the Coronavirus pandemic administrative authorities in Germany imposed curfews by means of administrative acts as well as regulations. The curfew is a single form of action that can take more than one legal form.

52 Hartmut Maurer & Christian Waldhoff, Allgemeines Verwaltungsrecht 199–200 (20th ed. 2020).

53 *Id.*

54 Barbara Remmert, *Schlichtes Verwaltungshandeln* (§ 17), *in* Allgemeines Verwaltungsrecht rn. 1–12 (Dirk Ehlers & Hermann Pünder eds., 15th ed. 2015). For instance, a *Rechtsverordnung* can either be contested in front of the Federal Constitutional Court or in front of the Higher Administrative Courts of the states. A *Verwaltungsakt* can in principle be contested before the administrative courts. While a *Verwaltungsakt* requires a hearing if it tends to interfere in citizens' individual rights, there is no such condition for a *Rechtsverordnung* or *Satzung*. A *Verwaltungsakt* on the one hand can be issued orally, whereas legal norms as the *Rechtsverordnung* and *Satzung* on the other hand have to be published in writing. And if an administrative agency disregards some formal requirement when issuing a *Verwaltungsakt*, this mistake can be cured, even in the judicial process. Opportunities to rectify errors in a *Rechtsverordnung* or *Satzung* are limited.

55 Franz-Joseph Peine & Thorsten Siegel, Allgemeines Verwaltungsrecht rn. 264 (13th ed. 2020).

56 Matthias Ruffert, *Verwaltungsakt* (§ 21), *in* ALLGEMEINES VERWALTUNGSRECHT rn. 1–9 (Dirk Ehlers & Hermann Pünder eds., 15th ed. 2015).
57 *See* Verwaltungsverfahrensgesetz [VwVfG] [Administrative Procedure Act], § 35. The Administrative Procedure Act also recognizes as a *Verwaltungsakt* a general directive (*Allgemeinverfügung*), which is distinguished from the classical *Verwaltungsakt* in that it can be directed to a larger number of addressees.
58 JÖRG IPSEN, ALLGEMEINES VERWALTUNGSRECHT rn. 290 (11th ed. 2019).
59 Rolf Stober, *Allgemeine Erschließung der Rechtsquellen und ihre Abgrenzung* (§ 24), *in* 1 VERWALTUNGSRECHT rn. 10 (Hans J. Wolff, Otto Bachof, Rolf Stober & Winfried Kluth eds., 13th ed. 2017).
60 Horst Dreier, Foreword to Article 1, *in* 1 GRUNDGESETZ KOMMENTAR rn. 124 (Horst Dreier ed., 3d ed. 2013).
61 Christian Bumke, *Verwaltungsakte* (§ 35), *in* 2 GRUNDLAGEN DES VERWALTUNGSRECHTS, *supra* note 48, rn. 155 ff.
62 VwVfG § 43.
63 HANS PETER BULL & VEITH MEHDE, ALLGEMEINES VERWALTUNGSRECHT MIT VERWALTUNGSLEHRE rn. 752 (9th ed. 2015).
64 Ruffert, *supra* note 56, rn. 24 ff.
65 WILFRIED ERBGUTH & ANNETTE GUCKELBERGER, ALLGEMEINES VERWALTUNGSRECHT MIT VERWALTUNGSPROZESSRECHT UND STAATSHAFTUNGSRECHT § 15, rn. 10 (10th ed. 2020). For a sophisticated approach to the issue, *see* Hans-Uwe Erichsen & Ulrich Knoke, *Bestandskraft von Verwaltungsakten* 2 NEUE ZEITSCHRIFT FÜR VERWALTUNGSRECHT 185 (1983).
66 Erichsen & Knoke, *supra* note 65, at 187 ff.
67 *See* Uwe Schmidt, Foreword to § 705, *in* ZIVILPROZESSORDNUNG KOMMENTAR rn. 104 (Monika Anders & Burkhard Gehle eds., 79th ed. 2021).
68 Ulrich Ramsauer, *Begriff des Verwaltungsaktes* (§ 35), *in* VERWALTUNGSVERFAHRENSGESETZ KOMMENTAR rn. 11 (Ulrich Ramsauer & Ferdinand O. Kopp eds., 22d ed. 2021).
69 MAURER & WALDHOFF, *supra* note 52 at § 9, rn. 40.
70 IPSEN, *supra* note 58, rn. 662–78. German doctrine distinguishes between being contrary to law (*rechtswidrig*) and being void (*nichtig*). *Verwaltungsakte* are void when they obviously suffer from especially grave legal errors and for that reason have no legal effect. VwVfG §§ 43(3), 44(1), (2).
71 Arnd Uhle, *Die Rechtsverordnung* (§ 24), *in* GESETZGEBUNG rn. 7.
72 On parliamentary norms, *see* PETER SCHINDLER, DATENHANDBUCH ZUR GESCHICHTE DES DEUTSCHEN BUNDESTAGES 1949 BIS 1999 2413–15 (1999). *See also* Max-Emanuel Geis, *Der Erlass von Satzungen* (§ 25), in GESETZGEBUNG, *supra* note 71, rn. 18; Uhle, *supra* note 71, rn. 8.
73 MICHAEL KLOEPFER, 1 VERFASSUNGSRECHT § 7, rn. 222 ff. (2011).
74 For a partially differing opinion, *see* Hermann Hill & Mario Martini, *Normsetzung und andere Formen exekutivischer Selbstprogrammierung* (§ 33), *in* 2 GRUNDLAGEN DES VERWALTUNGSRECHTS, *supra* note 15, rn. 16 ff.
75 Horst Dreier, Commentary on Article 20 (Democracy), in 2 GRUNDGESETZ KOMMENTAR rn. 120 (Horst Dreier ed., 3d ed. 2015).
76 MAURER & WALDHOFF, *supra* note 52, § 6, rn. 3–6.
77 Franz Reimer, *". . . einfach wieder die Folgerungsweise des Polizeistaates": Zur Unterscheidung von Aufgaben und Befugnissen im Polizeirecht*, *in* VERFASSUNGSSTAATLICHKEIT IM WANDEL: FESTSCHRIFT FÜR THOMAS WÜRTENBERGER ZUM 70. GEBURTSTAG 1047, 1056 (Dirk Heckmann, Ralf P. Schenke & Gernot Sydow Heckmann eds., 2013).
78 Winfried Kluth, *Gesetzmäßigkeit der Verwaltung und Vorbehalt des Gesetzes* (§ 30), *in* 1 VERWALTUNGSRECHT *supra* note 59, rn. 30.

79 Reimer, *supra* note 77, at 1056 ff.
80 Oliver Lepsius, *Gesetz und Gesetzgebung* (§ 12) *in* HANDBUCH DES VERFASSUNGSRECHTS: DARSTELLUNG IN TRANSNATIONALER PERSPEKTIVE rn. 61 ff. (Matthias Herdegen, Ralf Poscher, Johannes Masing & Klaus Ferdinand Gärditz eds., 20th ed. 2021); MAURER & WALDHOFF, *supra* note 52, § 6, rn. 12–15. For a differing opinion, *see* Bernd Grzeszick, Commentary on Article 20 (Right of Resistance), *in* GRUNDGESETZ KOMMENTAR rn 75 ff. (Günter Dürig, Roman Herzog & Rupert Scholz eds., 95th supplement 2021).
81 Martin Kment, Commentary on Article 80, *in* GRUNDGESETZ FÜR DIE BUNDESREPUBLIK DEUTSCHLAND KOMMENTAR rn. 13 (Hans D. Jarass & Bodo Pieroth eds., 16th ed. 2020). *See also supra* note 24 and accompanying text.
82 *See, e.g.*, Bundesverfassungsgericht [BVerfG] [Federal Constitutional Court] Aug. 8, 1978, 49 ENTSCHEIDUNGEN DES BUNDESVERFASSUNGSGERICHTS [BVERFGE] 89, 126.
83 *See, e.g.*, GG, art. 8 ("(1) All Germans shall have the right to assemble peacefully and unarmed without prior notification or permission. (2) In the case of outdoor assemblies, this right may be restricted by or pursuant to a law.").
84 Lepsius, *supra* note 80, rn. 61–68.
85 *See also* KLOEPFER, *supra* note 73, rn. 112.
86 GG, art. 19, para. 4, sentence 1.
87 Christian Ernst, Commentary on Article 19, *in* 1 GRUNDGESETZ KOMMENTAR rn. 110 (Ingo von Münch und Philip Kunig eds., 7th ed. 2021).
88 *See Verwaltungsgerichtsordnung* [VwGO] [Administrative Judicial Review Ordinance].
89 Helge Sodan, Commentary on § 42, *in* VERWALTUNGSGERICHTSORDNUNG GROSSKOMMENTAR rn. 364 ff. (Helge Sodan & Jan Ziekow eds., 5th ed. 2018).
90 BVerfG, Jan. 16, 1957, 6 BVERFGE 32.
91 6 BVERFGE 32, 36 ff. The right is rooted in Article 2, paragraph 1 of the Basic Law, which provides that "Every person shall have the right to free development of his personality insofar as he does not violate the rights of others or offend against the constitutional order or the moral law."
92 Kai-Uwe Riese, Commentary on § 113 VwGO, *in* VERWALTUNGSRECHT / VERWALTUNGS-GERICHTSORDNUNG KOMMENTAR rn. 30 (Friedrich Schoch & Jens-Peter Schneider eds., 41st supplement July 2022).
93 One cannot only challenge a burdensome *Verwaltungsakt*, but also, for instance, claim that one is legally entitled to a favorable *Verwaltungsakt* (say, the issuance of a license). Where *Verwaltungsakte* are concerned, there is in general a requirement to exhaust administrative remedies before proceeding to court. If the administration exercised discretion, not only the lawfulness of the challenged measure but also its expediency (*Zweckmäßigkeit*) is subject to review in the internal process. VwGO § 68, para. 1, sentence 1. One may also bring a legal challenge to administrative actions that have factual, not legal, effect, so-called *Realakte*. MAURER & WALDHOFF, *supra* note 52, § 15, rn. 7.
94 *See e.g.*, Eberhard Schmidt-Aßmann, *Einführung: Besonderes Verwaltungsrecht und Allgemeines Verwaltungsrecht. Zusammenwirken und Lerneffekte*, *in* BESONDERES VERWALTUNGSRECHT rn. 10 (Friedrich Schoch ed., 15th ed. 2013); Friedrich Schoch, Kapitel 2: *Polizei- und Ordnungsrecht*, *in* BESONDERES VERWALTUNGSRECHT rn. 151 (Friedrich Schoch ed., 15th ed. 2013).
95 IPSEN, *supra* note 58, rn. 512 ff.
96 MAURER & WALDHOFF, *supra* note 52, § 7, rn. 7 ff.
97 STEFFEN DETTERBECK, ALLGEMEINES VERWALTUNGSRECHT rn. 314 (19th ed. 2021).

98 IPSEN, *supra* note 58, rn. 530. Administrative discretion to answer the "if" question—that is, to determine whether the required condition exists or not—also exists in German law and goes by the name *Beurteilungsspielraum*. This is considered exceptional, however, as deciding whether conditions set by law are met or not is considered ultimately a matter of legal interpretation, on which courts should have the last word. Accordingly, a statute must make clear that the legislature intends to leave it to the administration to determine whether a condition obtains, *see* PEINE & SIEGEL, *supra* note 55, rn. 192 ff.; *see generally* Schönenbroicher, *Ermessen* (§ 40), *in* VERWALTUNGSVERFAHRENSGESETZ GROSSKOMMENTAR rn. 43 ff. (Thomas Mann, Christoph Sennekamp & Michael Uechtritz eds., 2d ed. 2019).

99 Schoch, *Gerichtliche Verwaltungskontrollen* (§ 50), *in* 3 GRUNDLAGEN DES VERWALTUNGSRECHTS, supra note 15, rn. 267.

100 Kai-Uwe Riese, Commentary on § 114 VwGO, *in* SCHOCH & SCHNEIDER, *supra* note 92, rn. 56 ff. (presenting the prevailing opinion). For an even more sophisticated approach, *see* Robert Alexy, *Ermessensfehler*, 41 JURISTENZEITUNG 701 (1986).

101 *See* MAURER & WALDHOFF, *supra* note 52, § 10, rn. 50.

102 LOTHAR MICHAEL & MICHAEL MORLOK, GRUNDRECHTE, rn. 605 ff. (7th ed. 2020).

103 Winfried Kluth, *Das Übermaßverbot*, 29 JURISTISCHE ARBEITSBLÄTTER 606 (1999).

104 Hans Hofmann, Commentary on Article 20, *in* GRUNDGESETZ KOMMENTAR rn. 72 (Bruno Schmidt-Bleibtreu, Hans Hofmann & Hans-Günter Henneke eds., 14th ed. 2018); Hans D. Jarass, Commentary on Article 20, *in* GRUNDGESETZ FÜR DIE BUNDESREPUBLIK DEUTSCHLAND KOMMENTAR, *supra* note 81, rn. 112; Grzeszick, *supra* note 80.

105 DETTERBECK, *supra* note 97, rn. 563.

106 Ulrich Ramsauer, *Nichtigkeit des Verwaltungsaktes* (§ 44), *in* VERWALTUNGSVERFAHRENSGESETZ KOMMENTAR, *supra* note 68, rn. 3 ff.

107 KLAUS SCHLAICH & STEFAN KORIOTH, DAS BUNDESVERFASSUNGSGERICHT pt. 4, rn. 134 ff. (12th ed. 2021).

108 *See* VwGO, § 47, para. 1, sentences 1 and 2 in connection with state laws. As a practical matter, standing doctrine limits those who can challenge an executive norm to those whose rights are affected. FRIEDHELM HUFEN, VERWALTUNGPROZESSRECHT § 19, 19–34 (2021).

109 MAURER & WALDHOFF, *supra* note 52, § 4, rn. 61–67.

110 On the so-called *Nichtigkeitsdogma*, *see, e.g.*, Barbara Remmert, Commentary on Article 80, *in* GRUNDGESETZ KOMMENTAR, *supra* note 80, rn. 137; *see generally* Anton Zimmermann, *Die Folgen der Rechtswidrigkeit von Rechtsnormen*, 48 JURISTISCHE ARBEITSBLÄTTER 249 (2018).

111 *See also* Reimer, *supra* note 77, at 1064.

4 Administrative Resilience

Stefanie Egidy

Introduction

Despite their heterogeneity, constitutions around the world call for institutional design features that promote and strengthen the resilience of public actors. This chapter argues for a concept of "resilience" that equips administrative actors with the necessary tools to address systemic challenges by recognizing their complex and dynamic nature. It leverages the current demand for institutional design arising from the rapidly advancing digital transformation of the executive sector and shows how resilience can guide the construction of the digital administrative state.

Resilient organizations provide stability and reliable reactions in the face of volatile situations. They are essential pillars of a democracy by forming an intricate support structure for providing collective goods, such as social peace, physical wellbeing, the protection of human rights, but also financial stability. Current challenges include crises of constitutional democracy, health emergencies, like most recently the Covid-19 pandemic, financial crises, and climate change.[1]

Administrative law plays a crucial role in generating, shaping, and safeguarding the resilience of the executive. This quality is an imperative of constitutional governance, not merely an aspiration of good public policy. When properly designed and applied, administrative law can provide the means to counter recent anti-democratic forces and bolster the strength of the administrative state. In this context, resilience describes the ability of organizations to overcome external shocks and, following a transition period, continue providing collective goods at prior levels while upholding predetermined normative values. Accordingly, an administrative actor is resilient when it can withstand threats or pressure, adapt to challenging conditions, and recover from adversity with its functioning and integrity intact.

This chapter focuses on the executive's role in responding to particular challenges, especially when faced with acute crises.[2] Its scope encompasses administrative actors from a local to a national level, covering municipal health agencies that respond to a bacterial outbreak, as well as central banks, which react to problems of national and even global magnitude. These administrative

DOI: 10.4324/9781003416036-4

actors have in the past been subject to pressure, threats, and even outright attacks. They operate within the legal framework set by the respective legislature and controlled by the competent courts, for instance the regulatory provisions of the U.S. Administrative Procedure Act (APA) and the U.S. Freedom of Information Act (FOIA) or its equivalents in other jurisdictions. Given their shared epistemological interest, this chapter draws on interdisciplinary insights from business organization and public administration research to inform administrative law.

The chapter begins by exploring the conceptual value of resilience. Carefully applied, the interdisciplinary notion of resilience promises to open up a new perspective on the construction of the administrative state. After carving out the relevant elements of administrative resilience, the analysis addresses its normative foundations. This section concludes by arguing that administrative law should embrace "resilience" as a guiding principle, instead of directly pursuing the normative goals of efficacy, legitimacy, and accountability.[3] The following part examines how administrative law can help build and strengthen administrative resilience. It begins by connecting the triggers of resilience with the corresponding mechanisms and proceeds to analyze the existing structure of the administrative state under the lens of resilience to identify resources of resilience. Combining both mechanisms and resources of resilience allows one to shift the perspective from analyzing existing laws to issues of institutional design. Here again, resilience has both positive and normative value. These insights create a demand for a theory of administrative resilience. The final part of the chapter tackles this challenge by exploring three central lines of inquiry that administrative law scholarship should emphasize: the ongoing technological transition from rule-based to predictive administration, the internal organizational structure of administrative organizations, and the role of information for administrative actors. Hence, this chapter aims to show how administrative law can equip administrative actors with the means necessary to withstand current challenges. These three aspects of administrative law offer a promising framework for reform that uses an interdisciplinary focus on resilience to strengthen the administrative state.

The Conceptual Value of Resilience

Reconceptualizing administrative law from a resilience perspective requires a narrow and precise definition of resilience that accounts for the interdisciplinary origins and applications of the concept.[4] This conceptual clarity provides the basis for exploring the descriptive dimension of resilience as a concept of public law, which hinges on its measurability as it is discussed in public administration research. Beyond its descriptive value, the concept of resilience has normative roots and implications relating to general constitutional principles. Without such a normative foundation, resilience might become an empty chiffre or mere political buzzword.[5] Only when anchored in common constitutional values does resilience turn into a normative task for lawmakers, legal interpreters, and scholars alike.

Interdisciplinary Evolution

The concept of resilience originates in engineering studies and material science.[6] In this context, resilience describes the specific characteristic of a material to revert back to its original state with its molecular integrity intact after experiencing an adverse influence, such as being pulled apart. Subsequently, the fields of psychology and ecology borrowed the resilience concept and applied it to humans and nature respectively.[7] Psychological research describes resilience as the ability of individuals to overcome significant adversity in their lived experience and ultimately to return to prior levels of functioning or life satisfaction.[8] The transfer from material science to human nature involves broadening the criterion of a return to the previous state because—in contrast to material—human beings will in most cases be cognizant of past adversity and collect memories as well as entrench reactions. A return to an identical state becomes impossible for humans. Therefore, the comparison between the two states of being has to allow for development and focus on the overall integrity of the system, not its concrete individual parameters. Consequently, evaluating psychological resilience depends on choosing the relevant points of comparison (such as wellbeing, the absence of stress symptoms, or mental health in general) and on selecting the methods for measuring the chosen parameters.[9] In a partially parallel development, ecology studies have integrated resilience into their framework.[10] Here, the starting point has a normative undertone, because the study of socio-ecological systems often tries to identify mechanisms that help preserve existing ecosystems.[11] Similar to psychology, however, the ecological understanding of resilience is open to acknowledge changes to a system by focusing on its overall integrity.[12]

This brief overview of the evolution of the concept of resilience allows us to distill its main components. Resilience constitutes a trait of a chosen subject, which surfaces only in reaction to a trigger.[13] Its relevance appears when observing the impact of a dynamic trigger in time by comparing the state of a system ex ante to an outcome ex post.[14] This evaluation allows one to draw inferences on the state of the system between both points in time and to determine its capacity to withstand external triggers. Such inference is particularly valuable when the inner workings of the subject of study remain hidden (as, for instance, in the mental processes of a human undergoing a trauma). Testing mechanisms to improve resilience are therefore mainly possible through trial and error.[15] The outcome measure of resilience lies on a sliding scale, which means that subjects can be more or less resilient.[16] Notably, resilience describes not how the subject itself reacts to a trigger, but whether and how far it recovers from the shock to its system.[17] The necessary length of time between the two states depends on the subject in question as well as the nature of the trigger. Only a within-subject comparison could indicate whether enough time has passed to conclude that a (full) recovery has failed to take place.

Relying on these efforts, this chapter understands resilience as the ability of administrative actors to absorb shocks or cope with adversity and still—potentially after a transitional phase in which the system is not functioning well or even at all—fulfil their function while maintaining their integrity (i.e., to adhere to their normative objectives).[18]

Descriptive Dimension in Public Law

Slowly, the interdisciplinary concept of resilience has found its way into public law discourse. Most analyses apply a resilience framework to the law itself asking whether legal systems, constitutions, or a specific set of laws prove to be resilient in light of specific triggers.[19] The contributions differ in their prescriptions. Some argue that the law, the constitution, or legal rules need to include mechanisms that allow it to be bent out of shape and snap back to its original shape when the strain is relieved.[20] This has sparked a discussion about the permissible level of deviation from the original state, the value or dangers of distinguishing normalcy and emergency, or the erosion caused by iterative events of adversity.[21] Others claim that there needs to be an alternative state of the law or set of legal rules for times of adversity, which emphasizes the effective functioning of law during crises.[22]

It is mainly in these contexts that legal scholarship explores how public actors contribute to the resilience of the law, for instance by continuing to enforce it during crises or by stressing its adaptive features.[23] To a lesser extent do contributions focus on state actors themselves as the subjects of resilience.[24] This might explain why legal studies on resilience often fail to engage with the neighboring disciplines of public administration and business management. As a result of this distinct focus on the resilience of the law, the analyses pay particular attention to the emergency–normalcy dichotomy to conceptualize periods of deviation from or non-enforcement of the applicable law and limit the role of state actors to their respective function of creating, interpreting, and enforcing legal rules.[25] The design and endowment of state actors only become relevant with regard to their contribution to preventing a turn towards emergency or ensuring a return to normalcy, for instance, through sunset clauses and budgetary safeguards.[26] Thus, studies on law and resilience pay little attention to the inner workings of administrative organizations and even less to the role of cognition and behavior of public officials. Filling this gap in legal scholarship requires merging the insights of administrative law scholarship with resilience analyses in studies of business organization and public administration.[27]

As an initial step, this approach requires explaining the specific legal nature and value of resilience. The concept of resilience as developed in organization theory, administrative science, and political science can be useful to evaluate and compare the resilience of administrative actors, but has no inherent legal relevance. This can change, when the legislature or the head of the executive imposes a mandate of resilience from the top down or when administrative agencies commit themselves to implement resilience as a program for their internal organization and decision-making bottom-up.[28] Both initiatives can transform resilience from a political chiffre into a legal obligation. However, since such attempts are still a rare occurrence, a more pertinent question concerns the normative foundation of administrative resilience, which the following section addresses.

So far at least, resilience is not yet an established positive concept in administrative law. Even though different disciplines engaging with the administration use it as an evaluative criterion,[29] no respective mandate exists in the current legal order, at least not in the United States or in European countries. In addition to evaluating the characteristics of administrative actors for their resilience capacity, it is also possible to evaluate different policy measures as to their effect on resilience.[30] Here, the specific research question shapes the understanding of resilience and due to the considerable heterogeneity in approaches, there is little consent on a definition of resilience as of yet.[31] Stripping resilience from its context threatens to drain the descriptive value of the concept. In response, it becomes important to follow a carefully tailored definition of resilience.

When used vaguely, one can question the descriptive value of resilience vis-à-vis other measures of organizational functioning, such as robustness, strength, durability, or efficacy.[32] Indeed, broadly understood, any measure that improves on the functioning of public actors faced with dynamic, intertemporal, and complex problems would count as a resource of resilience. Therefore, resilience can only contain its descriptive poignancy with a narrow definition. The core feature of resilience—that the competing concepts lack—is its status as a heterogeneous group of reactions meant to convey that the original system can be challenged, changed, or permanently altered by some force, but nevertheless retain its functioning and integrity in equilibrium without necessarily reverting back to its original state of being.[33] Accordingly, the concept of resilience is fluid in which type of reaction it describes. Moreover, resilience leads the focus away from the nature of the shock, threat, or challenge, to the characteristics that enable a system to show resilience. It often remains uncertain which types of features create resilience. There is no list of necessary or sufficient criteria. This, however, is not a weakness, but a strength of the concept.

Normative Foundations of Administrative Resilience

Administrative resilience is of normative importance in two ways. First, administrative resilience finds normative anchors in constitutional principles of liberal democracies. Second, increasing administrative resilience has normative implications.

First, absent any legislative, executive, or judicial mandates for resilience de lege lata, any demand for resilience has to arise from higher law, namely constitutional norms. The constitutional texts commonly make no mention of resilience. But also, the Federalist Papers developing a theory of U.S. American constitutionalism include no reference to resilience.[34] As a pure theoretical concept, resilience has no normative meaning. Put simply, resilience entrenches a status quo by demanding that the integrity of said status quo be unscathed in the course of adversity. A normative evaluation of resilience thus hinges on the evaluation of the status quo ex ante. Void of any qualifying assumptions, resilience can be both normatively desirable or undesirable depending on the entrenched prior state.[35] Therefore, it is essential to import a normative subtext into the requirement of resilience to leave the integrity of the status quo ex ante intact. This is more intuitive with regard to psychological resilience. Here, the initial benchmark includes measures that allude to social competence or self-acceptance.[36] Resilience then describes the ability to restore this status. An equivalent benchmark for administrative actors has to have constitutional roots.

Administrative actors need to be democratically legitimate, accountable, fulfill their assigned tasks, and adhere to higher law (including basic rights). Choosing these constitutional values as benchmarks connects resilience to a variety of constitutional demands. The rule of law requires administrative actions to conform to higher law independent of any adverse events. Ensuring that destructive forces cannot permanently undermine adherence to higher law serves the rule of law, as does reducing the time and intensity of a deviation from existing rules in times of crises.[37] The same is true for the adherence to basic rights and the provision of public goods. Once a state invests resources into building organizations and procedures to provide public goods such as public safety, clean water, or infrastructure, any contribution to its resilience ensures that the investment continues to benefit society.

The relationship between resilience and the principle of democracy is more complicated. At the outset, resilience describes the ability of a democracy to defend itself not only from external threats, but also from subversive antidemocratic forces that undermine integral elements of a liberal democracy. Adversity may not only challenge administrative organizations, but also function as a catalyst for fluctuations in public opinion.[38] A resulting policy change counts as resilient as long as it establishes a new equilibrium that shares the integrity and functioning of the prior state of policy.[39] Categorically denying such possibility would prevent any learning and run counter to the adaptive nature of resilience. Therefore, the integrity of one state of being has to be – to some extent – independent of a substantive policy change. However, there is one major caveat. The policy change itself has to be consistent with democratic principles, which excludes changes achieved through manipulation or anti-democratic forces from counting as resilient.[40]

Second, these considerations show that promoting resilience has normative implications. Selecting the parameters of a resilience framework cannot ignore this dimension, but has to take the underlying normative choices seriously. The importance of this finding becomes clearer when analyzing specific pillars of resilience. A prime example is the design of a technologically steered administrative governance. While using algorithmic tools can entrench an ex ante equilibrium and thereby strengthen resilience, they only further a normatively desirable state if their initial set-up is designed according to these goals.

Developing Administrative Resilience

This section maps the dimensions of resilience in order to explore the concept more closely and situate it relative to existing law and resilience research. It defines the relevant triggers and mechanisms underlying a dynamic that creates a demand for resilience. Based on this analysis, it lists potential resources for institutional resilience. Ultimately, it brings special attention to the behavioral dimension of subsuming administrative law under a resilience framework.

Triggers and Mechanisms

Resilience surfaces when an external shock destabilizes an equilibrium and sets in motion a response dynamic. The nature of this shock can take multifaceted forms. In response to a trigger, the subject can employ measures both to solve the actual challenge and to safeguard its own integrity. Triggers and responses are interdependent. Therefore, it is important to carve out the relevant triggers for administrative resilience and explore the underlying mechanisms.

Conceptually, two types of triggers can be distinguished. On the one hand, policy challenges pose a substantive task to the administration. The success of crisis management then depends on how well administrative actors solve this task, for instance, how fast and with how many casualties a country survives a pandemic. Measures of such success, however, concern the efficacy of crisis management, not the resilience of the responding organization. On the other hand, organizational threats challenge the integrity of the responding actor and have a systemic dimension.[41] How an organization handles this type of adversity can be expressed in terms of its resilience. Such systemic triggers can arise directly from policy challenges (simultaneously or successively) because crises can put pressure on an organization or complicate its functioning, as the Covid-19 pandemic did in various ways.[42] But there can also be indirect effects of crises or larger societal developments. Populism and the rise of anti-democratic forces are paradigmatic examples. These forces may feed off general policy crises and exert external pressure on the integrity of the executive as a part of their attempts to undermine the legal and governmental system more generally. Their methods range from clear-cut efforts to influence the processes of governance, e.g., through corruption, to much more subtle ways of weakening the integrity of the administration, e.g., through slowing down appointments or delegitimizing administrative actions in the public discourse.[43] Due to their inherently systemic nature, these triggers will serve as a reference point throughout the following analysis.

In addition to exploring the triggers of resilience, the mechanisms of resilience are worth paying attention to. Simply measuring two states of an organization fails to shed light on the phase in between these states and to explain the intermittent process. However, these elements matter for the outcome because it will be easier for an organization to recover from a phase of adversity the less severe and lasting its initial impact on the functioning and integrity of the system. Therefore, resilience relies not only on mechanisms that promote a speedy and full recovery back to the status quo ex ante, but also benefits from mechanisms that counter adversity directly and dampen its initial negative impact.[44] The more stable the equilibrium ex ante proves to be, the easier it is for an organization to recover that equilibrium. Mechanisms of resilience thus consist of preparation, transitional safeguards, and the ability to regenerate.

Resources

An important element of the resilience equation are the resources available to respond to adversity.[45] For administrative actors as a subject of resilience, the corresponding resources are their infrastructure and equipment as well as the legal framework that regulates their functioning—namely substantive administrative law as well as the law on administrative organization and procedure.[46]

The first and fundamental resource of resilience is the legislatively allocated funding to an administration, which is at the same time—by design—subject to political influence.[47] In the U.S. administrative system, for instance, the Federal Reserve is self-funded and thus independent from threats of budgetary cuts.[48] One way to increase resilience consists of stabilizing available funds and detaching them from political pressures.[49] The U.S. Federal Emergency Management Agency (FEMA) structure is a useful example of an administrative entity designed to provide funds for emergency relief. Even though FEMA itself can be subject to budget cuts, its budget is not tied to any concrete policy aim and therefore changes in funding require a justification on a similarly abstract level. In addition to monetary funding, administrative actors rely on access to quality personnel and equipment,[50] which are respectively regulated by the law governing the civil service and public procurement. Rules that allow for a flexible and speedy recruitment or acquisition can increase administrative resilience. The integrity of an equilibrium, however, is protected by rules that ensure the legitimacy and legality of these spending decisions, for instance an anti-corruption regime.

A second resource of resilience lies in substantive rules.[51] While substantive laws can themselves be a subject of resilience—the corresponding scholarship investigates whether adversity erodes adherence to the letter and spirit of these laws—they also contribute to the resilience of the administration itself.

Substantive rules guide as well as limit agency behavior and thereby stabilize administrative goals and means. This protects administrative actors from external pressure to change course, but also from internal attempts to undermine its goals or stretch the means as well as from implicit biases fueled by undue influence.[52] Stability is enforced within the bureaucratic hierarchy and through outside review, in particular, by the judiciary.[53] Substantive rules thus safeguard the integrity of administrative action during crises.

A third source of resilience are the rules governing administrative process and organization.[54] Instead of steering administrative behavior, they guide administrative cognition.[55] Civil servants are in charge of both recognizing and responding to adversity.[56] Accordingly, their cognitive abilities and capacity influence whether an administrative actor can readily identify adversity and initiate processes of resilience.[57]

Presenting these specific administrative traits as resources of resilience makes the implicit claim that their existence increases and their absence decreases resilience. This is an empirical question that is all too often ignored in legal scholarship. Answering it requires choosing and applying a method of measuring resilience. Resilience can be conceptualized as a composite variable consisting of several indicators. They can measure different aspects of an outcome equilibrium, such as the administrative actor's efficacy in providing public goods, its adherence to higher law, and its (perceived) legitimacy. In a model, each feature characterizing an organization could receive a value describing how much it contributes (or detracts) from the overall organizational resilience. This is complicated in case of interactions between the indicators. Econometrically, the interdependencies could be captured by an interaction term, but this will complicate the study of real-world-phenomena even further. Modeling such relationships also requires making assumptions about the causal connection between feature and outcome.[58] Such a model produces testable hypothesis that could be confirmed or disproven. In material science, it is possible to test in the lab whether changing one characteristic of a material strengthens or weakens it. The material can be put under stress to test whether it resorts to its original state. Such stress-testing in the lab is not possible in disciplines concerned with subjects and triggers that are difficult to replicate in the lab—be it for practical or ethical purposes. Still, organizations could use alternative ways of "stress-testing" government by conducting an independent review of vulnerabilities in a system or undertaking a simulation that tests resilience mechanisms akin to military exercises.[59] Furthermore, even the sole act of modeling administrative resilience could prove useful to explore the relevance of specific elements of administrative law, potentially also in a comparative dimension.

Institutional Design

Understanding the administrative legal framework as a resource of resilience raises the question of how to structure the administrative branch for resilience.[60] Responding to this demand is a constructive task of institutional design instead of a positive analysis of existing administrative rules.[61] The resulting change in perspective draws attention to the interaction between the cognition and the behavior of public officials, as well as the strategies of potential anti-democratic challengers.

This argument contains a positive and a normative claim. Normatively, administrative law needs to persist independent of externally triggered processes of corrosion. Therefore, the institutional design of administrative actors and mechanism choice relating to administrative processes have to evolve around resilience as one comparative measure. Positively, they can only do so when taking into account the behavioral and cognitive dimension with regard to the administrative personnel.[62] This perspective is present in public administration research, but often missing from administrative law scholarship.

Administrative actors mostly take action in relationship to private actors. The administration either responds to demands made by private actors, for instance when permitting a business venture or approving a factory, or it imposes demands upon private actors, such as enforcement actions against companies. Inherent in both types of relationships is an interaction dimension that has game theoretic relevance.[63] Game theory analyzes strategic interactions between rational agents. Therefore, it helps conceptualize the behavior of public actors who react to or anticipate the actions of others. The same is true for interactions in preparatory processes, such as the notice-and-comment procedure in administrative rule-making where private parties can give input and the rule-making actor has to respond.[64] Likewise, private actors including political parties can formally or informally influence the selection of agency staff. Additionally, other branches of government can put pressure on administrative agencies that can be political in nature, such as judges or legislative committees.

These interdependencies open up pathways for strategic attempts to utilize administrative processes for private interests especially from private and political actors seeking to undermine the democratic functioning of the executive itself. Examples are the strategic delay of appointments or a reduction in funds to achieve a specific policy goal.[65] While the previous section has emphasized a need to stress-test administrative processes with regard to specific triggers, this interactive dimension necessitates a sort of "strategy-proofing" with a prototypical "bad actor" in mind.[66] A behaviorally smart design of administrative actors has to begin by exploring tactics capable of undermining existing or prospective legal rules.[67] Since an erosion of rules most often unfolds by affecting the behavior of public officials instead of the rules themselves, said behavior warrants closer attention. Even without erosive forces, the behavioral assumptions and requirements of administrative legal rules have to be explored and made salient. This is a difficult task taken on by empirical legal studies and public administration research.[68] Administrative scholarship would therefore be well advised to incorporate these findings into the design, critique, and redesign of existing legal frameworks.

A similar argument applies to cognition. Legal rules shape which kinds of information public officials process and how they do so. For instance, an isolated structure of agencies hinders the merging of information in order to facilitate learning, whereas an integration of information systems could achieve the opposite. Even with a suitable legal framework in place, the integration of information partly depends on the cooperation of private actors and the receptiveness of public officials. Information that private actors strategically hide in a mountain of data or cognitive processing errors of the officials in charge reduce the likelihood that erosive tendencies are discovered, which in turn weakens resilience. In ideal conditions, an administrative system could identify its own breaking point to push back against or avoid accepting informational input that is likely to cause systemic damage.

Rethinking Resilient Administrative Law

One could process the analysis so far by outlining instruments and improvements of resilience in administrative law. However, such an endeavor will always be limited to a select number of instruments. Remedying current deficits, for instance, covers elements as diverse as workable public procurement rules, an effective anti-corruption regime, checks on erosive interpretations of administrative law, a right to a non-arbitrary allocation of funds, and an inclusion of learning mechanisms in law. Rather, this final section takes a more systemic approach and examines which areas of administrative law could most benefit from a resilience perspective and which structures need to be rethought. Correspondingly, it outlines which research questions can contribute to the adoption of such a perspective. Overall, this analysis shows how resilience theory offers a productive panorama in administrative law and demonstrates the value of empirical research in public administration.[69]

A first line of inquiry is the transformative nature of algorithmic administration. While the administration usually takes its administrative actions in individual one-directional processes limited to the specific case at hand, it is now increasingly in charge of implementing automated decision-making systems that guide its behavior. Administrative technology provides an opportunity to make salient all the institutional choices and behavioral assumptions that are typically lost in the realm of "administrative discretion". This should prompt a shift in administrative law away from regulating cumulative individual procedures towards the systematic organization of administrative procedure law at large.[70] A second strand of analysis addresses the informal norms and patterns of administrative decision-making. Due to their non-binding and non-enforceable nature, informal administrative rules are often neglected in analyses. However, they are crucial tools to steer cognition and behavior of public officials and have to be recognized in this capacity. A third avenue of exploration takes on the administration of information. Within the administrative system, information functions as a mediator between an external trigger and a public response. Thus, measuring and enhancing resilience requires a specific informational integrity, which extends the use of information in individual administrative processes to a systemic information management.

Programming Algorithmic Administration

In the past ten years, administrative processes have undergone a substantive structural shift towards the use of automated decision-making systems.[71] At one end of the spectrum lie administrative decisions produced through a fully automated process. These are mostly used for tasks of mass administration, most prominently in the case of tax assessments or social security notices of award.[72] At the other end of the spectrum lie administrative decisions that are almost fully processed by humans, but incorporate automatically processed information. The space in between is filled with administrative decisions that more or less integrate automated decision-aids.[73] Here, what I describe as "predictive administration" becomes increasingly relevant for administrative tasks.

Predictive analytics relies on automated data-processing to develop models that determine the probability of certain events occurring. Machine learning is a particularly powerful technique. It uses data sets to find patterns and develop models.[74] In this way, the program makes predictions for new inputs.[75] Predictive data analytics is already widely used by private companies, for example in marketing, when targeting consumers, or in lending decisions on the basis of credit scoring.[76] Government agencies are also making increasing use of these methods.[77] So far, the special case of *predictive policing* has attracted the most interest from the public-law community.[78] However, the methods of predictive analytics offer great potential for use with regard to administrative decisions more generally.[79] In the area of public supervision, for instance, predictive analytics can increase the efficiency of harm prevention by identifying potential hazards more precisely than individual human predictions based on empirical knowledge and intuition.[80] In this context, the use of predictive analytics can unfold a rationalizing potential, especially for discretionary supervisory activities.[81] This results in a paradigm shift for public administration: from rule-based decision-making, often relying on data sets provided by private companies, to continuous predictive decision-making through real-time risk indicators based on publicly available data, for example from *Google Analytics* or social media.[82]

This shift creates a strong regulatory demand. The proposed regulation of predictive analytics would impose legal constraints on internal administrative decision-making processes and enable effective control of predictive decisions.[83] It thus responds to a fundamental structural transformation. The use of technological innovation by regulatory agencies makes processes observable that otherwise occur primarily in human brains and internal agency procedures. At the same time, this development raises the question of how far the juridification of internal administrative law may advance. There is an inherent conflict between the administration's need for flexibility and the regulation of their inspection activity. But, in any case, the need for flexibility decreases once the administration chooses to commit itself to certain concepts, especially when purchasing and applying predictive software.

Administrative law has to process this transition from the traditional rule-based model of administration to a technology-based predictive administration.[84] This requires a turn in perspectives. So far, the focus lies on individual administrative decisions shaped through a legally deterministic process of specifically gathering information on a case-by-case basis and applying the law correspondingly. Instead, administrative decision-making programs are slowly taking a predictive turn demanding a programming of decisions ex ante.[85] That, in turn, requires a conceptualization of the organizational structure of the administrative decision-making process on a higher level. The automated decision-making system applies to all kinds of decisions and has to account for the systemic nature of its information-processing task.[86] Designing these algorithmic systems forces the administration to explicate its normative goals, thereby making the critical design features of such a system visible beyond the administrative body itself and allowing for external monitoring. The administration could productively use this development to increase its resilience.[87]

Until now, mechanism design of administrative decision-making has mainly become relevant with regard to the formalized allocation of scarce resources. A prominent example is school choice. Beyond such formal claims, e.g., to school placement, the regulation of the distribution of scarce administrative resources is rarely discussed, even though administrative actors commonly fulfill substantive or procedural participatory claims under the constraints of structurally limited attention and capacity for consistency.[88] In all these instances, administrative actors also apply certain parameters to allocate these resources. Yet, in contrast to formal claims to schooling or unemployment awards, they mostly do so implicitly and ad hoc without legislative steering and executive oversight. But when programming these decision-making steps, the administrative actor in charge would be required to determine at least the parameters of its predictive analysis explicitly.[89]

This has two consequences pertinent to administrative law. First, automated decision-making systems have to be designed for human use within the administration. Unfortunately, we know fairly little about systemic deficits of administrative behavior beyond the more general insights into heuristics and biases that mostly apply to administrative personnel as well.[90] Yet, the group dimension of decision-making as well as the impact of the legal limits that guide administrative behavior are both under-researched. Adding algorithmic governance to the mix requires a more intense analysis of the necessary human–machine interaction,[91] or more precisely bureaucrat–machine interaction. The results (or—bar any empirical studies—the current assumptions) have to inform the initial design choices for automated decision-making systems. This now provides an opportunity to use administrative resilience as a normative orientation and positive benchmark.[92] More concretely, algorithmic governance has to aim at compensating currently prevalent cognitive or behavioral deficits of administrative decision-making.

Second, administrative law needs to respond to these challenges by addressing critical design decisions in the phase preceding any individual decision-making, which is the phase of information collection and processing.[93] Often, administrative law only addresses individual cases once there is sufficient information calling for an administrative intervention. But the path up to this point so far escapes the attention of administrative law. Any use of the tools of predictive administration requires a legal framework to steer the technically necessary design choices. Substantively, the legal framework has to promote the rule of law and implement the principle of democracy. Organizationally, the idea of resilience could be a useful benchmark to influence the legal set-up. In particular, it might call upon administrative actors to incorporate empirically informed learning and evaluation mechanisms that demand the testing of algorithmic governance systems as well as the collection of information about their performance.[94]

Investigating Internal Operations

Administrative law consists of external and internal legal rules and procedures that guide administrative action.[95] The primary focus of both lawmaking efforts and legal scholarship is on rules with external effects vis-à-vis the citizens or administrative actors, such as most prominently the U.S. Administrative Procedures Act (APA), or other pieces of substantive legislation, such as the U.S. Endangered Species Act.[96] In addition to legislative measures, externally valid administrative law can also come from within the administration, most importantly from executive orders.[97] The attention on the laws' external effects mirrors the importance for citizens and correspondingly the judiciary, but also its function in the separation-of-powers system.[98] In consequence, administrative procedure has often been looked at through the lens of the individual and their rights (including procedural fairness), the contribution of a procedure to a correct or efficient outcome, and the political nature of its effects.[99] The lens of administrative resilience, however, requires looking at the contribution of organizational and procedural administrative rules to the systemic stability of administrative actors themselves.[100] With that, inner-administrative rules and mechanisms gain relevance.

Inner-administrative rules are an important tool of organizing government in a way that enables it to withstand pressure and threats.[101] Yet, they are often overlooked based on their seeming lack of external force. For instance, internal rules can impose a duty promptly to fill vacancies instead of allowing for a strategic delay of appointments. Moreover, internal administrative procedures can be proactively designed to secure the equality and due process of subsequent decision-making. Beyond these legal structures, it is important to consider behavioral insights to improve institutional responses to crises because the responsibility to lead administrative organizations ultimately falls to human decision-makers suffering from well-known cognitive constraints and biases.[102] Shaping their cognition and behavior through inner-administrative organization is a resource of resilience.

The most accessible way of evaluating these internal rules and procedures is the idea of "strategy-proofing" the administrative process mentioned above. It combines a careful evaluation of organizational structures of administrative actors with a focus on pathologies in the administrative process of enforcing legislative mandates. These pathologies can arise either from prototypically "bad" civil servants who consciously or even willfully undermine the normative goals of administrative action for their own gain or from "good" civil servants who face incentives that are misaligned with said normative goals, particularly in the form of democratic backsliding.[103] One example for the first scenario is corruption.[104] Here, a corrupt civil servant accepts a reward for acting in a certain way, usually in violation of existing rules.[105] The reward can be monetary, but also consist of a gain in political capital. An example for the second scenario is civil servants who take the opportunity to ease their workload by refraining from seeking information when enforcing legal obligations for private actors. Without information indicating an actionable situation, the officials formally act within their mandate not to open individual enforcement actions, but fail to comply with the spirit of the law.

In this regard, greater attention should be paid to the behavioral effects of administrative law. For what scholars cite as forces against backsliding are instruments based on cognition and social norms,[106] which can be encouraged or hindered by organizational and procedural mechanisms. Thus, a resilient administration needs an internal administrative law that incorporates the findings of behavioral and administrative sciences. Detailing the various instruments is a research agenda in and of itself.[107] Here, resilience could serve as a normative goal and evaluative benchmark.

Resilience calls for an entrenchment of a normatively desirable status quo in order to help administrative actors withstand external pressure and threats. Concretely, this means preventing prototypically "bad" actors from taking power and checking whether the incentive structure for "good" administrators conforms with the underlying normative goals.[108] The former is a difficult task that could easily conflict with democratic principles, particularly when the people elect civil servants who are open to undermining the existing order.[109] Therefore, it is important to ensure systemically that these choices actually comply with democratic processes. Moreover, the incentive structure has to ensure that administrative actors can continue to function despite a change in power. Currently, the U.S. President can often prevent an administrative agency from fulfilling its mandate by delaying the appointment of successors to a departing chief administrator in order to obstruct the agency from reaching the necessary quorum when this seems politically feasible.[110] Lowering quorum restrictions or setting up interim mandates could weaken this path to undermine administrative functioning.[111] This is especially important with regard to agencies that Congress has made independent from executive control. Other instruments address deficiencies in routine decision-making tasks, namely redundancies, backstops, and other stability enforcing mechanisms.[112] Lastly, the tool to review these structures for their strategy-proofness is stress-testing. The results of these stress tests then can inform administrative reform and thus require an administrative openness for learning.

Promoting Informational Integrity

Both aforementioned strategies center around the fundamental role of information for policy-making institutions.[113] Legislative as well as executive bodies around the world have a growing need for data that can form the basis for solving the complex challenges and crises they face.[114] Moreover, both branches constantly generate new insights with each law they enact and each action they take, as long as they pay attention to the experiences made with the application of the legal rules. These feedback loops provide an opportunity for public actors to scrutinize and improve policy choices.[115] The link between rule-making and information also fulfills an important accountability function. Counter-majoritarian forces can use the information generated to hold the legislature and the executive responsible for their normative choices. Moreover, acting upon a reliable empirical basis enables policy-makers to counter populist narratives. The provision and intertemporal protection of information against challenges of misinformation, concealment efforts, or outside threats are thus important tasks for all branches of government, who need to balance these demands with conflicting interests. While transparency is a crucial theme in areas as diverse as central banking and algorithmic governance, the role of information to strengthen the resilience of administrative actors in general has not been the subject of much research.

Moreover, the current integration of information in policy-making processes leaves a lot to be desired in most jurisdictions. Legislatures and rule-making agencies often fail to elucidate their epistemological interest, their underlying assumptions, their data-generation process, and the influence of different pieces of information. While lawmaking is—and needs to remain—an inherently political task, and democratic decision-making is not very conducive to a strict implementation of knowledge, the legislature and the executive sometimes commit themselves to explicitly resting their lawmaking efforts on an empirical basis. Therefore, I suggest deepening these efforts through three strategies that promote informational integrity in the policy-making process. They are not only suitable to shaping the decision-making stage, but are also relevant for an ex post observation of the consequences of specific choices that is necessary for their evaluation.

First, lawmaking institutions should think more deeply about adding the instrument of legislative experimentation to the toolbox.[116] Doing so would require much more than merely framing policy differences between different constituencies as a form of experimentation.[117] Most importantly, actual experimentation involves a deliberate process of setting up a hypothesis and coming up with a way to test it.[118] Ideally, an experiment involves a random allocation of participants to one of two groups, the treatment group and the control group.[119] This mechanism ensures that any deviation in outcome between the two groups is attributable to the treatment—at least in ideal conditions. While there are limited opportunities for implementing such a random draw, the initial task of formulating a sound and testable hypothesis is in itself a complex task that requires a commitment of policy-making actors to such a methodology and a cooperation with researchers experienced in the respective areas. Experimenting is a time-intensive task.[120] Hypotheses have to take a long-term approach and, therefore, would greatly benefit from the insights generated by the study of foresight.[121] In particular, one crisis could become an opportunity to learn and increase resilience for the next unforeseen event.[122] Formulating and testing explicit hypotheses in a crisis could prevent people and policy-makers alike from falling under the spell of the prevention paradox.[123]

A complementary strategy addresses the generation of institutional knowledge. Digital technology simplifies the collection, storage, processing, and distribution of large amounts of data. Beyond the individual nation-state, these data are important for private as well as foreign public actors. Establishing a resilient legal public information infrastructure could be a crucial step towards safeguarding the publicity of government data necessary for addressing upcoming challenges, such as climate change.[124] The infrastructure has to be reliable, quickly accessible, and secure. But without the appropriate legal framework, any technical choice regarding the infrastructure can be subject to change at will—at least as far as this is practically feasible, e.g., with regard to lock-in effects. Creating such a framework requires a careful analysis of its effects, especially because information has unique characteristics. Importantly, once shared, information effectively cannot be deleted. This feature can be used to deter public actors from deleting unwanted information by creating legal obligations to share with third parties who are independent or, at least, who share a different political composition or set up protected data mirroring systems.

Lastly, the technological transformation provides an opportunity for policy-making bodies to become more responsive to its citizens. Digital technology can provide the necessary infrastructure for creating a communicative space that allows citizens to interact and deliberate.[125]

Outlook

Resilience theory opens a productive panorama for administrative law. Its normative openness allows for an adoption to different real-world circumstances and offers flexibility to accommodate conflicting values. In contrast to one-directional normative goals that are generally applicable to administrative action, such as democratic legitimacy, rights protection, or administrative efficiency, a commitment to resilience requires an initial determination of a desirable status quo. This forces policy-making institutions to be more outspoken about their normative objectives, thus opening up a space for a larger debate. Moreover, resilience thinking allows the public administration to process crises and other shocks to the system dynamically and is therefore able to deal with complexity.[126] It replaces the common binary focus on a normatively desirable or undesirable outcome, which neglects to deal with the transitional phase in between, and provides tools to design mechanisms that help stabilize a normatively desirable equilibrium.

When applied to the administration, resilience theory also focuses on areas of administrative law that concern the organization and functioning of administrative agencies. This includes the funding and staffing of agencies, the digitization of administrative decisions, the informal regulation of internal processes, and the design of an informational infrastructure. The legal framework addressing these questions then becomes a resource of resilience. One particular strength of resilience is that it applies to a variety of shocks independent of the specific nature of a crisis. Correspondingly, the resources of resilience are not pre-determined and finite, but rather fluid. Thus, conclusively determining the various features of resilience is as impossible in law and political science as it is in psychology, which opens up a productive continuing discussion.

Moreover, the cognition and behavior of public officials gain relevance for the legal design of administrative organizations, which calls for an integration of the insights from public administration studies into administrative law. Instead of examining administrative law for any cognitive or behavioral deficits that its application can produce, resilience theory demands a more front-loaded general analysis of the interaction between legal rules and human decision-makers.

This suggested re-orientation of administrative law raises several questions. Most importantly, resilience theory has to propose ways to measure, evaluate, and compare the resilience of administrative actors. However, the fact that there exists no simplified numerical way of expressing resilience in the field of law cannot be held against the concept as such because the same is true for the current direct benchmarks, such as democracy or adherence to the rule of law. It is important to stress again that resilience would not replace these normative criteria, but add a layer that conceptualizes their fulfillment in a time dimension. A separate question concerns the justiciability of resilience. Adherence to resilience generally cannot be demanded before the courts as it is a principle of design, not an enforceable rule. Yet, it would still be possible for the legislature or the executive itself to commit to resilience and set up accountability mechanisms.

Ultimately, this chapter aims at developing the framework of resilience as a lens through which it is beneficial to observe the administrative state. It sheds light on various features that often go unnoticed when focusing on the legality of administrative action, arising from our concentration on judicial review and the rule of law. I call for prioritizing resilience in the design and set-up of administrative actors and for delving deeper into the relationship between administrative organization and human decision-making. Overall, resilience theory is a suitable tool to strengthen the administrative state.

Notes

1 Ferraro, Etzion, and Gehman (2015) analyze strategies to address such "grand challenges" from the perspective of organization theory.
2 See also Egidy (forthcoming) further exploring the potential contributions of technology to administrative resilience.
3 Rose-Ackerman (2021), pp. 1–10 unfolds the normative panorama of administrative policy-making; for example, Weiser (2017), pp. 2037–54 uses these parameters to evaluate experimental forms of policy-making.
4 See also Egidy (forthcoming), part II.
5 See Duit (2016), p. 365.
6 Martin-Breen and Anderies (2011), pp. 43–44; Humby (2014), p. 92.
7 For example, Den Hartigh and Hill (2022) draw on physics research to inform psychological resilience.
8 Werner and Smith (1979) trace the development of children born on the island of Kauai in a longitudinal study and study the interaction with risk factors, periods of stress, and trauma; see also Luthar, Cicchetti, and Becker (2000) critically reviewing the "construct of resilience."
9 See, e.g., Stein et al. (2019) measuring, among other things, mental health and wellbeing to determine functional resilience.
10 Holling (1973), p. 17; Wildavsky (1988).
11 See Craig (2020), pp. 1761–74 applying resilience theory to climate change; see also Ellis (2019); Monteiro de Lima Demange (2013), pp. 717–28.
12 See Craig (2020), pp. 1757–59; see also Benson and Garmestani (2011) critically analyzing the role of resilience for U.S. Natural Resource Management; see also Arnold and Gunderson (2013).
13 See, for example, Caza et al. (2020), pp. 342–43.
14 Marchant and Stevens (2017), pp. 244–45, 251–52.
15 Capano and Woo (2018), p. 434.
16 Hepfer and Lawrence (2022), p. 2; Kantur and Iseri-Say (2015) suggest an empirical measure.
17 See Marchant and Stevens (2017), p. 250.
18 See already Holling (1973).
19 For example, regarding the legal system: Ruhl (2011) and Hornstein (2011); regarding the law: Schotel (2022), pp. 374–76; regarding constitutions Contiades and Fotiadou (2015) and Ewing (2013).
20 Kahan (2005); Tribe and Gudridge (2004).
21 See for an overview Scheuerman (2006); Ferejohn and Pasquino (2004).
22 Ackerman (2004).
23 See, e.g., Fischman (2019), pp. 719–24; Cosens et al. (2020).
24 See Schildknecht (2015).
25 Contiades and Fotiadou (2015).
26 Ackerman (2004); Marchant and Stevens (2017), pp. 257, 262 view these features as a resource of resilience.
27 See from the field of public administration Duit (2016), pp. 373–77 and Hillmann and Guenther (2021); see from the business administration side Hepfer and Lawrence (2022) and Chen, Xie, and Liu (2021), who analyze the resilience of six companies (Southwest Airlines, Apple, Microsoft, Starbucks, Kyocera, and Lego).

28 Benson and Garmestani (2011) discuss the initiative of the U.S. Forest Service to achieve the resilience of the governed landscape. Such efforts could in the future also address the resilience of the institution itself.
29 See, i.a., the contributions to the symposium organized and summarized by Boin and Lodge (2016).
30 See Capano and Woo (2017), p. 417, who use the terminology of robustness in lieu of resilience.
31 See Hepfer and Lawrence (2022), pp. 6–8; see also endnote 4 for interdisciplinary literature reviews on the concept of resilience.
32 Giustiniano et al. (2018), pp. 1–4; sometimes, these terms are used interchangeably, see, e.g., Schildknecht (2015), pp. 433, 455 equating robustness with resilience.
33 Marchant and Stevens (2017), p. 247; but see Ansell, Sørensen, and Torfing (2023), p. 9 using robustness to refer to the quality described as resilience in this chapter; Capano and Woo (2017), pp. 401–06 view robustness as the retention of functionality, while resilience describes regaining a (new or old) equilibrium.
34 But see Hamilton in Federalist Paper No. 71, Cooke (1961) alluding to similar ideas: "When occasions present themselves, in which the interests of the people are at variance with their inclinations, it is the duty of the persons whom they have appointed to be the guardians of those interests, to withstand the temporary delusion, in order to give them time and opportunity for more cool and sedate reflection."
35 See also Hornstein (2011), p. 1552.
36 Ahern et al. (2006), pp. 120–21.
37 See Huq and Ginsburg (2018), pp. 94–99.
38 Romano (2014), pp. 28–32.
39 See Monteiro de Lima Demange (2013), pp. 700–06 in the realm of ecological resilience.
40 Lewandowsky et al. (2020), p. 57.
41 See Schildknecht (2015) drawing the relationship between systemic risk and resilience.
42 See Ţiclău, Hinţea, and Andrianu (2020) from a public administration point of view.
43 Glicksman and Hammond (2017), pp. 1669–86 provide evidence for a so-called "regulatory slop" of the Trump administration.
44 Duit (2016), pp. 366–67.
45 See Duchek (2020) detailing general resources of organizational resilience.
46 See Egidy (2024).
47 Schildknecht (2015), pp. 444–47, 462–63.
48 12 U.S.C. § 243; see also Barkow (2010), p. 44 providing further examples; but see Nash, Ruhl, and Salzman (2017) studying the impact of budget cuts on the outcome of agency performance.
49 See Rose (2021) using the Unemployment Trust Fund as a role model; see also Nash, Ruhl, and Salzman (2017), pp. 728–29, 744, 755–56 emphasizing the relevance of an agency's budget to its resilience.
50 Rose-Ackerman (2021), pp. 266–67; Freeman and Jacobs (2021), pp. 594–95, 615–20; Schildknecht (2015), pp. 460–61 argues that quality improves robustness.
51 Marchant and Stevens (2017), pp. 262–70.
52 See Ip (2017), pp. 177–87 analyzing the role administrative law as a debiasing device.
53 Rose-Ackerman, Egidy, and Fowkes (2015), pp. 77–93; but also internal review within the executive, see Livermore and Revesz (2013).
54 See Marchant and Stevens (2017), pp. 255–62.
55 See Hepfer and Lawrence (2022), pp. 17, 19–21 emphasizing the interdependence of cognition and resilience.
56 Ibid.
57 Ibid.

58 See Capano and Woo (2018), p. 428; for a formal model of agency behavior under a rationality assumption, see Posner (1972).
59 See Loo (2022); see Greenblott et al. (2019), p. 255 arguing to connect strategic foresight and simulations to "test the effectiveness of tactical responses to different kinds of threats and future conditions" in the U.S. federal bureaucracy; see also Ruhl and Katz (2015), p. 237 arguing to stress-test complex legal systems.
60 See Ansell, Sørensen, and Torfing (2023), pp. 12–13.
61 See instructively Capano and Woo (2018), pp. 428–33.
62 Hepfer and Lawrence (2022), pp. 17, 19–21; Rachlinski and Farina (2002), pp. 555–62.
63 Givati (2014).
64 Rose-Ackerman (2021), pp. 73–76.
65 See Freeman and Jacobs (2021), pp. 600–15 detailing the strategies of "structural deregulation."
66 See more extensively Egidy (forthcoming), part IV.B.
67 See Howlett (2020) exploring the "dark side of policy-making"; see also Huq and Ginsburg (2018), pp. 127–30 regarding constitutional retrogression in the executive.
68 See further Duit (2016), pp. 374–76.
69 Waye (2019), pp. 379–85. Yet, the costs of such an approach will have to be weighed against its benefits, see for adaptive management Doremus (2011).
70 See more extensively Egidy (forthcoming).
71 See extensively Coglianese and Lehr (2017) on the applications and legality of machine learning in the administration; Maciejewski (2017).
72 See Citron (2008), pp. 1256, 1259–60, 1263–64, 1268–71 with further examples of automated systems in the administration; see also Veale and Brass (2019), p. 123.
73 Citron (2008), pp. 1264–67.
74 See Finck (2020), pp. 658–59.
75 Athey (2017).
76 See on the legal limits Citron and Pasquale (2014).
77 See only Coglianese and Lehr (2017), pp. 160–67.
78 See, e.g., Ferguson (2017); Ferguson (2015); Meijer and Wessels (2019); A. Shapiro (2017); Berk (2021).
79 See Coglianese and Dor (2021), pp. 814–36 taking inventory of the uses of AI in the administration; Maciejewski (2017); see for predictive lawmaking Bagby and Packin (2021).
80 Ho and Altenburger (2019) critically discuss applications in food safety law; Mohler et al. (2015) address predictive policing; Hashimzade, Myles, and Rablen (2016) study tax audits.
81 Waye (2019), pp. 366–71; Bagby and Packin (2021); Kleinberg et al. (2015), p. 494.
82 See Waye (2019), pp. 370–71.
83 See in contrast Masur and Nash (2022) suggesting a strategy that makes government action more foreseeable by demanding private actors to make their predictions public.
84 See also Waye (2019), pp. 370–71.
85 Devins et al. (2017), pp. 373–75 emphasizes the importance of theory behind data.
86 Ibid., pp. 407–10.
87 Similarly with regard to regulatory technology, Bagby and Packin (2021), pp. 131–32; see also Egidy (forthcoming), part IV.C.
88 But see Glicksman, Markell, and Sevier (2020) empirically analyzing a specific type of mechanism choice.
89 Athey (2017) relating to the allocation of resources for fire or health inspections.
90 See, e.g., the review of Battaglio et al. (2019) identifying cognitive biases such as overconfidence in the public administration; see Rachlinski and Farina (2002); Ip (2017).

91 See Citron (2008), pp. 1264–67 detailing different types of interaction; see for experimental evidence Engel and Grgić-Hlača (2021).
92 Waye (2019), p. 378.
93 See Finck (2020), pp. 665–66.
94 Waye (2019), pp. 378–85.
95 Fisher and Shapiro (2021), pp. 119–23 thus rightly emphasize the role of administrative law to guide public administration.
96 Eskridge and Ferejohn (2001), pp. 1242–46.
97 See Rose-Ackerman (2021), pp. 72, 78–80 also addressing policymaking through, i.a., memoranda and informal rules.
98 See already Rose-Ackerman (1988), pp. 347–48.
99 Tyler (2003); McNollgast (1990); Mashaw (1990).
100 See Metzger and Stack (2017); Glicksman and Markell (2018); Markell and Glicksman (2014); S. A. Shapiro and Wright (2011).
101 Barnett (2020) provides the example of executive orders and agency regulations to set up rules that protect the impartiality of an agency adjudicator.
102 See Rachlinski and Farina (2002); see Grimmelikhuijsen et al. (2017) from a public administration perspective.
103 See Huq and Ginsburg (2018), pp. 127–30, 148–54; Howlett (2020), pp. 614–16.
104 See Rose-Ackerman (1975).
105 Huq and Ginsburg (2018), p. 129.
106 Nou (2019), pp. 356–62.
107 Egidy (forthcoming); Rachlinski and Farina (2002); Ip (2017).
108 See Rose-Ackerman (1975) with regard to corruption.
109 See Rose-Ackerman (2021), p. 78.
110 Freeman and Jacobs (2021), pp. 600–09.
111 But see Freeman and Jacobs (2021), pp. 600–03 outlining the structural problem of interim appointments.
112 Schildknecht (2015), pp. 456–58; Marchant and Stevens (2017), p. 267; Capano and Woo (2018), p. 430.
113 See Maciejewski (2017) detailing the role of data in (semi-) automated public administration.
114 But see Livermore (2017) on the downsides of producing socially harmful information.
115 See Schildknecht (2015), pp. 459–60 emphasizing the need of feedback for robustness.
116 See instructively Chien (2019); Gubler (2015).
117 See Wiseman and Owen (2018) presenting the spectrum of experimental federalism; see also Buzbee (2017).
118 Abramowicz, Ayres, and Listokin (2011); Ranchordás (2013), pp. 417–20, 423–24; Chien (2019), pp. 2339–42, 2343–46 in the context of experimentation in the administration.
119 Ranchordás (2013), pp. 421–24; but see Gubler (2015), pp. 558–61 discussing a non-technical form of experimentation via sunset clauses.
120 Thus Ferraro, Etzion, and Gehman (2015) promote a non-technical way of "distributed experimentation."
121 See for the practice and potential of foresight in the bureaucracy Greenblott et al. (2019); see Hines and Gold (2015) for the role of foresight in corporations; see Burrows and Gnad (2018) for foresight efforts in the policy-making arena; see Piirainen and Gonzalez (2015) stressing the need for a theoretical development of foresight studies; see also Fergnani and Chermack (2021).
122 But see Camacho (2009), pp. 47–50 for the potential deficits of information gathering.
123 See also Egidy (forthcoming), part IV.A.
124 See Cortez (2019); Landers (2019); Glicksman (2020), pp. 579–625.

125 See Rose-Ackerman (2021), pp. 269–71; see Ferraro, Etzion, and Gehman (2015) arguing in favor of a participatory architecture to increase robustness for solving complex challenges.
126 See only Craig (2020).

References

Abramowicz, Michael, Ian Ayres, and Yair Listokin. 2011. "Randomizing Law." *University of Pennsylvania Law Review* 159: 929–1005.

Ackerman, Bruce. 2004. "The Emergency Constitution." *The Yale Law Journal* 113: 1029–91.

Ahern, Nancy R., Ermalynn M. Kiehl, Mary Lou Sole, and Jacqueline Byers. 2006. "A Review of Instruments Measuring Resilience." *Issues in Comprehensive Pediatric Nursing* 29: 103–25.

Ansell, Christopher, Eva Sørensen, and Jacob Torfing. 2023. "Public Administration and Politics Meet Turbulence: The Search for Robust Governance Responses." *Public Administration* 101: 3–22.

Arnold, Craig Anthony (Tony), and Lance H. Gunderson. 2013. "Adaptive Law and Resilience." *Environmental Law Reporter* 43: 10426–43.

Athey, Susan. 2017. "Beyond Prediction: Using Big Data for Policy Problems." *Science* 355 (6324): 483–85.

Bagby, John W., and Nizan G. Packin. 2021. "RegTech and Predictive Lawmaking: Closing the Reglag Between Prospective Regulated Activity and Regulation." *Michigan Business & Entrepreneurial Law Review* 10: 127–77.

Barkow, Rachel E. 2010. "Insulating Agencies: Avoiding Capture through Institutional Design." *Texas Law Review* 89: 15–79.

Barnett, Kent. 2020. "Regulating Impartiality in Agency Adjudication." *Duke Law Journal* 69: 1695–1748.

Battaglio, R. Paul, Paolo Belardinelli, Nicola Bellé, and Paola Cantarelli. 2019. "Behavioral Public Administration *Ad Fontes:* A Synthesis of Research on Bounded Rationality, Cognitive Biases, and Nudging in Public Organizations." *Public Administration Review* 79: 304–20.

Benson, Melinda Harm, and Ahjond S. Garmestani. 2011. "Can We Manage for Resilience? The Integration of Resilience Thinking into Natural Resource Management in the United States." *Environmental Management* 48: 392–99.

Berk, Richard A. 2021. "Artificial Intelligence, Predictive Policing, and Risk Assessment for Law Enforcement." *Annual Review of Criminology* 4: 209–37.

Boin, Arjen, and Martin Lodge. 2016. "Designing Resilient Institutions for Transboundary Crisis Management: A Time for Public Administration." *Public Administration* 94: 289–98.

Burrows, Mathew J., and Oliver Gnad. 2018. "Between 'Muddling Through' and 'Grand Design': Regaining Political Initiative—the Role of Strategic Foresight." *Futures* 97: 6–17.

Buzbee, William W. 2017. "Federalism Hedging, Entrenchment, and the Climate Challenge." *Wisconsin Law Review*, 1037–1113.

Camacho, Alejandro E. 2009. "Adapting Governance to Climate Change: Managing Uncertainty through a Learning Infrastructure." *Emory Law Journal* 59: 1–77.

Capano, Giliberto, and Jun Jie Woo. 2017. "Resilience and Robustness in Policy Design: A Critical Appraisal." *Policy Sciences* 50: 399–426.

———. 2018. "Designing Policy Robustness: Outputs and Processes." *Policy and Society* 37: 422–40.

Caza, Brianna Barker, Michelle A. Barton, Marlys K. Christianson, and Kathleen M. Sutcliffe. 2020. "Conceptualizing the Who, What, When, Where, Why and How of

Resilience in Organizations." In *Research Handbook on Organizational Resilience*, edited by Edward H. Powley, Brianna Barker Caza, and Arran Caza, 338–53. Edward Elgar Publishing.

Chen, Ruijun, Yaping Xie, and Yingqi Liu. 2021. "Defining, Conceptualizing, and Measuring Organizational Resilience: A Multiple Case Study." *Sustainability* 13: 2517.

Chien, Colleen V. 2019. "Rigorous Policy Pilots: Experimentation in the Administration of the Law." *Iowa Law Review* 104: 2313–50.

Citron, Danielle Keats. 2008. "Technological Due Process." *Washington University Law Review* 85: 1249–1313.

Citron, Danielle Keats, and Frank Pasquale. 2014. "The Scored Society: Due Process for Automated Predictions." *Washington Law Review* 89: 1–33.

Coglianese, Cary, and Lavi M. Ben Dor. 2021. "AI in Adjudication and Administration." *Brooklyn Law Review* 86: 791–838.

Coglianese, Cary, and David Lehr. 2017. "Regulating by Robot: Administrative Decision Making in the Machine-Learning Era." *The Georgetown Law Journal* 105: 1147–1223.

Contiades, Xenophon, and Alkmene Fotiadou. 2015. "On Resilience of Constitutions. What Makes Constitutions Resistant to External Shocks?" *Vienna Journal on International Constitutional Law* 9: 3–26.

Cooke, Jacob E., Hrsg. 1961. *The Federalist*. Wesleyan University Press.

Cortez, Nathan. 2019. "Information Mischief Under the Trump Administration." *Chicago-Kent Law Review* 94: 315–48.

Cosens, Barbara A., J.B. Ruhl, Niko Soininen, and Lance Gunderson. 2020. "Designing Law to Enable Adaptive Governance of Modern Wicked Problems." *Vanderbilt Law Review* 73: 1687–1732.

Craig, Robin Kundis. 2020. "Resilience Theory and Wicked Problems." *Vanderbilt Law Review* 73: 1733–75.

Den Hartigh, Ruud J.R., and Yannick Hill. 2022. "Conceptualizing and Measuring Psychological Resilience: What Can We Learn from Physics?" *New Ideas in Psychology* 66: 100934.

Devins, Caryn, Teppo Felin, Stuart Kauffinan, and Roger Koppl. 2017. "The Law and Big Data." *Cornell Journal of Law and Public Policy* 27: 357–413.

Doremus, Holly. 2011. "Adaptive Management as an Information Problem." *North Carolina Law Review* 89: 1455–98.

Duchek, Stephanie. 2020. "Organizational Resilience: A Capability-Based Conceptualization." *Business Research* 13: 215–46.

Duit, Andreas. 2016. "Resilience Thinking: Lessons for Public Administration." *Public Administration* 94: 364–80.

Egidy, Stefanie. forthcoming. "Besonderes Verwaltungsrecht. Öffentliches Wirtschaftsrecht, Öffentliches Baurecht, Kommunale Selbstverwaltung." In *Öffentliches Recht als Verhaltensordnung. Ein neues Paradigma*, edited by Christoph Engel, Lawrence O'Hara, Stefanie Egidy, Yoan Hermstrüwer, Leonard Hoeft, and Pascal Langenbach. Mohr Siebeck.

———. forthcoming. "Resilient Administrative Technology." *Georgia Law Review* 58.

Ellis, Jaye. 2019. "Crisis, Resilience, and the Time of Law." *Canadian Journal of Law & Jurisprudence*, 305–20.

Engel, Christoph, and Nina Grgić-Hlača. 2021. "Machine Advice with a Warning about Machine Limitations: Experimentally Testing the Solution Mandated by the Wisconsin Supreme Court." *Journal of Legal Analysis* 13: 284–340.

Eskridge, William N. Jr., and John Ferejohn. 2001. "Super-Statutes." *Duke Law Journal* 50: 1215–76.

Ewing, K.D. 2013. "The Resilience of the Political Constitution." *German Law Journal* 14: 2111–36.

Ferejohn, John, and Pasquale Pasquino. 2004. "The Law of the Exception: A Typology of Emergency Powers." *International Journal of Constitutional Law* 2: 210–39.
Fergnani, Alessandro, and Thomas J. Chermack. 2021. "The Resistance to Scientific Theory in Futures and Foresight, and What to Do about It." *Futures & Foresight Science* 3: 1–16.
Ferguson, Andrew Guthrie. 2015. "Big Data and Predictive Reasonable Suspicion." *University of Pennsylvania Law Review* 163: 327–410.
———. 2017. "Policing Predictive Policing." *Washington University Law Review* 94: 1109–89.
Ferraro, Fabrizio, Dror Etzion, and Joel Gehman. 2015. "Tackling Grand Challenges Pragmatically: Robust Action Revisited." *Organization Studies* 36: 363–90.
Finck, Michèle. 2020. "Automated Decision-Making and Administrative Law." In *The Oxford Handbook of Comparative Administrative Law*, edited by Peter Cane, Herwig C. H. Hofmann, Eric C. Ip, and Peter L. Lindseth, 655–76. Oxford University Press.
Fischman, Robert L. 2019. "Letting Go of Stability: Resilience and Environmental Law." *Indiana Law Journal* 94: 688–725.
Fisher, Elizabeth, and Sidney Shapiro. 2021. "Disagreement about *Chevron*: Is Administrative Law the 'Law of Public Administration'?" *Duke Law Journal Online* 70: 111–37.
Freeman, Jody, and Sharon Jacobs. 2021. "Structural Deregulation." *Harvard Law Review*, 585–665.
Giustiniano, Luca, Stewart R. Clegg, Miguel P.e. Cunha, and Arménio Rego. 2018. *Theories of Organizational Resilience*. Edward Elgar Publishing.
Givati, Yehonatan. 2014. "Game Theory and the Structure of Administrative Law." *The University of Chicago Law Review* 81: 481–518.
Glicksman, Robert L. 2020. "Shuttered Government." *Arizona Law Review* 62: 573–635.
Glicksman, Robert L., and Emily Hammond. 2017. "Agency Behavior and Discretion on Remand." *Journal of Land Use* 32: 483–511.
Glicksman, Robert L., and David L. Markell. 2018. "Unraveling the Administrative State: Mechanism Choice, Key Actors, and Regulatory Tools." *Virginia Environmental Law Journal* 36: 319–85.
Glicksman, Robert L., David L. Markell, and Justin Sevier. 2020. "An Empirical Assessment of Agency Mechanism Choice." *Alabama Law Review* 71: 1039–1107.
Greenblott, Joseph M., Thomas O'Farrell, Robert Olson, and Beth Burchard. 2019. "Strategic Foresight in the Federal Government: A Survey of Methods, Resources, and Institutional Arrangements." *World Futures Review* 11: 245–66.
Grimmelikhuijsen, Stephan, Sebastian Jilke, Asmus Leth Olsen, and Lars Tummers. 2017. "Behavioral Public Administration: Combining Insights from Public Administration and Psychology." *Public Administration Review* 77: 45–56.
Gubler, Zachary J. 2015. "Making Experimental Rules Work." *Administrative Law Review* 67: 551–93.
Hashimzade, Nigar, Gareth D. Myles, and Matthew D. Rablen. 2016. "Predictive Analytics and the Targeting of Audits." *Journal of Economic Behavior & Organization* 124: 130–45.
Hepfer, Manuel, and Thomas B. Lawrence. 2022. "The Heterogeneity of Organizational Resilience: Exploring Functional, Operational and Strategic Resilience." *Organization Theory* 3: 1–29.
Hillmann, Julia, and Edeltraud Guenther. 2021. "Organizational Resilience: A Valuable Construct for Management Research?" *International Journal of Management Reviews* 23: 7–44.
Hines, Andy, and Jeff Gold. 2015. "An Organizational Futurist Role for Integrating Foresight into Corporations." *Technological Forecasting and Social Change* 101: 99–111.

Ho, Daniel E., and Kristen M. Altenburger. 2019. "When Algorithms Import Private Bias into Public Enforcement: The Promise and Limitations of Statistical Debiasing Solutions." *Journal of Institutional and Theoretical Economics* 175: 98–122.
Holling, C.S. 1973. "Resilience and Stability of Ecological Systems." *Annual Review of Ecology and Systematics* 4: 1–23.
Hornstein, Donald T. 2011. "Resiliency, Adaptation, and the Upsides of Ex Post Lawmaking." *North Carolina Law Review* 89: 1549–77.
Howlett, Michael. 2020. "Dealing with the Dark Side of Policy-Making: Managing Behavioural Risk and Volatility in Policy Designs." *Journal of Comparative Policy Analysis: Research and Practice* 22: 612–25.
Humby, Tracy-Lynn. 2014. "Law and Resilience: Mapping the Literature." *Seattle Journal of Environmental Law* 4: 85–130.
Huq, Aziz, and Tom Ginsburg. 2018. "How to Lose a Constitutional Democracy." *UCLA Law Review* 65: 78–169.
Ip, Eric C. 2017. "Debiasing Regulators: The Behavioral Economics of US Administrative Law." *Common Law World Review* 46: 171–97.
Kahan, Rebecca M. 2005. "Constitutional Stretch, Snap-Back, and Sag: Why *Blaisdell* Was a Harsher Blow to Liberty than *Korematsu*." *Northwestern University Law Review* 99: 1279–1313.
Kantur, Deniz, and Arzu Iseri-Say. 2015. "Measuring Organizational Resilience: A Scale Development." *Journal of Business, Economics and Finance* 4: 456–72.
Kleinberg, Jon, Jens Ludwig, Sendhil Mullainathan, and Ziad Obermeyer. 2015. "Prediction Policy Problems." *American Economic Review* 105: 491–95.
Landers, Renée M. 2019. "Mischief with Government Information Policy." *Chicago-Kent Law Review* 94: 593–606.
Lewandowsky, Stephan, Laura Smillie, David Garcia, Ralph Hertwig, Jim Weatherall, Stefanie Egidy, Ronald E. Robertson, et al. 2020. *Technology and Democracy. Understanding the influence of online technologies on political behaviour and decision-making, EUR 30422 EN, Publications Office of the European Union*. Luxembourg.
Livermore, Michael A. 2017. "The Perils of Experimentation." *The Yale Law Journal* 126: 636–708.
Livermore, Michael A., and Richard L. Revesz. 2013. "Regulatory Review, Capture, and Agency Inaction." *The Georgetown Law Journal* 101: 1337–98.
Loo, Rory van. 2022. "Stress Testing Governance." *Vanderbilt Law Review* 75: 553–613.
Luthar, Suniya S., Dante Cicchetti, and Bronwyn Becker. 2000. "The Construct of Resilience: A Critical Evaluation and Guidelines for Future Work." *Child Development* 71: 543–62.
Maciejewski, Mariusz. 2017. "To Do More, Better, Faster and More Cheaply: Using Big Data in Public Administration." *International Review of Administrative Sciences* 83: 120–35.
Marchant, Gary E., and Yvonne A. Stevens. 2017. "Resilience: A New Tool in the Risk Governance Toolbox for Emerging Technologies." *University of California, Davis, Law Review* 51: 233–71.
Markell, David L., and Robert L. Glicksman. 2014. "A Holistic Look at Agency Enforcement." *North Carolina Law Review* 93: 1–76.
Martin-Breen, Patrick, and J. Marty Anderies. 2011. "Resilience: A Literature Review." *Background Paper, The Bellagio Initiative*, available at: https://opendocs.ids.ac.uk/opendocs/handle/20.500.12413/3692, 1–64.
Mashaw, J.L. 1990. "Explaining Administrative Process: Normative, Positive, and Critical Stories of Legal Development." *Journal of Law, Economics, and Organization* 6: 267–98.
Masur, Jonathan S., and Jonathan Remy Nash. 2022. "Promoting Regulatory Prediction." *Indiana Law Journal* 97: 203–37.

McNollgast. 1990. "Positive and Normative Models of Procedural Rights: An Integrative Approach to Administrative Procedures." *Journal of Law, Economics, and Organization* 6: 307–32.

Meijer, Albert, and Martijn Wessels. 2019. "Predictive Policing: Review of Benefits and Drawbacks." *International Journal of Public Administration* 42: 1031–39.

Metzger, Gillian E., and Kevin M. Stack. 2017. "Internal Administrative Law." *Michigan Law Review* 115: 1239–1307.

Mohler, G.O., M.B. Short, Sean Malinowski, Mark Johnson, G.E. Tita, Andrea L. Bertozzi, and P.J. Brantingham. 2015. "Randomized Controlled Field Trials of Predictive Policing." *Journal of the American Statistical Association* 110: 1399–1411.

Monteiro de Lima Demange, Lia Helena. 2013. "The Principle of Resilience." *Pace Environmental Law Review* 30: 695–810.

Nash, Jonathan Remy, J.B. Ruhl, and James Salzman. 2017. "The Production Function of the Regulatory State: How Much Do Agency Budgets Matter?" *Minnesota Law Review* 102: 695–759.

Nou, Jennifer. 2019. "Civil Service Disobedience." *Chicago-Kent Law Review* 94: 349–81.

Piirainen, Kalle A., and Rafael A. Gonzalez. 2015. "Theory of and within Foresight—'What Does a Theory of Foresight Even Mean?'" *Technological Forecasting and Social Change* 96: 191–201.

Posner, Richard A. 1972. "The Behavior of Administrative Agencies." *The Journal of Legal Studies* 1: 305–47.

Rachlinski, Jeffrey J, and Cynthia R Farina. 2002. "Cognitive Psychology and Optimal Government Design." *Cornell Law Review* 87: 549–615.

Ranchordás, Sofia. 2013. "The Whys and Woes of Experimental Legislation." *The Theory and Practice of Legislation* 1: 415–40.

Romano, Roberta. 2014. "Regulating in the Dark and a Postscript Assessment of the Iron Law of Financial Regulation." *Hofstra Law Review* 43: 25–93.

Rose, Paul. 2021. "Toward a National Resilience Fund." *Northwestern University Law Review Online* 116: 41–67.

Rose-Ackerman, Susan. 1975. "The Economics of Corruption." *Journal of Public Economics* 4: 187–203.

———. 1988. "Progressive Law and Economics—and the New Administrative Law." *The Yale Law Journal* 98: 341–68.

———. 2021. *Democracy and Executive Power. Policymaking and Accountability in the US, the UK, Germany, and France*. Yale University Press.

Rose-Ackerman, Susan, Stefanie Egidy, and James Fowkes. 2015. *Due Process of Lawmaking. The United States, South Africa, Germany, and the European Union*. Cambridge University Press.

Ruhl, J.B. 2011. "General Design Principles for Resilience and Adaptive Capacity in Legal Systems—with Applications to Climate Change Adaptation." *North Carolina Law Review* 89: 1373–1403.

Ruhl, J.B., and Daniel Martin Katz. 2015. "Measuring, Monitoring, and Managing Legal Complexity." *Iowa Law Review* 101: 191–244.

Scheuerman, William E. 2006. "Emergency Powers." *Annual Review of Law and Social Science* 2: 257–77.

Schildknecht, Will. 2015. "Designing for Robustness: Overcoming Systemic Risk in the Political Branches." *California Law Review* 103: 433–66.

Schotel, Bas. 2022. "'Populism? It's Administrative Law, Stupid!': How Administrative Law Subverts Legal Resilience." In *Migrants' Rights, Populism and Legal Resilience in Europe*, edited by Vladislava Stoyanova and Stijn Smet, 1. Aufl., 355–76. Cambridge University Press.

Shapiro, Aaron. 2017. "Reform Predictive Policing." *Nature* 541: 458–60.

Shapiro, Sidney A., and Ronald F. Wright. 2011. "The Future of the Administrative Presidency: Turning Administrative Law Inside-Out." *University of Miami Law Review* 65: 577–620.

Stein, Murray B., Karmel W. Choi, Sonia Jain, Laura Campbell-Sills, Chia-Yen Chen, Joel Gelernter, Feng He, et al. 2019. "Genome-Wide Analyses of Psychological Resilience in U.S. Army Soldiers." *American Journal of Medical Genetics* 180: 310–19.

Ţiclău, Tudor, Cristina Hinţea, and Bianca Andrianu. 2020. "Adaptive and Turbulent Governance. Ways of Governing That Foster Resilience. The Case of the COVID-19 Pandemic." *Transylvanian Review of Administrative Sciences, Special Issue*, 167–82.

Tribe, Laurence H., and Patrick O. Gudridge. 2004. "The Anti-Emergency Constitution." *The Yale Law Journal* 113: 1801–70.

Tyler, Tom R. 2003. "Procedural Justice, Legitimacy, and the Effective Rule of Law." *Crime and Justice* 30: 283–357.

Veale, Michael, and Irina Brass. 2019. "Administration by Algorithm? Public Management Meets Public Sector Machine Learning." In *Algorithmic Regulation*, edited by Karen Yeung and Martin Lodge, 121–49. Oxford University Press.

Waye, Vicki. 2019. "Regtech: A New Frontier in Legal Scholarship." *Adelaide Law Review* 40: 363–86.

Weiser, Philip J. 2017. "Entrepreneurial Administration." *Boston University Law Review* 97: 2011–81.

Werner, Emmy E., and Ruth S. Smith. 1979. "A Report from the Kauai Longitudinal Study." *Journal of the American Academy of Child Psychiatry* 18: 292–306.

Wildavsky, Aaron. 1988. *Searching for Safety. Social Theory and Social Policy.* New York: Routledge.

Wiseman, Hannah J., and Dave Owen. 2018. "Federal Laboratories of Democracy." *University of California, Davis, Law Review* 52: 1119–91.

5 Bureaucrats as Temporary Leaders

Anne Joseph O'Connell

Professor Susan Rose-Ackerman is a prolific scholar, writing across a plethora of fields and methodologies.[1] Her record is inspiring and intimidating. Looking at her work that touches on civil servants and lower-level bureaucrats, I see three important themes. First, as an economist, Rose-Ackerman uses principal–agent models to propose improvements to bureaucrats' performance.[2] Specifically, she explores how institutional design—namely, "a workable scheme of economic incentives"—can promote competence and motivation in bureaucrats undertaking inspections and making benefits determinations.[3] Key to this work is her focus on motivations—of the bureaucratic agents, their principals, and governmental clients—and her presumed normative goal of improved performance, defined by social welfare.

Second, as a development and political economy scholar, Rose-Ackerman explores how a weak civil service contributes to government corruption in developing countries.[4] Her corruption work is vast and multifaceted, and bureaucrats play an important part. She examines how bribes function, for example.[5] And she explores solutions, where she downplays enforcement and returns to incentives.[6] She primarily promotes greater pay for civil servants but supports other reforms too, including the prevention of political hiring and firing of workers.[7]

Third, as a comparativist, Rose-Ackerman considers the points of connection and conflict between the United States and other developed countries (especially France).[8] In these comparisons, civil servants in the United States largely do not shine as bright as their European counterparts.[9] But she also explains how American bureaucrats can be more aligned with agency missions than political appointees and provide needed stability.[10] Rose-Ackerman, in addition, details the declining faith in civil servants across countries[11] and the critical role "an expert, career civil service" can play as "a chain of legitimacy from bureaucrats back to the electorate."[12]

I will return to these themes—considering bureaucrats in a principal–agent model, reducing civil servants' motivations to stray from agency missions, construing American bureaucrats as less elite (and less respected) compared to other European countries, and marking declining trust in civil servants—in various places below.

DOI: 10.4324/9781003416036-5

Agencies and Bureaucrats

Federal agencies arguably do more "lawmaking" than Congress and more "judging" than the federal courts.[13] While these agencies are typically led by Senate-confirmed appointees, the political layer is thin and has many vacancies. Career employees do the bulk of the agencies' critical work, as a matter of course and in staffing crises. For example, senior career officials at the Food and Drug Administration oversee over 17,000 other employees in inspecting food, testing medical devices, and approving drugs and vaccines (including those for COVID-19), among other important duties.[14] In the State Department, career employees perform a broad range of tasks, including advising on foreign affairs, training diplomats, and adjudicating visa applications.[15]

Federal career workers reflect the American public more than members of Congress, federal judges, or political appointees.[16] They are, however, "older, whiter, more educated, and more likely to be male than the average U.S. resident."[17] Of the approximately two million federal employees, there were over 644,111 veterans in FY 2020, 30 percent of the federal workforce.[18] The U.S. Postal Service, which is not included in the two million count above, is the third largest civilian employer after Walmart and Amazon. Its workers are more diverse than the country's labor force: Over 40 percent of the agency's workers, "including mail carriers, postal clerks, and mail sorters and processors," are persons of color.[19] Rose- Ackerman shows how the American bureaucracy is less elitist than its European counterparts.[20] In her view, that has costs—for instance, in respect they receive and in their skill levels.

Many call these agency workers "civil servants," but that label is not always technically correct. Every nonmilitary job in an executive agency has two defining (and often overlapping) components: its payment classification and its appointment process.[21] The appointments process is broken into two primary categories: civil service positions filled by a merit process (the competitive service) and positions "excepted" from the traditional merit system (the excepted service). There is also the Senior Executive Service, but it is much smaller, comprising less than half of one percent of the workforce.[22] Outside the SES, federal workers are split between the competitive and excepted services. In December 2022, just under 71 percent of positions fell into the competitive service, and about 29 percent were in the excepted service.[23] Many excepted service positions, however, are nonpolitical jobs. When I refer to "career" or "nonpolitical" workers, I mean federal agency officials who are essentially chosen for their expertise and merit through nonpolitical mechanisms.

Federal agencies' nonpolitical workers have suffered in recent years. They have also stepped up, including by filling critical vacant political jobs. I turn next to the undermining of the government's nonpolitical workforce, particularly during the Trump Administration. Amidst reorganizations, constrained budgets and pay, government shutdowns, and White House directives, long-serving agency employees have fled the government. The morale of many who stayed plummeted. In my view, the "losers" are the American taxpayers and all who rely on federal agencies, and the "winners" are government contractors, on whom agencies increasingly rely, often at considerable cost. Rose-Ackerman takes a different view, at least in part—seeing the use of government contractors as a good alternative to lesser-skilled bureaucrats in certain contexts.[24] But she also cares deeply about agency missions and worries about political appointees and contractors undermining nonpolitical workers and their performance.[25]

Crisis for Government Workers

Trust in the federal government is abysmally low. In 2022, only one-fifth of surveyed Americans noted that they "trust the federal government to do what is right just about always/most of the time."[26] Public leaders sometimes foster this mistrust. President Reagan liked to joke: "The nine most terrifying words in the English language are: I'm from the Government, and I'm here to help."[27] In setting up the National Performance for Reinventing Government, President Clinton stressed: "Our goal is to make the entire Federal Government less expensive and more efficient, and to change the culture of our national bureaucracy away from complacency and entitlement toward initiative and empowerment."[28] President Trump labeled career officials as the "deep state" throughout his presidency, including calling the State Department "the Deep State Department" and accusing the "deep state" at the FDA of deliberately slowing COVID-19 vaccines and treatments.[29] A top White House official during his Administration called for "the deconstruction of the Deep State."[30]

By contrast, President Biden praised career diplomats at the State Department at the start of his term: "I believe in you. We need you badly. And I'm going to have your back—that, I promise you—just like you're going to have the backs of the American people."[31] In a 2021 Executive Order, Biden said, "career civil servants are the backbone of the Federal workforce, providing the expertise and experience necessary for the critical functioning of the Federal Government."[32] Biden has coupled his praise with demands on career workers, including a directive on improving "customer" experiences.[33] This directive explicitly links bureaucratic performance to trust in government.[34] Rose-Ackerman's work has also focused on the customer–client experience, emphasizing the promise of "customer" feedback to improve bureaucratic service of the public's needs.[35]

Although some politicians like cutting red tape, efficiency is just one governmental objective. Accountability and stewardship of taxpayer dollars also matter. (All three feature in Rose-Ackerman's work.) Interestingly, low levels of trust in the federal government in the United States stem, in part, from reactions to political officials, rather than career workers. According to a 2022 survey by the Pew Research Center, when queried about political appointees in federal agencies, 42 percent of those surveyed said they have at least a "fair amount of confidence" in those officials. But when queried about career agency workers, 61 percent have that level of confidence in them.[36] That number may be trending downwards, as Rose-Ackerman has shown declining trust in bureaucrats in recent years.[37]

We have witnessed numerous interventions that have undermined agency career workers' morale and willingness to serve. First, given the barriers to shifting agency procedures and policies, Presidents like to reorganize the federal bureaucracy—often without sufficient buy-in from agency workers.[38] In the Trump Administration, the Department of Agriculture sent most of its Economic Research Service and its National Institute of Food and Agriculture from Washington, D.C. to the Kansas City area. The Department of Interior moved much of the D.C. headquarters staff of the Bureau of Land Management to Grand Junction, Colorado. (The Biden Administration has decided to move BLM's headquarters back to Washington, D.C.)

More accurately, the agencies sent the positions away, but the people did not follow. At the research entities in the Department of Agriculture, a former leader claimed that most of the workers left the agency instead of moving.[39] Despite a recent round of hiring, the staff at both the Economic Research Service and the National Institute of Food and Agriculture has decreased by about one-third since 2016.[40] In the Bureau of Land Management, close to 90 percent of affected workers quit (or found other jobs).[41] Morale also plummeted in the USDA organizations. In 2019, employee satisfaction sat at 36.5 and 20.3 (on a 100-point scale) at the Economic Research Service and the National Institute of Food and Agriculture, respectively—drops of more than 30 points at each agency since 2016.[42]

Second, until recently, Congress had largely tamped down meaningful growth in both agency budgets and employee pay. The 2011 Budget Control Act placed yearly limits on discretionary defense and nondefense spending through FY 2021.[43] The Act enforced these caps through sequestration (that is, automatic spending cuts).[44] Sequestration, which drove downsizing and froze hiring in some entities, is also linked to lower agency morale.[45] The size of the federal workforce (excluding the postal service) has remained essentially flat since the mid-1950s—hovering at around two million employees.[46] Although government spending has increased in the intervening decades, private contractors, states and local governments, and nongovernmental organizations have played increasing roles.[47] With recent legislation, this was starting to change. For example, the Inflation Reduction Act provided the Internal Revenue Service and connected agencies with nearly $80 billion in supplemental funding "to bolster taxpayer services and enforcement of the tax code, among other purposes."[48] A recent legislative compromise to suspend temporarily the debt limit does, however, take back over $11 billion of this IRS allotment and freeze discretionary spending at many other agencies for fiscal year 2024, the latter of which "may remind federal employees of the spending caps-era that followed the 2011 Budget Control Act."[49]

According to the Congressional Budget Office, federal workers with a high school or college degree earn more than their counterparts (by education level) in the private sector, but those with a professional degree or doctorate receive about a quarter less than their private peers.[50] This education–salary divergence comports with Rose-Ackerman's comparative work on the eliteness (or not) of American and European nonpolitical government workers.[51] Salary increases, however, have been uncertain in recent years. President Trump proposed such minor increases that Congress overrode his recommendations twice, enacting a 3.1 percent jump in 2020 and a 1.9 percent increase in 2019 after the five-week shutdown.[52] Despite urgent calls in 2017 and 2018 from the National Academy of Public Administration, no headway was made to update pay and job classification procedures for career workers that were largely defined over seven decades ago.[53] Rose-Ackerman has shown the corrosive effects of similar constraints on civil servant salaries outside the United States.[54]

Third, Congress and the White House have increasingly failed to keep the government open. There have been 21 shutdowns (some partial) since 1976.[55] In the most recent shutdown, from December 22, 2018 to January 25, 2019, 380,000 federal workers were furloughed, and 420,000 essential workers had to work without pay.[56] Soon after the shutdown, almost 90 percent of excepted service workers noted worsening morale (compared to before the shutdown) in a Federal News Network survey.[57] The head of human capital at the Department of Commerce warned that "the recurring possibilities of the government shutting down due to lapsed funding could be an impediment to recruiting young people."[58]

Fourth, President Trump issued many directives that undermined the career workforce in the federal government. He started his term with a nearly three-month hiring freeze.[59] In 2018, he issued three executive orders to make it easier to remove federal workers, to cut the time that workers can spend on union activities, and to renegotiate contracts between agencies and their unions.[60] In 2020, President Trump tried to create "Schedule F," which would have moved considerable numbers of career employees "in confidential, policy-determining, policy-making, or policy-advocating positions" out of the competitive service and into a new series of the excepted service, with no protection from removal.[61] President Biden rescinded these last four orders.[62] A future Republican President is likely to return to the policies.

These interventions have contributed to departures and lower morale of agency workers, but their consequences go deeper. To start, governmental operations suffer. After the relocations, the productivity of the Agriculture Department's Economic Research Service dropped by half (as measured by its research reports).[63] Sponsored research by the National Institute of Food and Agriculture is receiving less supervision and oversight.[64] Each departure of a career worker can represent years or decades of lost expertise. These losses are also felt outside of the government.

The CBO estimated that the last government shutdown, which lasted five weeks, "delayed approximately $18 billion in federal discretionary spending for compensation and purchases of goods and services and suspended some federal services," resulting in a $3 billion cut in GDP.[65] Harder to measure are the resulting delays in agency initiatives. The Partnership for Public Service's report on the shutdown detailed how "a short-term shutdown can do lasting, and sometimes irreparable, harm."[66] For instance, the Federal Aviation Administration had planned to hire over 1,400 air traffic controllers in FY 2019; the shutdown made them cut that goal by over one-third.[67]

While career workers in the federal bureaucracy have suffered, their overseers—political appointees—have often been missing. I next address issues at the top of federal agencies.

Dysfunction of Political Appointments Process

Given the importance of agency leaders, one might think that keeping top jobs in the administrative state filled would be a priority for both the President and Congress. Instead, there are vast gaps in confirmed agency leadership up and down the organization charts. As of August 15, 2022, for the 809 positions being tracked by the Partnership for Public Service and the *Washington Post*, the Biden Administration had only 442 confirmed leaders (and 152 term appointees or holdovers). Over 130 nominations were pending in the Senate, but over 80 jobs lacked a formal nominee.[68]

Vacancies are not unique to the Biden or Trump Administrations. In a study of most Senate-confirmed jobs at cabinet departments and free-standing executive agencies from 1977 to 2005, I found, on average, between 15 and 25 percent of positions did not have confirmed or recess appointed leaders.[69] Things have gotten worse since 2005, and both the White House and the Senate are to blame. I first discuss lags in nominations before turning to confirmation delays and acting officials.

Nomination Lags

According to research by Professor David Lewis and Mark Richardson, the last three completed Administrations (George W. Bush, Barack Obama, and Donald Trump) did not submit a single nomination in their first two years for, on average, nearly 30 percent of vacant Senate-confirmed agency positions.[70] While President Trump had the worst record, failing to submit a nomination in his first two years for 36 percent of posts, the figure was over one-quarter for President Obama. President Obama also submitted far fewer agency nominations in his final two years than other recent two-term Presidents.[71]

At the end of December 2021, compared to the past four Administrations, President Biden had submitted fewer agency nominations (counting concurrent nominations separately) than all of his predecessors but President Trump.[72] President George W. Bush, who also had a slow start to transition planning, had submitted about a hundred more agency nominations to the Senate than his successor by the end of 2001.

The Biden Administration has made significant strides in diversifying agency leadership—but that takes time.[73] According to research by Kathryn Dunn Tenpas, at the 300-day mark, women made up half of the 140 confirmed appointees to the 15 cabinet departments, and nearly 40 percent were persons of color.[74] These are marked increases from previous Administrations. Finding leaders outside the largely white and male pool of former appointees (the "in-and-outers" as Hugh Heclo called them) may take longer, as does the process of vetting potential nominees with limited or no government paper trails.

The sluggishness in nominations is, in part, also the result of the Federal Vacancies Reform Act of 1998 (Vacancies Act) and specific agency succession provisions, along with delegations of authority—all of which provide the White House with an easy alternative to the traditional appointments process for many positions. I discuss acting officials more below.

Confirmation Delays

Official nominations are just the start of the appointments process. As I have found, over 20 percent of agency nominations between the start of President Reagan's Administration and the end of President Obama's failed to get confirmed, with most being returned by the Senate (nearly one-third of President Obama's nominations were returned or withdrawn).[75] For those nominations that the Senate did confirm (sometimes on the second or third nomination), the confirmation process took two months under President Reagan but increased to four months under President Obama.[76] Returns and delays did not improve under President Trump.[77]

Comparing confirmations, at the end of December 2021, the Senate had approved fewer agency nominees under President Biden than Presidents Clinton, Bush, and Obama.[78] President Biden barely beat out President Trump.[79]

A major chokepoint in staffing agency positions at the start of the Biden Administration was the Senate. Agency picks often lost out to legislation and judicial nominees. The delays in agency confirmations since President Biden took office do not rest entirely, however, on the legislative and judicial priorities of the White House and the Senate. Despite changes to Senate rules decreasing support needed to move a nomination to a confirmation vote as well as debate time for lower-level appointees, members can still draw out the process.[80]

Acting Leaders

During nomination lags and confirmation delays, acting officials operate as stand-in leaders in many agencies, with the exception of top positions in independent regulatory commissions and boards. Reliable information on acting leaders is very hard to come by for a wide set of Senate-confirmed positions, however. In a 2019 "staffing snapshot" of 301 Senate-confirmed positions in cabinet departments, I determined that confirmed officials filled 64.1 percent of these positions, while acting leaders sat in 13.3 percent.[81] The functions of the remaining 22.6 percent were presumably being carried out through delegation orders, or not at all. Professor Christina Kinane examined all Senate-confirmed positions in cabinet departments annually from 1977 to 2016: In approximately 11,000 position-year observations, just over 80 percent were filled by confirmed appointees, nearly 11 percent were filled by acting officials, and about 9 percent had no one listed.[82]

Using data I collected on the highest agency positions, under Presidents Obama and George W. Bush, acting Cabinet Secretaries served (or a complete vacancy existed), as a fraction of the total days of an Administration, 2.7 and 1.6 percent of the time, respectively. By contrast, in the first three years of the Trump Administration, acting Secretaries served for 9.9 percent of the days.[83] The final year was similar. President Trump, for example, had no confirmed Secretary of Homeland Security after he pushed out Kirstjen Nielsen in April 2019 through to the end of his term. Similarly, until President Trump took office, the EPA's head was much more likely to be a confirmed official than an acting one. Under Presidents George W. Bush and Obama, acting Administrators served for just 8.1 and 5.5 percent, respectively, of their Administrations. Under President Trump, however, an acting EPA Administrator led the agency for slightly under one-quarter of his first three years.[84]

In sum, President Trump's expressed adoration of acting leaders[85] named what had been previously unspoken: Modern Presidents have relied heavily on acting officials. In the following section, I combine the attention to career workers and their missing overseers in considering how nonpartisan agency officials step into top roles temporarily.

Career Workers as Acting Leaders

Despite intentional or unintentional measures undermining agency workers, the federal workforce has continued to serve the public in critical ways. One of these ways has received little public attention, but it raises interesting issues: Senior career officials often step in to fill political roles while the appointments process churns. The agents become (temporarily) the principals (and in some ways function more like the elite European civil servants that Rose-Ackerman describes).

In my view, Congress should encourage their service in acting roles and in carrying out delegated authority when there are staffing gaps, particularly in Inspector General positions.

Since 1998, the Vacancies Act has permitted certain officials—first assistants, other Senate-confirmed appointees, and qualifying senior agency workers (political and career)— temporarily to fill covered Senate-confirmed roles.[86] The time limits for acting officials can extend to several years if the White House submits formal nominations.[87] When the time limits run out, agencies typically delegate the nonexclusive duties of the vacant positions downward, often to career workers.[88]

Presidents Trump and Biden turned to career agency workers at the start of their Administrations for the highest agency jobs, as acting Cabinet Secretaries. On his first day, President Trump had only two confirmed Secretaries. For the remaining thirteen slots, he relied on four Senate-confirmed officials from the Obama Administration and nine career officials.[89] At the Departments of Agriculture and Treasury, those career acting Secretaries served for months. Only later in his Administration did President Trump turn to nonconfirmed political officials—among others, Matthew Whitaker and Peter O'Rourke—to take on top acting roles at the Departments of Justice and Veterans Affairs, respectively.[90]

President Biden had no confirmed Secretaries on Inauguration Day. He used holdover Senate-confirmed officials from President Trump's Administration at the Departments of Defense and Homeland Security, and thirteen nonconfirmed agency officials at the start. Of the thirteen, twelve came from the agencies' career leadership.[91]

Career acting officials are prevalent in lower-level Senate-confirmed positions throughout the federal bureaucracy. Consider, for example, the General Counsel of the Environmental Protection Agency. Since the Office of the General Counsel was created in 1983 (as a Senate-confirmed role) until the end of the Trump Administration, there have been more acting General Counsels at the EPA than confirmed and recess appointed ones, treating service across Administrations separately.[92] Of the seventeen acting General Counsels, only two were Senate-confirmed to other roles; five were political officials, and ten came from the career ranks.[93]

The three dozen Senate-confirmed IG jobs have long been plagued by vacancies.[94] The IG job at the Defense Department lacked a Senate-confirmed occupant for close to seven years.[95] As of end of May 2023, the Department of the Treasury and the State Department haven't had a confirmed IG for more than 1,430 and 1,100 days, respectively.[96]

Until the last Administration, skilled senior career officials in the IG office typically have served as acting IGs or carried out the duties of the role through delegation once the Vacancies Act's time limits ran out. For instance, after the last confirmed IG left the Defense Department in January 2016, Glenn Fine, the Principal Deputy IG, became the acting IG and then continued doing the job through delegated authority when the acting time limits ran out in late 2017. In April 2020, however, President Trump submitted a formal nomination for the DOD IG job, which allowed him to turn to the Vacancies Act to name a new acting IG to replace Fine, Sean O'Donnell.[97]

Consider also Christi Grimm, the current confirmed IG at the Department of Health and Human Services. She joined the Department's Office of the Inspector General in 1999 and rose to the Principal Deputy IG job in early 2020. In May 2020, President Trump said that he was getting rid of her after she reported "severe shortages" in hospital supplies during the pandemic, but he did not carry through on that threat.[98] Grimm remained as the Principal Deputy IG, carrying out the vacant job's duties through delegation. The arrival of the Biden Administration restarted the time limits for acting service, allowing her to regain the acting title. Biden then nominated her for the job (and the Senate confirmed her)—a career worker who became a political appointee.

President Trump did carry through with other IG removals. At Secretary of State Mike Pompeo's request, the President fired the Department's IG and, as with Fine's replacement, turned to the Vacancies Act to go around the career deputy IG to pick a political appointee outside the IG office. (O'Donnell, President Trump's pick for acting IG at DOD, was a confirmed IG at the EPA.) President Trump also replaced the career acting IG for the Department of Transportation with a new interim political official with no IG experience.[99]

The firings and the political replacements generated considerable attention at the Capitol and beyond. In 2022, Congress passed legislation restricting acting IGs to senior staff members in IG offices, all of whom are selected in a nonpartisan fashion, and to confirmed IGs at other agencies.[100]

In the first best world, according to many commissions, scholars (myself included), and other commentators, there would be fewer lower-level Senate-confirmed positions in federal agencies. Congress rarely takes action, however, to pare down those slots.[101] Acting officials, particularly those drawn from the career ranks, may be a realistic and desirable solution for jobs outside of independent commissions and boards.[102] As an alternative to Congress reverting Senate-confirmed jobs to political positions chosen by the President or the agency head, the Vacancies Act permits senior career officials to serve temporarily.

In some sense, acting officials drawn from the career ranks resemble the elite civil servants Rose-Ackerman describes in European countries.[103] Nonpolitical leaders can stem the politicization of the bureaucracy.[104] But such career leaders still operate in political jobs. They are both "the political actors [who] set the goals" and the "expert professionals [who] carry them out in a competent and cost-effective way," in Rose-Ackerman's formulation of "performance accountability."[105] Their motivations are complex—and may shift in moving from an agent to a principal role.[106] They may not be the "best" person in terms of social welfare. But the combination of expertise and some political accountability may be desirable. And the possibility of such acting service may encourage good career officials to stay in government service.[107] Career actings, of course, are not without issues—legal and normative, to which I now turn, along with several reform proposals.

Policy and Legal Issues

The current appointments process for filling key federal agency jobs is not working effectively—not at the White House and not in the Senate. Acting officials and delegations of authority do permit large parts of the government to function, at least on some level, while that process plays out. But, at times, interim leaders and delegation serve as more than stop-gap measures—becoming, as a practical matter, the dominant way of staffing agency leadership positions, and, along the way, often undermining agency performance and political accountability and generating legal concerns.

Many commentators see acting leaders negatively, as "substitute teachers," who lack the necessary authority in a classroom (or agency).[108] Even though they have the same formal authority as confirmed leaders, acting officials are less able to wield it because they get less buy-in from the employees who work beneath them, relevant congressional committees, and the public.[109]

Acting leaders have also been forcefully critiqued as politically unaccountable. While acting officials often possess the stability, knowledge, and management experience necessary for their positions, a common criticism is that they are unqualified because they have not been vetted by the Senate.[110] But consider ambassadorial posts: The State Department's foreign service officers who step in temporarily to run embassies almost certainly know more than political appointees selected as a result of their campaign contributions.[111]

The conventional dislike of acting officials sits in some tension with repeated calls for cuts to the number of agency positions requiring Senate confirmation. In some sense, the frequent use of acting officials—at least in lower-level positions—functionally accomplishes what Congress often fails to do formally. But commentators rarely think about acting officials in that light.

In addition, decisions made by acting leaders—particularly those drawn from the career ranks—may face increased legal risks. Some legal challenges are constitutional—namely, whether non-Senate-confirmed officials can temporarily serve in top agency positions.[112] In short, these highest positions are considered principal offices: Is a nonconfirmed acting official in such a job a principal officer under the Appointments Clause? In 1898, the Supreme Court said no—that such an interim official was an inferior officer.[113]

This is not a trivial matter. As noted above, President Biden entered the White House with thirteen acting Cabinet Secretaries who had not been confirmed to another post, while President Trump had nine such officials on his first day.[114] From July 2021 when President Biden fired Andrew Saul as head of the Social Security Administration to December 2023 when Martin O'Malley was confirmed and sworn in, Kilolo Kijakazi was serving as the acting Commissioner, arguably a principal office under the Appointments Clause.[115] Kijakazi is the Deputy Commissioner for Retirement and Disability Policy—an unconfirmed job. While all the lower courts to rule on the question found, correctly in my view, Matthew Whitaker's service as acting Attorney General under President Trump constitutional,[116] questions persist because those courts relied on an 1898 Supreme Court case that seems to be in tension with more recent decisions.[117]

Other legal questions are statutory. Among the disputes, there is controversy over whether agencies can name first assistants (who are default acting leaders under the Vacancies Act) after a vacancy occurs.[118] This is an issue when the staffing of the first assistant position changes with a new administration, such as Deputy Secretaries and many Principal Deputies to Assistant Secretaries. But it is less of an issue if the first assistant role is a career position, such as the Principal Deputy Assistant Administrator for International and Tribal Affairs at the EPA. Career workers at that level do not typically resign with a new administration.

Reforms

We do not live in a first best world. Balancing accountability and government functioning is tricky. I suggest two reforms that center on career workers serving temporarily as agency leaders.

First, Congress should restrict nonconfirmed acting officials in the highest Senate-confirmed positions—such as Cabinet Secretaries—to those who have substantial agency expertise. Currently, in addition to first assistants and other Senate-confirmed officials, senior agency workers can take on certain vacant Senate-confirmed positions in the federal bureaucracy if they have spent at least 90 days in the agency in the year prior to the vacancy and are paid at least at the GS-15 level.[119] Three months is not very long. This final Vacancies Act category should be restricted to senior officials who have worked in the agency for at least five years prior to the vacancy. This modification would have barred Whitaker from serving as acting Attorney General, while allowing Michael Young, who had worked for the Agriculture Department for over twenty-five years, to serve as acting Secretary of Agriculture at the start of the Trump Administration.[120] With such a change, any agency workers taking on top acting roles will likely be drawn from the career ranks and will bring critical expertise.[121]

Second, Congress should reduce permitted time limits for acting officials in the most important agency positions. Although the Vacancies Act's time limits are longer than those of prior statutes, determining precisely how long any given acting official can serve presents a puzzle fit for a math class. If there is no pending nomination, acting officials generally can serve for only 210 days from the vacancy's start date, unless the vacancy exists when a new President takes office (or comes within the next sixty days); if that is the case, acting officials can serve for an additional 90 days.[122] Nominations lengthen the permitted tenure of temporary leaders. Acting officials may serve during the pendency of two nominations to the vacant position. If each nomination fails, a new 210-day period of service runs from the date of the failure.[123]

The Accountability of Acting Officials Act[124] would reduce the 210-day periods to 120 days for principal offices, but still allow for acting service during two pending nominations.[125] Reducing the time periods for such acting service (without pending nominations) is a compelling reform. To start, these are the very highest agency jobs, where political accountability concerns are the greatest. The traditional appointments process helps make agencies accountable to the American public, and shorter time limits will create incentives for the White House to send nominations to the Senate. Moreover, there are constitutional concerns with having nonconfirmed acting officials at the top of agencies—concerns that deepen with the length of tenure.[126]

Conclusion

This chapter has largely focused on senior career workers in the American bureaucracy.

Returning to themes in Rose-Ackerman's work, I have examined how these workers can be both agents and principals (looking like high-level bureaucrats in European nations), how their motivations may be well aligned with agency missions and good governance, and sadly how they are often criticized by commentators.[127] Rose-Ackerman's work in this area, from economics to anti-corruption to comparative law, provides helpful insights, not just in my research on political appointees and career officials but for anyone interested in agency staffing.

Notes

1 As a student, I was lucky to take Administrative Law from Susan Rose-Ackerman and to write my required SAW paper under her careful and demanding supervision. I would not have had the career path I have been fortunate to travel without her mentorship. Jeffrey Capelouto, Taylor Nicholas, Grace Rybak, and Caroline Hunsicker provided exceptional research assistance on this chapter, which draws from my congressional testimony on these issues.

2 *See* ECONOMICS OF ADMINISTRATIVE LAW (Susan Rose-Ackerman ed., 2008); Susan Rose-Ackerman, *Reforming Public Bureaucracy through Economic Incentives?*, 2 J. L. ECON. & ORG. 131 (1986) [hereinafter Rose-Ackerman, *Reforming Public Bureaucracy*].

3 Rose-Ackerman, *Reforming Public Bureaucracy*, *supra* note 2, at 133.

4 *See* BONNIE PALIFKA & SUSAN ROSE-ACKERMAN, CORRUPTION AND GOVERNMENT (2d ed. 2018); Susan Rose-Ackerman, CORRUPTION AND GOVERNMENT: CAUSES, CONSEQUENCES, AND REFORM (1999); Tina Søreide & Susan Rose-Ackerman, *Corruption in State Administration*, *in* THE RESEARCH HANDBOOK ON CORPORATE CRIME AND FINANCIAL MISDEALING 195 (Jennifer Arlen, ed., 2018); Susan Rose-Ackerman, *The Challenge of Poor Governance*, *in* HOW TO SPEND $50 BILLION TO MAKE THE WORLD A BETTER PLACE 77 (Bjørn Lomborg ed., 2006); Silvia Colazingari & Susan Rose-Ackerman, *Corruption in a Paternalistic Democracy: Lessons from Italy for Latin America*, 113 POL. SCI. Q. 447 (1998); Jonathan Rodden & Susan Rose-Ackerman, *Does Federalism Preserve Markets?*, 83 VA. L. REV. 1521 (1997); Susan Rose-Ackerman, *The Law and Economics of Bribery and Extortion*, 6 ANN. REV. L. & SOC. SCI. 217 (2010); Susan Rose-Ackerman, *The Role of the World Bank in Controlling Corruption*, 29 L. & POL'Y INT'L BUS. 93 (1997); Susan Rose-Ackerman, *Corruption: Greed, Culture, and the State*, 120 Yale L. J. Online (2010), https://www.yalelawjournal.org/forum/corruption-greed-culture-and-the-state; Mgmt. Dev. & Governance Div., Bureau for Pol'y & Programme Support, U.N. Dev. Programme, *Corruption and Good Governance: Discussion Paper 3* (1997).

5 Rose-Ackerman, *The Challenge of Poor Governance*, *supra* note 4, Mgmt. Dev. & Governance Div., *supra* note 4.

6 Colazingari & Rose-Ackerman, *supra* note 4; Rose-Ackerman, *The Role of the World Bank in Controlling Corruption*, *supra* note 4.

7 Søreide & Rose-Ackerman, *supra* note 4; Mgmt. Dev. & Governance Div., *supra* note 4.

8 SUSAN ROSE-ACKERMAN, DEMOCRACY AND EXECUTIVE POWER: POLICYMAKING ACCOUNTABILITY IN THE US, THE UK, GERMANY, AND FRANCE (2021) [hereinafter ROSE-ACKERMAN, DEMOCRACY AND EXECUTIVE POWER].

9 Thomas Perroud & Susan Rose-Ackerman, *Impact Assessment in France: U.S. Models and French Legal Traditions*, 20 Eur. Pub. L. 649 (2014); Thomas Perroud & Susan Rose-Ackerman, *Policymaking and Public Law in France*, 19 Colum. J. Eur. L. 225 (2013).

10 Susan Rose-Ackerman, *"Slash and Burn" in the U.S. Congress and the Trump Administration: Permanent Damage or Short-Term Setback?*, 170 Revue Française d'Administration Publique 421, 429 (2019) [hereinafter Rose-Ackerman, *Slash and Burn*]; Susan Rose-Ackerman, Diane A. Desierto & Natalia Volosin, *Hyper-Presidentialism: Separation of Powers without Checks and Balances in Argentina and Philippines*, 29 Berkeley J. Int'l L. 246 (2011); Susan Rose-Ackerman, *Regulation and Public Law in Comparative Perspective*, 60 U. Toronto L. J. 519 (2010).

11 Palifka & Rose-Ackerman, *supra* note 4; Rose-Ackerman, *Slash and Burn*, *supra* note 10; Susan Rose-Ackerman, *Administrative Law and Democracy*, *in* The Oxford Handbook of Comparative Administrative Law 1075 (Peter Cane et al. eds., 2021).

12 Rose-Ackerman, Democracy and Executive Power *supra* note 8, at 105.

13 Agency "lawmaking" consists mostly of regulations. According to Federal Register tables, between 1976 and 2021, agencies annually published between 2,964 (in 2019) and 7,745 (in 1980) final rules in the Federal Register. In addition, according to the Government Accountability Office's database, in the period of 1997 to 2021, "major rules," which are rules expected to have an annual economic impact of at least $100 million or other significant economic effects, ranged between an annual low of 49 (in 2017) and a high of 140 (in 2020). To compare, looking at two-year Congresses between 1977 and 2020, enacted laws ranged from 284 (for the 112th Congress) to 804 (for the 95th Congress). *Statistics and Historical Comparison*, Govtrack, https://www.govtrack.us/congress/bills/statistics. Agencies also adjudicate. For instance, in FY 2019, the Social Security Administration decided over 2.3 million initial claims for disability benefits (and presided over 790,000 hearings). Soc. Sec. Admin., Annual Performance Report Fiscal Years 2019–2021 44, 46 (2020), https://bit.ly/3akmSWA. There are also many agency adjudications involving veterans and immigrants, among others. To compare, in 2021, the federal appellate courts saw nearly 44,000 filings and district courts received over 421,000 filings for both civil and criminal matters. *Caseload Statistics Data Tables*, U.S. Courts, https://www.uscourts.gov/statistics-reports/caseload-statistics-data-tables.

14 Patrizia Cavazzoni, Peter Marks, Susan Mayne, Judy McMeekin, Jeff Shuren, Steven Solomon, Janet Woodcock & Mitch Zeller, *Senior FDA Career Executives: We're Following the Science to Protect Public Health in Pandemic*, USA Today (Sept. 10, 2020), https://bit.ly/3pTeEd3.

15 Cory R. Gill, Cong. Rsch. Serv., R45203, U.S. Department of State Personnel: Background and Selected Issues for Congress 17–18 (2018), https://bit.ly/37h7qIF.

16 Rachel Augustine Potter, Bending the Rules: Procedural Politicking in the Bureaucracy 190–91 (2019).

17 *Id.* at 189–90.

18 Office of Pers. Mgmt., Employment of Veterans in the Federal Executive Branch, Fiscal Year 2020, at 2 (2022).

19 Drew Desilver & Katherine Schaeffer, *The State of the U.S. Postal Service in 8 Charts*, Pew Rsch. Ctr. (May 14, 2020), https://pewrsr.ch/3jLSkA3.

20 *See* Perroud & Rose-Ackerman, *Impact Assessment in France*, *supra* note 9, at 8–9 (contrasting the U.S. bureaucracy with "a government largely staffed by elite civil servants" in France); Perroud & Rose-Ackerman, *Policymaking and Public Law in France*, *supra* note 9, at 302 (describing "elite civil servants" in France).

21 There are three major payment categories: "blue-collar, white-collar, and top-level management positions." David E. Lewis, The Politics of Presidential Appointments: Political Control and Bureaucratic Performance 20 (2008).
22 Office of Pers. Mgmt., FedScope: Federal Workforce Data: Employment December 2022 (2022), https://www.fedscope.opm.gov/employment.aspx.
23 *Id.*
24 Palifka & Rose-Ackerman, *supra* note 4, at 201; Rose-Ackerman, *Slash and Burn*, *supra* note 10, at 430.
25 Rose-Ackerman, Democracy and Executive Power, *supra* note 8, at 78; Rose-Ackerman, *Slash and Burn*, *supra* note 10, at 430.
26 Pew Rsch. Ctr., Americans' Views of Government: Decades of Distrust, Enduring Support for Its Role 10 (2022), https://www.pewresearch.org/politics/2022/06/06/americans-views-of-government-decades-of-distrust-enduring-support-for-its-role/.
27 Ronald Reagan, News Conference (Aug. 12, 1986) (transcript available from the Ronald Reagan Presidential Library & Museum), https://bit.ly/3jQe3Ha.
28 William J. Clinton, Remarks Announcing the Initiative to Streamline Government, 29 Weekly Comp. Pres. Doc. 350 (Mar. 3, 1993), https://bit.ly/3rXk2OT.
29 Peter Baker, Lara Jakes, Julian E. Barnes, Sharon LaFraniere & Edward Wong, *Trump's War on the "Deep State" Turns Against Him*, N.Y. Times (Oct. 23, 2019), https://nyti.ms/2ZdthMO; Donald J. Trump, Press Conference (Mar. 20, 2020) (transcript available from C-SPAN), https://bit.ly/3ajZN6b; Laurie McGinley, Carolyn Y. Johnson & Josh Dawsey, *Trump without Evidence Accuses "Deep State" at FDA of Slow-Walking Coronavirus Vaccines and Treatments*, Wash. Post (Aug. 22, 2020), https://wapo.st/3jVZ4LO.
30 Baker, Jakes, Barnes, LaFraniere & Wong, *supra* note 29.
31 Dan Diamond, Lisa Rein & Juliet Eilperin, *Trump Left Behind a Damaged Government. Here's What Biden Faces as He Rebuilds It*, Wash. Post (Feb. 6, 2021), https://wapo.st/2N8MWLp.
32 Exec. Order No. 14,003, *Protecting the Federal Workforce*, 86 Fed. Reg. 7,231, 7,231 (Jan. 27, 2021).
33 Exec. Order No. 14,058, *Transforming Federal Customer Experience and Service Delivery to Rebuild Trust in Government*, 86 Fed. Reg. 71,357, 71,358 (Dec. 13, 2021).
34 *Id.* at 71,357.
35 Rose-Ackerman, *Reforming Public Bureaucracy*, *supra* note 2, at 134, 141.
36 Lee Rainie, Scott Keeter & Andrew Perrin, Pew Rsch. Ctr., Trust and Distrust in America 16 (2019), https://pewrsr.ch/3rWWBmO.
37 Rose-Ackerman, *Administrative Law and Democracy*, *supra* note 11, at 1091.
38 James Q. Wilson, Bureaucracy: What Government Agencies Do and Why They Do It 282 (1989).
39 Frank Morris, *USDA Research Agencies "Decimated" by Forced Move. Undoing the Damage Won't Be Easy*, NPR (Feb. 2, 2021), https://n.pr/3pV5oVR.
40 Diamond, Rein & Eilperin, *supra* note 31.
41 Juliet Eilperin, *Trump Officials Moved Most Bureau of Land Management Positions Out of D.C. More than 87 Percent Quit Instead*, Wash. Post (Jan. 28, 2021), https://wapo.st/3jl1IdA.
42 Emily Badger, Quoctrung Bui & Alicia Parlapiano, *The Government Agencies that Became Smaller, and Unhappier, Under Trump*, N.Y. Times (Feb. 1, 2021), https://nyti.ms/36N7hwf; P'ship for Pub. Serv, Best Places to Work in the Federal Government, Agency Report: Bureau of Land Management, https://bit.ly/3qfZXRD. The Trump Administration also tried to merge the Office of Personnel Management into the General Services Administration. Congress refused to permit the merger in the National Defense Authorization Act of 2020 and solicited

a study of the issues (including cost implications) from the National Academy of Public Administration. Erich Wagner, *House Committee Investigates Whether Officials Misled Congress on OPM-GSA Merger*, GOV. EXEC. (July 1, 2020), https://bit.ly/38sgE6b.

43 CONG. RSCH. SERV., R46752, EXPIRATION OF THE DISCRETIONARY SPENDING LIMITS: FREQUENTLY ASKED QUESTIONS 1 (2021), https://crsreports.congress.gov/product/pdf/R/R46752.

44 CONG. RSCH. SERV., R44874, THE BUDGET CONTROL ACT: FREQUENTLY ASKED QUESTIONS 1 (2019), https://bit.ly/3qq6x8c.

45 P'SHIP FOR PUB. SERV., GOVERNMENT DISSERVICE: OVERCOMING WASHINGTON DYSFUNCTION TO IMPROVE CONGRESSIONAL STEWARDSHIP OF THE EXECUTIVE BRANCH 21 (2015), https://bit.ly/3b3S9fj.

46 Paul C. Light, *The True Size of Government Is Nearing a Record High*, BROOKINGS (Oct. 7, 2020), https://brook.gs/37co3Fe.

47 JOHN J. DILULIO, JR., BRING BACK THE BUREAUCRATS: WHY MORE FEDERAL WORKERS WILL LEAD TO BETTER (AND SMALLER!) GOVERNMENT 14–19 (2014).

48 CONG. RSCH. SERV., INSIGHT, IRS-RELATED FUNDING IN THE INFLATION REDUCTION ACT (Aug. 9, 2022), https://crsreports.congress.gov/product/pdf/IN/IN11977.

49 Eric Katz, *Debt Limit Deal Would Save Feds' Paychecks, But Freeze Agency Spending*, GOV'T EXEC. (May 30, 2023), https://www.govexec.com/management/2023/05/debt-limit-deal-would-save-feds-paychecks-freeze-agency-spending/386877/.

50 CONG. BUDGET OFFICE, COMPARING THE COMPENSATION OF FEDERAL AND PRIVATE-SECTOR EMPLOYEES, 2011 TO 2015, at 2 (2017), https://bit.ly/3agS490.

51 *See supra* note 20.

52 Nicole Ogrysko, *Federal Pay Parity for Civilian Employees Should Continue in 2021, House Members Say*, FED. NEWS. NETWORK (July 10, 2020), https://bit.ly/2ZgHxEr.

53 NAT'L ACAD. OF PUB. ADMIN., NO TIME TO WAIT: BUILDING A PUBLIC SERVICE FOR THE 21ST CENTURY 1 (2017), https://bit.ly/3shLPbk; NAT'L ACAD. OF PUB. ADMIN., NO TIME TO WAIT, PART 2: BUILDING A PUBLIC SERVICE FOR THE 21ST CENTURY (2018), https://bit.ly/3bvWR61 (identifying recommended reforms to address problems identified in 2017 report).

54 Susan Rose-Ackerman, *The Political Economy of Corruption*, *in* CORRUPTION AND THE GLOBAL ECONOMY 21, 47 (Kimberly Ann Elliott, ed., 1997).

55 CONG. RSCH. SERV., RL 34680, SHUTDOWN OF THE FEDERAL GOVERNMENT: CAUSES, PROCESSES, AND EFFECTS 3–4 (2018), https://bit.ly/3amgzkY. The latest were: November 14 to 19, 1995; December 16, 1995 to January 6, 1996; October 1 to 13, 2013; January 19 to 22, 2018; and December 22, 2018 to January 25, 2019. CONG. RSCH. SERV., R41759, PAST GOVERNMENT SHUTDOWNS: KEY RESOURCES 9–13 (2019), https://bit.ly/2N7oYjt.

56 P'SHIP FOR PUB. SERV., SHUTDOWN LETDOWN: HOW THE LONGEST SHUTDOWN IN U.S. HISTORY DID LASTING DAMAGE TO OUR GOVERNMENT AND THE PEOPLE IT SERVES 3 (2019), https://bit.ly/3pp7sEy.

57 Nicole Ogrysko, *Excepted Employees Say Shutdown Did Irreparable Damage to Morale*, FED. NEWS. NETWORK (Jan. 30, 2019), https://bit.ly/2ZuozdP.

58 P'SHIP FOR PUB. SERV., *supra* note 56, at 10.

59 Memorandum on Hiring Freeze, 82 Fed. Reg. 8,493 (Jan. 25, 2017). The freeze ended April 12, 2017. Brian Naylor, *Trump Lifting Federal Hiring Freeze*, NPR (Apr. 12, 2017), https://n.pr/3aguysK.

60 Exec. Order No. 13,836, 83 Fed. Reg. 25,329 (June 1, 2018); Exec. Order No. 13,837, 83 Fed. Reg. 25,335 (June 1, 2018); Exec. Order No. 13,839, 83 Fed. Reg. 25,343 (June 1, 2018).

61 Exec. Order No. 13,957, 85 Fed. Reg. 67,631 (Oct. 26, 2020).
62 Exec. Order No. 14,003, 86 Fed. Reg. 7,231 (Jan. 27, 2021); *see also* Erich Wagner, *Biden Signs Executive Order Killing Schedule F, Restoring Collective Bargaining Rights*, Gov. Exec. (Jan. 22, 2021), https://bit.ly/3qlWp0g.
63 Morris, *supra* note 39.
64 *Id.*
65 Cong. Budget Office, The Effects of the Partial Shutdown Ending in January 2019 1 (2019), https://bit.ly/3jOOcix.
66 P'ship for Pub. Serv., *supra* note 56, at 3.
67 *Id.* at 4.
68 *Biden Political Appointee Tracker*, Wash. Post, https://www.washingtonpost.com/politics/interactive/2020/biden-appointee-tracker/ (last visited Aug. 15, 2022).
69 Anne Joseph O'Connell, *Vacant Offices: Delays in Staffing Top Agency Positions*, 82 S. Cal. L. Rev. 913, 962, 965 (2009) [hereinafter O'Connell, *Vacant Offices*].
70 David E. Lewis & Mark D. Richardson, *The Very Best People: President Trump and the Management of Executive Personnel*, 51 Presidential Stud. Q. 57, tbl.1 (2021).
71 Anne Joseph O'Connell, *Staffing Federal Agencies: Lessons from 1981–2016*, Brookings Inst. (Apr. 17, 2017), https://www.brookings.edu/research/staffing-federal-agencies-lessons-from-1981–2016/ [hereinafter O'Connell, *Staffing Federal Agencies*].
72 Anne Joseph O'Connell, *End of Year Appointments Press*, Brookings Inst. (Dec. 29, 2021), https://www.brookings.edu/blog/up-front/2021/12/29/end-of-year-appointments-press/ [hereinafter O'Connell, *End of Year Appointments*].
73 Mariel Padilla, *Biden Promised the Most Diverse Administration Ever. Here's How He's Doing*, The 19th (Apr. 30, 2021), https://19thnews.org/2021/04/biden-promised-the-most-diverse-administration-ever-heres-how-hes-doing/.
74 Kathryn Dunn Tenpas, *Biden's Confirmations Progress at the 300-day Mark*, Brookings Inst. (Nov. 24, 2021), https://www.brookings.edu/blog/fixgov/2021/11/24/bidens-confirmations-progress-at-the-300-day-mark/.
75 O'Connell, *Staffing Federal Agencies*, *supra* note 71.
76 *Id.*
77 Carlos Galina, *Joe Biden's First Year in Office: Nominations and Confirmations*, P'ship for Pub. Serv., (Jan. 10, 2022), https://presidentialtransition.org/publications/joe-bidens-first-year-in-office/.
78 O'Connell, *End of Year Appointments*, *supra* note 72. In percentage terms of submitted nominations, President Biden fell last (just 53 percent of his agency picks were confirmed by the end of 2021). Presidents Trump, Obama, Bush, and Clinton saw 60, 69, 66, and 73 percent, respectively, of their agency nominations confirmed by the end of December of their first years.
79 *Id.*
80 Michael Crowley, *Empty Desks at the State Department, Courtesy of Ted Cruz*, N.Y. Times (Oct. 2, 2021), https://www.nytimes.com/2021/10/02/us/politics/senate-confirmation-cruz-nominations.html; Morgan Keith, *Sen. Tom Cotton Refused to Confirm U.S. Attorney Nominees in Blue States Until Sen. Dick Durbin Apologized for Interrupting Him 9 Months Ago*, Bus. Insider (Dec. 12, 2021), https://www.businessinsider.com/tom-cotton-confirm-us-attorney-nominees-dick-durbin-interrupted-2021-12; Kevin Freking, *Sluggish Pace of Confirmations Vexes Biden White House*, Associated Press (Oct. 24, 2021), https://apnews.com/article/joe-biden-donald-trump-barack-obama-ted-cruz-george-w-bush-ec0045ca948d4c2862e9c9a855631b51.
81 Anne Joseph O'Connell, *Actings*, 120 Colum. L. Rev. 613, 655 (2020).
82 Christina M. Kinane, *Control without Confirmation: The Politics of Vacancies in Presidential Appointments*, 115 Am. Pol. Sci. Rev. 599, 606 (2021).

83 O'Connell, *Actings*, *supra* note 81, at 646. For information on variation by agency and the type of acting official (first assistant, other confirmed official, nonconfirmed political official, nonconfirmed career official), *see id.* at 644 tbl.2, 648 tbl.5. For historical comparisons (1789–2005), *see* ANNE JOSEPH O'CONNELL, ADMIN. CONF. U.S., ACTING AGENCY OFFICIALS AND DELEGATIONS OF AUTHORITY 25–27 (2019), https://www.acus.gov/report/final-report-acting-agency-officials.

84 O'Connell, *Actings*, *supra* note 81, at 651. There has been greater use of acting officials in EPA's Deputy Administrator and General Counsel slots across all recent Administrations. *Id.*

85 John T. Bennett, *Frustrated by "My Generals," Trump Turns to "My Actings,"* ROLL CALL (Jan. 14, 2019), https://www.rollcall.com/news/whitehouse/frustrated-generals-trump-turns-actings. Early in his Administration, President Trump claimed that "in many cases, we don't want to fill [Senate-confirmed] jobs." Cody Derespina, *Trump: No Plans to Fill "Unnecessary" Appointed Positions*, FOX NEWS (Feb. 28, 2017), https://www.foxnews.com/politics/trump-no-plans-to-fill-unnecessary-appointed-positions.

86 These roles arise almost entirely in cabinet departments and executive agencies. *See* O'Connell, *Actings*, *supra* note 81, at 627–29.

87 *Id.* at 630–31.

88 Admin. Conf. of the U.S., Recommendation 2019–7, Acting Agency Officials and Delegations of Authority, 84 Fed. Reg. 71,352 (Dec. 27, 2019).

89 Anne Joseph O'Connell, *Waiting for Confirmed Leaders: President Biden's Actings*, BROOKINGS INST. (Feb. 4, 2021), https://www.brookings.edu/research/president-bidens-actings/ [hereinafter O'Connell, *Waiting for Confirmed Leaders*].

90 O'Connell, *Actings*, *supra* note 81, at 673.

91 O'Connell, *Waiting for Confirmed Leaders*, *supra* note 89.

92 O'Connell, *Actings*, *supra* note 81, at 650 tbl. 6. From January 20, 2020 to the end of the Trump Administration, there was one additional acting General Counsel, David Fotouhi.

93 *Id.* at 652 tbl. 8. The additional acting official since my analysis in *Actings*, Fotouhi, appears to be a political official, having joined the agency in 2017. *About EPA's Acting General Counsel: David Fotouhi*, ENV'T PROT. AGENCY (Jan. 19, 2021), https://19january2021snapshot.epa.gov/aboutepa/about-epas-acting-general-counsel_.html.

94 The Council of the Inspectors General on Integrity and Efficiency, among others, tracks IG vacancies online. *See Inspector General Vacancies*, COUNCIL OF THE INSPECTORS GEN. ON INTEGRITY AND EFFICIENCY, https://www.oversight.gov/ig-vacancies.

95 *The Honorable Robert P. Storch*, DOD OFFICE OF THE IG, https://www.dodig.mil/Biographies/Bio-Display/Article/3239269/the-honorable-robert-p-storch/; Glenn Fine, *After Six Years, It's Time to Confirm a Defense Department Inspector General*, DEFENSE ONE (Oct. 21, 2022), https://www.defenseone.com/ideas/2022/10/after-six-years-its-time-confirm-defense-department-inspector-general/378777/.

96 *Inspector General Vacancies*, *supra* note 94.

97 PN1714–116th Congress (2019–2020), *Nomination of Jason Abend, of Virginia, to be Inspector General, Department of Defense*, 116th Congress (2020), https://www.congress.gov/nomination/116th-congress/1714; Anne Joseph O'Connell, *Watchdogs at Large*, BROOKINGS INST. (Aug. 6, 2020), https://brook.gs/3rMeQeS.

98 *Id.*

99 Catherine Lucey & Gordon Lubold, *Behind Trump's Removal of Inspectors General: Support for His Agenda*, WALL ST. J. (May 21, 2020), https://on.wsj.com/3biLLAV.

100 Bob Bauer & Jack Goldsmith, *Inspector General Reform in the NDAA*, LAWFARE (Dec. 23, 2022, 2:01 PM), https://www.lawfareblog.com/inspector-general-reform-ndaa.
101 For a rare example, *see* Presidential Appointment Efficiency and Streamlining Act of 2011, Pub. L. No. 112–166, 126 Stat. 1283 (2012).
102 A recent study found that acting officials are "significantly more likely to fill high-capacity positions when presidents seek to expand an agency's policy reach," while these positions are more likely to be left without confirmed or acting leaders when Presidents seek to reduce agency activity. Kinane, *supra* note 82, at 612.
103 *See supra* note 20.
104 *See* David J. Barron, *Foreword: From Takeover to Merger: Reforming Administrative Law in an Age of Agency Politicization*, 76 GEO. WASH. L. REV. 1095 (2008) (showing how personnel decisions can politicize the bureaucracy).
105 ROSE-ACKERMAN, DEMOCRACY AND EXECUTIVE POWER, *supra* note 8, at 18.
106 *See* Rose-Ackerman, *Reforming Public Bureaucracy*, *supra* note 2.
107 *See* PALIFKA & ROSE-ACKERMAN, *supra* note 4.
108 Russell Berman, *President Trump's "Substitute Teacher" Problem*, ATLANTIC (Apr. 17, 2017), https://www.theatlantic.com/politics/archive/2017/04/president-trumps-substitute-teacher-problem/523101.
109 O'Connell, *Actings*, *supra* note 81, at 697.
110 *Id.* at 698–99.
111 *See* Ryan M. Scoville, *Unqualified Ambassadors*, 69 DUKE L. J. 71, 118–40 (2019). A GAO survey of acting Inspectors General found that all but one believed "having an acting IG had no impact on the OIG's [Office of Inspector General] ability to plan and conduct work." U.S. GOV'T ACCOUNTABILITY OFFICE, GAO-18–270, INSPECTORS GENERAL: INFORMATION ON VACANCIES AND IG COMMUNITY VIEWS ON THEIR IMPACT 17 (2018), https://www.gao.gov/assets/700/690855.pdf. Almost one-quarter of employees, however, contended there was a negative impact. *Id.* The GAO also found that employees generally liked internal acting IGs. *Id.* at 19, 31. Interestingly, nearly half of the acting IGs thought their temporary status had a negative effect on employee management. *Id.* at 21.
112 *See* O'Connell, *Actings*, *supra* note 81, at 658–60.
113 United States v. Eaton, 169 U.S. 331, 343 (1898).
114 O'Connell, *Waiting for Confirmed Leaders*, *supra* note 89.
115 Jamie Rathjen, *O'Malley Sworn In as New Social Security Commissioner*, BLOOMBERG LAW (Dec. 21, 2023), https://news.bloombergtax.com/payroll/omalley-sworn-in-as-new-social-security-commissioner.
116 O'Connell, *Actings*, *supra* note 81, at 665 n.255.
117 Thomas A. Berry, *Are 13 Current Cabinet Members Unconstitutional?* CATO INSTITUTE: CATO AT LIBERTY (Jan. 21, 2021), https://www.cato.org/blog/are-13-current-cabinet-members-unconstitutional. The Supreme Court did recently cite that 1898 case favorably. *See* United States v. Arthrex, 141 S. Ct. 1970, 1985 (2021) (citing United States v. Eaton, 169 U.S. 331, 343 (1898)). For more on my views on this legal issue, *see* O'Connell, *Actings*, *supra* note 81, at 660–66.
118 O'Connell, *Actings*, *supra* note 81, at 675–79.
119 5 U.S.C. § 3345(a)(3).
120 O'Connell, *Actings*, *supra* note 81, at 712.
121 To be fair, late in a President's second term, acting leaders could be political officials who started early in the first term. *Id.*
122 5 U.S.C. §§ 3346(a)(1), 3349(a)(b).
123 VALERIE C. BRANNON, CONG. RSCH. SERV., R44997, THE VACANCIES ACT: A LEGAL OVERVIEW 14 fig. 2 (2020), https://crsreports.congress.gov/product/pdf/R/R44997/5.
124 H.R. 2994, 117th Cong. (2021).

125 The 210-day period ran out for the Secretary of Commerce position during President Obama's Administration in 2013, leaving the cabinet department without an acting leader for over four months before the White House nominated Penny Pritzker. Permitting acting officials to serve during two nominations seems important for several reasons. Issues arise during the vetting process, and the Senate or the White House should not feel pressured into accepting a problematic nominee. Many agency nominees also fail to get confirmed on their first submission; Loretta Lynch would be one example. Specifically, some vacancies occur shortly before the intersession recess. Even if the same party controls the Senate and the White House, Congress struggles to confirm nominations to top cabinet posts that are made close to the year's end.

126 While every lower court to rule on this constitutional concern upheld Whitaker's service, they relied on the Supreme Court's 1898 decision in *United States v. Eaton*, which seemingly treated someone serving *temporarily* in a principal office as an *inferior* officer. *See United States v. Smith*, 962 F.3d 755, 762–65 (4th Cir. 2020); O'Connell, *Actings*, *supra* note 81, at 655 nn. 255–56 (collecting other cases). I believe nonconfirmed acting officials can constitutionally serve in principal offices under these time limits. *Id.* at 660–66.

127 In other work, I am exploring the reverse, in some sense—how political appointees can look more like career civil servants. *See, e.g.*, H.R. 6066 (117th Cong.) (legislative proposal to make director of Office of Personnel Management "appointed without regard to political affiliation").

Selected References

Silvia Colazingari & Susan Rose-Ackerman, *Corruption in a Paternalistic Democracy: Lessons from Italy for Latin America*, 113 Pol. Sci. Q. 447 (1998).

Anne Joseph O'Connell, *Actings*, 120 Colum. L. Rev. 613, 655 (2020).

Anne Joseph O'Connell, *End of Year Appointments Press*, Brookings Inst. (Dec. 29, 2021).

Anne Joseph O'Connell, *Staffing Federal Agencies: Lessons from 1981–2016*, Brookings Inst. (Apr. 17, 2017).

Anne Joseph O'Connell, *Waiting for Confirmed Leaders: President Biden's Actings*, Brookings Inst. (Feb. 4, 2021).

Bonnie Palifka & Susan Rose-Ackerman, Corruption and Government (2d ed. 2018).

Thomas Perroud & Susan Rose-Ackerman, *Impact Assessment in France: U.S. Models and French Legal Traditions*, 20 Eur. Pub. L. 649 (2014).

Thomas Perroud & Susan Rose-Ackerman, *Policymaking and Public Law in France*, 19 Colum. J. Eur. L. 225 (2013).

Susan Rose-Ackerman, *Administrative Law and Democracy*, *in* The Oxford Handbook of Comparative Administrative Law 1075 (Peter Cane et al. eds., 2021).

Susan Rose-Ackerman, *The Challenge of Poor Governance*, *in* How to Spend $50 Billion to Make the World a Better Place 77 (Bjørn Lomborg ed., 2006).

Susan Rose-Ackerman, Democracy and Executive Power: Policymaking Accountability in the US, the UK, Germany, and France (2021).

Susan Rose-Ackerman, *Reforming Public Bureaucracy Through Economic Incentives?*, 2 J. L. Econ. & Org. 131 (1986).

Susan Rose-Ackerman, *The Role of the World Bank in Controlling Corruption*, 29 L. & Pol'y Int'l Bus. 93 (1997).

Susan Rose-Ackerman, *"Slash and Burn" in the U.S. Congress and the Trump Administration: Permanent Damage or Short-Term Setback?*, 170 Revue Française d'Administration Publique 421 (2019).

6 The Creation of the Modern American Civil Service and the (Constitutional) Limits of German Influence

Matthias Rossbach

Introduction[1]

The relationship between democracy and bureaucratic expertise is one of the central themes of Susan Rose-Ackerman's work.[2] It is one of her fundamental achievements to analyze this relationship from a comparative perspective and to inspire scholars from all over the world to follow this path. The different administrative and constitutional traditions of the United States and Germany have always played a central role in her comparative work.[3] The influence of German concepts on American administrative law has recently become subject of debate and criticism.[4] Against this backdrop, this chapter analyzes the creation of the modern American civil service in the late 19th century and the (constitutional) limits of German influence.

In modern times, the American founders were the first who had to answer the pivotal question that arises in every democracy: how should the personnel system of the executive branch be designed in order to realize the principle of popular sovereignty?[5]

When this question occurred in Germany at the beginning of the Weimar Republic in 1919 and again during the founding of the Federal Republic of Germany in 1949, traditional civil service principles had already influenced German administration for more than a century.[6] When the "venture of democracy" was undertaken in Germany,[7] the first codification of the essential principles of the civil service was more than 100 years in the past: beginning with the Prussian General Land Law (Allgemeines Landrecht für die Preußischen Staaten) of 1794, but more completely with the Bavarian Hauptlandespragmatik of 1805.[8] When democracy finally prevailed in 1918/1919, "the bureaucratic machinery continued to work almost undisturbed."[9] The Reich Civil Service Act of 1873 remained in force,[10] and with Articles 128 to 130 of the Weimar Reich Constitution, the longstanding civil service principles were given constitutional status.

In the United States, by contrast, republicanism and the principle of popular sovereignty had shaped the executive branch and the selection of its personnel long before the emergence of a modern administration with regulatory agencies and a professional civil service in the late 19th century. During the

DOI: 10.4324/9781003416036-6

Philadelphia Convention and its aftermath, the American founders attributed paramount importance to the power to appoint and to remove executive officers.[11]

The founders tried to reach their self-proclaimed aim of choosing "virtuous characters" through a political process.[12] The nomination of officers by the President should tie the decision back to the people and thereby ensure republican "responsibility"; requiring the consent by the Senate "would be an excellent check upon a spirit of favoritism in the President, and would tend greatly to prevent the appointments of unfit characters" who did not have the necessary republican "virtue."[13] This political process is now enshrined in the Appointments Clause of Article 2 of the U.S. Constitution. In this way, the American founders designed the federal appointments process as a means to realize republicanism and self-government: "as the President was to nominate, there would be responsibility, and as the Senate was to concur, there would be security."[14]

Civil service reform in the United States began more than 80 years after the founding.

The reformers of the 1870s and 1880s criticized the so-called spoils system of the previous decades in which the vast majority of officeholders were selected through partisan political criteria.[15] They called for reforming the personnel system by adopting European concepts.[16] The breakthrough for civil service reform was caused by the assassination of President James Garfield by a disappointed Republican Party supporter who had not been nominated for a diplomatic post in Paris.[17] It led to the Pendleton Act of 1883, which remained in effect until the Civil Service Reform Act of 1978.[18] Its basic principles continue to this day.[19] The Pendleton Act allowed the President to establish a Civil Service Commission to set rules for civil service entrance examinations based on professional criteria.[20] This basic idea led to the foundation of a competitively selected civil service. It serves below the layers of political appointees who are chosen by the President with (or without) the consent of the Senate—as prescribed in the Appointments Clause (and in its Excepting Clause specifying when the consent of the Senate is not necessary).

Was the civil service reform of the late 19th century an import of "alien ideas" into the American system that contradicts the Constitution and the founders' ideals?[21] Accusations of this kind are part of a criticism that the American administrative state has been facing since the end of the 19th century.[22] Philip Hamburger's book is a recent example for criticism of foreign—especially German—influence on administrative law in general.[23] This is often supported by the fact that leading reformers of the late 19th century were influenced by German administrative law and state theory and admired the efficiency of German, especially Prussian, administration.[24]

This chapter will show that the civil service reform of the late 19th century was not a departure from the principles of self-government that characterized the constitutional law on executive personnel since the founding, nor did it lead to a German-style career civil service in the United States.[25] The present

American personnel system is the product of a specifically American development. The chapter proceeds in the following steps:

First, it will argue that the original "constitutional language"[26] of the founders was still very much present in the discourse of the *early* civil-service reformers. For them, the idea of efficiency remained secondary to the first motive of eliminating the grievances that the spoils system had caused. In this context, the strength of the principle of republican virtue was apparent: the necessary changes were justified by the need to return to the republican ideals of the constitutional fathers; the previous practice was criticized as corruption.

Second, although reformers were influenced by German ideas, they were aware of the limits to the implementation of German administrative practices in the United States. They even actively stressed the impossibility of transplanting German ideas into American law.

Third, the chapter will argue that European civil service models—both English and German—were not adopted without significant changes. They were adapted to American constitutional principles and American constitutional law.

This chapter thus shows the strength of the preceding constitutional tradition in the United States vis-à-vis an emerging concept of a competitively selected civil service. At the same time, the question of the constitutionality of the competitively selected civil service remains debated until today—fueled by cases like *Lucia v. SEC.*[27] The crucial question is where to draw the line between positions that fall under the rules of the competitively selected civil service and those that do not.

Motives and Models of Early Reformers of the U.S. Civil Service

From the perspective of practical politics, the introduction of civil service examinations in 1883 was less an adoption of European ideas than an attempt—at least partially—to retain power. Republicans feared defeat in the 1884 elections, and the introduction of civil service examinations would result in a newly elected Democratic president firing fewer (Republican-appointed) personnel, because he could not select successors according to political criteria.[28] Substantive requirements for personnel selection should lead to de facto protection against dismissals; the incentive for political dismissal is removed if the possibility of political replacement does not exist.[29] This mechanism provided presidents with an incentive to expand the scope of these civil service principles—which Franklin D. Roosevelt later did in order to secure his New Deal agenda.[30]

In addition, the President could free himself from the political claims of Congress seeking to influence personnel selection and thus strengthen his position.[31] Hence, section 10 of the Pendleton Act contained a prohibition against considering the recommendations of members of Congress insofar as the Pendleton Act applied to hiring. Because it also allowed the President to unilaterally determine which positions were subject to the Act, he thus had the weakening of Congress in his own hands.[32] This explains the rapid expansion of the Pendleton Act's reach in subsequent decades: In 1883 it covered only ten percent of the total executive staff; by 1952 its share had increased to 86 percent.[33]

But the preservation of power alone cannot explain the reform agenda. Rather, the Pendleton Act was also the victory of a campaign against the "corruption" of the spoils system that had begun in the 1860s and was based primarily on moral arguments.[34] The reformers justified the changes with the need to return to the ideals of the founding generation:[35] "What we want is to intrench the principle and practice of Washington in the law," said one of the leading reformers, George William Curtis, in a speech in 1869.[36] Curtis analyzed George Washington's personnel practice and concluded that the latter had selected only according to the criteria of "ability, integrity, and fitness."[37] Curtis considered this exemplary, as well as Washington's alleged restraint in personnel selection: "They are words that should blaze in gold over the doors of the White House."[38] The practice of the spoils system, in contrast, has led to "intrigue and corruption," he said: "economy, patriotism, honesty, honor, seem to become words of no meaning."[39]

The strong influence of the republican principles adopted by the founding generation was evident: The republican ideal of personnel selection embraced by the founders and developed from an orientation toward "virtue" and the "common good" was seen as exemplary. The classical republican dichotomy of "corruption" versus "virtue" (which was later famously analyzed by Pocock, Bailyn, and Wood) once again shaped the discourse.[40] The difference between the reformers and the founding generation, however, was that the reformers no longer solely relied on the political process to realize the republican ideal of "virtue" in personnel selection. They wanted to secure the practical implementation of those ideals through substantive legal standards.[41]

The civil service reformers of the second half of the 19th century sought to return to the values of the founding generation and to fight those groups that were oriented toward self-interest—"factions", as Madison would call them.[42] In particular, they singled out (fairly or unfairly) the party politicians organizing the spoils system at the state and local levels.[43] Curtis refers to them as a "ring or clique of professional politicians" who were an "oligarchy."[44] Parties as such were not questioned. However, they should be reduced to their "legitimate" purpose: according to Curtis, the goal of parties should not be the distribution of offices, but the realization of their program through legislation.[45]

The reformers achieved their first successes even before the passage of the Pendleton Act. In 1871, a first Civil Service Commission was set up, although it ended its work in 1875 due to a lack of budgetary resources.[46] But its work prepared for the decisive step in 1883.

The reformers' role model was not Germany, but Britain. Although other European countries, including Prussia, were also considered, the most important model of the early civil service reformers was the reform of the civil service in England. [47] It had been reformed just one year earlier—in 1870—with the goal of combating patronage and orienting appointment processes to the merit of the candidate.[48] This reform in England included the introduction of an examination system that was administered by an independent Civil Service Board[49]—similar to the first Civil Service Commission in 1871. American reformers were in close contact with major English reformers like Stafford Northcote and Charles Edward Travelyan.[50] Dorman Eaton, who had a major influence on the wording of the Pendleton Act, had previously published a book on "Civil Service in Great Britain" in which he argued for the adoption of essential elements of the English civil service. [51]

Even before the Pendleton Act, Congress passed a law that highlighted the motives of the civil service reformers. In 1876, it prohibited executive personnel from demanding money from other employees in the executive branch for political purposes.[52] This measure was intended to strike at the heart of the corruption that reformers had diagnosed. At the same time, it struck at one of the main mechanisms of the spoils system—albeit imperfectly because it did not include sums of money that had to be paid by public officials to persons outside the executive branch.[53] The constitutionality of this law was upheld by the Supreme Court in the case *Ex parte Curtis* in 1882.[54] The court explicitly upheld both of the reformers' goals—"efficiency and integrity in the discharge of official duties"—as constitutional.[55] However, it should be noted that the 1876 Act did not refer to offices whose appointments are made by the President with the consent of the Senate. Thus, from the outset, it was concerned with offices at lower levels of the hierarchy. Nevertheless, the Supreme Court's pronouncements were a vindication of the reformers' agenda and contributed to the passage of the Pendleton Act just one month after the December 1882 ruling.[56]

German Influence and Its Limits

"The civil service of Prussia is indebted for its world-renowned efficiency and purity—1. To the common law of Prussia, which contains the provision that 'nobody shall be appointed to a public office unless he possesses the competent qualifications and has produced evidence of his fitness'," reads a report by Thomas A. Jenckes for the House of Representatives from 1868, which is considered one of the foundational texts of the reform movement.[57] As mentioned above, increasing the efficiency of the civil service was only the second motive for the early reformers—behind moral restoration—but it was always mentioned as well.[58] Increasing efficiency became dominant as a motive after the Pendleton Act was passed: the Progressive Movement placed it at the center of its agenda from the late 1880s onward. This agenda was directed towards administration by politically neutral experts.[59] Their product was not only the creation of independent regulatory commissions, but also an expansion of the reach of the civil service rules of the Pendleton Act.[60]

Although the Pendleton Act itself was influenced more by British models, Germany was a model for these developments and not only in terms of administrative efficiency. Leading representatives of the Progressive movement such as Woodrow Wilson and Frank Goodnow were also influenced by German state theory.[61] Both are considered to have brought the concept of the separation of politics and administration to the United States.[62] In doing so, they justified the political neutrality and independent position of subordinate executive personnel and certain higher officials—and thereby advocated for a civil service system similar to the German model.[63] But on closer examination, they also stressed the limits of German influence on American law and they did not support a complete adoption of continental concepts:

Woodrow Wilson

Wilson—like many so-called progressives of his time—was influenced by German political and administrative science. At Johns Hopkins University, he was a student of Herbert B. Adams, who was a student of Johann Caspar Bluntschli in Heidelberg.[64] Thus, Wilson also quoted Bluntschli[65] in his contribution "The Study of Administration" of 1887 on the necessity of a separation between politics and administration: "administration lies outside the proper sphere of politics."[66] Here, Wilson paraphrases Bluntschli, who regards politics as the task of the statesmen, and administration as the task of the "technical offices."[67] It is precisely this argument that Wilson adopts when he calls for a "technically schooled" civil service.[68] He complained that there was too much education in political science in the U.S. and too little emphasis on "technical knowledge": "It is an education which will equip legislators, perhaps, but not executive officials."[69]

But Wilson at the same time recognized the problems of transforming continental ideas into American law:

> We should not like to have had Prussia's history for the sake of having Prussia's administrative skill; and Prussia's particular system of administration would quite suffocate us. It is better to be untrained and free than to be servile and systematic. Still there is no denying that it would be better yet to be both free in spirit and proficient in practice.[70]

This strong statement against the pure implementation of German ideas is corroborated by more concrete examples. In particular, Wilson sees the problems of the German separation between civil service and the society, which is a characteristic feature of the civil service law tradition established by the Bavarian Hauptlandespragmatik:[71]

> a distinct, semi corporate body with sympathies divorced from those of a progressive, free-spirited people, and with hearts narrowed to the

> meanness of a bigoted officialism. Certainly such a class would be altogether hateful and harmful in the United States.[72]

Wilson thus strongly criticizes the German administration, whose efficiency he had previously praised. According to him, the efficiency of the German civil servant stems from an "esprit de corps": "He serves, not the public, but an irresponsible minister."[73]

Therefore, Wilson demands that access to the civil service examinations must be open in principle to all social classes: in his opinion it is necessary to

> draw the administrative personnel of the government by some free and open process from out the general body of the nation, without preferring in the selection one class or order or social station or blood or condition to another, if only fit and capable persons be found for each function.[74]

Of course, it has to be noted at this point that the practice of Wilson's administration was far from meeting these standards. Wilson's racism led to the de facto exclusion of African-Americans from leadership positions and to strict segregation in the civil service.[75] Blake Emerson shows that this practice was rightly sharply criticized by W.E.B. Du Bois and others and that it did not meet democratic standards.[76]

In contrast to the German tradition, Wilson also sees the necessity of the dependence of the administration on public opinion: Although public officials should enjoy protection against dismissal in his opinion, a dismissal should be possible if the official does not show "allegiance to the policy of the government"[77] that is directly responsible to the people.[78] Like Stein in Prussia, Wilson relies on the "leadership" of "statesmen" with "true spirit."[79] But like the American founders, he sees the necessity for a link back to the people as guaranteed by elections and by mechanisms of public opinion.[80]

Wilson thus attempts a balancing act: he wants to adopt basic European structures because he considers the "business of administration" to be identical in both monarchies and democracies.[81] At the same time, however, he sees the dangers of this adoption and argues for adapting continental concepts to the principles of American constitutional law:

> If we would employ [the science of administration], we must Americanize it, and that not formally, in language merely, but radically, in thought, principle, and aim as well. It must learn our constitutions by heart; must get the bureaucratic fever out of its veins; must inhale much free American air.
>
> [. . .]
>
> We have only to filter it through our constitutions, only to put it over a slow fire of criticism and distil away its foreign gases.[82]

Frank Goodnow

A similar ambivalence can also be observed in the work of Frank Goodnow, known among other things for his seminal work on comparative administrative law.[83] He most clearly articulated the separation of politics and administration in his monograph "Politics and Administration."[84] Goodnow was also influenced by German thought, was a student of Rudolph von Gneist in Berlin[85] and of Francis Lieber, who had emigrated to the United States.[86] This influence is already evident in the starting point of his book, "Politics and Administration." He refers to Gneist as the first to focus attention on the "importance of administrative institutions."[87] In Germany and England, Goodnow argues, public opinion would also separate politics from administration.[88] This separation would have effects on organization and administrative personnel: "there should be organized a force of governmental agents absolutely free from the influence of politics."[89]

The search for truth, the similarity of administration to judicial and business activities are Goodnow's arguments for separating administration from politics.[90] From this he draws consequences for administrative personnel and demands that those who perform such activities enjoy security of tenure "like judges."[91] This security, he argues, is necessary because the required expertise can only be acquired through many years of experience.[92] This classic argument for legitimacy through expertise played an important role not only in the Progressive period of the early 20th century but also in the New Deal—then combined with the need for effective "management"—and was ultimately used to justify both protection from dismissal for subordinate officeholders and the existence of independent agencies.[93]

However, Goodnow also acknowledges that limits to these arguments exist in American constitutional law: first, he acknowledges the constitutional problems associated with his demand for protection of public officials against dismissal. He therefore says: "That this can be accomplished by any changes in the law may, perhaps, be doubted."[94] Instead, he wants to bring about such protection through the mechanisms of public opinion.[95] Second, Goodnow takes into account popular sovereignty as a constitutional principle and draws from it a consequence that continues to shape the American personnel system to this day: protection against removal of high executive officeholders, who have broad discretionary powers, is incompatible with the principle of "popular government." Goodnow connects the President's right to remove with the extent of the exercise of discretion by the respective officeholder and therefore demands protection against removal only for the "lower ranks" of the civil service.[96]

The principle of popular sovereignty, thus, limits the efficiency postulate. Goodnow also stresses the dangers of efficiency as an absolute postulate: "since it tends to further the formation of an immense governmental machine whose very efficiency may make it dangerous to the existence of popular government."[97]

As much as Prussia serves as a model in terms of efficiency, and as much as Goodnow *is* influenced by German ideas, he stresses the limits of adopting German concepts:

> Thus a strong administration, where the party organization is weak, may nullify the popular will through the control which the administration has, and in the nature of things must have, over the elections. This is largely true at the present time of Germany, and has been true in the past in France. [98]

Overall, the reformers' desire for efficiency did not lead to disregard for principles of American constitutional law: the principle of democracy is given higher priority, at least in the rhetoric of the reformers, than the desire for a more efficient administration. However, it should at least briefly be mentioned that, on the other hand, the principle of separation of powers is heavily criticized by the reformers: Goodnow argues that separation of powers threatens the "harmony" between the articulation of the will of the state and its execution.[99] John Rohr thus concludes that Goodnow adopts a concept that in practice amounts to the superiority of one power over the other and thereby ultimately the concept of a parliamentary system.[100]

The Modern American Civil Service: Adapting Civil Service Concepts to Constitutional Law

When—one hundred years after the establishment of the Prussian "Ober-Examinations-Kommission"[101] and more than eighty years after the Philadelphia Convention—the introduction of examinations for access to the general[102] civil service was discussed in America, constitutional concerns were raised immediately. Attorney General Amos Akerman argued in 1873 that civil service examinations might violate the Appointments Clause.[103] These objections exemplify the fact that in the United States—unlike in Germany—the Constitution precedes the emergence of a career civil service. It was thus necessary to adapt European civil service concepts to American constitutional law. There could be no complete adoption of foreign models.

The constitutional concerns were numerous—and so were the necessary adaptations and thus the differences between the American civil service and its European counterparts:

Appointments Clause

The most important concern pertained to the Appointments Clause of Article 2 of the U.S. Constitution. It contains an enumeration of those who hold the appointing power: the President with the consent of the Senate or—if determined by Congress—the President alone, or courts of law or heads of departments. Amos Akerman and others thus feared that the introduction of civil service examinations would give the appointing power to the examiners and thus to somebody who is not enumerated in the Appointments Clause:

> An enactment that the President shall appoint to a certain office the person adjudged by the examiners to be the fittest, is not different in constitutional principle from an enactment that he shall appoint John Doe to that office. In neither case are his judgment and will called into exercise.[104]

Thus, an examination system ran the risk of transferring the decision to the Civil Service Board: "that board would virtually be the appointing power. [. . .] That Congress cannot give such authority, I think is manifest."[105]

But American reformers found a solution to these concerns. This solution was later enshrined in U.S. civil service law by the Pendleton Act of 1883 and continues to have consequences today. This solution has three components that are aimed at reconciling the civil service system with the Appointments Clause:

Rule of Three and Other Models

First, the examining boards selected by the Civil Service Commission were not given the right to make final decisions on personnel selection. Rather, the examiners were to certify and rank the candidates; the selection itself was then made by the holder of the appointing power "among those graded highest as the results of such competitive examinations."[106] The word "among" indicates that this selection should not be limited to any one person. In this way, the statute satisfies the need, cited by Akerman, to leave sufficient discretion to the constitutional appointing power. Chief Justice Taft took up this demand in the case *Myers v. United States* and defined it as the limit of statutory restrictions on executive nominating power.[107] Understood in this way, the Civil Service System is not a shift of personnel power to a review board, but rather a substantive requirement that candidates be members of a group of persons certified by the review board.[108] Akerman was unwilling to say how narrowly the group might be defined. Like many constitutional problems, this is "a question of degree."[109]

In practice, the Rule of Three (or, at times, the Rule of Four) was applied, according to which the appointing authority was free to select from the best three candidates certified by the review board.[110] This Rule of Three still exists today: 5 U.S.C. § 3317 prescribes a corresponding requirement for the Office of Personnel Management, which since the Civil Service Reform Act of 1978 has been one of two successor agencies to the Civil Service Commission:[111] "The Office of Personnel Management shall certify enough names from the top of the appropriate register to permit a nominating or appointing authority who has requested a certificate of eligibles to consider at least three names for appointment to each vacancy in the competitive service."

However, this rule has been dead letter since 2010 when President Obama directed the executive branch to apply exclusively the alternative category model standardized in 5 U.S.C. § 3319.[112] According to this model, candidates are not ranked, but are placed in two or more categories. The appointing authority may then select from among the candidates in the top category.[113] This model gives the appointing authority greater leeway than the traditional Rule of Three and is therefore even more likely to meet constitutional requirements.[114]

Limits of the Civil Service System

Second, the Pendleton Act clarifies that the rules of the competitive civil service system do not apply to offices subject to the advice-and-consent procedure.[115] A similar provision is still in force today (5 U.S.C. 2102 (a)).[116] Thus, the personnel that fall under the default rule of the Appointments Clause (nomination by the President, confirmation by the Senate) are not part of the competitive civil service. This also protects the Senate's right of confirmation. According to the plan of the founders, Senate consent should be the means of quality assurance for the most important positions in the executive branch.[117] It should be noted that while the advice-and-consent process is constitutionally mandatory only for principal officers, it is also the constitutional default rule for inferior officers: it applies as long as Congress has not expressly delegated the power of appointment of an inferior officer to the President alone or to a head of department.[118]

Control by the President Over the Scope of the Civil Service

Third, the civil service system was designed to give the President control over its development and its scope. The law was essentially designed as an enabling statute on the basis of which the President could issue rules which the Civil Service Commission was to help him prepare ("aid the President, as he may request, in preparing suitable rules for carrying this act into effect").[119] Only by taking into account these rules should the Civil Service Commission issue further regulations for carrying out the examinations.[120]

Thus, the President was able to determine the scope of the civil service system: initially, it extended only to 10 percent of the executive branch's personnel.[121] The President and the Secretaries (on his instructions) had the right to extend the scope to other parts of the executive branch. Later presidents made intensive use of this, so that the civil service grew continuously until the middle of the 20th century.[122]

To this day, the President has control over the scope of the civil service by having the right to exempt positions from civil service rules (5 U.S.C. § 3302). By using this authority, employees are exempted in 5 CFR § 213.101 et seq. in different "Schedules." In particular, this includes so-called Schedule C positions, which are defined under 5 CFR § 213.3301 (a) as "positions which are policy-determining or which involve a close and confidential working relationship with the head of an agency or other key appointed officials." This category of positions, created by President Eisenhower, includes employees on the management staffs of departments and other agencies, such as personal assistants, communications staff, and congressional liaison offices.[123]

This limited scope of the civil service was intended from the beginning: President Chester Arthur stated that the Pendleton Act covered only "subordinates whose duties are purely administrative and have no legitimate connection with the triumph of any political principles."[124]

In terms of current legal doctrine, as framed by *Lucia v. SEC*,[125] one could argue that these employees do not even fall within the scope of the Appointments Clause because they do not constitute "Officers of the United States."

Conclusion

Overall, the civil service reformers took the requirements of the Appointments Clause into consideration from the outset. This is not to argue that every legal scholar would agree that the current civil service is in complete conformity with all requirements of the Appointments Clause. The point is rather that the reformers of the 1870s and the 1880s did their best to respect the Appointments Clause and especially the appointing power of the President. It can even be claimed that the Pendleton Act strengthened the President's position vis-à-vis the heads of departments because the establishment of the Civil Service Commission led to centralization.[126] These findings are confirmed by the following dialogue during a Senate hearing with the chairman of the first Civil Service Commission from the 1870s, George William Curtis, on American reform legislation:[127]

Senator Dawes:	Do you not think, therefore, that the character of the [civil service] commission itself would depend very largely upon the disposition of the Executive?
Mr. Curtis:	Necessarily.
Senator Dawes:	Then would not the Pendleton bill be just as likely to be put to its enemies to nurse as any other bill?
Mr. Curtis:	I think we agree that we are dealing with human nature.
Senator Dawes:	No one of us can hope for much good out of a hostile, aggressive political opponent of this measure in the Executive chair, can we?
Mr. Curtis:	No.
Senator Dawes:	Therefore you trust the whole of it to him?
Mr. Curtis:	That is where the Constitution places the appointing power.

No Separation of Civil Service and Society: A Democratic Civil Service

As mentioned above, the reformers of the late 19th century were convinced that a civil service in a democracy must not be separated from society.[128]

They argued against the German and British version of a civil service with an "esprit de corps," a "civil service class", and in favor of a civil service that is part of the society.[129] The civil service of the United States should be open and not create a self-contained bureaucracy.[130] This is also consistent with Alexis de Tocqueville's earlier observation that "American civil servants remain indistinguishable from the mass of the citizens."[131]

This theoretical demand, which was derived from the principle of democracy, had concrete consequences in the civil service legislation: firstly, the Pendleton Act included a provision against the mechanism of self-recruitment within a civil service class, which—in contrast—was explicitly welcomed in the Bavarian tradition that characterized Germany.[132] Section 9 prohibited the enlistment of more than two members of a family in the civil service.[133] Moreover, in continuity with George Washington's practice, the Pendleton Act also ensured representativeness geographically by mandating a proportionally equitable distribution.[134]

Furthermore, the Pendleton Act stipulated that entrance examinations must be "practical in character" and related to the needs of the service to be performed.[135] This was directed against requiring formal academic education for the admission to the entrance examination.[136] This prohibition of a minimum education requirement is laid down in 5 U.S.C. § 3308 to this day. A degree may be required only as an exception when the duties of the job cannot be performed otherwise. This prohibition of a minimum education requirement also mirrors the personnel ideal of the "common man" that was put forward in the times of the so-called "Jacksonian Democracy."[137] It combined the concept of popular sovereignty with the demand for equal access as well as representativeness of the civil service.[138]

In the legislative process that led to the Pendleton Act, the Senate deleted a provision that allowed entry into the civil service only at the lowest level—which was the case in England and is still the default rule in Germany.[139] A possible motive for this move can be found in an address by President Chester Arthur in 1881, in which he criticized both the restriction of entry to the entry-level post provided for in England and the age limit there.[140] Arthur explicitly opposes a career system, according to which higher offices can only be attained through promotions from the entry-level office:

> There are many persons who fill subordinate positions with great credit, but lack those qualities which are requisite for higher posts of duty; and, besides, the modes of thought and action of one whose service in a governmental bureau has been long continued are often so cramped by routine procedure as almost to disqualify him from instituting changes required by the public interests. An infusion of new blood from time to time into the middle ranks of the service might be very beneficial in its results.[141]

From Arthur's speech, two reasons can be identified for allowing an entry on all levels, which has been part of U.S. civil service law from the beginning: first, to make the civil service as broadly accessible as possible, especially independent of the candidate's age; and second, the fear that without such a provision, the civil service would become inflexible, contrary to the public interest. Both reasons can be traced back to the principle of democracy, as Paul van Riper pointedly notes:

> From 1883 to this day, one may enter the American public service at almost any level and at almost any age. Indeed, the adoption of age and other restrictions tending to prevent this mobility have been on many occasions, and often still are, bitterly attacked as "undemocratic".[142]

Openness and permeability continued to characterize the Civil Service: although the Classification Act of 1923 structured the civil service, it did not create a career system in the German sense, in which a civil servant's career follows a clear path of offices, starting at the entry level, but rather ensured that access to higher ranks was open not only to members of the civil service, but also to applicants from outside.[143]

Today, 5 U.S.C. § 5101 et seq. establish a rank-in-position system that—with exceptions, e.g. for the Foreign Service and the military—does not provide for a personal career ladder (rank-in-person system), but rather evaluates positions or offices according to their duties, for which candidates can apply from within and from outside.[144] Hiring is "at the minimum rate of the appropriate grade" pursuant to 5 U.S.C. § 5333. Thus, only the rate is the lowest for a new hire. The grade is based on the duties of the particular position for which one is applying, so it can be a grade in a higher range even for new hires from outside. In fact, from 1990 to 2005, between 25 and 33 percent of all new hires were in the high grades GS 12–15; the average age of new hires in these grades in 2005 was 43.5 years.[145]

The scope of protection against removal

In contrast to German practice, the Pendleton Act provided no protection against removal.[146] It only protected an employee from being fired for lack of partisan political activity or for lack of partisan political contributions, which clearly sought to stop the operation of the spoils system of the previous decades.[147] However, the reformers of 1883 were reluctant to enshrine further protection against dismissals in law. In this respect, the strength of the constitutional paradigm was also evident. The Pendleton Act confirmed the so-called Decision of 1789.[148] This term refers to a debate in the first Congress over the establishment of the Department of Foreign Affairs during which the view that the President has the sole and unrestricted right of removal by virtue of constitutional law narrowly prevailed over three other positions.[149] Until the 1950s, the Decision of 1789 and its affirmation in *Myers v. United States* meant that civil service employees enjoyed no constitutional protection against removal.[150] The doctrine of privilege was developed as a supporting concept, according to which the employee had no "right" to his employment.[151] As late as 1950, this doctrine was upheld by courts—as exemplified in the famous D.C. Circuit Court decision in *Bailey v. Richardson*, which refused to find a possible violation of the first, fifth, and sixth amendment.[152]

On the sub-constitutional level, limited protection against removal was only gradually introduced after the Pendleton Act: President McKinley issued an executive order in 1897 stating that no one who had attained office through examinations could be dismissed without cause ("except for just cause"). President Theodor Roosevelt clarified this in 1902 by stating that only those reasons that "promote the efficiency of the service" could serve as cause.[153] In 1912, the Lloyd-La Follette Act codified this directive into law, and it remained the primary standard for dismissal of competitive civil service employees until 1979.[154] However, the intensity of judicial review was initially weak and did not increase until the mid-20th century.[155] The legal provisions were not regarded as implying that the employee had a right to judicial review of whether such a cause actually existed.[156] The law was interpreted to mean that no formal fact-finding was required before dismissal, and, therefore, no court could subsequently review whether a cause actually existed.[157]

The reason for the increase in removal protection beginning in the 1950s was not a stronger constitutional role for the civil service as an institution; rather, it was a consequence of an increase in fundamental rights protection throughout the constitutional order—mainly caused by the "Civil Rights Revolution."[158] Protests by African-Americans against the discrimination in the civil service, which had persisted since George Washington, led to a first executive order by President Roosevelt in 1941, which related solely to the Armed Services Administration.[159] Executive Orders 10590 (President Eisenhower) and 11246 (President Johnson) as well as 11375 (President Johnson) prohibited any discrimination in the civil service on the basis of race, skin color, religion, national origin, and gender.[160] The Civil Rights Act of 1964—the legislative centerpiece of the Civil Rights Revolution—articulated non-discriminatory access to public service as a programmatic principle.[161]

The two landmark rulings *Elrod v. Burns*[162] in 1976 and *Branti v. Finkel*[163] in 1980 finally led to a break with the Decision of 1789 because they granted executive officeholders individual constitutional protection against removal for specific reasons.[164]

However, the rulings still cannot be seen as establishing a constitutional lifetime principle comparable to the German civil service; this is made clear in the subsequent case law:

> The First Amendment is not a tenure provision protecting public employees from actual or constructive discharge. The First Amendment prevents the government, except in the most compelling circumstances, from wielding its power to interfere with its employees' freedom to believe and associate, or to not believe and not associate.[165]

In addition, *Elrod v. Burns* and *Branti v. Finkel* were accompanied by sharp dissenting opinions. The conservative justices in *Elrod v. Burns* began their dissenting opinion by saying: "The Court holds unconstitutional a practice as old as the Republic, a practice which has contributed significantly to the democratization of American politics."[166] The 2010 ruling in *Free Enterprise Fund v. PCAOB*[167] was a sign that their opinion was increasingly gaining traction in the case law.[168] The decision, authored by Chief Justice Roberts and supported by Justices Scalia, Kennedy, Thomas, and Alito, was a commitment to the Decision of 1789 and thus to the President's right to remove: "Since 1789, the Constitution has been understood to empower the President to keep these officers accountable—by removing them from office, if necessary."[169]

On the one hand, the court in *Free Enterprise Fund* showed restraint by not taking away the independence of the Securities and Exchange Commission (SEC). Thus, it did not break with the principles of the seminal case of *Humphrey's Executor*,[170] regarded as the cornerstone of the "for cause"—protection for the heads of independent agencies and, therefore, as an important part of the administrative state.[171] However, *Free Enterprise Fund* declared the dismissal protection for the board of the PCAOB (Public Company Accounting Oversight Board) unconstitutional because there were *two* levels between the president and the PCOAB in which statutory dismissal protection (dismissal only for cause) should operate.[172]

Justices Breyer, Stevens, Ginsburg, and Sotomayor responded with a dissenting opinion based on functionalist arguments that invoked the Necessary and Proper Clause to justify, among other things, Congress's right to establish two layers of removal protection.[173] They also accused the majority of de facto challenging the constitutionality of the competitive civil service within independent agencies, where two layers of removal protection exist.[174]

The same conflict appeared in the 2020 case of *Seila Law v. CFPB*, in which the five-person majority (Justices Roberts, Alito, Kavanaugh, Thomas, and Gorsuch) declared unconstitutional the rule that the head of the Consumer Financial Protection Bureau (CFPB) can be fired by the President only for "inefficiency, neglect, or malfeasance"—that is, only for *cause* and not *at will*.[175] In doing so, it adopted *Free Enterprise Fund's* reasoning and referenced the line of precedents upholding the President's right to remove—beginning with the Decision of 1789.[176] In doing so, the majority construed *Humphrey's Executor* narrowly: according to them, *Humphrey's* applied only to agencies with a multimember board composed of experts and balanced along partisan lines, and not to the single agency head case at issue in *Seila*.[177] The four-person minority (Justices Kagan, Sotomayor, Ginsburg, and Breyer) criticized the majority's fixation on the number of people in management.[178] Rather, they argued for a functional criterion.[179]

This glimpse[180] into the development of the law on removal protection paradigmatically demonstrates that the U.S. Constitution has shaped civil service law not only in its creation, but that constitutional developments have also been reflected in the further development of civil service law. The debate about the extent of the removal power of the President can legitimately be called the longest debate in American constitutional history because it started in the first Congress, which produced the aforementioned Decision of 1789. And since then, the debate has never ended. It is framed by constitutional principles like democratic accountability as well as by "constitutional moments" such as the New Deal and the Civil Rights Revolution.[181] In this way, American civil service law reflects the constitutional development of the United States.

The Strength of Traditions and Recent Developments

The strength of the preceding constitutional tradition in the United States vis-à-vis an emerging concept of a competitively selected civil service is similar to the strength of the long-standing administrative civil service tradition in Germany vis-à-vis the new post-war constitution.

The dominance of the German administrative tradition was directly experienced by Americans after the Second World War. In 1950, the American Allied High Commissioner demanded several changes to the German federal government's draft of a Provisional Personnel Act, which—purged of specifically National Socialist provisions—essentially corresponded to the German Civil Service Act of 1937.[182] In spite of the clear demands of the Allies, the German federal government only made a few changes. The demand to give so-called outsiders, who were not members of the civil service, a better chance to enter its ranks was rejected on the grounds that this would contradict the German career system.[183] In the end, the Americans gave up their resistance—not without visible annoyance, which John McCloy expressed in a personal letter to Chancellor Konrad Adenauer (translated from German):

> From the beginning, one of our main objectives was to promote the establishment in Germany of a healthy democratic form of government which would reflect the diverse views of the German people and be accountable to them. . . . Our concern for the introduction of certain minimum reforms of the traditional German civil service system arose solely from the conviction that the bureaucracy of a country must support, and not be able to hinder, the maintenance of effective control of government by the citizens. We . . . are disappointed in what the Federal Government has accomplished in the field of civil service.[184]

The aim of this chapter was to show the (opposite) strength of the tradition of the American Constitution in the formative phase of the modern U.S. civil service in the late 19th century.

Although the reformers were influenced by English and German concepts, they advocated for necessary adaptations of civil service concepts to the American constitutional tradition and realized them in practice. Of course, this does not mean that every legal scholar would agree that the current civil service is in complete conformity with all constitutional requirements. Quite the contrary: this question is at the core of a major debate that has been unfolding in recent years.

This debate mirrors two opposing currents in the development of the U.S. civil service: on the one hand, the personnel system of the Jacksonian democracy, which was based on the constitutional paradigms including the Decision of 1789, but brought the rotation of officeholders to an extreme; on the other hand the competitively selected civil service system founded in the 1880s. These two opposing currents formed the basis of the New Deal of the 1930s, which was also significantly realized through the personnel system: the potential of a President with strong personnel power, founded in Jacksonian Democracy, was combined with the concept of a politically neutral administration that would efficiently enforce comprehensive economic and social reforms.[185] This dichotomy remains the basis of American public service to this day; today's personnel system is a product of both currents.[186]

However, it is important to stress that (at their respective origins) neither of these currents is fundamentally antagonistic to the Constitution and to the founders' "constitutional language." Both act under the umbrella of the American constitutional tradition. They just interpret it differently. These differences can be observed in famous recent cases like *Seila Law v. CFPB*[187] and *Lucia v. SEC.*[188]

Lucia v. SEC dealt with the definition of the term "Officer of the United States," which is crucial for the interpretation of the Appointments Clause. This clause only applies to officers and not to "mere employees."[189] Even before *Lucia*, the Supreme Court determined that a person qualifies as an officer if he or she exercises "significant authority pursuant to the laws of the United States."[190] A large part of the civil service does not fulfill this condition, and thus—as the Supreme Court itself has stated—does not belong to the category "Officers of the United States."[191] They are thus outside the scope of the Appointments Clause and do not raise constitutional concerns. However, the interpretation of "significant authority" and thus the exact reach of the constitutional requirements is still unclear. *Lucia v. SEC* did not conclusively clarify these ambiguities, but only ruled that the Administrative Law Judges (ALJs) of the SEC exercise "significant authority" and are therefore officers.[192] What is now being discussed is the extent to which this decision can be applied to other ALJs as well as to other officers of agencies.[193] The consequences would be broad; in many cases these employees are not appointed by the Head of Department,[194] as prescribed in the Appointments Clause. Classifying them as officers would result in their appointment violating the Constitution.

The Trump administration used the ruling in *Lucia vs. SEC* as a political opportunity to generally exempt ALJs from the competitive civil service selection process by creating a new category of Excepted Service (Schedule E).[195] As a consequence, ALJs are no longer subject to competitive hiring procedures. Rather, the respective agency head can make a selection in which the only binding criterion is the "license to practice law." The Executive Order creating Schedule E was explained as follows:

> As evident from recent litigation, Lucia may also raise questions about the method of appointing ALJs, including whether competitive examination and competitive service selection procedures are compatible with the discretion an agency head must possess under the Appointments Clause in selecting ALJs. Regardless of whether those procedures would violate the Appointments Clause as applied to certain ALJs, there are sound policy reasons to take steps to eliminate doubt regarding the constitutionality of the method of appointing officials who discharge such significant duties and exercise such significant discretion.[196]

This exemplifies that the conflict between different constitutional interpretations is also a political battle. The core question is where to draw the line between the competitively selected civil service on the one hand, and the exempted service or the political appointees on the other hand. As shown above, since the 19th century, these questions have always had two sides in the United States: a legal and a political side. And as the aforementioned dialogue between one of the framers of the modern civil service, George William Curtis, and Senator Dawes in the 1870s shows, the ultimate decision on the extent of the competitive civil service rests with the President.[197] The Constitution defines limits to the extension of civil service principles, but it does not define a minimum scope for the competitive civil service. And here, a final and perhaps crucial difference between the German and the American civil service tradition becomes evident: Germany has an explicit constitutional guarantee of a career civil service, due to which the civil service as an institution is beyond ordinary politics. In the United States, the extent of the competitive civil service is ultimately not only a legal, but also a political decision. The courts give an important framework. But the final answer to the crucial question of where to draw the line between positions that fall under the rules of the competitively selected civil service and those which do not probably will be given by the political process—and most likely this answer will never be final.

Notes

1 This chapter contains translations of texts from my doctoral thesis, which analyzes the relationship between the normative claim of a specifically democratic constitutional law and the choice of personnel in the executive branch of the United States of America—with a focus on the constitutional theory, the genesis, and the development of the law on appointments and removals. It was published as: MATTHIAS ROSSBACH, DAS PERSONAL DER REPUBLIK. ENTSTEHUNG UND ENTWICKLUNG EINES DEMOKRATISCHEN PERSONALVERFASSUNGSRECHTS DER EXEKUTIVE AM BEISPIEL DER VEREINIGTEN STAATEN VON AMERIKA (2020).

The idea for my doctoral thesis arose during my LL.M. studies at Yale Law School. For her great support and for numerous enriching conversations on this topic, I would like to express my very special thanks to Professor Susan Rose-Ackerman.

2 Cf. SUSAN ROSE-ACKERMAN, DEMOCRACY AND EXECUTIVE POWER: POLICYMAKING ACCOUNTABILITY IN THE US, THE UK, GERMANY, AND FRANCE (2021); Susan Rose-Ackerman, *Administrative Law and Democracy*, in: THE OXFORD HANDBOOK OF COMPARATIVE ADMINISTRATIVE LAW 1075 (Peter Cane et al. eds., 2021).

3 SUSAN ROSE-ACKERMAN, CONTROLLING ENVIRONMENTAL POLICY: THE LIMITS OF PUBLIC LAW IN GERMANY AND THE UNITED STATES (1995); Susan Rose-Ackerman, *American Administration Law Under Siege: Is Germany a Model?* 107 Harvard Law Review 1279 (1994).

4 PHILIP HAMBURGER, IS ADMINISTRATIVE LAW UNLAWFUL? 447 ff. (2014).

5 ROSSBACH, *supra* note 1, at 589.

6 Ibid.

7 Cf. HORST DREIER / CHRISTIAN WALDHOFF (eds.), DAS WAGNIS DER DEMOKRATIE (2018).

8 Cf. BERND WUNDER, GESCHICHTE DER BÜROKRATIE IN DEUTSCHLAND 28 ff. (1986); HANS HATTENHAUER, GESCHICHTE DES DEUTSCHEN BEAMTENTUMS 99 ff., 195 ff. (1993).

9 WOLFGANG RUNGE, POLITIK UND BEAMTENTUM IM PARTEIENSTAAT 16 (1965).

10 Cf. HATTENHAUER, *supra* note 8, at 346.

11 Cf. ROSSBACH, *supra* note 1, at 59 ff., 87 ff., 155 ff., 213 ff., 589.

12 Cf. ROSSBACH, *supra* note 1, at 146, especially on the role of Marbury v. Madison in this context.

13 ALEXANDER HAMILTON, FEDERALIST NO. 76. On the genesis of the federal appointments process in depth cf. ROSSBACH, *supra* note 1, at 229 ff.

14 Gouverneur Morris, September 7, 1787, as cited in: MAX FERRAND, THE RECORDS OF THE FEDERAL CONVENTION OF 1787, VOL. 2, 539 (1966).

15 On the spoils system in depth: ROSSBACH, *supra* note 1, at 520 ff.; CARL R. FISH, THE CIVIL SERVICE AND THE PATRONAGE (1904); MATTHEW A. CRENSON, THE FEDERAL MACHINE (1975).

16 *See infra* Motives and Models of Early Reformers of the U.S. Civil Service.

17 ROSSBACH, *supra* note 1, at 531. Cf. JERRY L. MASHAW, CREATING THE ADMINISTRATIVE CONSTITUTION 238 (2012); BRIAN J. COOK, BUREAUCRACY AND SELF-GOVERNMENT 65 (1996). In depth on civil service reform in the late 19th century: ARI HOOGENBOOM, OUTLAWING THE SPOILS (1968); PAUL VAN RIPER, HISTORY OF THE UNITED STATES CIVIL SERVICE 60 ff. (1958).

18 On this reform work: Carolyn Ban / Patricia Ingraham, *Legislating Bureaucratic Change*, *in*: LEGISLATING BUREAUCRATIC CHANGE: THE CIVIL SERVICE REFORM ACT OF 1978, 1 (Carolyn Ban / Patricia Ingraham eds., 1984).

19 DAVID H. ROSENBLOOM, THE FEDERAL SERVICE AND THE CONSTITUTION 63 (2014).

20 Pendleton Act of January 16, 1883, 22 Stat. 404 (1883), section 2.

21 Woodrow Wilson had anticipated this reproach; cf. Woodrow Wilson, *The Study of Administration*, 2 Political Science Quarterly 197, 202 (1887). On the role of an abstract idea of the state in the American discourse, e.g. WILLIAM F. WILLOUGHBY, THE GOVERNMENT OF MODERN STATES 22 (1936).

22 Cf. for a classic exposition of the conservative critique of the administrative state Gary Lawson, *The Rise and Rise of the Administrative State*, 107 Harvard Law Review 1231 (1994). For the classic justification, *see* JAMES LANDIS, THE ADMINISTRATIVE PROCESS 1 ff. (1938). For an overview: Susan Rose-Ackerman, *The*

Regulatory State, in: THE OXFORD HANDBOOK OF COMPARATIVE CONSTITUTIONAL LAW 671 (2012, Michael Rosenfeld / András Sajo (eds.)).

23 PHILIP HAMBURGER, *supra* note 4, at 447 ff. (2014).

24 Wilson, *supra* note 21, at 204: "admirable system." Cf. Robert D. Miewald, *The Origins of Wilsons's Thought. The German Tradition and the Organic State*, in: POLITICS AND ADMINISTRATION 17 f. (Jack Rabin / James S. Bowman eds.); Christian Rosser, *The Role of Foreign Ideas in Identity Formation: The Hegelian Roots of Early American Public Administration*, in: THE EUROPEAN PUBLIC SERVANT. A SHARED ADMINISTRATIVE IDENTITY? 135, 142 (Fritz Sager / Patrick Overeem eds., 2015). *See also* PATRICK OVEREEM, THE POLITICS–ADMINISTRATION DICHOTOMY 57 ff. (2012).

25 The difference between the American and the German career civil service is also emphasized by FRITZ MORSTEIN MARX, EINFÜHRUNG IN DIE BÜROKRATIE 202 (1959).

26 BRUCE A. ACKERMAN, WE THE PEOPLE, VOL. 1, 316 (1993).

27 Lucia v. SEC, 585 U.S. ___, 138 S.Ct. 2044 (2018).

28 Cf. in detail: HOOGENBOOM, *supra* note 17, at 236 ff. He points (at 247) to the debates in Congress, in which one senator described the law as a "bill to perpetuate in office the Republicans who now control the patronage of the Government."

29 On this point also: MASHAW, *supra* note 17, at 236 ff.

30 The Ramspeck Act of 1940 gave Roosevelt the ability to extend the scope of civil service rules to positions that had previously been legally exempt. The result was to protect in particular those civil servants who supported the New Deal agenda. Cf. Sidney Milkis, *The Presidency and Political Parties*, in: THE PRESIDENCY AND THE POLITICAL SYSTEM 309 ff. (Michael Nelson ed., 11th ed. 2018).

31 MASHAW, *supra* note 17, at 236.

32 *See infra* The Modern American Civil Service: Adapting Civil Service Concepts to Constitutional Law.

33 Cf. PATRICIA INGRAHAM, THE FOUNDATION OF MERIT 30 ff. (1995); FISH, *supra* note 15, at 229 ff.

34 WILLIAM E. NELSON, THE ROOTS OF AMERICAN BUREAUCRACY 1830–1900, 119 (1982). *See also* LEONARD D. WHITE, THE REPUBLICAN ERA. A STUDY IN ADMINISTRATIVE HISTORY, 1869–1901, 295 ff. (1965); FREDERICK C. MOSHER, DEMOCRACY AND THE CIVIL SERVICE 68 (1982).

35 *See also* ROSENBLOOM, *supra* note 19, at 60 ff.; COOK, *supra* note 17, at 66 f.

36 George William Curtis, *Civil Service Reform. An Address Before the American Social Science Association at its Meeting in New York in October 1869*, in: ORATIONS AND ADDRESSES OF GEORGE WILLIAM CURTIS, VOL. II, 1, 19 (Charles Eliot Norton ed., 1894). On Curtis' role: VAN RIPER, *supra* note 17, at 78 ff.

37 Curtis, *supra* note 36, at 33.

38 Curtis, *supra* note 36, at 6. On the frictions between Washington's ideals and the reality of the early Republic: ROSSBACH, *supra* note 1, at 129 ff.

39 Curtis, *supra* note 36, at 13.

40 John G. A. Pocock, *Virtue and Commerce in the Eighteenth Century*, 3 Journal of Interdisciplinary History 119 (1972); JOHN G. A. POCOCK, THE MACHIAVELLIAN MOMENT 507 ff. (1975/2016); BERNARD BAILYN, THE ORIGINS OF AMERICAN POLITICS (1968); GORDON S. WOOD, THE CREATION OF THE AMERICAN REPUBLIC, 1776–1787 (1969/1998). Even if the concept of virtue was not mentioned explicitly by Curtis, the words "honesty," "honor," and "patriotism" used by Curtis ultimately meant precisely the orientation toward the common good that was associated with "virtuous characters" in Washington's time. Thus HOOGENBOOM, *supra* note 17, at 21 also concludes that reformers tend to see themselves as preservers of virtue. *See also* ROSENBLOOM, *supra* note 19, at 60 and 67; BARRY D.

KARL, EXECUTIVE REORGANIZATION AND REFORM IN THE NEW DEAL 6 (1963). Cf. ROSSBACH, *supra* note 1, at 98 ff.
41 Cf. ROSSBACH, *supra* note 1, at 313 ff.
42 JAMES MADISON, FEDERALIST NO. 10.
43 KARL, *supra* note 40, at 6. Cf. also David H. Rosenbloom, *Politics and Public Personnel Administration. The Legacy of 1883*, in: CENTENARY ISSUES OF THE PENDLETON ACT OF 1883, 1, 4 (Rosenbloom ed., 1982).
44 George William Curtis, *Machine Politics and the Remedy*, in: ORATIONS AND ADDRESSES OF GEORGE WILLIAM CURTIS, VOL. II, 145, 149 (Charles Eliot Norton ed.,1894); *see also* ROSENBLOOM, *supra* note 19, at 59.
45 George William Curtis, *The Relation between Morals and Politics. Illustrated by the Civil Service System*, in: ORATIONS AND ADDRESSES OF GEORGE WILLIAM CURTIS, VOL. II, 119, 135 (Charles Eliot Norton ed., 1894). Cf. also WHITE, *supra* note 34, at 300.
46 Cf. VAN RIPER, *supra* note 17, at 68 ff.; FISH, *supra* note 15, at 213 f.; DAVID E. LEWIS, THE POLITICS OF PRESIDENTIAL APPOINTMENTS 16 (2008). Prior to this, there had already been examinations in specific fields, for example in parts of the military and for clerks in the postal service; cf. MASHAW, *supra* note 17, at 183.
47 Cf. for the consideration of other countries for example THOMAS A. JENCKES, THE CIVIL SERVICE. REPORT FROM THE JOINT SELECT COMMITTEE ON RETRENCHMENT, MADE TO THE HOUSE OF REPRESENTATIVES OF THE UNITED STATES, MAY 14, 1868, 185 ff. (1868). On the influence of the British model: RICHARD E. TITLOW, AMERICANS IMPORT MERIT (1982); VAN RIPER, *supra* note 17, at 65 ff.; David L. Dillman, *Civil Service Reform in Comparative Perspective*, in: LEGISLATING BUREAUCRATIC CHANGE 203, 204 ff. (Patricia Ingraham / Carolyn Ban eds., 1984).
48 VAN RIPER, *supra* note 17, at 65 ff.
49 COLIN PILKINGTON, THE CIVIL SERVICE IN BRITAIN TODAY 18 ff. (1999).
50 VAN RIPER, *supra* note 17, at 65 f.
51 DORMAN EATON, CIVIL SERVICE IN GREAT BRAIN 363 ff. (1880).
52 An act making appropriations for the legislative, executive, and judicial expenses of the Government for the year ending June 13, 1877 and other purposes of August 15, 1876, 19 Stat 143 (1876), Section 6; cf. ROSENBLOOM, *supra* note 19, at 64 f.
53 Cf. ROSENBLOOM, *supra* note 19, at 64 f.
54 Ex parte Curtis, 106 U.S. 371 (1882).
55 Ex parte Curtis, 106 U.S. 371, 373 (1882).
56 VAN RIPER, *supra* note 17, at 90 f.
57 JENCKES, *supra* note 47, at 136; cf. VAN RIPER, *supra* note 17, at 66; STEPHEN SKOWRONEK, BUILDING A NEW AMERICAN STATE 47 ff. (1982).
58 MOSHER, *supra* note 34, at 68; NELSON, *supra* note 34, at 121.
59 Cf. SKOWRONEK, *supra* note 17, at 68 ff.; MOSHER, *supra* note 34, at 73 ff.
60 SKOWRONEK, *supra* note 17, at 68 ff.
61 Cf. Sylvia D. Fries, *Staatstheorie and the New American Science of Politics*, 34 Journal of the History of Idea 391 (1973); Miewald, *supra* note 24, at 17.
62 An overview of the standard narrative as well as a critique is provided by OVEREEM, *supra* note 24, at 3 ff. Most prominent representative of this narrative: DWIGHT WALDO, THE ADMINISTRATIVE STATE 105 ff. (1984).
63 Wilson, *supra* note 21, at 216; FRANK J. GOODNOW, POLITICS AND ADMINISTRATION 88 (1900).
64 Miewald, *supra* note 24, at 18; Rosser, *supra* note 24, at 142.
65 JOHANN CASPAR BLUNTSCHLI, LEHRE VOM MODERNEN STAAT. THEIL 3: POLITIK ALS WISSENSCHAFT 467 (1876).
66 Wilson, *supra* note 21, at 210. Cf. ROSSBACH, *supra* note 1, at 538 ff.

67 Bluntschli, *supra* note 65, at 467.
68 Wilson, *supra* note 21, at 216.
69 Wilson, *supra* note 21, at 215 f.
70 Wilson, *supra* note 21, at 207.
71 Cf. Rossbach, *supra* note 1, at 408 ff.
72 Wilson, *supra* note 21, at 216.
73 Wilson, *supra* note 21, at 221.
74 Woodrow Wilson, Notes for Lectures in a Course on Constitutional Government, 1898–1900; *see* Ronald J. Pestritto, Woodrow Wilson and the Roots of Modern Liberalism 241 (2005).
75 Cf. Eric S. Yellin, Racism in the Nation's Service (2013).
76 Blake Emerson, The Public's Law 76 f. (2019).
77 Wilson, *supra* note 21, at 216.
78 Wilson, *supra* note 21, at 216 f.
79 Wilson, *supra* note 21, at 217.
80 Wilson, *supra* note 21, at 217.
81 Wilson, *supra* note 21, at 218.
82 Wilson, *supra* note 21, at 207 and 219.
83 Frank J. Goodnow, Comparative Administrative Law (1893).
84 Goodnow, *supra* note 63.
85 In the preface to Comparative Administrative Law (*supra* note 83, at VI) Goodnow writes: "The author deems it necessary to acknowledge how much he is indebted to the published works and personal influence felt in lectures he has heard, of Professor Rudolph von Gneist, of the University of Berlin, Germany."
86 Oliver Lepsius, Verwaltungsrecht unter dem Common Law 266 f. (1997); cf. on Lieber's influence and the transfer of German state theory to the United States also Fries, *supra* note 61, at 391.
87 Goodnow, *supra* note 63, at 5. Cf. Rossbach, *supra* note 1, at 542 ff.
88 Goodnow, *supra* note 63, at 85.
89 Goodnow, *supra* note 63, at 85.
90 Goodnow, *supra* note 63, at 85.
91 Goodnow, *supra* note 63, at 87.
92 Goodnow, *supra* note 63, at 87.
93 The classic exposition in the New Deal: Landis, *supra* note 22, at 13 f., 26 ff., 87 ff.; Cook, *supra* note 17, at 128 ff.; on the debate in Germany: Christoph Möllers, Gewaltengliederung 121 ff. (2005); Andreas Voßkuhle, *Expertise und Verwaltung*, in: Allgemeines Verwaltungsrecht—zur Tragfähigkeit eines Konzepts 637 (Hans-Heinrich Trute et al. eds., 2008).
94 Goodnow, *supra* note 63, at 121.
95 Goodnow, *supra* note 63, at 121: "That it will be accomplished, as soon as an educated and intelligent public opinion demands it, is a moral certainty."
96 Goodnow, *supra* note 63, at 90 f.
97 Goodnow, *supra* note 63, at 90.
98 Goodnow, *supra* note 63, at 90 f.
99 Goodnow, *supra* note 63, at 23. For further analysis: Rossbach, *supra* note 1, at 544 ff.
100 John A. Rohr, To Run a Constitution 86 ff. (1986). On the frictions with the constitutional concepts of the founders also Overeem, *supra* note 24, at 163.
101 Wilhelm Bleek, Von der Kameralausbildung zum Juristenprivileg 77 (1972).
102 Prior to this, there had been examinations in specific fields, *see supra* note 46.
103 Amos T. Akerman, *Opinion on the Civil-Service Commission*, 13 Opinions of Attorneys Generals 516, 523 (1873). Rossbach, *supra* note 1, at 339 ff.

104 Akerman, *supra* note 103, at 523.
105 Akerman, *supra* note 103, at 523.
106 Pendleton Act of January 16, 1883, 22 Stat. 404 (1883); *see also* VAN RIPER, *supra* note 17, at 104.
107 Myers v. United States, 272 U.S. 52, 128 (1926). Cf. Hanah M. Volokh, *The Two Appointment Clauses: Statutory Qualifications for Federal Officers*, 10 Journal of Constitutional Law 745, 753 (2008). On statutory restrictions of the appointment power cf. ROSSBACH, *supra* note 1, at 313 ff.
108 Akerman, *supra* note 103, at 524.
109 Akerman, *supra* note 103, at 525.
110 INGRAHAM, *supra* note 33, at 25; OLIVER P. FIELD, CIVIL SERVICE LAW 10 (1939); VAN RIPER, *supra* note 17, at 104.
111 The second successor agency is the Merit Service Protection Board, which is primarily responsible for internal administrative legal protection against adverse personnel decisions and prohibited practices. Cf. Patricia W. Ingraham, *The Civil Service Reform Act of 1978: Its Design and Legislative History*, in: LEGISLATING BUREAUCRATIC CHANGE 13, 17 (Patricia Ingraham / Carolyn Ban eds., 1984); KATHERINE C. NAFF / NORMA M. RICCUCCI / SIEGRUN F. FREYSS, PERSONNEL MANAGEMENT IN GOVERNMENT 13 (2014).
112 NAFF et al., *supra* note 111, at 261; NORMA M. RICCUCCI, PUBLIC PERSONNEL MANAGEMENT 137, 143 (2012).
113 However, it is limited by veterans' preference legislation; *see* 5 U.S.C. § 3319 (c)(2).
114 FIELD, *supra* note 110, at 10, regards the Rule of Three as providing sufficient scope for the appointment power. Critically: Jennifer L. Mascott, *Who Are "Officers of the United States"?* 70 Stanford Law Review 443, 552 f. (2018).
115 Pendleton Act of January 16, 1883, 22 Stat. 404 (1883), Section 7: "nor, unless by direction of the Senate, shall any person who has been nominated for confirmation by the Senate be required to be classified or to pass an examination." Cf. INGRAHAM, *supra* note 33, at 28.
116 5 U.S.C. § 2102 (a) (1) (B): "except . . . (B) positions to which appointments are made by nomination for confirmation by the Senate, unless the Senate otherwise directs."
117 For an analysis of the debates of the founders cf. ROSSBACH, *supra* note 1, at 262 ff.
118 Cf. ROSSBACH, *supra* note 1, at 230.
119 LEWIS MAYERS, THE FEDERAL SERVICE 48 (1922); VAN RIPER, *supra* note 17, at 108 f.
120 Pendleton Act of January 16, 1883, 22 Stat. 404 (1883), Section 2: "Said commission shall, subject to the rules that may be made by the President, make regulations for, and have control of, such examinations." Cf. NAFF et al., *supra* note 111, at 7.
121 MASHAW, *supra* note 17, at 239.
122 *See supra* note 30; for an overview: INGRAHAM, *supra* note 33, at 31 and 34; LEWIS, *supra* note 46, at 19 f.
123 LEWIS, *supra* note 46, at 11 ff.
124 CHESTER A. ARTHUR, SECOND ANNUAL MESSAGE (December 4, 1882).
125 Lucia v. SEC, 138 S.Ct. 2044 (2018). *See infra* The Strength of Traditions and Recent Developments.
126 NAFF et al., *supra* note 111, at 7.
127 THE CIVIL SERVICE COMMISSION, THE CIVIL SERVICE OF THE UNITED STATES. REPORT TO THE PRESIDENT 169 (April 15, 1874). The dialogue already refers to the (failed) predecessor legislation of 1871.

128 *See supra* German Influence and Its Limits.
129 *See supra* German Influence and Its Limits.
130 MOSHER, *supra* note 34, at 69; VAN RIPER, *supra* note 17, at 101.
131 ALEXIS DE TOCQUEVILLE, DEMOCRACY IN AMERICA 236 (2003); cf. ROSSBACH, *supra* note 1, at 493 f.
132 Cf. ROSSBACH, *supra* note 1, at 407 ff., 490 ff., and 548 ff.
133 22 Stat. 406 (1883), Section 9.
134 22 Stat. 404 (1883), Section 2. For Washington's practice cf. ROSSBACH, *supra* note 1, at 123 ff.
135 Pendleton Act, Section 2, 22 Stat. 403 (1883); *see also* ROSENBLOOM, *supra* note 19, at 63.
136 MOSHER, *supra* note 34, at 69: "There was provided no link between the entrance system and the products of any particular universities, as in Britain, nor was there any link to the products of universities in general."
137 MARVIN MEYERS, THE JACKSONIAN PERSUASION 30 f. (1957); CRENSON, *supra* note 15, at 22 ff.; JAMES A. MORONE, THE DEMOCRATIC WISH 82 (1998).
138 Cf. ROSSBACH, *supra* note 1, at 479 ff.
139 MOSHER, *supra* note 34, at 69; ROSENBLOOM, *supra* note 19, at 63; for England: EATON, *supra* note 11, at 324; for Germany: ROSSBACH, *supra* note 1, at 551.
140 CHESTER A. ARTHUR, FIRST ANNUAL MESSAGE (December 6, 1881).
141 ARTHUR, *supra* note 140.
142 VAN RIPER, *supra* note 17, at 101.
143 BERNARD SILBERMAN, CAGES OF REASON 281 (1993). Cf. ROSSBACH, *supra* note 1, at 551 f.
144 NAFF et al., *supra* note 111, at 258 f.; JOSEPH N. CAYER, PUBLIC PERSONNEL ADMINISTRATION IN THE UNITED STATES 56 ff. (1996). The introduction of the Senior Executive Service in the late 1970s, however, also brought with it a rank-in-person system for this sector (*see* 5 U.S.C. § 5382 f.).
145 U.S. MERIT SYSTEMS PROTECTION BOARD, REPORT, IN SEARCH OF HIGHLY SKILLED WORKERS 5, 11 (2008); cf. ROSSBACH, *supra* note 1, at 552.
146 VAN RIPER, *supra* note 17, at 101 ff; ROSENBLOOM, *supra* note 19, at 66 ff.
147 22 Stat. 404 (1883).
148 VAN RIPER, *supra* note 17, at 103.
149 Cf. J. DAVID ALVIS / JEREMY D. BAILEY / F. FLAGG TAYLOR, THE CONTESTED REMOVAL POWER, 1789–2010, 16 ff. (2013); COOK, *supra* note 17, at 36 ff.; LEONARD D. WHITE, THE FEDERALISTS. A STUDY IN ADMINISTRATIVE HISTORY 20 ff. (1948/1956); CHARLES C. THACH, THE CREATION OF THE PRESIDENCY 1775–1789, 140 ff. (1922); Saikrishna Prakash, *New Light on the Decision of 1789*, 91 Cornell Law Review 1021 (2006). For an analysis of the debate in the First Congress cf. ROSSBACH, *supra* note 1, at 404 ff.
150 For details cf. ROSSBACH, *supra* note 1, at 452 ff.
151 Cf. Gerald E. Frug, *Does the Constitution Prevent the Discharge of Civil Service Employees?* 124 University of Pennsylvania Law Review 942, 961 f. (1976); ROSENBLOOM, *supra* note 19, at 10 ff.; ROSSBACH, *supra* note 1, at 518 ff.
152 Bailey v. Richardson, 182 F. 2d 46 (D.C. Cir. 1950).
153 MAYERS, *supra* note 119, at 496; Frug, *supra* note 151, at 956 f.
154 MAYERS, *supra* note 119, at 497; Frug, *supra* note 151, at 958 f.
155 Cf. ROSENBLOOM, *supra* note 19, at 67 f.; ROSSBACH, *supra* note 1, at 452 ff.; RONALD JOHNSON / GARY LIBECAP, THE FEDERAL CIVIL SERVICE SYSTEM AND THE PROBLEM OF BUREAUCRACY 66 ff. (1994).
156 Richard A. Merrill, *Procedures for Adverse Actions against Federal Employees*, 59 Virginia Law Review 196, 199 (1973); Howard C. Westwood, *The "Right" of an Employee of the United States against Arbitrary Discharge*, 7 George Washington

Law Review 212, 231 (1938); Frug, *supra* note 151, at 958; MAYERS, *supra* note 119, at 498.

157 Cf. MAYERS, *supra* note 119, at 498 (text and fn. 1); Anonymous, *Note: Review of Removal of Federal Civil Service Employees*, 52 Columbia Law Review 787, 792 ff. (1952).

158 On the "civil rights revolution" in general: BRUCE A. ACKERMAN, WE THE PEOPLE, VOL. 3. CIVIL RIGHTS REVOLUTION (2014).

159 For the discrimination in the civil service since Washington cf. ROSSBACH, *supra* note 1, at 120 ff. Regarding Executive Order 8802 of June 25, 1941 cf. NAFF et al., *supra* note 111, at 324.

160 For details on this development, cf. ROSSBACH, *supra* note 1, at 456 ff. and NAFF et al., *supra* note 111, at 324 ff.; ROSENBLOOM, *supra* note 19, at 67 ff.

161 78 Stat. 254 (1964), section 701(b). On the role of the Civil Rights Act: WILLIAM ESKRIDGE / JOHN FEREJOHN, A REPUBLIC OF STATUTES 7 (2010).

162 Elrod v. Burns, 427 U.S. 347 (1976).

163 Branti v. Finkel, 445 U.S. 507 (1980).

164 Leah M. Bishop, *Patronage and the First Amendment after Elrod v. Burns*, 78 Columbia Law Review 468 (1978); Barry P. Biggar, *Patronage and Public Employment after Branti v. Finkel*, Pace Law Review 423 (1981); Susan Lorde Martin, *Patronage Employment: Limiting Litigation*, 49 San Diego Law Review 669 (2012); Kevin J. O'Connor, *Rutan v. Republican Party of Illinois: Federal Court's Expanding Role in Political Patronage Employment Decisions*, 24 Connecticut Law Review 641, 642 ff. (1992).

165 Rutan v. Republican Party of Illinois, 497 U.S. 62, 76 (1990).

166 Elrod v. Burns, 427 U.S. 347, 376 (1976) (Powell, J., dissenting).

167 Free Enterprise Fund v. PCAOB, 561 U.S. 477 (2010). *See* Patricia L. Bellia, *PCAOB and the Persistence of the Removal Puzzle*, 80 The George Washington Law Review 1371 (2012); Michael J. Gerhardt, *On Candor, Free Enterprise Fund, and the Theory of the Unitary Executive*, 22 William & Mary Bill of Rights Journal 337 (2013); Harold J. Krent, *Federal Power, Non-Federal Actors: The Ramifications of Free Enterprise Fund*, 79 Fordham Law Review 2425 (2011); Ronald J. Krotoszynski, Jr, *Cooperative Federalism, The New Formalism, and the Separation of Powers Revisited: Free Enterprise Fund and the Problem of Presidential Oversight of State-Government Officers Enforcing Federal Law*, 61 Duke Law Journal 1599 (2012); Jerome Nelson, *Administrative Law Judges' Removal "Only For Cause": Is That Administrative Procedure Act Protection Now Unconstitutional?* 63 Administrative Law Review 401 (2011); Neomi Rao, *A Modest Proposal: Abolishing Agency Independence in Free Enterprise Fund v. PCAOB*, 79 Fordham Law Review 2541 (2011); Kevin M. Stack, *Agency Independence After PCAOB*, 32 Cardozo Law Review 2391 (2011); Peter L. Strauss, *On the Difficulties of Generalization—PCAOB in the Footsteps of Myers, Humphrey's Executor, Morrison and Freytag*, 32 Cardozo Law Review 2255 (2011).

168 The decision is also seen as a sign of a "new formalism"; *see* Krotoszynski, *supra* note 167, at 1615 ff. Cf. also Gillian E. Metzger, *Foreword: 1930s Redux: The Administrative State under Siege*, 131 Harvard Law Review 1, 2 (2017).

169 Free Enterprise Fund v. PCAOB, 561 U.S. 477, 483 (2010).

170 Humphrey's Executor v. United States, 295 U.S. 602 (1935).

171 Free Enterprise Fund v. PCAOB, 561 U.S. 477, 483 (2010): "The parties do not ask us to reexamine any of these precedents, and we do not do so." Similarly, also at page 487: "The parties agree that the Commissioners cannot themselves be removed by the President except under the Humphrey's Executor standard."

172 Free Enterprise Fund v. PCAOB, 561 U.S. 477, 495 (2010).

173 Free Enterprise Fund v. PCAOB, 561 U.S. 477, 515 (2010).
174 Free Enterprise Fund v. PCAOB, 561 U.S. 477, 538 et seq. (2010) (Stevens, J., dissenting).
175 Seila Law v. CFPB, 140 S.Ct. 2183, 2191 (2020).
176 Seila Law v. CFPB, 140 S.Ct. 2183, 2197 et seq. (2020).
177 Seila Law v. CFPB, 140 S.Ct. 2183, 2199 et seq. (2020).
178 Seila Law v. CFPB, 140 S.Ct. 2183, 2240 (2020) (Kagan, J., concurring in the judgment in part and dissenting in part).
179 Seila Law v. CFPB, 140 S.Ct. 2183, 2225 (2020) (Kagan, J., concurring in the judgment in part and dissenting in part).
180 For a detailed overview of the development cf. ROSSBACH, *supra* note 1, at 436 ff.
181 For the term "constitutional moment" cf. Bruce A. Ackerman, *The Storrs Lectures: Discovering the Constitution*, 93 Yale Law Journal 1013, 1022 (1984); for its application to the constitutional law of executive personnel cf. ROSSBACH, *supra* note 1, at 389, 479, 531, 587.
182 On this in detail: UDO WENGST, BEAMTENTUM ZWISCHEN REFORM UND TRADITION 110 and 130 (1988). Cf. ROSSBACH, *supra* note 1, at 14.
183 German Federal Archives, BArch. B 136/494, sheet 102.
184 German Federal Archives, BArch. B 136/494, sheet 106.
185 Cf. Cass R. Sunstein, *Constitutionalism after the New Deal*, 101 Harvard Law Review 421, 508 (1987): "The New Deal alternative was both to increase the power of the presidency and to create the modern administrative agency, comprised of technically sophisticated officials promoting the public interest."
186 Cf. also Herbert Kaufman, *The Growth of the Federal Personnel System*, in: THE FEDERAL GOVERNMENT SERVICE 7, 30 (Wallace S. Sayre and others eds., 1954): "all values however have been recognized in some measure all of the time"; Anonymous, *Developments in the Law. Public Employment*, 97 Harvard Law Review 1611, 1619 ff. (1984).
187 Seila Law v. CFPB, 140 S.Ct. 2183 (2020); *see supra* The Modern American Civil Service: Adapting Civil Service Concepts to Constitutional Law.
188 Lucia v. SEC, 138 S.Ct. 2044 (2018).
189 Cf. ROSSBACH, *supra* note 1, at 365 ff.
190 Buckley v. Valeo, Page 424 U.S. 1, 126 (1976); Freytag v. Commissioner, 501 U.S. 868, 881 (1991).
191 Free Enterprise Fund v. PCAOB, 516 U.S. 477, 506 (2010): "many civil servants within Independent Agencies would not qualify as, 'officers of the United States,' who exercise[e] significant authority pursuant to the laws of the United States." On the uncertainties and ambiguities: Strauss, *supra* note 167, at 2279 ff.
192 Lucia v. SEC, 138 S.Ct. 2044 (2018).
193 Cf. Samuel A. Schwartz, *Lucia v. SEC: The Ambiguity of the Appointments Clause Continues, Sending Tremors Coursing throughout the Administrative State*, Journal of Business and Technology Law Proxy 1, 14 ff. (2019).
194 Kent Barnett, *Resolving the ALJ Quandary*, 66 Vanderbilt Law Review 797, 810 f. (2013). On the problem of defective appointment, *see also* Jennifer L. Mascott, *Constitutionally Conforming Agency Adjudication*, Loyola Journal of Regulatory Compliance 22, 23 f. (2017).
195 Executive Order 13483, July 10, 2018; cf. Mascott, *supra* note 114; ROSSBACH, *supra* note 1, at 382 f. and 582 f.
196 Executive Order 13483, July 10, 2018.
197 *See supra* note 127.

Bibliography

Ackerman, Bruce A., *The Storrs Lectures: Discovering the Constitution.* 93 Yale Law Journal 1013 (1984)

Ackerman, Bruce A., We the People, Vol. 1 (1993)

Ackerman, Bruce A., We the People, Vol. 3. Civil Rights Revolution (2014)

Alvis, J. David/Bailey, Jeremy D./Taylor, F. Flagg, The Contested Removal Power, 1789–2010 (2013)

Anonymous, *Developments in the Law. Public Employment*, 97 Harvard Law Review 1611 (1984)

Anonymous, *Note: Review of Removal of Federal Civil Service Employees*, 52 Columbia Law Review 787 (1952)

Bailyn, Bernard, The Origins of American Politics (1968)

Ban, Carolyn/Ingraham, Patricia, *Legislating Bureaucratic Change*, in: Legislating Bureaucratic Change: The Civil Service Reform Act of 1978, 1 (Carolyn Ban/Patricia Ingraham eds., 1984)

Barnett, Kent, *Resolving the ALJ Quandary*, 66 Vanderbilt Law Review 797 (2013)

Bellia, Patricia L., *PCAOB and the Persistence of the Removal Puzzle*, 80 The George Washington Law Review 1371 (2012)

Biggar, Barry P., *Patronage and Public Employment after Branti v. Finkel*, Pace Law Review 423 (1981)

Bishop, Leah M., *Patronage and the First Amendment after Elrod v. Burns*, 78 Columbia Law Review 468 (1978)

Bleek, Wilhelm, Von der Kameralausbildung zum Juristenprivileg (1972)

Bluntschli, Johann Caspar, Lehre vom modernen Staat. Theil 3: Politik als Wissenschaft (1876)

Cayer, Joseph N., Public Personnel Administration in the United States (1996)

Cook, Brian J., Bureaucracy and Self-Government (1996)

Crenson, Matthew A., The Federal Machine (1975)

Dillman, David L., *Civil Service Reform in Comparative Perspective*, in: Legislating Bureaucratic Change 203 (Patricia Ingraham/Carolyn Ban eds., 1984)

Dreier, Horst/Waldhoff, Christian (eds.), Das Wagnis der Demokratie (2018)

Eaton, Dorman, Civil Service in Great Brain (1880)

Emerson, Blake, The Public's Law (2019)

Eskridge, William/Ferejohn, John, A Republic of Statutes (2010)

Field, Oliver P., Civil Service Law (1939)

Fish, Carl R., The Civil Service and the Patronage (1904)

Fries, Sylvia D., *Staatstheorie and the New American Science of Politics*, 34 Journal of the History of Idea 391 (1973)

Frug, Gerald E., *Does the Constitution Prevent the Discharge of Civil Service Employees?* 124 University of Pennsylvania Law Review 942 (1976)

Gerhardt, Michael J., *On Candor, Free Enterprise Fund, and the Theory of the Unitary Executive*, 22 William & Mary Bill of Rights Journal 337 (2013)

Goodnow, Frank J., Comparative Administrative Law (1893)

Goodnow, Frank J., Politics and Administration (1900)

Hamburger, Philip, Is Administrative Law Unlawful? (2014)

Hattenhauer, Hans, Geschichte des deutschen Beamtentums (1993)

Hoogenboom, Ari, Outlawing the Spoils (1968)

Ingraham, Patricia W., *The Civil Service Reform Act of 1978: Its Design and Legislative History*, in: Legislating Bureaucratic Change 13 (Patricia Ingraham/Carolyn Ban eds., 1984)

INGRAHAM, PATRICIA, THE FOUNDATION OF MERIT (1995)
JOHNSON, RONALD/LIBECAP, GARY, THE FEDERAL CIVIL SERVICE SYSTEM AND THE PROBLEM OF BUREAUCRACY (1994)
KARL, BARRY D., EXECUTIVE REORGANIZATION AND REFORM IN THE NEW DEAL (1963)
Kaufman, Herbert, *The Growth of the Federal Personnel System*, in: THE FEDERAL GOVERNMENT SERVICE 7 (Wallace S. Sayre and others eds., 1954)
Krent, Harold J., *Federal Power, Non-Federal Actors: The Ramifications of Free Enterprise Fund*, 79 Fordham Law Review 2425 (2011)
Krotoszynski, Ronald J., Jr, *Cooperative Federalism, The New Formalism, and the Separation of Powers Revisited: Free Enterprise Fund and the Problem of Presidential Oversight of State-Government Officers Enforcing Federal Law*, 61 Duke Law Journal 1599 (2012)
LANDIS, JAMES, THE ADMINISTRATIVE PROCESS (1938)
Lawson, Gary, *The Rise and Rise of the Administrative State*, 107 Harvard Law Review 1231 (1994)
LEPSIUS, OLIVER, VERWALTUNGSRECHT UNTER DEM COMMON LAW (1997)
LEWIS, DAVID E., THE POLITICS OF PRESIDENTIAL APPOINTMENTS (2008)
Martin, Susan Lorde, *Patronage Employment: Limiting Litigation*, 49 San Diego Law Review 669 (2012)
Mascott, Jennifer L., *Constitutionally Conforming Agency Adjudication*, Loyola Journal of Regulatory Compliance 22 (2017)
Mascott, Jennifer L., *Who Are "Officers of the United States"?* 70 Stanford Law Review 443 (2018)
MASHAW, JERRY L., CREATING THE ADMINISTRATIVE CONSTITUTION (2012)
MAYERS, LEWIS, THE FEDERAL SERVICE (1922)
Merrill, Richard A., *Procedures for Adverse Actions against Federal Employees*, 59 Virginia Law Review 196 (1973)
Metzger, Gillian E., *Foreword: 1930s Redux: The Administrative State under Siege*, 131 Harvard Law Review 1 (2017)
MEYERS, MARVIN, THE JACKSONIAN PERSUASION(1957)
Miewald, Robert D., *The Origins of Wilsons's Thought. The German Tradition and the Organic State*, in: POLITICS AND ADMINISTRATION 17 (Jack Rabin/James S. Bowman eds.)
Milkis, Sidney, *The Presidency and Political Parties*, in: THE PRESIDENCY AND THE POLITICAL SYSTEM 309 (Michael Nelson ed., 11th ed. 2018)
MÖLLERS, CHRISTOPH, GEWALTENGLIEDERUNG (2005)
MORONE, JAMES A., THE DEMOCRATIC WISH (1998)
MORSTEIN MARX, FRITZ, EINFÜHRUNG IN DIE BÜROKRATIE (1959)
MOSHER, FREDERICK C., DEMOCRACY AND THE CIVIL SERVICE (1982)
NAFF, KATHERINE C./RICCUCCI, NORMA M./FREYSS, SIEGRUN F., PERSONNEL MANAGEMENT IN GOVERNMENT (2014)
Nelson, Jerome, *Administrative Law Judges' Removal "Only For Cause": Is That Administrative Procedure Act Protection Now Unconstitutional?* 63 Administrative Law Review 401 (2011)
NELSON, WILLIAM E., THE ROOTS OF AMERICAN BUREAUCRACY 1830–1900 (1982)
O'Connor, Kevin J., *Rutan v. Republican Party of Illinois: Federal Court's Expanding Role in Political Patronage Employment Decisions*, 24 Connecticut Law Review 641 (1992)
OVEREEM, PATRICK, THE POLITICS–ADMINISTRATION DICHOTOMY (2012)
PESTRITTO, RONALD J., WOODROW WILSON AND THE ROOTS OF MODERN LIBERALISM (2005)
PILKINGTON, COLIN, THE CIVIL SERVICE IN BRITAIN TODAY (1999)

POCOCK, JOHN G.A., THE MACHIAVELLIAN MOMENT (1975/2016)

Pocock, John G.A., *Virtue and Commerce in the Eighteenth Century*, 3 Journal of Interdisciplinary History 119 (1972)

Prakash, Saikrishna, *New Light on the Decision of 1789*, 91 Cornell Law Review 1021 (2006)

Rao, Neomi, *A Modest Proposal: Abolishing Agency Independence in Free Enterprise Fund v. PCAOB*, 79 Fordham Law Review 2541 (2011)

RICCUCCI, NORMA M., PUBLIC PERSONNEL MANAGEMENT (2012)

RIPER, PAUL VAN, HISTORY OF THE UNITED STATES CIVIL SERVICE (1958)

ROHR, JOHN A., TO RUN A CONSTITUTION (1986)

Rose-Ackerman, Susan, *Administrative Law and Democracy*, in: THE OXFORD HANDBOOK OF COMPARATIVE ADMINISTRATIVE LAW 1075 (Peter Cane et al. eds., 2021)

Rose-Ackerman, Susan, *American Administration Law Under Siege: Is Germany a Model?* 107 Harvard Law Review 1279 (1994)

ROSE-ACKERMAN, SUSAN, CONTROLLING ENVIRONMENTAL POLICY: THE LIMITS OF PUBLIC LAW IN GERMANY AND THE UNITED STATES (1995)

ROSE-ACKERMAN, SUSAN, DEMOCRACY AND EXECUTIVE POWER: POLICYMAKING ACCOUNTABILITY IN THE US, THE UK, GERMANY, AND FRANCE (2021)

Rose-Ackerman, Susan, *The Regulatory State*, in: THE OXFORD HANDBOOK OF COMPARATIVE CONSTITUTIONAL LAW 671 (Michael Rosenfeld/András Sajo eds., 2012)

Rosenbloom, David H., *Politics and Public Personnel Administration. The Legacy of 1883*, in: CENTENARY ISSUES OF THE PENDLETON ACT OF 1883, 1 (Rosenbloom ed., 1982)

ROSENBLOOM, DAVID H., THE FEDERAL SERVICE AND THE CONSTITUTION (2014)

ROSSBACH, MATTHIAS, DAS PERSONAL DER REPUBLIK. ENTSTEHUNG UND ENTWICKLUNG EINES DEMOKRATISCHEN PERSONALVERFASSUNGSRECHTS DER EXEKUTIVE AM BEISPIEL DER VEREINIGTEN STAATEN VON AMERIKA (2020)

Rosser, Christian, *The Role of Foreign Ideas in Identity Formation: The Hegelian Roots of Early American Public Administration*, in: THE EUROPEAN PUBLIC SERVANT. A SHARED ADMINISTRATIVE IDENTITY? 135 (Fritz Sager/Patrick Overeem eds., 2015)

RUNGE, WOLFGANG, POLITIK UND BEAMTENTUM IM PARTEIENSTAAT (1965)

Schwartz, Samuel A., *Lucia v. SEC: The Ambiguity of the Appointments Clause Continues, Sending Tremors Coursing throughout the Administrative State*, Journal of Business and Technology Law Proxy 1 (2019)

SILBERMAN, BERNARD, CAGES OF REASON (1993)

SKOWRONEK, STEPHEN, BUILDING A NEW AMERICAN STATE (1982)

Stack, Kevin M., *Agency Independence After PCAOB*, 32 Cardozo Law Review 2391 (2011)

Strauss, Peter L., *On the Difficulties of Generalization—PCAOB in the Footsteps of Myers, Humphrey's Executor, Morrison and Freytag*, 32 Cardozo Law Review 2255 (2011)

Sunstein, Cass R., *Constitutionalism after the New Deal*, 101 Harvard Law Review 421 (1987)

THACH, CHARLES C., THE CREATION OF THE PRESIDENCY 1775–1789 (1922)

TITLOW, RICHARD E., AMERICANS IMPORT MERIT (1982)

TOCQUEVILLE, ALEXIS DE, DEMOCRACY IN AMERICA (2003)

Volokh, Hanah M., *The Two Appointment Clauses: Statutory Qualifications for Federal Officers*, 10 Journal of Constitutional Law 745 (2008)

Voßkuhle, Andreas, *Expertise und Verwaltung*, in: ALLGEMEINES VERWALTUNGSRECHT—ZUR TRAGFÄHIGKEIT EINES KONZEPTS 637 (Hans-Heinrich Trute et al. eds., 2008)

WALDO, DWIGHT, THE ADMINISTRATIVE STATE (1984)

WENGST, UDO, BEAMTENTUM ZWISCHEN REFORM UND TRADITION (1988)

Westwood, Howard C., *The "Right" of an Employee of the United States against Arbitrary Discharge*, 7 George Washington Law Review 212 (1938)

WHITE, LEONARD D., THE FEDERALISTS. A STUDY IN ADMINISTRATIVE HISTORY (1948/1956)
WHITE, LEONARD D., THE REPUBLICAN ERA. A STUDY IN ADMINISTRATIVE HISTORY, 1869–1901 (1965)
WILLOUGHBY, WILLIAM F., THE GOVERNMENT OF MODERN STATES (1936)
Wilson, Woodrow, *The Study of Administration*, 2 Political Science Quarterly 197 (1887)
WOOD, GORDON S., THE CREATION OF THE AMERICAN REPUBLIC, 1776–1787 (1969/1998)
WUNDER, BERND, GESCHICHTE DER BÜROKRATIE IN DEUTSCHLAND (1986)
YELLIN, ERIC S., RACISM IN THE NATION'S SERVICE (2013)

7 The Neoliberal Turn of Contemporary French Administrative Law

Thomas Perroud

Introduction: Neoliberalism and Administrative Law

The neoliberal project is equally economic, political, and legal, and is reflected in specific techniques. Most studies in the field identify neoliberalism with a preference for markets techniques (vouchers) over public intervention, for privatization[1] over public options and for contracting-out instead of direct provision. In political science, neoliberalism has been broadly conceptualized as an attack on the state, whether by stripping it of its core functions to give them to private actors or by promoting globalization along with free-market policies.[2]

My aim in this paper is to identify neoliberalism with specific legal techniques of constitutional importance and not outcomes or results. Indeed, neoliberal administrative law corresponds to a specific relationship to legality. It is, more precisely, the creation of mechanisms that make it possible to neutralize Parliament's will (statutes) under the cover of a managerial discourse and to weaken administrative checks and balances.

Classic administrative law was characterized by two features. First, it was liberal in spirit. Its goal was to control administrative power (hence a very generous rule on standing allowing the citizen easy access to the judge to challenge administrative decisions).[3] Also, the idea of the separation of powers was at the very center of the French administrative structure. In the same vein, this liberalism was clearly evident in the concept of public and private spheres as shaped by administrative judges who constrained state intervention in the economy. Such containment was also perceptible in the moral sphere: administrative activities could not impose a particular version of morality. All of this has radically changed today.

At the same time, classical administrative law was characterized by the desire to ensure the preeminence of representative democracy. Judges were formerly to ensure the preeminence of statutory law; today, in contrast, they are incrementally increasing the possibilities for neutralizing it. The judiciary thus developed a new legality by overhauling the hierarchy of norms. In addition, through the establishment of independent administrative authorities in the 1980s, the administration has become exempt from democratic accountability to the Parliament.

DOI: 10.4324/9781003416036-7

To sum up, in French administrative law, neoliberalism is characterized by two structural elements: it is an anti-liberal ideology, on the one hand, and an anti-democratic one, on the other.

Anti-Liberal Characteristics of Contemporary French Administrative Law

Liberalism is not a homogeneous movement. In administrative law, it translated into structures and mechanisms with the purpose of reining in and controlling administrative power. On the one hand, traditional liberalism is embedded in the structures and controls of administrative action.

Controlling Power in Administrative Structures: The Weakening of Separations

The ideal of controlling and balancing power was at the heart of French administrative institutions. Based on the US experience, Jon Michaels shows that privatization policies weakened what he calls the administrative separation of powers.[4] As applied to France, this argument helps to explain the very peculiar conceptions of administrative separation present in French administrative law.

First, the principle of the separation of administrative courts and active administration is receding (*séparation de la juridiction administrative et de l'administration active*). This principle has two sides: on the one hand, this principle justified the transfer of administrative litigation from the administration itself to the judge. But, on the other hand, the principle implied judicial deference towards the administration. Jacques Chevallier clearly showed that this principle was established in the period between 1872 and 1905.[5] It clearly limits the powers of the administrative judge over the administration, prohibiting, for instance, injunctions or the judicial remaking of administrative decisions. In classic French administrative law, the judge could only quash an administrative decision. In that sense, the French administrative judges were much weaker than their common law counterparts.

The 1980s ushered in a counter movement that profoundly changed this relationship, in particular by introducing the injunction.[6] But more recently, the rise of "full jurisdiction review" constitutes the clearest rupture. "Full jurisdiction review" is the power of the administrative judge to remake an administrative decision. This power is enshrined in law for certain cases and now has a general basis in the field of administrative sanctions.[7] In these cases, the judge becomes the administration, with the power to change the decision reviewed. This is a radical constitutional change. Although Parliament assigned a power to the administration, the judge gets the final say.

Next, the principle of the separation of administrative and judicial authorities (*principe de séparation des autorités administratives et judiciaires*) also underwent a notable change. This principle comes from the dual nature of the French court system, the civil law courts with the *Cour de Cassation* at the top and the administrative courts headed by the *Conseil d'Etat*. This principle was first elaborated during the French Revolution and prohibits civil judges from intervening in administrative action.[8] This principle was merely symbolic for two hundred years because Parliament remained free to assign appeals to either the administrative or the civil judge. It was given a constitutional status in 1987 by the Constitutional Court in order to protect the jurisdiction of the administrative courts.[9]

Several things have begun to interfere with this demarcation line.

First, Parliament gave jurisdiciton to some challenges brought against prominent agencies to the civil judge instead of to the administrative one. At the beginning of the 1980, neoliberalism in France developed as a critique of administrative action with the promotion of privatization policies and the rise of competition law. The administrative courts were critiqued as an archaic judicial model. Parliament transferred from the administrative court to the civil courts the power of review of a key agency, namely the Competition Authority (*Conseil de la concurrence* now renamed *Autorité de la concurrence*) and later did the same for some decisions of the financial markets authority (Commission des opérations de bourse now renamed Autorité des marchés financiers) and several others. I have argued elsewhere that this transfer represents a privatization of the control over the administration.[10] The Conseil d'Etat itself even felt the need to lobby the Constitutional Council to get a constitutional protection of its competence.[11]

More recent developments have shifted these demarcation lines, but in the other direction, towards increasing the competence of the administrative judge to rule on civil liberties. Administrative judges had no competence in assuring the protection of civil liberties, which had been under the sole protection of the civil judge. When the administration violated a liberty, for instance, the right of property, the civil judge was competent and could sanction the administration. The Constitution of the Fifth Republic states: "No one may be arbitrarily detained. The judicial authority, guardian of individual freedom, shall ensure the respect of this principle under the conditions provided for by law." The administrative judge has always been suspected of bias towards the administration; hence, the protection of civil liberties necessitated the intervention of an independent judge. However, today, even this line has shifted.

In French administrative law, *voie de fait* and *emprise irrégulière* were two cases where the civil judge could sanction violations of people's rights and had full powers to do so. A *voie de fait* is an administrative act that illegally cancels a property right or that violates an individual freedom. These infringements are so serious that the act loses its administrative character and falls under the control of the judicial judge. Being very close to the executive, the administrative judge was not the proper adjudicatory forum. In the French legal culture, the administrative judge has always been thought of as a protector of the administration. Similarly, *emprise irrégulière* covers any violation of private property by the administration. In these two cases, the civil judge regains competence to sanction the administration and order compensation or restoration of the situation.

Here again, the lines have shifted. Two cases by the *Tribunal des Conflits*—the court that adjudicates on jurisdictional conflicts between the civil and administrative legal orders—have increased the competence of the administrative judge on these disputes.[12] Since the 1980s and 1990s, the Conseil d'Etat has worked to neutralize the stigma attached to itself as a protector of the interests of administration and managed to regain competence in these very symbolic fields. Its new powers helped it to justify the claim that, technically, it is as well equipped as the civil judge to sanction the administration—ignoring the fact that the constitutional preference for the civil judge was also justified by the closeness of the Conseil d'Etat to the executive and not solely by the fact that the administrative judge lacked injunctive powers.

As a result, we are losing a symbol, one that had made the civil judge the arbiter of the most serious attacks by the administration on fundamental rights. Meanwhile, the administrative judges themselves have not changed; they remain very close to the government. The extension of the administrative judge's competence to the protection of fundamental freedoms is also clear in the context of the state of emergency.[13] French freedoms are increasingly under the control of judges close to the administration.

This naturally leads us to the third line of protection shielding against administrative arbitrariness: the weakening separation between administrative and judicial police (*séparation des polices administratives et judiciaires*). In order to contain the power of the police, French law sought to separate the spheres of two police activities called administrative and judicial. The focus of administrative police (*police administrative*) is to prevent breaches of public order,[14] whereas the judicial police (*police judiciaire*) aims to sanction criminal offenses. The two are most of the time intertwined; that's why the jurisprudence is not perfectly clear. Administrative police authorities are part of the administration whereas judicial police authorities are judges and magistrates.

This separation has gradually melted away. The most worrying blow was delivered by the Dieudonné case. Dieudonné is a successful comedian and humorist who was convicted on several occasions before the criminal courts for the anti-semitic nature of some of his shows. In France, racist, anti-semitic public speech is punishable by a criminal sanction.[15] The only legal sanction against the abuse of freedom of expression was therefore *ex-post* and by a judge independent of the executive.

On the occasion of a show entitled "The Wall," members of the public asked for the banning of the show. The law did not allow such a preliminary ban. The Minister of the Interior at the time, Manuel Valls, issued a circular asking the prefects, at the local level, to take the place of the mayors who had not banned the performances.[16] In other words, the executive used its police powers to force local administrative officials to ban the show. The comedian challenged the bans in Orléans, Nantes, and other cities before the first instance administrative tribunal and then before the Conseil d'Etat. In a 2014 decision, the Conseil d'Etat upheld the bans, thereby redefining *police administrative* at the expense of the criminal judge and free speech.[17]

As a scholar explains,[18] these ordinances undermine the autonomy of *police administrative* by integrating crime prevention into its missions. The Council of State now considers that *police administrative* authorities have the competence to prevent the occurrence of offenses:

> It is incumbent upon the authority vested with *police administrative* powers to take the necessary, appropriate and proportionate measures to prevent the commission of criminal offenses likely to constitute a disturbance of public order without excessively infringing on the exercise by citizens of their fundamental freedoms.[19]

This case merges police administrative and police judiciaire by giving the former a mission attributed traditionally to the latter, at the expense of fundamental rights. In fact, this jurisprudence now authorizes administrative authorities to ban a show.

Another significant development has been the rise in administrative sanctions since the 1980s. In France, liberalism had barred the administration from imposing sanctions; if administrators wanted to sanction non-compliance with the law, they had to refer the matter to the criminal judge, who had a monopoly in adjudicating the matter.[20] A major manifestation of the neoliberal penality,[21] as Bernard Harcourt calls it, is, in France, the massive use of sanctions that bypasses the judge. Most agencies in the field of competition law, financial services regulation, or the regulation of network industries were awarded such a power, which also means that they wield regulatory as well as sanctioning powers. They are enforcing their regulations, which is not in the tradition of French administrative law. As we will show later, this choice can be explained by sociological reasons: shielding white-collar offenders from the stigma of a criminal trial.

All these separations were akin to internal checks and balances. This system is now weakened, giving the administration more power over citizens.

Administrative Justice and the Moderation of Administrative Power: The Decline of Standing in French Administrative Law

The protection against abuses of administrative power was also ensured by very generous rules on standing. Access to the French administrative judge was easy, ensuring protection against abuses and a very tight control of how the administration executes the law.

In about 1900, the Council of State established judicial review as a general interest remedy, opening the doors of its courtroom widely. We are now witnessing an opposite trend. Urban planning law has seen the most sophisticated techniques that block access to the judge in the name of legal security.

"Legal security" has been promoted by the Council of State itself since the 1990s.[22] Under this rubric, the beneficiaries of authorizations or contracts with the administration should not be under constant threat of a challenge. Because the country faces an important housing shortage, construction times should be shorter. Restriction of access to the court is part of this business-friendly policy. The same trend is visible in the law of public contracts where third parties are now denied access to the courts.[23]

This policy has limited standing for associations and NGOs. Associations have had standing to bring challenges before administrative judges since the 1906 landmark case of *Syndicat des patrons coiffeurs de Limoges*.[24] In the field of urban law, an important business-friendly reform of 2018 bars associations incorporated for less than a year from bringing a case to challenge a building permit, thereby preventing access for ad hoc associations created for the purpose of helping citizens to challenge a permit.[25] The alleged reason given by the government was to prevent "abusive" challenges. The French Constitutional Council has found no breach of the fundamental right of access to justice although there is absolutely no link between the abusive nature of an appeal and the date of incorporation of an association.[26]

Additionally, the same developments arise for unilateral acts based on the 2019 *Czabaj* case that, in the name of legal certainty again, prevents appeals against individual administrative decisions in certain cases.[27] The default time limit to bring a challenge against an administrative decision is two months after the notice of the decision is received.[28] However, if the notification fails to mention how to challenge the decision and the time limit, it used to be the rule that the decision could be challenged anytime. That rule was undermined by the Czabaj case, in the name of legal security.

Finally, a clear attack against access to justice was rendered on May 18th, 2018, *Fédération des finances et des affaires économiques de la CFDT (no 414583)*. Paul Cassia rightly argues that it amounts to a "symbolic and very real violence against litigants,"[29] as it restricts access to a judge for applicants who wish to challenge collaterally (i.e., after a final decision) the procedural irregularities of a decision.

Clearly, in recent cases, the Conseil d'Etat has deviated from the spirit of classical administrative law. Some might object: What about the *Fairvesta* decision which, by contrast, permits litigation for a new category of soft law?[30] But this is where the differential treatment of interests becomes the most striking. The judge in the Fairvesta judgment carried out a ranking of interests, and held that only soft law acts with notable economic effects may be justiciable.[31] This statement is shocking because administrative judges have never given any special treatment to economic interests. Doing so here is all the more shocking when contrasted with the high barriers for legal action by private individuals or associations in urban planning litigation.[32] The difference in treatment gives the impression that the Council of State serves "Big Capital," to use Frédéric Rolin's expression.[33] Later, however, the Council of State opened judicial review to all kinds of soft law acts, irrespective of their effect.[34]

A New Political Economy

Liberalism in classic French administrative law manifested itself through principles of containment. At the cost of an anachronism, one could say that French administrative jurisprudence contained Thatcherite or Reaganite principles.[35] Early cases held that public bodies could not create economic activities in competition with private companies. There was even a correlation between standing and economic intervention visible in the 1901 *Casanova* case[36] where the the Conseil d'Etat gives standing to local taxpayers to challenge decisions that have an effect on the local budget. Economic actions of the administration were subject to the principle of subsidiarity. It was only after the 1929 crisis that the Conseil d'Etat accepted a more nuanced approach to public intervention: the administration could only step in and take the place of a private initiative and offer a public service when there was a market failure.[37] This requirement was abolished in 2006 in the *Ordre des avocats au barreau de Paris* (Order of Lawyers at the Paris Bar).[38]

Similarly, since 2000, if a public entity applies for a public procurement contract, the Council of State has held that the public entity and the private person must be considered equal.[39] Later, the judge tempered this approach by requiring proof of public interest.[40] The judgment quoted above thus aligns the jurisprudence relating to the application for a contract with that regarding the offering of a public service. However, in both cases, the court no longer assumes that private initiative must be protected from the intrusion of public power.[41] The principle of non-intervention is over and done with. The Council of State has even published guidance on the economic action of public persons.[42]

The state is treated as a normal actor. At the same time, the Conseil d'Etat integrates competition law with public interest criteria. The jurisprudence answers the question raised by Foucault and that defines neoliberalism: "How can the overall exercise of political power be modeled on the principles of a market economy?"[43] The most influential theorist on the use of market mechanisms to control public services is Julian Le Grand, who wrote: *The Other Invisible Hand: Delivering Public Services through Choice and Competition*.[44] In 1991, he defined quasi-market mechanisms to include public policies whose goal is to reconfigure public action to imitate market mechanisms with the purpose of reining in public services and making them more efficient. Establishing a quasi-market involves a change in the role of the state which is no longer the one financing and providing the service.[45] The state restricts itself to the role of the financer in order to introduce competition among the various suppliers.

Today, economic action by public bodies is in fact oriented towards the protection of markets. The influence of these ideas is visible in the case law of the Conseil d'Etat, which was inspired by the cases of the European Court of Justice that imposed respect for competition law (that has constitutional status in the European Union) as a principle of State action.[46] The judgment kickstarting this change was rendered in 1997, in *Millions et Marais*,[47] followed by the decision *Société EDA*[48] and the opinion *Société L et P Publicité SARL*[49] and *Société Jean-Louis Bernard Consultants.*[50] The Council of State now requires that all administrative activity respect the integrity of the market: "once accepted in principle [by the High Court judges], such an intervention must not be carried out in a way that, the particular situation in which this public entity would find itself compared to other operators acting on the same market, would distort the free interplay of competition on the latter."[51] The Société EDA case is very revealing because it concerns a public decision involving the management of the public domain that can have an effect on a market. The Conseil d'Etat recognizes no hierarchy for the different general interests involved: competition law and the protection of the market are on the same level as the preservation of the public domain.

Thus, neoliberalism has changed the substance of administrative action to make room for competition law and market principles. We can also see this very clearly in the central role played by public procurement law. Also, for the first time, under the code that regulates the use of public properties, public bodies are being recognized as officially having a right of property over the public domain.[52] The basic idea, here, is to allow public entities to earn more from their properties using devices similar to those applicable to the use of private property.

A New Moral Order

All the principles constraining State action in the private sphere have fallen one after the other. The last one disappeared in the 1990s. Administrative bodies enjoy inherent police powers aimed at protecting the public order (i.e., preventing disruptions of public security, public hygiene, and public tranquility; a functional equivalent in the common law would be public nuisance and breach of the King's peace). The public order in question was always said to be "material and exterior": no moral questions could be used to argue that a disruption of public order required intervention. Mayors could not use their police powers to uphold a moral order. This changed in the 1990s with the dwarf-tossing case. In this case a mayor decided to ban this activity in the town as contrary to human dignity. The Conseil d'Etat upheld the ban, holding that human dignity belonged to the public order.[53] This was indeed an increase of administrative powers. It also poses a democratic issue because local police powers are not powers that need democratic approval by municipal councils, this is an inherent power of the mayor that must be used to avoid liability for the municipality.

The traditional conception of public order ensured the protection of liberty and prevented police authorities from imposing their moral order on different communities. Admittedly, the Council of State was never clear on the question of morals even before the judgment on dwarf-tossing was rendered.[54] Likewise, the *Société Les films Lutétia* case of 1959 allows mayors to prohibit the screening of certain films that could create unrest.[55] The film in question was *Le feu dans la peau* (Fire under the Skin), banned by the mayor of the city of Nice. But the case law was restricted to cinema and required some proof of unrest. The jurisprudence is vast; many mayors have tried to ban specific motion pictures.

The *Commune de Morsang-sur-Orge* case on dwarf-tossing shows a great deal of paternalism. The government commissioner Frydman, in his conclusions, does not hesitate—speaking about dwarf-tossing—to draw a parallel with Nazism when speaking of the *untermensch*. It is symptomatic of the new moral order born in the post–Cold War era with the fall of the Berlin Wall.[56] It is also a time when French society has to face its past, its role in the collaborating with Germany during the war and the extermination of Jews.

Finally, secularism also redefined the nature of public services. All signs of religion are banned from public schools in order to prevent face veils.[57] Formerly, only civil servants were barred from wearing religious signs or expressing any religious preference. However, recent cases have blurred the line concerning the showing of nativity scenes during the Christmas season. The law of 1905 concerning the separation of the churches and the state is clear.[58] According this law: "The Republic ensures freedom of conscience. It guarantees the free exercise of worship subject only to the restrictions hereinafter enacted in the interest of public order" and, under the terms of its Article 2: "The Republic does not recognize, salary or subsidize any cult." For the implementation of these principles, Article 28 of this same law provides that: "It is forbidden, in the future, to raise or affix any religious sign or emblem on public monuments or in any public place whatsoever, with the exception of buildings used for worship, burial grounds in cemeteries, funeral monuments as well as museums or exhibitions". In 2016, the Conseil d'Etat reread the law to allow in some instances, in some places, the erection of Christmas creches.[59] The Conseil d'Etat relaxed its jurisprudence for the sake of the Catholic tradition. Its holdings imply that although the face veil cannot have a plurality of meanings, the Christmas creche can.

The boundaries that formerly demarcated the French administration's scope of action have changed dramatically. The Council of State does not restrict State intervention and even promotes it (let us not forget that the protection of public order is not an option for the administration but indeed an obligation). The goals of administrative action are thus profoundly disrupted, increasingly realigning the system of public action with that of corporate logic.[60] It is thus apparent that contemporary French administrative law, by rendering access to the judge more precarious for ordinary citizens, has given up on containing state intervention that promotes neoliberal policies.

What remains now is to study the anti-democratic character of this law.

Anti-democratic Characteristics of Contemporary French Administrative Law

The anti-democratic nature of contemporary administrative law arises from a new concept of legality and to the new forms of action that allow the administration to escape democratic control. Here, I will highlight the role of independent administrative authorities, privatization, and the so-called shareholder and contracting state.

A Neoliberal Legality

The key concept of French administrative law is that of the hierarchy of norms. The courts' role is to uphold this hierarchy with the Constitution at the top, statutes next, and administration decisions below (individual decisions being the lowest form of norm, below administrative rules). The Council of State has remade this hierarchy, to the detriment of statutory law. Since the Third Republic, the Council of State had rooted its legitimacy in statutory law. Judicial review, with its very generous standing rules, aimed at enforcing the will of Parliament over administrative actions. All the tools were in place to ensure that the will of the parliament was respected. For instance, even non-governmental organizations (NGOs) has had standing to bring challenges since 1906.[61]

The Council of State, more than ten years after the Cour de Cassation,[62] downgraded the status of Acts of Parliament. It held that international law was above statutory law in a 1989 *Nicolo* judgment and extended the holding to European Union law.[63] This jurisprudence means that the executive, which is almighty in international affairs, can override statutes by reference to international law. The change was not balanced by constitutional changes ensuring more checks on international treaty making, which are still secret and mainly discretionary processes. Article 53 of the French Constitution gives Parliament only a veto power on the ratification of treaties.[64] The legislator is left out of diplomatic negotiations. Hence, the executive is at the center of public action and with the power of the administration further reinforced.

The development of *in concreto* review, introduced by the Council of State in the *Ms. Gonzalez-Gomez* case, deepens the trend.[65] This decision allows the judge to neutralize the enforcement of a law in a specific case if he or she deems that the application of the law would excessively breach a fundamental right. The case concerned a request addressed to the French administration to perform a post-mortem insemination in Spain. However, the law prohibited the export of gametes to carry out this type of insemination, a procedure prohibited in France. The Conseil d'Etat held that although the law was legal in general, in this particular instance—*in concreto*—where a Spanish national intended to perform a legal act in Spain (although illegal in France) the application of the law for Ms Gonzalez-Gomez would disproportionately breach her rights. In other words, *in concreto* review has the potential to create as many micro-hierarchies of norms as there are cases.

What is less well known is the bottom-up reconstruction of the hierarchy of norms, which is not exclusively the product of the efforts of the Council of State. In certain technical fields where financial stakes are important, as for example in urban planning law, tax law, or labor law, a real reconstruction of the hierarchy of norms occurs from the bottom up by limiting the downwards effects of statutes.[66] In tax matters, tools for neutralizing the law are old, since the norm dates from 1927, and allows for decisions of the administration to prevail over the law.[67] But, recently, the use of the *rescrits* in fiscal, social, and financial laws, which allows the citizen to ask the administration to take a position on the interpretation of a norm that can prevail over the law, reinforces the supremacy of lower-ranked rules in the hierarchy of norms over those adopted by the community.[68] It was the simplification program, launched in 2004,[69] that revived this movement, although support for the *rescrit* emerged in the 1990s.[70]

The *rescrit* is clearly a victory of powerful interests that managed to impose the idea that administrative interpretation—even *contra legem*—can prevail over the law.

Labor law has also recently seen a process of inversion when it comes to the hierarchy of norms. Labor law has long[71] applied specific conflict-of-law rules. However, the El Khomri reform created "micro-hierarchies" and "micro legal orders" within the different types of acts in this area[72] that in some instances allowed norms negotiated by unions to prevail over statutes. Bourdieu's analysis identifies neoliberalism with reforms influenced by economists who, in this case, provided the scientific underpinnings for these changes. Economists Gilbert Cette and Pierre Cahuc even campaigned for the transformation of the hierarchy of norms.[73] The report by State Councilor Jean-Denis Combrexelle ratified this approach.[74]

Contemporary techniques for depriving the law of effect abound, as illustrated by the development of the statutory "right to error." Under this provision, a taxpayer can be exempted from tax penalties if he willingly rectifies the errors on his forms.[75] This new technique was designed after the failure of the simplification program (whose main achievement was probably to entrench the doctrine of "positive silence," that is, if the administration fails to answer a request, it is presumed to have accepted the request). The idea, defended by some councilors of state, is to deprive the law of effect because simplification failed.[76] It is the approach now taken to deregulation, with the introduction of so-called "liquid" administrative law.[77]

We have also previously mentioned the limited scope of the procedural flaws that may be invoked to support judicial review, which we believe is also a symptom of this anti-democratic development. The new rules in public contracts litigation, restricting the possibility of judicial review of public contracts deemed illegal, contribute to the same trend.[78]

The force of the law is therefore considerably weakened, reducing the leeway of the national community to take decisions on its own fate. These are not the only undemocratic aspects of contemporary administrative law. Since the 1980s, the administration also has been developing forms of action that escape parliamentary control.

Three of these are especially important: the rise of independent administrative authorities, the privatization of state functions, and the development of the state as an owner or contractor.

Independent Agencies and White-Collar Crime

The rise of independent administrative authorities is a well-known phenomenon. In Europe, these agencies were created to oversee the privatization and deregulation of the utilities sector. The purpose was to isolate the regulation of a sector from the influence of elected politicians. This is a neoliberal aspect in itself, but not the only one.

In France, enforcement of competition law and financial services law was entrusted exclusively to administrative agencies. The Competition Authority is the equivalent of the Federal Trade Commission and the *Autorité des marchés financiers* is the equivalent of the Securities and Exchange Commission. However, unlike in the United States, there is no private enforcement of these laws and very little criminal enforcement, although most administrative offenses in these sectors have equivalents in criminal law (insider trading, for instance, can be punished by administrative or criminal proceedings). This creates the impression, especially for financial services law, that powerful people are tried behind closed doors before administrative agencies that cannot sentence them to jail. Hence, some sociologists argue that the development of administrative agencies in France can be understood as a way for powerful people to get a more comfortable venue to be tried and not face the infamy of a criminal trial.

Administrative law is central in the class struggle over penalities levied on different types of offenses. Lascoumes uses Foucault's analytical tools to make sense of the growth of administrative agencies in France.[79] Foucault distinguishes two types of *illégalismes* (translated as illegality, although this translation is contested[80]): *l'illégalisme des droits* and *l'illégalisme des biens.*[81] The former includes breaking legal rules that establish the regulatory framework for economic and social activity, holding property rights constant. The latter violates the laws governing property rights. Feldman explains the difference thus: "The penal reform strategy aimed to draw a clear line of division between these two categories. From out of this division, the illegalism of rights (cheating, violating regulations, exploiting loopholes, and embezzlement) became increasingly out of reach to those without large sums of capital at their disposal, and, at the same time, property crimes (the "illegalisms of goods") became a permanently tempting alternative to wage labor, as independent methods of securing a livelihood, such as grazing or foraging on the ever-more enclosed commons, became impossible.[82]

Administrative agencies, as Lascoumes shows for France, can be a way to treat *l'illégalisme des droits* differently from *l'illégalisme des biens.* White-collar crimes in the former category are channeled to special tribunals or agencies that avoid the stigma of criminal trials.[83] In contrast, ordinary property offenses are heard in the regular criminal courts.

In sum, the creation of administrative agencies can be considered neoliberal in the sense that it is associated with the special treatment awarded to white-collar crimes in France from the 1980s.

Towards the Privatization of Administrative Justice?

The privatization of state functions is also a means to remove certain functions from mechanisms of democratic accountability. Following a wave of privatizations in the 1980s, France continued along this path, but in areas that go to the very heart of sovereignty. At first, the Council of State, as well as the Constitutional Council, made sure that sovereign functions remained with the state—even if the jurisprudence of the constitutional judges is highly volatile on this point.[84] But one should seriously question the effectiveness of this jurisprudence at a time when local authorities are privatizing parking meters, parking, and speeding tickets. Every time, the argument put forward is that of efficiency: privatization appears to provide a better-quality service at a lower cost—an assertion that has been strongly questioned by well-founded studies.[85] In the case of the United States, Jon Michaels' important work documents the anti-democratic effects of this approach. The contemporary trend of merging market and state or, to use Jon Michaels' expression, of making the government a "politicized business," has the effect of sidelining the expertise of civil servants and the role of civil society in the development of public policies, rendering the state more authoritarian. [86] As Michaels states:

> [T]he mixing of government and market forces leads to an increase in state power to the detriment of the private sector, threatening to destabilize the liberal democratic order. More fundamentally, this mixture increases the power of the executive at the expense of the Congress and the civil service, threatening the constitutional and administrative separation of powers.[87]

In other words, the ideal of limited government contradicts that of a privatized government because the privatized functions find themselves outside the control mechanisms developed in traditional constitutional and administrative law. These functions are also beyond the mechanisms of private law. The privatization of state functions aims to deprive society of the means to control the state and influence its policy. It increases citizens' alienation from their state, thereby revealing the true nature of this process: it is a process of political alienation.

The scope of privatized functions also is not well controlled. As a case study, I examined the contract Paris signed to outsource parking tickets and the resolution of disputes arising from the fines.[88] The contract is interesting from the neoliberal perspective because it assumes that users are rational actors. Also, and more importantly, it outsources administrative justice to a private actor to deal with administrative disputes.

Shareholder State

To conclude this panorama, consider a contemporary feature of public action: the "shareholder state." The privatization program never produced the neutral state ideologues dreamt about. Most public services were put on the financial markets with the state as a shareholder. This new feature creates an identity crisis for the state. Should it behave like a normal shareholder? What should its proper role be? This new shareholder role puts the public right of ownership at the center of public action.

An agency was created to manage state assets: States Participations Agency (*Agence des participations de l'État*).[89] This agency's remit is to promote the proprietary interests of the state over all other goals.

Again, we are seeing a development whose rationale is the state's right of ownership, which requires civil servants to get involved in protecting and protecting the financial value of state assets. This type of action is far removed from traditional accountability mechanisms: Parliament can hardly understand the daily actions of this body, which nevertheless has a decisive impact on the delivery of public services but whose actions are not justiciable.

The Toulouse Airport case is interesting to study because it shows all the ambiguities of this new mission. The State Participations Agency signed a shareholders' agreement with the company that agreed to take over the airport in which the state's goals appeared to be captured. The contract actually transfers the decision to the private company.

Is the state as a shareholder still the state? The shareholders' agreement for the airport shows how the state can align its will to that of a private person and abdicate its other functions, especially its democratic ones. It pledges to conform to the will of the investor, a commitment appearing as the final stage in the privatization of the state.

In summary, this essay has attempted to provide insight into what neoliberalism could mean for administrative law. Our method consisted of identifying what was essential to classical administrative law in order to reflect on the structural changes that French administrative law is experiencing today.

Two adjectives describe the neoliberal administrative law agenda: it is both anti-liberal and anti-democratic. A neoliberal administration is stronger, less controlled, and less accountable than one that conforms to democratic values and the rule of law.

Notes

1 J. Freeman, Martha Minow, Government by Contract—Outsourcing the American Democracy, HUP, 2009; J. D. Michaels, Constitutional Coup: Privatization's Threat to the American Republic, HUP, 2017.

2 Quinn Slobodian, Globalists. The End of Empire and the Birth of Neoliberalism, HUP, 2018.

3 American readers may need to be reminded that "liberalism" in European legal discourse stands for a state that promotes individual freedom, the market economy, and limited state intervention. It is not associated with overall left-of-center social policies, as the term is used in the US.

4 J. Michaels, Constitutional Coup: Privatization's Threat to the American Republic, HUP, 2017.

5 J. Chevallier, L'élaboration historique du principe de séparation de la juridiction administrative et de l'administration active, LGDJ, 1970.
6 Law of 8 February 1995.
7 V. Conseil d'État, 16 février 2009, Société ATOM. (If an administrative penalty is challenged, the administrative judge is always given full powers to quash and vary a decision.)
8 Law of 16–24 août 1790, art. 13. This law gives administrative action immunity from any challenge. Revolutionaries feared judges. They were wary that they would paralyze the reforms of the French Revolution. Also see Decree of 16 fructidor an III (2 September 1795). This situation ended when Napoléon created the Conseil d'Etat in 1799.
9 Conseil constitutionnel, Decision n° 86–224 DC of 23 January 1987, Loi transférant à la juridiction judiciaire le contentieux des décisions du Conseil de la concurrence.
10 T. Perroud, « La Cour d'appel de Paris est-elle vraiment un juge administratif ? », Droit administratif, 2017 no 5, pp. 23–31.
11 T. Perroud, Décision Conseil de la concurrence, in J. Chevallier, J. Caillosse, D. Lochak, T. Perroud, Les grands arrêts politiques de la jurisprudence administrative, Lextenso, 2019.
12 Tribunal des conflits, 17 juin 2013, no 3911, Bergoend c. ERDF Annecy Léman; Tribunal des conflits, 9 décembre 2013, no 3931, Époux Panizzon c. Commune de Saint-Palais-sur-mer; Conseil d'État, ord., 23 janvier 2013, Commune de Chirongui, no 365262.
13 See for instance S. Hennette-Vauchez, La Démocratie en état d'urgence. Quand l'exception devient permanente, Seuil, 2022.
14 Public order is defined by: public security, public tranquility, public hygiene. The administrative authority is empowered by law to prevent all acts breaching them and the decision is reviewed by administrative courts.
15 Racist insult (Article 23 and 29 of the Law of 1881 on freedom of the press), racist defamation (Article 23 of the Law of 1881 on freedom of the press), or provocation to discrimination, hatred, or racist violence are punishable (Article 24 of the Law of 1881 on freedom of the press).
16 Circulaire du ministre de l'Intérieur à destination des préfets, Lutte contre le racisme et l'antisémitisme—manifestations et réunions publiques—Spectacles de M. Dieudonné M'Bala M'Bala, 6 janvier 2014.
17 Conseil d'Etat, ord., 9 janvier 2014, Ministre de l'Intérieur / Soc. Les Productions de la Plume et Dieudonné M'Bala M'Bala, n° 374508.
18 J. Petit, « Les ordonnances Dieudonné : séparer le bon grain de l'ivraie », AJDA, 2014, 866.
19 Conseil d'État, 9 November 2015, no 376107, concl. A. Bretonneau, AJDA, 2015 p. 2508; See also P. Bon, « Le but de la police administrative générale après l'affaire Dieudonné », RFDA, 2016, p. 791.
20 There is a general provision in the criminal code allowing administrative authorities to prosecute non-compliance with administrative acts or regulations: R. 610–5 of the Penal Code.
21 B. E. Harcourt, Neoliberal Penality, op. cit.
22 See L'urbanisme, pour un droit efficace, La Documentation française, 1992. Recently, Chr. Maugüé, Propositions pour un contentieux de l'urbanisme plus rapide et plus efficace, http://www.cohesion-territoires.gouv.fr/IMG/pdf/2018.01.11_rapport_contentieux_des_ autorisations_d_urbanisme.pdf.
23 Conseil d'État, Ass., 4 April 2014, no 358994, Département du Tarn-et-Garonne. The case allowing third parties to challenge the illegality of the award of an administrative contract is: Conseil d'État, 4 August 1905, Martin, Lebon, p. 749.

24 Conseil d'Etat, du 28 December 1906, no 25521.
25 Article L. 600–1-1 of the Urban Code.
26 For a critique see: T. Perroud, J. Graefe, The French Constitutional Council's Problem with Impartiality: The Constitutional Council's "Association La Sphinx" decision of 1 April 2022, VerfBlog, 2022/6/03.
27 Conseil d'État, 13 July 2019, Czabaj, no 387763.
28 R. 421–1 of the Code of administrative justice.
29 P. Cassia, « Le Conseil d'État abîme les principes de légalité et de sécurité juridique », Le Blog de Paul Cassia, 22 May 2018.
30 Conseil d'État, Ass., 21 March 2016, no 368082, Société Fairvesta International GmbH.
31 *Ibidem.*
32 See the detail described by C. Maugüe and C. Barrois de Sarigny, « 2018 : une nouvelle étape de la spécificité du contentieux de l'urbanisme », RFDA, 2019, p. 33.
33 F. Rolin, « Le droit administratif est-il au service du Grand Capital ? », AJDA, 2016, p. 921.
34 Conseil d'État, 12 June 2020, GISTI, no 418142.
35 The Conseil d'Etat in the Winkell case even accepted the laying off of public servants who had been on strike (Conseil d'Etat, du 7 août 1909, Winkell, no 37317).
36 Conseil d'État, 29 March 1901, Casanova, no 94580.
37 Conseil d'État, 30 May 1930, Chambre syndicale du commerce en détail de Nevers, Rec. Lebon, p. 583.
38 Conseil d'État, Ass., 31 May 2006, Ordre des avocats au barreau de Paris, no 275531.
39 Conseil d'État, Sect., 16 October 2000, Société Jean-Louis Bernard Consultants, no 222208. See also Conseil d'État, 10 July 2009, Département de l'Aisne, no 324156.
40 See Conseil d'État, 30 December 2014, Société Armor SNC, no 355563.
41 Conseil d'État, 16 October 2000, Compagnie méditerranéenne d'exploitation des services d'eau, RFDA, 2001 p. 106.
42 Conseil d'État, Guide des outils d'action économique, La Documentation française, 2018.
43 M. Foucault, op. cit., p. 136.
44 J. Le Grand, *The Other Invisible Hand: Delivering Public Services through Shoice and Competition* (Princeton University Press, 2007). See also J. Dixon, J. Le Grand, and P. Smith, Can Market Forces Be Used for Good? Kings Fund, 2003; « Quasi-Markets and Social Policy », The Economic Journal, vol. 101, no 408 (September 1991), pp. 1256–1267.
45 (« Quasi-Markets and Social Policy », art. cit. [n. 1], p. 1257).
46 See for instance the cases involving the combination of regulatory and commercial functions by public bodies that is deemed to be a breach of competition law by the ECJ: Italy v Commission ("British Telecommunications") [1985] ECR 510.
47 Conseil d'État, 3 November 1997, Société Yonne Funéraire, Société Intermarbres, Société Million et Marais, no 169907.
48 Conseil d'État, 26 March 1999, Société EDA, no 202260.
49 Conseil d'État, 22 November 2000, Société L et P Publicité SARL, no 223645.
50 Conseil d'État, 8 November 2000, Société Jean-Louis Bernard Consultants, no 222208.
51 Conseil d'État, Ass., 31 May 2006, Ordre des avocats au barreau de Paris, no 275531.
52 Code général de la propriété des personnes publiques in force since 1 July 2006.
53 Conseil d'État, Ass., 27 October 1995, Commune de Morsang-sur-Orge et Ville d'Aix-en-Provence.

54 P.-H. Teitgen, La police municipale : étude de l'interprétation jurisprudentielle des articles 91, 94 et 97 de la loi du 5 avril 1884, Sirey, 1934.
55 Conseil d'État, 18 December 1959, Société Les films Lutétia, no 36385.
56 P. Frydman, « L'atteinte à la dignité de la personne humaine et les pouvoirs de police municipale. À propos des 'lancers de nains' », RFDA, 1995, 1204.
57 Loi n° 2004–228 du 15 mars 2004 encadrant, en application du principe de laïcité, le port de signes ou de tenues manifestant une appartenance religieuse dans les écoles, collèges et lycées publics.
58 Loi du 9 décembre 1905 concernant la séparation des Églises et de l'Etat.
59 Conseil d'État, Ass., 9 November 2016, Commune de Melun c. Fédération départementale des libres penseurs de Seine-et-Marne, no 395122 and Conseil d'État, Ass., 9 November 2016, Fédération de la libre pensée de Vendée, no 395223.
60 See J. Chevallier, « La juridicisation des préceptes managériaux », Politiques et Management Public, vol. 11, no 4, 1993, pp. 111–134; J. Caillosse, L'État du droit administratif, LGDJ, 2017; La constitution imaginaire de l'administration : recherches sur la politique du droit administratif, PUF, 2008.
61 Conseil d'Etat, du 28 décembre 1906, syndicat des patrons coiffeurs de Limoges, no 25521.
62 Cour de Cassation, ch. mixte, 24 May 1975, no 73–13.556.
63 Conseil d'État, 20 October 1989, Nicolo, Rec. Lebon, p. 190.
64 Article 53 of the Constitution.
65 Conseil d'État, 31 May 2016, Mme Gonzalez-Gomez, RFDA, 2016, p. 755.
66 See, H. Jacquot, « Sur la règle de la compatibilité limitée en droit de l'urbanisme », in Mélanges en l'honneur d'Yves Jégouzo, Dalloz, 2009, p. 607 ; J. Trémeau, « L'urbanisme et le Palais-Royal », in Mélanges en l'honneur du président Bruno Genevois, Dalloz, 2008, pp. 1049–1062.
67 F. Grabias, La tolérance administrative, Dalloz, 2018, p. 49.
68 B. Plessix, « Le rescrit en matière administrative », Revue juridique de l'économie publique, no 657, October 2008, study 8; B. Plessix, « Le droit à l'erreur et le droit au contrôle », RFDA, 2018, p. 847; A.-L. Girard, « Le rescrit », RFDA, 2018, p. 838.
69 See Act of 9 December 2004 on the simplification of the law, empowering the government to take by ordinance any measure to "allow the taxpayer to invoke the doctrine and decisions of the administration relating to the rights and taxes collected and recovered according to the terms of the customs code" (24, 6) and to "allow taxpayers to invoke the circulars and ministerial instructions published; allow taxpayers to invoke the interpretation of the fiscal body on their situation regarding the legislation relating to contributions and social security contributions" (52, 1 and 2). See in social matters the ordinance of 6 June 2005. See P. Deumier, « La "doctrine administrative" : une interprétation opposable », RTD civ., 2006, 69.
70 B. Oppetit, « La résurgence du rescrit », D., 1991, 105.
71 Cass. soc., 17 July 1996: « en cas de conflit de normes, c'est la plus favorable au salarié qui doit recevoir application » (in the event of a conflict of rules, the rule most favorable to the employee must be applied). See P. Deumier, Introduction au droit, LGDJ, 2017, 4th ed., no 312.
72 The two expressions were coined by Fl. Canut and Fr. Géa, « Le droit du travail, entre ordre et désordre (première partie) », Droit social, 2016, 1038.
73 G. Cette, « On n'a pas tout fait contre le chômage de masse », Le Monde Économie, 4 March 2017 : « Dans une tribune au Monde, l'économiste Gilbert Cette (AFSE, université d'Aix-Marseille) plaide pour la réforme du SMIC et de la formation professionnelle, et l'inversion de la hiérarchie des normes conventionnelles. » See the report by P. Cahuc here : https://www.tresor.economie.gouv.fr/Ressources/12415_quelle-articulation-des-normes-en-droit-du-travail.

74 J.-D. Combrexelle, La négociation collective, le travail et l'emploi, Rapport au Premier ministre, France Stratégie, September, 2015.
75 Act 2018–727 of 10 August 2018 for a state serving a trustful society.
76 T. Tuot, Audition before the special committe of the Senate, 14 February 2018. G. Dumont, « La loi ESSoC, révolution ou involution ? », AJDA, 2018, p. 1815.
77 The term is from Dumont (n. 76).
78 Conseil d'État, Ass., 4 April 2014, Tarn-et-Garonne; P. Delvolvé, « Les limitations dans le temps de l'invocation des vices de forme et de procédure affectant les actes réglementaires—Des arguments pour ?», RFDA, 2018, p. 665.
79 P. Lascoumes, Des erreurs, pas des fautes : La gestion discrète du droit des affaires (Déviance et contrôle social), Centre de recherches sociologiques sur le droit et les institutions pénales, 1985; P. Lascoumes, G. Moreau-Capdevielle, Justice pénale et délinquance d'affaires, ministère de la Justice, 1983; E. Serverin, P. Lascoumes, T. Lambert, Transactions et pratiques transactionnelles : sujets et objets des transactions dans les relations conflictuelles de droit privé et de droit public. Economica, 1987.
80 Alex J. Feldman, Foucault's Concept of Illegalism, European Journal of Philosophy 28 (2): 445–462 (2020).
81 M. Foucault, Surveiller et punir : Naissance de la prison, Gallimard, 1993, esp. parts 2 and 4.
82 Alex J. Feldman, Foucault's Concept of Illegalism, art. cit., pp. 7–8.
83 P. Lascoumes, Des erreurs et pas des fautes, op. Cit., p. 129.
84 Conseil d'État, Ass., 17 June 1932, Ville de Castelnaudary; Const. Council., 10 March 2011, no 2011–625 DC, Loi d'orientation et de programmation pour la performance de la sécurité intérieure.
85 Chr. Hood and R. Dixon, in A Government that Worked Better and Costs Less? OUP, 2015.
86 J. Michaels, Constitutional Coup, Privatization's Threat to the American Republic, Harvard University Press, 2017.
87 *Ibidem*, p. 126.
88 T. Perroud, "Privatisation, Contrats Administratifs et Droits Fondamentaux. L'exemple du Marché Public du Stationnement Payant à Paris," RDLF 2020 chron. n° 82 (available here: http://www.revuedlf.com/droit-administratif/privatisation-contrats-administratifs-et-droits-fondamentaux-lexemple-du-marche-public-du-stationnement-payant-a-paris/).
89 Decree no 2004–963 of 9 September 2004 establishing.

8 Law and Monetary Policy

From Limited Judicial Review to Parliamentary Scrutiny in the European Monetary Union

Joana Mendes

During the decade-long process of EU integration, integration through law has placed the Court of Justice of the European Union (CJEU) at the center of the complex economic, political and social dynamics that have involved states, corporations and citizens in the shaping of EU law. At the same time, the deepening of integration, and of tensions between the legal orders of the Member States and of the Union, led the CJEU to extend the veil of the law to areas where judicial adjudication fits uneasily. Monetary policy is one such area: a contentious policy field where central banks' decisions diffusely and indirectly touch virtually every household and business, interacting with the political decisions of politically accountable governments.

At the height of the eurozone sovereign debt crisis, and later in a period of relative normalcy, the CJEU adjudicated two high-profile cases—*Gauweiler* and *Weiss*—in a largely similar manner.[1] It seemingly struck the delicate balance between, on the one hand, preserving the discretion of the European Central Bank (ECB) in exercising an EU exclusive competence and, on the other, setting boundaries assuring that the ECB acts lawfully when pursuing its mandate within the limits set by the Treaty norms. Legal interpretation, assisted by the deployment of legal principles—proportionality and reason-giving—purportedly have allowed the Court to provide judicial review suitable for the degree of complexity of monetary policy decisions, enabling it to control possible manifest errors of assessment, and, hence, filter out blatant instances of illegality of central bank decisions.[2] When the ECB also became active in banking supervision, the extension of the Court's customary administrative law–like methodology to the deeply political realm of money supply regulation seemed to preserve the rule-of-law canon of the EU: like any other institution, the ECB is subject to judicial review.[3] The matter was, nevertheless, hotly debated, when in May 2020 the German Federal Constitutional Court (FCC) set aside the CJEU judgment on *ultra vires* grounds, given the EU court's highly deferential examination of proportionality.[4]

This jurisprudential development is potentially relevant in comparative terms. In the US, there have been recent calls to critically assess whether the idiosyncratic features of central banking justify deviations from 'normal' administrative law recipes, and, specifically, how to attune judicial review to the

DOI: 10.4324/9781003416036-8

new world of central banking.[5] From this perspective, the solutions of EU law could be appealing. Against this background, this chapter takes the discussion of judicial review triggered by the *Gauweiler* and *Weiss* judgments as a starting point to assess the role that the legal principles deployed in judicial review can have in monetary policy.[6] It argues that those judgments have shown that the conventional methodology that the CJEU has applied to review complex technical assessments reveals the weaknesses, rather than the ability, of courts to control or structure the discretion exercised by central banks. Yet, the judgments do point the way to the role that the legal techniques developed by the CJEU—and, hence, the law that structures discretionary decision-making—may nevertheless have in a different institutional setting: the monetary dialogue between the ECB and the European Parliament. It has emerged as an institutional practice that aims to render the ECB accountable to the Parliament but which has important limitations as an accountability forum.

The chapter starts by outlining the main layers of legality that placed the CJEU at the core of constitutional turmoil in the EU and contrasts judicial review of monetary policy decisions in EU law and in US law. Despite the many pages that have already been dedicated to the *Gauweiler* and *Weiss* judgments of both the CJEU and the German FCC, it is important to return to them to contrast the positions of three different judiciaries on the possibilities of judicial review of monetary policy. None of these positions has convincingly justified *judicial* control over central bank measures. Yet, zooming in on the legal principles that were deployed in the conflicting judgments of the FCC and the CJEU in *Weiss*—proportionality, care and reasons—the chapter argues that they are, indeed, important tools to secure external scrutiny of central bank measures. They provide parameters of reasoning that the ECB must deploy in its decision-making and can unveil the value judgments that central bankers necessarily make when assessing the conditions, criteria and implications of monetary policy decisions and the processes through which they define the content of monetary policy. They can be used to assess how compromises between competing interests have been struck and, hence, to question and contest the choices made, and, possibly, through ex post scrutiny, change the course of monetary policy. Yet, even if law supports these processes, this is not a task for the courts, whose control necessarily leads to a binary outcome of legality/illegality. It is, on the contrary, a type of scrutiny that parliaments can and must deploy when enhancing the mechanisms through which they hold accountable one of the most powerful institutions in modern government and whose independence must not exempt it from public scrutiny. The chapter argues that the deployment of such legal principles can help to overcome some of the weaknesses of the "monetary dialogue" that emerged as the main institutional practice of the European Parliament in seeking to hold the ECB accountable. It concludes that this proposal cannot tackle the deep democratic challenges of the EMU, but can nevertheless help to improve the much-needed parliamentary scrutiny of the actions of the ECB.

Judicial Review of Monetary Policy Decisions: A Comparative Note

The European Central Bank before Two European Courts: Two Cases, Three Episodes of a Saga

The *Gauweiler* and the *Weiss* judgments were both triggered by the constitutional complaints of a group of German academics, lawyers and politicians who mobilized the FCC, and indirectly the CJEU, to act against two unconventional, monetary policy measures adopted by the European Central Bank (ECB): the ECB's Outright Monetary Transactions (OMT) program of 2012 and the Public Sector Purchase Programme (PSPP) of 2015. In their contention, the ECB was, through those programs, supporting the economies and financing the budgets of the Member States in need, in breach of its mandate and of the Treaty prohibition of monetary financing, and, as a result, of the sovereign rights of the German Parliament, as well as, by implication, their own right to vote. The formal link was straightforwardly formulated thus: "if the Bundestag . . . loses competences, the right to vote guaranteed [by the Constitution] loses substance."[7] Concretely, the constitutional complaints were directed at preserving the political economy model that the Treaty has enshrined, against the circumstances that, since the early 2010s, pushed the ECB to expand its actions beyond the strict price stability mandate that had guided the bank's operation before the global financial crisis. The bank had become the stronghold of secure financial stability in the eurozone through measures whose obvious economic effects no longer allowed the ECB to present itself as a technocratic institution insulated from political choices.

In her dissenting opinion to the FCC order in the *Gauweiler* case, judge Gertrude Lübbe-Wolff warned that the German court was putting itself in an impossible position in a double sense: not only had it held the action admissible in novel terms that lacked "determinative standards" set in previous case law;[8] but it also was wholly unclear what action would be required if the CJEU were to find the OMT decision *ultra vires*. In her view, lack of action by national sovereign institutions with regard to measures taken at the EU level could not be subject to a constitutional complaint in the case of *Gauweiler*, where the applicants protested the inaction of the German Parliament and Government that, they argued, amounted to a violation of German sovereign rights. If it had succeeded, there was no explicit constitutional mandate that specified in substantive terms "the content and reach of the alleged duty to act."[9] No rule determined what the German Parliament and Government would be *legally* bound to do with a view to remedying the claimed omission. Lübbe-Wolff was adamant: "one ought to refuse being sent on grand desert tours that will not lead to any spring."[10] The claims in *Gauweiler* did not succeed—both the CJEU and the FCC upheld the legality of OMT[11]—but the final outcome of *Weiss* confirmed Lübbe-Wolff's warnings more than seven years later.

Having overcome the admissibility hurdles, both at national and EU level, *Gauweiler* set the terms of judicial review that the CJEU later repeated in *Weiss*, despite the very different circumstances of the programs subject to review.[12] The main legal devices that have enabled the Court on both occasions to uphold the legality of the ECB measures were the following. First, the Court delimited the mandate of the ECB, specifically the boundaries between monetary and economic policy, by reference to the goals of the measures adopted and the need to preserve the transmission of monetary policy through the means chosen by the ECB.[13] Second, starting from the premise of the ECB's wide discretion, the CJEU applied a proportionality test and concluded that the ECB had committed no "manifest error of assessment" in determining the necessity and appropriateness of the measure.[14] Third, it identified the characteristics of the program that, in its view, prevented it from circumventing the prohibition of monetary financing.[15] In *Gauweiler*, the FCC accepted the CJEU ruling, and the constitutional claims were dismissed. A few years later it admitted the same constitutional complaints in relation to the PSPP. In its preliminary reference to the CJEU, the FCC expressed strong doubts on the proportionality of the program. Yet, this time, the FCC rejected the ruling of the CJEU, in a judgment that disrupted the world of European law for the months that followed its pronouncement in May 2020.[16] Its main objection was to the way the CJEU assessed the proportionality of the PSPP's intended monetary effects and the unintended economic side effects.[17] Although the FCC raised concerns about the CJEU's assessment that PSPP did not circumvent the prohibition of monetary financing, it accepted its position on this point.[18]

The position of the FCC could hardly have been stronger and demonstrated, a contrario, how proportionality *cannot* be a norm of judicial control of the ECB's discretion.[19] For the first time, it held that a legal act of an EU institution was not binding on Germany.[20] In its view, the CJEU had acted *ultra vires* by having "[accepted] positions asserted by the ECB without closer scrutiny" and "[allowing] the ECB to expand—gradually and in a manner that is not necessarily noticeable from the outset—its competences on its own authority."[21] Because of how the CJEU had applied proportionality, its judgment was "simply not comprehensible" and thus "objectively arbitrary." The turmoil that ensued, the judgment's strong terms and the manifold discussions around primacy seemed to signal a major turning point in EU law. And yet, within the deadline set by the Court, the president of the Bundestag and the German finance minister simply declared that the information that the Bundesbank had sent were sufficient to meet the proportionality assessment as the FCC had required.[22] In May 2021, "the FCC announced that there will be no further constitutional check of the documents."[23] The German Parliament and Government had acted as prompted by the FCC, but, aside from the regular use of the language of proportionality in the ECB measures and public speeches, little, if anything, was gained in terms of accountability of its actions. The "grand desert tours" manifestly did "not lead to any spring." Beneath the major clash between the two high courts that seemed to imperil the longstanding process of mutual constitutional adjustment, they had both revealed—in deeply distinct ways—their incapacity to weigh in on monetary policy measures adopted by an independent central bank.[24]

Non-Justiciability of the Fed's Monetary Policy Decisions

From a comparative perspective, the very possibility of judicial review of the monetary policy decisions of central banks appears an exception. In other jurisdictions, the outcome of the very few judicial challenges against central banks' monetary policy decisions seem to place them outside the realm of justiciability. This argument is advanced here solely by relying on US law.

Raichle v Federal Reserve Bank of New York, a federal appellate case from 1929, 16 years after the establishment of the Federal Reserve System, is the relevant precedent. It held that questions raised by measures pertaining to the setting of interest rates are, most likely, of a political nature.[25] In this judgment, despite the fact that the US Court of Appeals did not apply the political questions doctrine, it found "persuasive" the argument of the defendant that "upon the facts alleged the questions raised are political, and not justiciable."[26] In an oft-cited passage of that judgment, the Court held that:

> It would be an unthinkable burden upon any banking system if its open market sales and discount rates were to be subject to judicial review. Indeed, the correction of discount rates by judicial decree seems almost grotesque, when we remember that conditions in the money market often change from hour to hour, and the disease would ordinarily be over long before a judicial diagnosis could be made.[27]

The case pertained to the banks' actions to raise interest rates, for which the plaintiff claimed compensation for damages. The Court noted "the broad purposes of the Act and the wide powers of supervision and control given to the Federal Reserve Board over the whole Reserve System."[28] It also outlined the tools that the Federal Reserve Banks had at their disposal. The explicit mention in the enabling statute of purchases and sales in the open market meant that this was, in itself, a lawful tool. The question, then, was whether it had been rendered unlawful because of the purpose for which it had been mobilized: to reduce the volume of collateral or brokers' loans, the effect that had caused damage to the plaintiff, to increase interest rates.[29] In other words, the court assessed whether this tool and purpose had been appropriate. The Court saw no basis to consider it unlawful:

> We can see no basis for the contention that it is a tort for a Federal Reserve Bank to sell its securities in the open market, to fix discount rates which are unreasonably high, or to refuse to discount eligible paper, *even though its policy may be mistaken and its judgment bad.* The remedy sought would make the courts, rather than the Federal Reserve

> Board, the supervisors of the Federal Reserve System, and would involve a cure worse than the malady. . . . . If [the bank] proceeds in good faith through open market operations and control of discount rates to bring about a reduction of brokers' loans, it commits no legal wrong.[30]

The cited passages indicate that, in matters of monetary policy, accountability for monetary policy decisions is not a task for courts. One analysis, however, notes a detail that could unlock a possible judicial basis for review: bad faith on the part of the bank, however difficult to ascertain by courts, can generate a "legal wrong."[31] Still, *Raichle* stands today as a hallmark of central bank exceptionalism when it comes to judicially determined fetters on discretion, which make these powerful institutions mostly "invisible" in "court-centered [paradigms] of administrative law."[32] David Zaring summarizes the Fed's subjection to judicial review, in particular its Open Markets Committee (FOMC) as follows: "a combination of *Chevron* deference, unwilling potential plaintiffs, and, most importantly, the lack of a standard for reviewability identified by Judge Hand in *Raichle*, has made the agency extremely difficult to judicially supervise."[33] Supervision of the FOMC remains with the Federal Reserve Board, and the economic impacts that its monetary policy decisions may have on individuals remain an indirect and general effect of macroeconomic decisions.[34] On this account, these decisions should remain largely exempt from judicial review.

A Different Continent, a Different Time

Reasons similar to those the US Court of Appeals invoked in *Raichle* in 1929 arguably apply to gauging the effects of a program for the purchase of government bonds on the financing conditions and needs of Member States (at stake in *Weiss*). The deployment of instruments of monetary policy raises political questions that challenge justiciability. Yet, in the EMU, the law delimits the authority of the bank in terms that allow litigants to contest the political economic tenets of monetary policy decisions (as *Gauweiler* and *Weiss* illustrate).[35] Practice has shown since 2010 that even a narrow mandate of price stability can be redefined through administrative and judicial interpretation, showing the illusion of rule-bound monetary policy. But even as the ECB returned to the core business of interest rate regulation in 2022, in the aftermath of the Covid-19-induced economic slowdown and the rise of energy prices, the strong political stakes of monetary policy decisions are evident.[36] There are, therefore, important prudential reasons for limiting judicial review, beyond the vague justification that "questions of monetary policy are usually of a controversial nature."[37]

From this perspective the standard on which the CJEU settled, while not perfect, could stand for "meaningful oversight of the agency without unduly intervening in its zone of expertise," as called for across the Atlantic.[38] And yet, the judgment of the CJEU in *Weiss* gives little support to the conclusion that the Court is capable of exercising "meaningful oversight" over the actions of the ECB and, still less, that it has found its proper role as the overseer of legality in an area that, admittedly, presents a fundamental challenge. The Court simply confirmed the ECB's own position that it has "*full* discretion to use its instruments, as necessary to carry out its tasks and fulfil its mandate."[39] It sanctioned both the Treaty norms—the ECB defines monetary policy—and the institutional practice that has enabled the ECB to define the boundaries of its own mandate, through the policy measures it has adopted since its inception and, much more visibly, in the past decade.[40]

The Untapped Potential of the *Weiss* Saga[41]

The volumes of articles and commentaries written on *Weiss* focused on primacy, judicial dialogue and on different understandings of proportionality. However, they largely ignored the substantial issues behind the case: the meaning of central bank independence when the bank holds massive amounts of government and corporate bonds, and the viability of an EMU whose political economic tenets are virtually set in stone in Treaty norms.[42] Most analyses have also largely downplayed the transformative potential of the judicial clash. Beyond the criticism to both judgments, beyond the heated debate on the terms and possibilities of judicial "dialogue" between high courts, and beyond the contention over different interpretations of legal rules, the case of *Weiss* revealed the need to acknowledge and address the limits of proceeding through legal tweaking. In addition, it highlighted the dysfunctionality and deep democratic flaws of the EMU.[43] Yet, three years on, these issues linger, dormant in the apparent calm brought by the retreat of the ECB into inflation curbing and price stability. The tension between legal stasis (which *Weiss* ultimately reinforced) and central bank dynamism (arguably unstoppable), noted by Martin Höpner, has not subsided.[44]

Against this background, and failing Treaty reform, the quest continues for a "meaningful oversight" of the ECB that does not "unduly [intervene] in its zone of expertise" (however the limits of "unduly" interference may be defined). Here, too, both the FCC and the CJEU judgments in *Weiss* give important pointers, although neither judgment was able to advance them fruitfully.

Proportionality as a Procedural Requirement in the FCC Judgment

There is little doubt that the judgment of the FCC aimed at preserving the Maastricht settlement of a narrow Treaty mandate, as the ECB interpreted it in the first decade of its existence, and pursued by a depoliticized central bank. Its insistence on proportionality, however, belied that very settlement. By requiring that proportionality includes a "balancing of the competing interests" implicated by the consequences of the measure chosen by the ECB,[45] the FCC in fact assumed that what the ECB must do—and does—beyond a neutral and purely expertise-based monetary policy that can be distinguished from economic policy decisions that are the competence of the democratic institutions of the Member States, and coordinated at the EU level with the "support" of the ECB.[46] The FCC requested that "the program's monetary policy objective and its economic policy effects be identified, weighed and balanced against one another"; and that the ECB provide "a prognosis as to the PSPP's economic policy effects [and] an assessment of whether any such effects were proportionate to the intended advantages in the area of monetary policy."[47] It further identified that the "relevant economic policy effects of the PSPP" may include: "the risk of creating real estate and stock market bubbles as well as the economic and social impact on virtually all citizens, who are at least indirectly affected inter alia as shareholders, tenants, real estate owners, savers or insurance policy holders."[48] The Court seemed particularly concerned with the PSPP's "considerable risk of losses for private savings," specifically, pension schemes; the rise of real estate prices with "sharp increases—especially regarding residential property in major cities— . . ., which possibly already come close to creating a 'market bubble'"; with access to cheap credit that PSPP enabled, thereby "[allowing] economically unviable companies to stay on the market"; with "the risk that the ESCB becomes dependent on Member State politics as it can no longer simply terminate and undo the programme without jeopardizing the stability of the monetary union."[49]

The division of tasks in the relationship between the ECB and the reviewing court—the CJEU, which in this instance the FCC replaced—is clear according to the FCC. It is not up to the court "to decide . . . how such concerns are to be weighed exactly in the context of a monetary policy decision; rather, the point is that such effects, . . . must not be completely ignored"; "it would have been incumbent upon the ECB to weigh these effects and balance them, based on proportionality considerations, against the expected positive contributions to achieving the monetary policy objective the ECB itself has set."[50] That is not only because of the ECB's relative technical competence, but also because that operation enables the Court to control "whether it was still proportionate to tolerate the economic and social policy effects of the PSPP, problematic as they may be in respect of the order of competences, or, possibly, at what point they have become disproportionate."[51] In the case of *Weiss*, the "lack of balancing and lack of stating the reasons informing such balancing" meant that the ECB had breached proportionality as a requirement that guides the delimitation of competences in EU law.[52]

There is little point in rehearsing here the many critiques that this aspect of the judgment has raised.[53] What I wish to highlight is not whether the Court could have required such a balancing from the ECB (because it lacked the competence to adjudicate on the legality of an act of an EU institution, because it applied too strict a test of judicial review, or because it relied on a parochial approach to proportionality), but the procedural duty that the FCC derived from proportionality.[54] The FCC presumed that the principle of proportionality is a tool that can be deployed both as a norm of conduct by the

ECB and as a norm of control by the courts when controlling the exercise of monetary powers.

Care and Reasons as Procedural Requirements in the CJEU Judgment

The two courts converge with regards to the ability of judicial review to weigh in on matters of monetary policy. Their judgments are premised on the idea that general principles of law can be mobilized by the courts as a means of controlling their discretion, even if they resort to such principles in radically different ways. In addition to proportionality, the CJEU indicated in both *Gauweiler* and *Weiss* two other procedural duties: careful and impartial examination and the duty to give reasons. These feature often in case law that examines, in various fields of law, the bounds of legality in an exercise of discretion, in combination or isolated from a control of proportionality. In *Weiss*, in particular, the Court seemed to treat the review of monetary policy as just another instance of review of discretion.[55]

Yet, contrary to what it stated in both judgments, the CJEU did not deploy these legal principles to control the ECB's discretion, and it ended up couching in legal language the decision-making of the ECB—through its reasoning based on proportionality and care—without asserting control.[56] The problem here is not only the high degree of deferral given to the ECB decision, and, in particular, to its expertise, expressed by the Court when referring, in both judgments, to the principle of care ("given that questions of monetary policy are usually of a controversial nature and *in view of the ESCB's broad discretion, nothing more can be required* of the ESCB *apart from that it use its economic expertise* and the necessary technical means at its disposal to carry out that analysis *with all care and accuracy*").[57] The problem is that the Court took at face value the information the ECB provided and the arguments it put forward.[58] When looking for manifest errors of assessment—for which it conflated care and proportionality[59]—the Court examined the measure, its characteristics, against the justification given by the ECB, for the means chosen and the ends *as interpreted by the ECB*.[60] It did so, mostly, if not exclusively, based on the measure itself, without external references that could serve as normative yardsticks of assessment. This way of proceeding may be explained by the court's rules of procedure in preliminary reference actions, that condition the Court's inquisitorial powers, and justified by limited judicial review of monetary policy decisions. Yet, it remains true that these general principles of law have not operated as judicial safeguards that balance out the discretion of the authority subject to control. If they are to function as tools of *control* of discretion, care and proportionality require an examination of the decision-maker's process that must go beyond an analysis of the facts and arguments brought forward by the author of the measure challenged. They presuppose probing external evidence and assessing alternatives, or, at least, the processes followed to assess alternatives. Care, as a tool of control, presumes that there is some yardstick, external to the measure itself, that allows the court to assess the relevance of the factors considered. Proportionality requires, at least, that the adequacy and necessity of the measure be probed in view of possible alternatives. The Court of Justice did neither in its *Weiss* judgment. In the words of the much-criticized judgment of the FCC, the CJEU "[accepted] positions asserted by the ECB without closer scrutiny," in a way that cannot prevent a situation in which the ECB gets "to expand . . . its competences on its own authority."[61]

Regarding the duty to give reasons, the Court treated the PSPP decision as it does any act of the EU institutions. According to the formula that the Court also cited in *Weiss*, the statement of reasons:

> must show clearly and unequivocally the reasoning of the author of the measure in question, so as to enable *the persons concerned* to ascertain the reasons for the measure and to enable *the Court* to exercise its power of review, [but] it is not required to go into every relevant point of fact and law.[62]

This way of "proceduralising rationality" allows for a much-needed flexibility in adjusting judicial review of procedural duty to the circumstances of each case and avoiding turning it into review of the substantive legality of the act.[63] It also allows the Court to adapt a duty that applies indistinctly to all the legal acts of the institutions to their legal effects, e.g., by distinguishing the scope of the duty to state reasons of an individual measure and of a measure intended to have general application.[64] The EU courts consistently emphasize that the specific requirements of the duty to give reasons depend on the circumstances of each legal act, in particular, on the substance and wording of the measure, the nature of the reasons given, the interests that the persons directly and individually concerned may have in obtaining explanations, the context of the measure, and "the whole body of rules governing the matter in question."[65]

When deployed in judicial proceedings, the duty to give reasons operates as a norm of control, which, as the cited passage indicates, is instrumental for two purposes: to enable *the persons concerned* to ascertain the reasons for the measure and to enable *the Court* to exercise its power of review. This is also how the Court applied its case law on the duty to give reasons in *Weiss*: it outlined all the elements that had been brought before the Court, whether included in the decision under review or generally published by the ECB, considering that these "supplement the reasoning given in the decisions by setting out, in detail, the economic analyses underpinning the decisions, the various options considered by the Governing Council and the reasons justifying the choices made, in the light, in particular, of the observed and anticipated effects of the PSPP."[66] Only in one point it dismissed laconically the concerns of the FCC with regard to reasons. The CJEU considered that the absence of publication of details relating to the black-out period was outside the scope of the duty to give reasons, because "the purpose of such publication would be to show the precise content of the measures adopted by the ESCB rather than the reasons justifying those measures."[67]

This treatment of reasons in *Weiss* follows the longstanding case law of the Court. The problem does not lie here, but rather in the narrow function of the duty to give reasons when used as a tool of judicial review. As filtered through the case law of the Court, the duty to give reasons has lost its original wide scope in EU law.[68] This occurred because of the Court's need to strike a difficult balance between compliance with the duty to give reasons while being unable to review their substance, which is off-limits to the courts. The duty to give reasons has been enshrined in the Community Treaties since the 1950s, applicable first only to some of the acts of the High Authority of the European Coal and Steel Community and of the Commission and of the Council of the European Economic Community. This duty was, first and above all, "a guarantee against arbitrary action, [aimed at] enabling ***the public to understand and investigate the actions of the executive invested with important powers***."[69] In the case of monetary policy, there are two reasons to favor reviving the original meaning that the duty to give reasons had in EU law. First, the economic, social and political consequences of ECB decisions have far-reaching effects (which, in a model of monetary dominance, constrain significantly the fiscal policies of Member States). Second, the judicial review has had a very limited effect on reigning in monetary policy following the *Weiss* saga. Just like the other general legal principles that the CJEU mobilized in *Weiss*, the duty to give reasons served less to control than to support the strong powers that the ECB has acquired in the EU institutional system. But the realization of the potential that the duty of reasons—in the meaning it originally had in EU law—is not a task for the courts, but is one for the European Parliament and for national parliaments. The rest of the chapter develops this argument, by drawing on the economic dialogue that the ECB maintains with the European Parliament. Before proceeding, however, the next section clarifies the potential that these three *legal* principles have for "meaningful oversight" of the ECB.

Untapped Potential

The FCC resorted to the principle of proportionality as part of the balancing operation that the ECB must conduct to be sure that it fully considers the various socio-economic effects of the measures it pursues in carrying out its mandate. As Isabel Feichtner has argued, an obligation to evaluate the distributive effects of monetary policy measures—documented in one single procedure (in the guise of impact assessment reports)—would facilitate external scrutiny and could define the content of monetary policy.

The point, to be clear, is not to have "an *ex post* rationalization in a report" but a process of decision-making that considers alternatives in view of their effects, alternatives which may replace the originally planned course of action. Parliaments, as Feichtner indicates, should be the accountability fora for compliance with a principle of proportionality as a tool for gauging the distributive effects of monetary policy.[70] Given the lack of clarity about what interests must be balanced, if the court were to assess that balancing by deploying proportionality as a legal principle, it would manifestly go beyond what courts can do.[71] Determining "whether it was still proportionate to tolerate the economic and social policy effects of the PSPP . . ., or, possibly, at what point they have become disproportionate"[72]—or at what point economic implications become the primary objective of a measure and are not merely secondary to a monetary policy measure—is not something that can be ascertained on the basis of the law. The FCC presumed wrongly that the principle of proportionality could serve as a norm of control *by the courts* when controlling the exercise of monetary powers to this effect. In contrast, the same tool can be used by parliaments to force, through *ex post* controls, a process of self-reflection that the ECB must conduct and document in ways that make the stakes accessible, ascertainable and contestable by the European Parliament.

For this purpose, the principle of careful and impartial assessment offers a solid basis for an external scrutiny of how the ECB went about assessing relevant factors when carrying out the various studies that the preparation of monetary policy measures requires. Much like proportionality—applied in the demanding reading of the FCC—careful and impartial examination is a tool that can pierce through the complexity of decision-making and tease out the conditions, the criteria and the implications of monetary policy decisions. The fact that it has developed in EU law through case law, as an aspect of good administration, does not mean that it cannot also be used by the Parliament for that purpose. In fact, these tools cannot be deployed in monetary policy by the institution that developed them—the Court—without that scrutiny bringing it too close to a substitution of judgment. The lack of external legal yardsticks provided by legal norms challenges the judicial application of these principles. In addition, assessment by the Court can only lead to one of two outcomes: the legality or the illegality of a contested measure. It risks, therefore, distortions of policy decisions that can be detrimental to the ECB's mandate.[73] And yet, as the outcome of *Weiss* has demonstrated, a fully deferential approach to the expertise of the ECB is not a viable alternative. It amounts only to a semblance of control, which may "crowd out other forms of accountability"; by endorsing the legality of policy measures even if on thin grounds, it risks substituting for political debate.[74]

Proportionality and care, practiced by the ECB, must be accompanied by a duty to give reasons. In the original meaning this duty had in EU law, reasons ought not be provided to satisfy "persons concerned" or to support the task of reviewing courts, but, instead, to facilitate public understanding, even if only of a knowledgeable public, composed of Member States and of parliamentary representatives. The revival of this way of understanding the duty to give reasons is particularly needed when the actions of the ECB affect the economic policy decisions that are, constitutionally, the premise of the Member States, whether or not there has been a breach of the vertical division of competences. Such a statement of reasons is likely to reveal how different groups and interests are advantaged and disadvantaged by the ECB's policy measures. But it may not necessarily be the task for the Court reviewing the legality of judicially contested measures to enforce this constitutional dimension of the duty to give reasons. Even if it is a *legal* duty, its purpose is not to support judicial review of legality, or protect the rights of the persons concerned. Rather, this constitutional dimension is meant to support a public understanding of how the public actions of the EU institutions are contributing to the achievement of the objectives of EU integration. Concretely, it can enable a judgment of the compromise achieved between competing public interests, of the choices made by the decision-maker when defining a specific course of action, established through legally defined purposes. As such, the duty to give reasons functions as a self-regulatory measure for the deciding body, an instrument to facilitate a substantiated judgment of the conditions, criteria and implications of the acts it adopts. This process may not only facilitate a change in the content of monetary policy, given the opening of the decision-making procedure that it may enable, but it may also support the scrutiny of the political overseers and, in particular, of the European Parliament. This function of the duty to give reasons is arguably a component of the duty of cooperation that the deciding institutions owe to those that, in a democratic polity, must hold them to account.[75]

Like any other institution, the ECB is bound to abide by the law that brought it into existence, which is subject to different legal interpretations guided by varying policy choices. The principles of proportionality, care and reasons can unveil the intertwinement between legal interpretations and policy choices that ground the ECB's action. Outside the Court, they can serve as a channel to expand the range of actors who participate in the accountability fora of the ECB—not the Court or the persons concerned, seen as the litigants who have stakes in the case they brought to court, but the representatives of the citizens in the Parliament. By mobilizing the tools that the courts have developed for their function of control, parliamentarians are not restricted to the role of an impartial umpire who, in that role, must not cross the boundaries of what would be an "undue" interference with the powers that the Treaty legally warrants.

Two objections can be raised against applying this set of legal principles to the ECB: its independence and the possibility of fostering an undesirable amount of judicial litigation. Independence, however, cannot be understood as isolating the ECB from "meaningful scrutiny," nor can it be understood in the absolute terms that have enabled the ECB to decide the terms of its own mandate.[76] As much as the boundaries of ECB mandate have evolved, so too must the understanding of independence evolve under the Treaty. Its independence, much like its discretion, cannot be "full" to the point of obliterating substantive accountability to democratic institutions.[77] In addition, the ECB's high degree of independence is a reason *for*, not against, a closer scrutiny of its policy measures.

Even if done *ex post*, such scrutiny can, in time, influence the course of monetary policy that the ECB chooses and the considerations that it brings into its decision-making. Importantly, this change that, following Isabel Feichtner,

I indicate as a possible effect of applying a demanding view of proportionality, combined with care and reasons as just explained, need not happen in the form of instructions to the ECB. Legally, it cannot. By force of Article 130 TFEU (Treaty on the Functioning of the European Union), the ECB cannot receive instructions from any Union or national institution, and these must not seek to influence either the ECB or national central banks. But changes can come from within the institution, triggered by successive processes of *ex post* scrutiny, in which a larger scope of interlocutors of the ECB—not only the markets but also political overseers—assesses the terms of the ECB's policy measures with formal *and* material powers of accountability. Surely, the combined application of general legal principles in support of heightened parliamentary scrutiny does not suffice to induce such a result. What I propose here—focused only on the role of general principles of law—must be one element among other mechanisms of accountability. Namely, the European Parliament has called for "a more meaningful advisory role in the appointment process" in the procedure to appoint members of the ECB's Executive Council, on which it is consulted.[78]

Finally, and turning to the second possible objection, the heightened parliamentary accountability stemming from mobilizing legal principles may indeed create incentives for judicial litigation. The EU courts could be faced with more legal challenges that may strike at the core of the ECB discretion, as *Gauweiler* and *Weiss*. Yet, two points counter this objection. First, the full deference to the discretion of the ECB that the Court upheld in the two instances and the ensuing light-touch deployment of proportionality and reasons are arguably important deterrents to litigants seeking a judgment of illegality of monetary policy decisions. Second, if such cases arise, a light-touch type of scrutiny—although not the full empowerment that *Weiss* enabled—can be further justified *if* a stronger "meaningful scrutiny" is being exercised by other account holders. That is not the case currently, as will be seen in the next section. In those conditions, judicial review could be part of a triangular relationship of accountability that involves the parliament and the courts.

Parliamentary Scrutiny of ECB

The accountability of the ECB towards the European Parliament draws essentially on the Monetary Dialogue. The "dialogue" refers to the exchange of information that occurs in quarterly meetings between the Parliament's ECON Committee and the ECB President, based on MEPs' questions on the ECB's conduct of monetary policy.[79] This institutional practice resulted from the initiative of the Parliament and the willingness of the ECB to draw on the ECB's duty to "address an annual report on the activities of the ESCB and on the monetary policy of both the previous and current year to the European Parliament."[80] As such, this norm provides for a very limited channel of accountability (although it has, since 2016, generated an exchange between the two institutions in the form of ECB statements).[81] The motivations of the Parliament are well documented in a report of 1998. Starting from the premises that "monetary policy is not . . . neutral" and that "the independence of a central bank bestows upon it a weighty responsibility for economic and social development," the Parliament noted the ECB's "unprecedented degree of independence," the significance of the power to define price stability and, thereby, influence economic growth, investment and employment.[82] Such power, the Parliament noted, requires a corresponding "high degree of transparency of monetary-policy decisions" and a "high level" of democratic accountability, unmatched by the "embryonic form" envisaged in the Treaty.[83] The Parliament also added that demanding democratic accountability can support a "high degree of credibility and trustworthiness of the future ECB."[84]

Since the outset, the ECB seems to have been convinced of the advantages of establishing regular contacts with the Parliament, but the forum has proven a rather limited means to effectively scrutinize the ECB.[85] In 2009, an analysis of the first decade of monetary dialogue noted that the discussions lacked focus and were superficial; in this light, the willingness of the ECB to subject itself to parliamentary scrutiny was more window dressing than effective commitment to democratic accountability.[86] Recent studies have confirmed the limits of monetary dialogue and its weaknesses as a form of substantive accountability.[87] Lack of focus and of interaction remain a problem, with commentators suggesting the need for "a more inquisitive style of questioning" and for opportunities of follow-up questions.[88] Diessner, in particular, pointed out the "acute awareness" of MEPs "of the limited input into the EBC's decision-making," which he attributes to the ECB's extreme independence.[89] Yet, as much as this extreme independence has been an institutional practice in the two decades of the ECB's existence, it stems from an understanding of the degree of independence that is not a necessity under the wording of Article 130 TFEU. Although EPs cannot give instructions to the Bank, independence cannot be a limit to close scrutiny of the ECB's past actions. The Treaty is sparse in defining the ECB's accountability, but nothing in its wording indicates that a high degree of independence must not be followed by a demanding degree of accountability, as requested by the Parliament since the outset and in line with the various public statements of members of the ECB in this regard.[90] The EP can pass an *ex post* substantiated judgment on the merits of the ECB's monetary policy decisions, on the conditions of their adoption, on the criteria that led to the specific configurations of a decision or a program and on its implications. Passing a substantiated judgment *ex post facto* does not amount to "seek or take instructions" that Article 130 TFEU precludes.

The much-needed improvements to make the EP an effective accountability forum for monetary policy require, in addition to suggestions to change the format and composition of the meetings, that the MEPs' requests for information and justification on how the ECB delivers its mandate be focused, relevant and significant.[91] The deployment of the principles of proportionality and of careful and impartial examination by MEPs in the quarterly meetings can support this process, both at the preparation stage and by informing follow-up questions. They provide a reasoning structure that can guide both decision-making and the processes of control of those decisions. They enable MEPs to pierce through the political and technical complexity involved in monetary policy decisions. As much as they allow courts to tap into the logic of executive decision-making, assess the reasonableness of decisions taken in the exercise of discretion and how the examination conducted by the decision-makers supported the technical and value judgments that their decisions incorporate, they can also support the Parliament in the same process. If used to strengthen the monetary dialogue, they will be part of a process that is intended to trigger political debate, to probe alternatives and to facilitate a substantiated judgment, without the constraints of a binary decision of legality/ illegality. The lack of sanction—which several commentators pointed out as a weakness of the monetary dialogue—is not a necessary obstacle to substantive accountability, if the process of information exchange and justification can deliver a public justification that can espouse an informed contestation, balance out the information asymmetry and, thereby, create an actual "dialogue" which, in turn, can influence the course of future actions of the ECB.

Integration through Law by the Parliament, Not Democracy

Integration through law has been the "most powerful narrative of EU law."[92] Although it dominated throughout much of the decades that preceded the European sovereign debt crisis, the developments of EU integration that have unfolded since have arguably shown the limits of this way of conceiving the role of law in the EU. Other perspectives are emerging and my proposal to rely on law to counterbalance the power that the ECB retains in the EMU governance structure may seem, at the very least, anachronistic. As long as the EMU retains its original design, the power imbalances that it crystalizes will be maintained.[93] The "legal fix" through general principles to induce contestation within the process of monetary policy decision-making, a democratic debate and justification of these decisions mediated through parliamentary accountability, will operate against the background of Treaty norms that were *meant* to insulate the ECB not only from national governmental politics but also from the other EU institutions.[94]

The constraints on democracy that stem from the over-constitutionalization of the Treaties are particularly strong in the case of the EMU.[95] These are institutional, since fundamental political trade-offs involved in setting interest rates and inflation targets are entrusted to a central bank that has acquired an unparalleled degree of independence.[96] But, importantly, they are also substantive. The Treaty perpetuates a monetarist paradigm of political economy: price stability is *the* goal of monetary policy, which must be attained without prejudice to supporting economic policy goals (Articles 119(2) and 127(1) TFEU); money is a neutral medium of economic exchange, inflation a quantitative phenomenon regulated through interest rates and, in any event, without interferences in the functioning of "an open market economy with free competition, favouring an efficient allocation of resources" (Articles 119(2), 127(1) and 123 TFEU); the participating states must ensure sound public finances (Articles 119(3), 123 and 126 TFEU). This framework defines at a constitutional level the boundaries within which any redistributive choices ensuing from monetary policy decisions are taken. The Treaty, therefore, favours specific policy outcomes in the trade-offs that must be struck between competing policy interests implicated in monetary policy decisions.[97] As such, it closes off the possibilities of open and inclusive monetary policy making that I propose could follow from a heightened parliamentary accountability.

My proposal in this chapter is intended to force a democratic deliberation and justification that was avoided by design when the EMU was set up. It faces at least two hurdles. First, the current EMU is built on a purposeful depoliticization of money, that served not only the deepening of European integration but also the preferences of governments to avoid responsibility for the distributional choices entailed in monetary policy decisions.[98] Second, if governments have abdicated political responsibility for controversial—and, potentially, politically costly—decisions, parliamentarians may also wish to hide behind the ECB independence to shy away from the type of substantive accountability that I am advocating.[99] Since the sovereign debt crisis, however, the subjugation of the economic policies of elected national governments to the monetary stance of the ECB lost the benefit of the technocratic justification for the ECB's independence and the appearance of neutrality that the ECB had secured. That subjugation persists no matter whether the ECB decides to pursue expansive or restrictive monetary policies, and how it may perceive its role at a given point in time. Maintaining the current EMU design means maintaining a managerial modus of economic government, alienated from democratic processes, that restricts these processes also fundamentally at the national level.[100] Neither Treaty norms nor a return to the "normal" business of central bankers of curbing inflation that we are witnessing in 2023 can hide the eminently political character of the regulation of money. Parliamentarians may be aware that the political costs of lack of accountability may be higher than pursuing the non-consequential forms of dialogue that has existed hitherto.

As long as the EMU operates within the current Treaty framework, the proposal I make cannot amount to any form of democratization. Yet, I would like to suggest that, in the current stage of the EMU, giving more importance to the law in monetary policy as a support of parliamentary accountability can be a means to open possibilities of limited reform within the current Treaty framework. It can be a step in the direction of increased parliamentary scrutiny, which, short of Treaty reform, remains an important step to take. It can unveil the political stakes of the criteria of monetary policy decisions as well as its implications and, possibly, in conjunction with other triggers, force the consideration of alternatives. Presently, the evolution of central banking and the transformations that the interpretation of the Treaty—*a contrario sensu* if need be—fall within the sole purview of the central bank, within a system that includes the national central banks. Formal account holders—be they courts or parliaments—must find ways to be effective voices in that process.

Notes

1 Case C-62/14, *Gauweiler*, Judgment of the Court (Grand Chamber) of 16 June 2015, ECLI:EU:C:2015:400 (henceforth, *Gauweiler*), and C-493/17, *Weiss*, Judgment of the Court (Grand Chamber) of 11 December 2018, ECLI:EU:C:2018:1000 (henceforth, *Weiss*).
2 K. Lenaerts, "Proportionality as a Matrix Principle Promoting the Effectiveness of EU Law and the Legitimacy of EU action—Keynote Speech," in ECB Legal Conference 2021, *Continuity and Change—How the Challenges of Today Prepare the Ground for Tomorrow* (2022), 27–42, 30–33 (https://www.ecb.europa.eu/pub/pdf/other/ecb.ecblegalconferenceproceedings202204~c2e5739756.en.pdf).
3 Referring to "the methodological approach followed by the Court," idem, 33.
4 BVerfG, Judgment of the Second Senate of 5 May 2020—2 BvR 859/15, ECLI: DE:BVerfG:2020:rs20200505.2bvr085915 (henceforth, 'FCC, *Weiss*').
5 P. Conti-Brown, Y. Listokin and N. R. Parrillo, "Towards an Administrative Law of Central Banking" (2021) *Yale Journal on Regulation* 38(1), 1; S. Ostrowski, "Judging the Fed" (2021) *Yale Law Journal* 131(2), 726.
6 This chapter advances the argument I first made in J. Mendes, "Constitutive Powers and Justification: The Duty to Give Reasons in EU Monetary Policy," forthcoming in M. Dawson et al. (eds.), *Towards Substantive Accountability in EU Economic Governance* (CUP, forthcoming), where I ask whether law can support political accountability, irrespective of concrete instances of judicial review.
7 Peter Huber (2019), "The ECB under the Scrutiny of the *Bundesverfassungsgericht*," in ECB Legal Conference 2019, "Building Bridges: Central Banking Law in an Interconnected World" (April 2019), pp. 28–46 at p. 36 (https://www.ecb.europa.eu/pub/pdf/other/ecb.ecblegalconferenceproceedings201912~9325c45957.en.pdf).
8 The Court held their plea admissible based on a possible breach of the right to vote protected by Article 38(1) of the German Basic Law before an *ultra vires* act of the ECB.
9 Dissenting Opinion of Justice Lübbe-Wolff on the Order of the Second Senate of 14 January 2013, ECLI:DE:BVerfG:2014:rs20140114.2bvr272813, para 16 to 20.
10 Idem, para 23. She added: "the problem of indeterminateness and indeterminability of what is positively due . . . will remain virulent as a problem of indeterminateness and, accordingly, unenforceability of what the Court decides" (para 24). For an exhaustive analysis of the other constitutional dimensions of this reference, see, among many, M. Wendel, "Exceeding Judicial Competence in the Name of Democracy: The German Federal Constitutional Court's OMT Reference" (2014) *European Constitutional Law Review* 10(2), 263.
11 Among the many analyses of the case, its outcome is documented here: A. Pliakos and G. Anagnostaras, "Saving Face? The German Federal Constitutional Court Decides Gauweiler" (2017) *German Law Journal* 18(1), 213.
12 On these differences, see M. Dani et al., "It's the political economy . . .! A moment of truth for the eurozone and the EU" (2021) *International Journal of Constitutional Law* 19(1), 309.
13 *Gauweiler*, para 46–52; *Weiss*, para 53–70.
14 *Gauweiler*, para 66–92, in particular para 74 and 75; *Weiss*, para 56 and 71–97, in particular 73 and 91.
15 *Gauweiler*, para 93–127; *Weiss*, para 102 and following.

16 See, among many, the special collection "European Constitutional Pluralism and the PSPP Judgment," *German Law Journal* 2020 24(4) and the symposium on "The PSPP Judgment of the Bundesverfassungsgericht," *International Journal of Constitutional Law* 2021 19(1).
17 FCC, *Weiss*, para 153 and 176–178.
18 FCC, *Weiss*, para 184 and 197.
19 This argument has been developed in more detail in Dani et al. (n 12) and Mendes (n 6).
20 Para 119.
21 FCC, *Weiss*, para 142 (in relation to the objectives of the measure) and para 156 (in relation to the CJEU's application of the principle of proportionality).
22 D. Utrilla, "Three Months after Weiss: Was Nun?" EU Law Live, 5 August 2020 (https://eulawlive.com/three-months-after-weiss-was-nun/).
23 German Federal Constitutional Court judgment of 18 May 2021 2 BvR 1651/15 ECLI:DE:BVerfG:2021:rs20210429.2bvr165115.
24 For detail, see Dani et al. (n 12).
25 *Raichle v. Federal Reserve Bank of New York*, 34 F.2d 910 (2d Cir. 1929), 15 July 1929.
26 See, further, Ostrowski (n 5), 752 (holding that Raichle "somewhat blurs the line between non-justiciability and extreme deference," yet concluding that "at bottom, it matters little whether this precedent is best read as a merits decision subject to enormous deference or a holding on justiciability—the takeaway is the same").
27 *Raichle*, at 915, cited at S. Egidy, "Judicial Review of Central Bank Actions: Can Europe Learn from the United States?" in ECB Legal Conference 2019, "Building Bridges: Central Banking Law in an Interconnected World" (2019), pp. 53–76, 57 (https://www.ecb.europa.eu/pub/pdf/other/ecb.ecblegalconferenceproceedings201912~9325c45957.en.pdf); D. Zaring, "Law and Custom on the Federal Open Market Committee" (2015) *Law and Contemporary Problems* 78(3), 157, at 175; and Ostrowski (n 5), 735.
28 *Raichle*, at 913.
29 *Raichle*, at 915. The plaintiff had argued that "the bank during the year 1928 illegally engaged in a course of conduct, which it is still continuing, that had for its object an arbitrary reduction of brokers' loans and a general reduction of security prices"; furthermore, the Federal Reserve Bank had "'arbitrarily and unreasonably raised' the rediscount rate which it charges to its member banks, 'for the purpose and with the effect of raising interest rates generally" with the result that "interest rates [had] become unreasonable, and plaintiff [had been damaged by being obliged to pay such rates for borrowed money, and by having the value of his securities depreciated through the sale of securities by persons unwilling or unable to pay these rates" (*Raichle*, at 911).
30 *Raichle*, at 915, emphasis added.
31 Egidy (n 27) 58, identifying here an "outer limit" to the wide deference of *Raichle*.
32 Conti-Brown (n 5) 5.
33 Zaring (n 27) 175. See, further, p. 176. On the changes of the Federal Reserve System, see, succinctly, Ostrowski (n 5), 735–736.
34 Which explains the lack of standing: Conti-Brown et al. (n 5), 5, footnote 13.
35 See, further, "Parliamentary Scrutiny of ECB" below.
36 Discussing the nature of inflation and showing its political stakes, see I. Weber et al., "Inflation in Times of Overlapping Emergencies: Systemically Significant Prices from an Input–Output Perspective" (2022) Economics Department Working Paper Series 340. See also A. Tooze, "Now Is a Time of Tough Choices—Including on the 2% Inflation Target," *Financial Times*, 29 June 2023.
37 *Weiss*, para 90: *Gauweiler*, para 75.

38 Ostrowski (n 5), 761.

39 https://www.ecb.europa.eu/ecb/orga/accountability/html/index.en.html (accessed 27 June 2023, emphasis added).

40 Mendes (n 6). The different proposals on the interpretation of the ECB's mandate that have been advanced since 2021, following the ECB's strategic review, fail to address a fundamental point: in the current state of EU law, the ECB gets to choose which of the many goals of the secondary mandate it gets to pursue and this is a fundamental political choice (see, in particular, M. Ioannidis and C. Zilioli, "Climate Change and the Mandate of the ECB: Potential and Limits of Monetary Contribution to European Green Policies" (2022) *Common Market Law Review* 59(2), 363 and N. de Boer and J. van 't Klooster, "The ECB, the Courts, and the Issue of Democratic Legitimacy after Weiss" (2020) *Common Market Law Review* 57(6), 1717). The fact that its choice for climate change can be explained through a policy of appointments (J. Deyris, "Too Green to Be True? Forging a Climate Consensus at the European Central Bank" (2023) *New Political Economy*) and the argument that, unlike in other policy areas, climate change is guided by strict benchmarks set by political institutions (see Ioannidis and Zilioli, idem) does not alleviate the democratic concerns raised by leaving such a choice in the hands of an extremely independent institution.

41 This section draws on arguments briefly advanced in J. Mendes, "General Principles of Law in Monetary Policy: In the Hands of Courts?" in D. Fromage (ed.), *Jacques Ziller: A European Scholar* (European University Institute, 2022), 2–14, DOI: 10.2870/098663.

42 Treaty revision has become politically untenable and, yet, central bank policies changed throughout the world. Among many, A. Tooze, "The Death of the Central Bank Myth," Foreign Policy, 13 May 2020.

43 Dani et al. (n 12), arguing that Weiss represented a missed opportunity for constitutional transformation.

44 Martin Höpner, "Proportionality in the PSPP Saga: Why Constitutional Pluralism Is Here to Stay and Why the Federal Constitutional Court Did Not Violate the Rules of Loyal Conduct" (2022) *European Papers* 6(3), 1527, at 1535–1536.

45 FCC, *Weiss*, para 138.

46 Article 127 TFEU. See, on this argument, de Boer and van 't Klooster (n 40).

47 FCC, *Weiss*, para 165 and 168.

48 Idem, para 173.

49 Idem, para 173–175.

50 Idem, para 173 and 176.

51 Idem, para 176.

52 Idem, Weiss, para 177.

53 See, among many, M. Wendel, "Paradoxes of Ultra-Vires Review: A Critical Review of the PSPP Decision and Its Initial Reception" (2020) *German Law Journal* 21(5), 979.

54 See also I. Feichtner, "The German Constitutional Court's PSPP Judgment: Impediment and Impetus for the Democratization of Europe" (2020) *German Law Journal* 21(5), 1110.

55 *Weiss*, para 30 ("in situations such as that at issue in the present case, in which an EU institution enjoys broad discretion, a review of compliance with certain procedural safeguards—including the obligation for the ESCB to examine carefully and impartially all the relevant elements of the situation in question and to give an adequate statement of the reasons for its decisions—is of fundamental importance").

56 On this point, I am using the analysis that appeared in Mendes (n 41).

57 *Gauweiler*, para 75; *Weiss*, para 90, emphasis added.

58 *Weiss*, para 74 ("it follows from recital 3 of Decision 2015/774, from the documents published by the ECB . . . and from the observations submitted to the

Court"), 75 ("it can be seen from the documents before the Court"), 76 (restating recital 4 of Decision 2015/774), para 77 (relying on statements of the ECB). The reasoning includes general references to "observations" and "documents" that refer, presumably, to all that can be submitted to the Court according to Article 23 of the Statute, as well as those that the Court may request according to Article 24 of the Statute. See also *Weiss*, para 80 (where the Court situates its examination of whether PSPP went "manifestly beyond what is necessary" to maintain price stability in the context of PSPP, as described by the ECB); para 82 and 83 to 92. The effects of successively renewed short periods, which the Court mentions, are not identified in the judgment (para 85 and 86); there is only a circular mention to the necessity of the PSPP based on the temporary nature of the program: "the PSPP has, from the start, been intended to apply only during the *period necessary for attaining the objective sought* and is therefore temporary in nature" (para 84). Similarly, the effects of the limitations placed on the volume of bonds that may be acquired was also not identified (para 87 to 89); also here one is confronted with a circular reference: "that amount . . . was regularly revised in order to *restrict it to what was necessary in order to achieve the stated objective*" (para 88).

59 V. Kosta, "Proportionality and Discretion in EU Law: In Search of Clarity," in ECB Legal Conference 2021, *Continuity and Change—How the Challenges of Today Prepare the Ground for Tomorrow* (2022) pp. 98–102.

60 *Weiss*, para 78 and 91.

61 FCC, *Weiss*, para 142 (in relation to the objectives of the PSPP) and para 156 (in relation to the application of proportionality). Similarly, Egidy (n 27).

62 *Weiss*, para 31, emphasis added.

63 P. Craig, *EU Administrative Law*, 3rd ed. (OUP, 2018), 318–320. The term "proceduralising rationality" is from J. L. Mashaw, *Reasoned Administration and Democratic Legitimacy. How Administrative Law Supports Democratic Government* (CUP, 2018), 117. The analysis on reasons that follows has been much expanded in Mendes (n 6).

64 As reflected in *Weiss*, para 32.

65 *Weiss*, para 33, which does not include the specification of all these parameters but follows this same line (for those, see, among many, Case C-15/10, *Etimine v Secretary of State for Work and Pensions*, ECLI:EU:C:2011:504, para 114, or Case T-122/15, *Landeskreditbank v ECB*, ECLI:EU:T:2017:337 para 124).

66 *Weiss*, para 36 (the analysis on the duty to give reasons is in para 30 to 43).

67 *Weiss*, para 43.

68 J. Mendes, "The Foundations of the Duty to Give Reasons and a Normative Reconstruction," E. Fisher, J. King and A. Young (eds.), *The Foundations and Future of Public Law* (OUP, 2020), 299–321.

69 Joined Cases 36, 37, 38–59 and 40–59, *Präsident et al. v High Authority*, Opinion AG Lagrange, at 451 (emphasis added), cited and analyzed by Mendes, idem, 313–314. On the scope of the duty, see Article 15 of the Treaty establishing the European Coal and Steel Community (Article 30 imposed the same duty on the judgments of the Court) and Article 190 of the Treaty establishing the European Economic Community.

70 Feichtner (n 54) 1100.

71 On how this lack of determination affects the application of the principle of proportionality in monetary policy, see S. Egidy, "Proportionality and Procedure of Monetary Policy-Making" (2021) *International Journal of Constitutional Law* 19(1), 292–293, and Toni Marzal, "Making Sense of the Use of Proportionality in the Bunderverfassunsgericht's PSPP Decision" (2020) *Revue des Affaires Européennes* 2, 441.

72 FCC, *Weiss*, para 176.

73 I take this point from Mendes (n 41).

74 Egidy (n 27) 69.
75 Article 13(2) TEU ("The institutions shall practice mutual sincere cooperation") read in coordination with Article 10(1) and (2) TEU arguably give textual support to a legal duty as proposed in the text.
76 See further, Mendes (n 6).
77 See further, Dawson et al. (n 6). On the claim of "full discretion," see n 39.
78 European Parliament Resolution of 10 February 2021 on the European Central Bank Annual report 2020 (2020/2123(INI)), point 35. On the importance of appointments for ideational changes, see Deyris (n. 40).
79 For details, see R. Lastra, "Accountability Mechanisms of the Bank of England and of the European Central Bank," Study for the Committee on Economic and Monetary Affairs, Policy Department for Economic, Scientific and Quality of Life Policies, European Parliament, 2020, p. 24; K. Whelan, "Accountability at the Fed and the ECB," Study for the Committee on Economic and Monetary Affairs, Policy Department for Economic, Scientific and Quality of Life Policies, Luxembourg, 2020, 17; G. Claeys and M. Domínguez-Jiménez, "How Can the European Parliament Better Oversee the European Central Bank?" Study for the Committee on Economic and Monetary Affairs, Policy Department for Economic, Scientific and Quality of Life Policies, Luxembourg, 2020, 20.
80 Article 284(3) TFEU (replicated in Article 15.3 of the Protocol (No 4) on the Statute of the European System of Central Banks and of the European Central Bank (OJ C 202/230). The same report needs to be addressed to the Council and the Commission, and also to the European Council. On the legal framework of the ECB's parliamentary accountability, see F. Amtenbrink and K. van Duin, "The European Central Bank before the European Parliament: Theory and Practice after 10 Years of Monetary Dialogue" (2009) *European Law Review* 34(4), 561, at 565–570, pointing out the proactive roles of the EP and of the ECB in establishing the monetary dialogue and the significance of this practice against the background of very thin legal provisions.
81 European Parliament Resolution of 25 February 2016 on the European Central Bank Annual Report for 2014 (2015/2115(INI)), para 35; feedback on the input provided by the European Parliament as part of its resolution on the ECB Annual Report 2014 (https://www.ecb.europa.eu/pub/pdf/other/20160407__feedback_on_the_input_provided_by_the_european_parliament_en.pdf). Codifying this practice, see European Parliament Decision of 1 June 2023 on the arrangements in the form of an exchange of letters between the European Parliament and the European Central Bank on structuring the practices for interaction in the area of central banking (2023/2026(ACI)), under ECB's Annual Report.
82 European Parliament, "Report on Democratic Accountability in the 3rd Phase of EMU 23 March 1998," Committee on Economic and Monetary Affairs and Industrial Policy, Rapporteur: Mrs Christa Randzio-Plath, points 1 and 2. (I am using the French version, which reads at points differently from the English translation "L'indépendance d'une banque centrale lui confère une lourde responsabilité au niveau du développement économique et social.")
83 The corresponding yardstick is clear in the text of the resolution that followed the report: European Parliament, "Resolution on Democratic Accountability in the Third Phase of EMU" (OJ C 138, 04/05/1998) p. 177, point 4.
84 Report on democratic accountability, point 5.
85 Amtenbrink and van Duin (n 80), 570.
86 Idem, 581–582. ("For the ECB president the current arrangements provide him with the perfect venue to parade his openness in the conduct of monetary policy and the ECB's readiness to subject itself to external review of its performance.")
87 On substantive accountability, see Dawson et al. (2023) (n 6); see also M. Dawson et al., "Reconciling Independence and accountability at the European Central Bank:

The False Promise of Proceduralism" (2019) *European Law Journal* 25(1), 75. In detail, on the limits, see S. Diessner, "The Promises and Pitfalls of the ECB's 'Legitimacy-as-Accountability' towards the European Parliament Post-Crisis" (2022) *The Journal of Legislative Studies* 28(3), 402 405–410. Noting that "dialogue" can be just a "'lecture' or statement by the ECB President to MEPs," see Lastra (n 79), 28; observing that it "is not well suited to the necessary detailed exploration of the various complex monetary policy issues that have emerged in recent years," see Whelan (n 79), 17.

88 Whelan (n 79), 17. Stressing the same lack of focus already noted in 2009, see Claeys and Domínguez-Jiménez (n 79), 12. No changes to the current practice appear in the recent accountability "arrangements" established between the ECB and the EP (see EP Decision, n 81, under "Hearings before the ECON committee"), despite the intentions of the Parliament manifested in the preamble of the Parliament's decision (see recital H).

89 Diessner (n 87), 407.

90 For example, Y. Mersch, "Central bank independence revisited" European Central Bank (2017), https://www.ecb.europa.eu/press/key/date/2017/html/sp170330.en.html.

91 A. Akbik, *The European Parliament as an Accountability Forum: Overseeing the Economic and Monetary Union* (Cambridge University Press, 2022), 190–196, in particular 191–193 (although this study does not cover the monetary policy dialogue, many of its insights are relevant in this context).

92 C. Joerges, "Why European Legal Scholarship Should Become Aware of Karl Polanyi: The Great Transformation and the Integration Project" (2022) *European Law Open* 1(4), 1067.

93 Feichtner (n 54) 1094.

94 S. Mudge and A. Vauchez, "Dependence on Independence. Central Bank Lawyers and the (Un)making of the European Economy," (2022) *Economy and Society* 51(4), 584.

95 On the argument of over-constitutionalisation, see D. Grimm, "The Democratic Costs of Constitutionalisation. The European Case" (2015) *European Law Journal* 21(4), 460.

96 On those trade-offs, see Tooze (n 36) and P. Heimberger and L. Steininger, "ECB Interest Rate Hikes Will Damage Climate Protection Policies," *EUROPP—European Politics and Policy or the London School of Economics*, 15 August 2022.

97 A. Peychev, "The Primacy of the European Central Bank: Distributional Conflicts between Theory and Practice in the Pursuit of Price Stability" (2023) *European View* 22(1), 48, at 52.

98 S. Eich, *The Currency of Politics* (Princeton, 2023), 195–201, J. Leaman, *The Bundesbank Myth. Towards a Critique of Central Bank Independence* (Palgrave, 2001), 225–241.

99 I am grateful to Susan Rose-Ackerman for this point.

100 Dani et al. (n 12).

9 Administrative Democracy and Federalism

*Athanasios (Akis) Psygkas**

Mediating the potential tension between technical expertise and democratic accountability in administrative policy-making has been a cornerstone of Susan Rose-Ackerman's path-breaking work in comparative administrative law.[1] One of her earlier books comparing environmental law and policy in Germany and the United States turned the spotlight on public input in administrative policy-making—what I will call "administrative democracy"—as an important policy reform that would address weaknesses in the democratic accountability of German environmental regulation.[2] Ten years later, Rose-Ackerman explored this fundamental tension in the context of Central and Eastern European new democracies and offered a reform agenda that included administrative democracy as a mechanism for moving "from elections to democracy."[3] In her latest book *Democracy and Executive Power*, Rose-Ackerman emphasized democratic values as central to the exercise of executive power and defended public consultation and reason-giving as key contributors to the democratic accountability of administrative policy-making.[4]

In her earlier work on policy-making accountability, Susan Rose-Ackerman turned the spotlight on other institutional design options, notably federalism (or, more broadly, decentralization).[5] This second theme offers a fruitful lens through which to view administrative democracy. In a seminal 1980 article, Rose-Ackerman offered a significant qualification to well-established arguments in favour of federalism.[6] One traditional argument is that diverse governmental entities in a decentralized regime promote innovation by lowering the costs of policy experimentation because there are more individual loci of experimentation as opposed to a uniform, centrally, and *a priori* mandated standard.[7] According to Justice Brandeis's famous expression, states can serve as "democratic laboratories."[8] Rose-Ackerman challenged the general claim that federalism enhances innovation by expositing

* Professor Susan Rose-Ackerman's scholarship not only inspired my work in comparative administrative law and interest in institutional design, but, even more fundamentally, provided a new lens through which to view law more broadly. I also wish to thank Western Law students Juliano Baggieri (JD'24), Karen Hakim (JD'23), and Stephen Warner (JD'25) for excellent research assistance.

DOI: 10.4324/9781003416036-9

a model predicting that "[i]f state and local governments are supposed to be 'laboratories,' then . . . few useful experiments will be carried out in them."[9] Rose-Ackerman's model gave rise to a wide range of responses in the economics and political science literature.[10] A 2009 account assessed three decades of responses and concluded that Rose-Ackerman's main claim that states will not innovate at the socially optimal level still stands.[11]

My aim here is to bring together administrative democracy and federalism as a (contested) engine for policy experimentation, innovation, and diffusion. I hypothesize an ideal type of federal–state interaction that can lead to the development of effective administrative democracy. This scheme consists of feedback loops, whereby the center adopts a particular accountability mechanism, potentially in the form of a minimum standard, that it can impose on the periphery or indirectly influence the periphery to adopt. The component entities of the federal system "download" this minimum standard and are free to move beyond it and to experiment with procedural modes that operationalize it and may enhance public accountability in the periphery. Some of these good practices might be subsequently "uploaded" onto the center and be generalized or spread across state borders. I explore how this hypothesis plays out in three examples of "federal" or decentralized systems:[12] the United States (US), the European Union (EU), and Canada.

The first section provides conceptual clarifications that set the scene for my main argument regarding the interactions between federalism and administrative democracy. The second section argues that the US case is primarily a story of "downloading" but makes a normative claim in favour of "uploading" as well. The federal model has had a significant, albeit indirect, influence on state administrative procedures. At the same time, the reverse course of influence is normatively appealing. States may serve as useful, even if undertapped, sources of inspiration for procedural regulatory reform at the federal level. The third section of the chapter provides an example from the EU of direct "downloading" of procedural mandates but suggests that the EU's decentralized regime also creates institutional opportunities for "uploading" that would be beneficial. The fourth section suggests that, while "downloading" is absent from Canada because the country lacks a federal notice-and-comment process, participatory mechanisms do exist at the provincial level. Normatively, Canada could serve as an example of potential "uploading" that would facilitate the transition to a general federal mandate for public participation in administrative policy-making. The final section of the chapter concludes.

Delineating the Scope of Federal–State Interactions in the Context of Administrative Democracy

Administrative democracy pertains to the direct relations between administrative agencies and citizens and emphasizes public input in the policy-making process.[13] There is significant overlap between the idea of administrative democracy and social accountability; the latter has three main components—transparency, reason giving, and participation.[14] My focus here is on direct citizen involvement in administrative decisions of general applicability, which can take the form of public consultations/notice-and-comment procedures on drafts of administrative rules or policies.[15]

I use the term "federalism" broadly to capture a wide variety of decentralized regimes. The defining characteristic of a federal system for my purposes is the division or sharing of power across multiple levels, and, in the administrative context, it implies a network of administrative authorities that operate both at the center (that is, federal administrative agencies) and the periphery (that is, state or provincial administrative agencies). Under this approach, all three country cases discussed here present federal features in the sense that administrative power is exercised by public authorities at both the national and subnational levels. Most importantly, administrative agencies in both the center and the periphery employ their own decision-making processes and are subject to diverse modes of democratic accountability; this feature, in turn, gives rise to opportunities for innovation and learning across boundaries. This multi-level structure is the minimum institutional precondition for the federal–state interface in the context of administrative democracy. Beyond this minimum, the degree of administrative integration and coordination between the national and subnational administrative agencies varies. For example, the literature on comparative federalism describes "administrative federalism" (or "regulatory federalism") as a system in which the national entities assume responsibility for the overall design of substantive policies and programs with the subnational entities tasked with the implementation and administration of these national policies and programs.[16] Administrative federalism is contrasted with "jurisdictional federalism" where "each order of government operates within its own sphere, responsible for both policy and administration."[17]

Both the United States and the European Union have been accurately described as systems of "regulatory federalism."[18] In the United States, federal actors (i.e., Congress and the president) "have acknowledged the relationship between federalism and administrative government, incorporating the states as central players in major federal regulatory schemes."[19] In the European Union, substantive regulatory frameworks have been put in place at the center—i.e., the EU level—with national authorities acting as full-fledged enforcers.[20] This institutional choice creates a system of regulatory federalism or "managed decentralization."[21] By contrast, the Canadian case is closer to dual jurisdictional federalism.[22]

These helpful schematic representations, however, do not fully capture the complex institutional realities of evolving federal systems. In the United States, the "continuous readjustment of the respective regulatory competencies of Congress and the states" has resulted in a system "in a perpetual state of locomotion describable as kaleidoscopic rather than linear in nature."[23] In Canada, the "classical paradigm" of dual federalism with strictly delineated and exclusive spheres of jurisdiction for the federal and provincial governments has given way to a "modern paradigm" of flexible or cooperative federalism that recognizes a high degree of overlap and interplay between the orders of government and facilitates cooperation among them.[24]

Finally, my approach is distinct from an important strand of "administrative federalism" in US scholarship, which asks how administrative law may protect federalism values, such as enhancing states' input in federal agency decision-making.[25] The focus in this strand of the literature is on the allocation of authority among different actors vertically and horizontally (i.e., between Congress and federal agencies) with a concomitant emphasis on doctrines such as agency preemption of state law.[26] This work views administrative law as an avenue for realizing federalism values. My focus, instead, is on how federalism may advance or structure administrative law values, notably democratic accountability. I also explore potential synergies between federalism and administrative law,[27] but my focus is on accountability *processes* rather than the allocation of substantive policy-making authority.

This emphasis on procedural rather than substantive policy distinguishes my approach from earlier work that has engaged the "states as laboratories" idea—and Susan Rose-Ackerman's skeptical view of it—in a host of policy domains, including healthcare and health systems,[28] environmental policy,[29] bilingual education policy,[30] and the rights of criminal suspects.[31] The emphasis on procedural innovation and diffusion instead of substantive policy innovation has important implications for the forms of federal–state interface and adds a different dimension to Rose-Ackerman's model.[32]

In the context of the case studies in this chapter, namely, procedural experimentation and innovation driven by administrative authorities, a fundamental assumption of Rose-Ackerman's model is missing. That is to say, contrary to elected officials, agency officials are not motivated by electoral gains precisely because they do not need re-election to keep their job; some may, in fact, enjoy fixed terms. However, bureaucrats may still be sensitive to a reluctance by elected officials to undertake novel, risky policy because politicians may be able to leverage their capacity to alter an agency's budget or policy authority.[33] This is less of a concern in the case of independent administrative agencies, which are insulated from political interference.

A further dynamic may be at play and promote experimentation and innovation. This has been described in the literature as "policy evangelism": officials may experiment with novel policies because they value the possibility of their innovation being emulated "whether out of love for humanity, ideology, social status, or simple hubris."[34] This introduces "reputational competition"—administrative agencies in the periphery may have incentives to come up with novel accountability mechanisms because of the associated reputational benefits. Regardless of the motives of state-level agencies, innovation with respect to democratic accountability may also occur because novel procedures would be only one part of a bundle that includes a host of substantive regulatory measures; as a result, the risk of failure is hedged.[35]

Hence, procedural experimentation in federal systems is possible, but this is only part of the story. Administrative federalism involves a series of multidirectional interactions between the different levels of government. One direction is top-down: the center adopts a particular accountability mechanism, which may only be a baseline requirement, that it can then impose on the periphery or indirectly influence the periphery to institute. The component entities of the federal system "download" this minimum standard and are free (or even encouraged) to exceed this minimum standard. This subnational experience can then be "uploaded" onto the center and inform the development of national procedures or spread horizontally within the federal system.

This schematic depiction does not capture all the nuances of the complex networked relations between administrative authorities at different levels of government. These relations depend on the background constitutional and administrative structures in each country and the depth of these administrative networks. For example, the center may have the authority to impose procedural standards on the periphery in some case studies (e.g., in the EU) but not in others (e.g., in Canada). In other cases, this influence across levels of government is indirect and potentially more difficult to establish. However, the ideal type I put forward offers both a descriptive account of how administrative democracy developed in federal systems and a normative account of how federalism creates valuable sources of learning that can advance the goals of effective democratic accountability for administrative policy-making. The three cases highlight different descriptive and normative elements aiming to shed light on the interaction between administrative democracy and federalism.

The United States

Federal–State Interface and Administrative Procedures: A Story of "Downloading"

The United States was the leader in developing administrative democracy mechanisms. Hence, domestic, comparative, and global administrative law scholarship has focused on the notice-and-comment (or informal rulemaking) procedures outlined in section 553 of the federal Administrative Procedure Act (APA) of 1946 as elaborated by federal courts. This provision stipulates that, when making rules having binding effect on private parties, the federal agency must provide notice of its proposal, an opportunity for interested parties to comment, and "a concise general statement" of the basis and purpose of the rules. This open-ended and transparent notice-and-comment process will not necessarily involve an oral hearing, but the agency must accept "written data, views, or arguments"[36] and respond to qualitatively important comments submitted during the process.[37] Although federal administrative law and the procedures formalized by the federal APA are clearly important, I argue here that state-level administrative experience is an instructive repository of procedures and practices and provides a more textured picture of US administrative law.[38]

The "basic blueprint for rulemaking" set out in the federal APA has also been an institutional fixture at the state level.[39] Many of the general concepts and broad frameworks of the federal APA were adopted by the states when they developed their own administrative procedures, but the channel of influence was indirect.[40] Indeed, in the same year that Congress enacted the federal APA, the National Conference of Commissioners on Uniform State Laws—also known as the Uniform Law Commission (ULC)—adopted the Model State Administrative Procedure Act (MSAPA) of 1946.[41] Section 2(3) of the MSAPA provided that "prior to the adoption of any rule . . . the adopting agency shall as far as practicable, publish or otherwise circulate notice of its intended action and afford interested persons opportunity to submit data or views orally or in writing."

The parallel histories leading to the adoption of the federal APA and the MSAPA demonstrate the common origins of federal and state administrative law as well as common concerns regarding the democratic legitimacy of administrative rulemaking. The American Bar Association (ABA) has been described as being at the origin of both acts.[42] Federal legislative reform was first proposed by an ABA Special Committee in the 1930s, but it was not until 1946 that the federal APA was passed.[43] At the same time, similar developments were occurring at the state level in the late 1930s, with an ABA Committee producing reports and a draft act, which was submitted to the ULC.[44] The ULC ultimately approved the MSAPA in October 1946 after the enactment of the federal APA. E. Blythe Stason, who was involved in both processes, outlined how debates around the federal administrative process informed the development of the MSAPA.[45] Indeed, the fact that the ULC "purposefully waited to adopt the 1946 MSAPA until after the federal [APA] was actually adopted suggests that the federal act played an important role in this state law development."[46] However, this role was indirect and mediated through the MSAPA. The states did not copy (or "download") detailed provisions of the federal APA directly but rather relied on the 1946 MSAPA (and later revisions, notably the 1961 MSAPA) as they were developing state APAs. Therefore, since the MSAPA was influenced by the federal APA, the borrowing was indirect.[47]

The institutional choice of a model act as opposed to a uniform act was significant. Indeed, the 1946 MSAPA was short; its thirteen sections included only major principles of administrative law, with the particular details left to each state.[48] The same deliberate choice was made in the 1961 revisions of the MSAPA. This drafting approach shifted in the more detailed, but less influential, 1981 MSAPA. The latest revision in 2010 was lengthier than the 1961 Act but shorter and less detailed than the 1981 Act.[49] The design features of a model act, which has been the model followed for all MSAPAs and defined especially the more influential 1946 and 1961 versions, are especially relevant for my argument here as they facilitate experimentation by striking a balance between uniformity and flexibility (or diversity). By setting out common general principles—in this context, a general requirement for public participation in rulemaking—the model act prompts states to adopt baseline procedural requirements (uniformity) without stipulating the precise procedural details which are up to the states (diversity).[50] Therefore, the model act jumpstarts institutional conversations about designing administrative processes that are flexible and fit for purpose for each state. This feature allows for experimentation and innovation at the state level and may enable a different type of influence from the states to the federal level (what I have described as "uploading") or across state lines. This direction of influence has been studied less[51] but is normatively appealing.

State–Federal Interface and Administrative Procedures: In Favor of "Uploading"

The skeletal nature of the MSAPA and its diverse implementation across multiple states suggests that states can become learning sites in the context of administrative process. State experience may provide insights into both the benefits and perils of procedural reform that are also relevant at the federal level because section 553 of the federal APA only offers a "skeletal framework" for informal rulemaking processes.[52] The legislative history of the federal APA illustrates that the notice-and-comment process was only a minimal requirement on which federal agencies had broad discretion to add further procedural layers as they saw fit.[53] The Act thus set in motion a process of experimentation drawing on individual agency experience. My argument is that this reservoir of institutional experience can and should be expanded to include not only federal but also state agencies. This would be an example of "uploading" from the periphery to the center developed in the aftermath of "downloading" from the center to the periphery, thus closing the feedback loop.

Previous work has shed light on examples of federal procedural reform drawing on state experience. One example is the definition of "rule" in section 551(4) of the federal APA as an "agency statement of general or particular applicability and future effect." This federal definition has been criticized for not focusing on "general applicability" and instead using as the defining characteristic of a rule its "future effect."[54] According to the same account, the appropriate definitional fix for section 551(4) "lies readily at hand [in the 1981] Model State Administrative Procedure Act,"[55] which defines "rule" as "an agency statement of general applicability that implements, interprets, or prescribes (i) law or policy, or (ii) the organization, procedure, or practice requirements of an agency."[56] Interestingly, the requirement for prospectivity had originally been copied from the federal APA into the 1946 MSAPA but then subsequently dropped in the 1961, 1981, and 2010 versions of the MSAPA.

The second example involves stakeholder engagement in the initial drafting stage of agency rulemaking—that is, an earlier stage in the rulemaking process than the point at which notice-and-comment requirements are normally triggered. In Texas, section 5(f) of the Administrative Procedure and Texas Register Act (APTRA) of 1975 provided that an agency may use informal conferences and consultations, or appoint committees of experts, interested persons, or representatives of the general public to advise it with respect to any contemplated rulemaking. Texas had copied this provision not from the 1946 or 1961 MSAPA, which included no equivalent provision, but from the Wisconsin Administrative Procedure Act.[57] The statutory recognition of informal conferences and consultations as well as advisory committees at the state level was significant both because it added a procedural layer that facilitated earlier stakeholder involvement and because it predated the recognition of negotiated rulemaking processes at the federal level. Negotiated rulemaking refers to a process whereby an agency, with the assistance of a neutral adviser, known as "convenor," brings together an advisory committee, composed of representatives of identifiable affected interests and agency officials, who try to reach consensus on a proposed rule.[58] Even though a version of negotiated rulemaking (without the convenor) was in effect in Texas since 1976, it was not until the 1980s that negotiated rulemaking started receiving more attention,[59] through Recommendations from the Administrative Conference of the United States (ACUS).[60] The formal statutory endorsement of negotiated rulemaking at the federal level would come in 1990.[61]

A third example pertains to the agency rulemaking record for proposed rules, illustrating that the federal–state interface is a two-way street that can reinforce common underlying principles. The text of the federal APA did not provide a clear requirement for a rulemaking record for informal (notice-and-comment) processes. There was no such requirement in section 553 and the stipulation in section 706(2) that "the court shall review the whole record or those parts of it cited by a party" was originally understood as referring only to formal rulemaking.[62] Early on, the Supreme Court expanded the scope of "administrative record" to cover informal agency proceedings, but this broader application "has given rise to uncertainty and experimentation as agencies and courts have worked to implement the administrative record concept—at times inconsistently."[63] In 1974 ACUS issued a Recommendation outlining administrative materials that should be part of the rulemaking record under notice-and-comment procedures,[64] and similar language was used in a 2013 ACUS Recommendation.[65] Revisions of the federal APA to include a requirement for an official agency rulemaking record were proposed in 1979 but did not move forward.[66] By contrast, statutory provisions on official rulemaking records, containing material similar to those in the two ACUS Recommendations, were available at the state level. Relevant language was endorsed in both the 1981 and the 2010 MSAPAs,[67] and incorporated into state APAs.[68] Explicit statutory mandates for agency rulemaking records illustrate how rulemaking record provisions can be formalized. As a normative matter, state experience should add further impetus towards amending the federal APA with the aim of institutionalizing and providing further clarity to current federal practice. Overall, this example illustrates the feedback loop between the center and the periphery. Although the center—in this context, the ACUS in response to US Supreme Court cases—took the initiative and inspired the periphery to endorse them, it is the periphery that actually innovated through the explicit statutory incorporation of these requirements.

A similar idea is at play in the fourth example, the "direct final rulemaking" process. This process, set out in section 310 of the 2010 MSAPA, may be used if a state agency "proposes to adopt a rule which is expected to be noncontroversial." The agency must provide notice of the noncontroversial rule and the opportunity for the public to object to the adoption of the rule. If no objection is received within the public comment period, the rule becomes final. If an objection is received, the agency must give notice of the objection, and it then proceeds with the normal rulemaking process, which requires a public comment period under section 306. The "direct final rulemaking" process was reflected in federal practice and was discussed and recommended in a 1995 ACUS Recommendation.[69] However, it is not expressly provided for in the federal APA, although it could be justified by the federal Act's "good cause" exemption from notice-and-comment procedures.[70] At the state level, the ACUS recommendation is the default requirement under section 310 of the MSAPA. As Ronald Levin, who was a consultant to ACUS when it made this recommendation, has suggested, if states enact section 310, "their action will serve as a good test of the workability of the ACUS recommendation."[71] These would be laboratories of procedural experimentation in action and could provide empirical support for a similar federal APA reform.

The final example pertains to guidance documents, that is, agency statements that are not legally binding and "advise the public on how the agency proposes to exercise discretion or interpret law."[72] Guidance is an umbrella term covering both policy statements and interpretive rules.[73] This is an "essential and ubiquitous instrument of administration" because it facilitates consistency, predictability, and promptness in administrative action, thus saving time and resources for both the agencies and the regulated entities.[74] Agencies issue an enormous volume of guidance that far exceeds rulemaking.[75] In addition, agencies often adhere to guidance rigidly and regulated parties have incentives to follow guidance, which may result in guidance operating as *de facto* binding.[76] The federal APA exempts guidance documents from notice-and-comment requirements.[77] It requires publication of these documents before an agency can rely on them against a third party,[78] but when Congress enacted this publication requirement, it expressly opted against applying additional participatory procedures to the issuance of guidance.[79]

The volume and practical importance of guidance documents, coupled with the exemption from APA's notice-and-comment requirements, gave rise to reform proposals. As early as 1976, ACUS recommended that agencies should normally use notice-and-comment processes prior to issuing guidance and, in the absence of pre-promulgation notice-and-comment, agencies should publish the guidance document with an invitation for public comment and then evaluate the guidance in the light of comments received.[80] In 1992, ACUS urged agencies to put in place procedures that provide affected persons with a fair opportunity to "challenge the legality or wisdom" of policy statements and "suggest alternative choices in an agency forum that assures adequate consideration by responsible agency officials."[81] In 2017, ACUS recommended that agencies "afford members of the public a fair opportunity to argue for lawful approaches other than those put forward by a policy statement or for modification or rescission of the policy statement."[82] If there has been no public participation at the pre-adoption stage, the agency "should consider offering an opportunity for public participation after adoption."[83] An analogous approach was adopted in a 2019 ACUS Recommendation for interpretive rules.[84]

As this discussion was unfolding at the federal level, there were parallel developments at the state level. Contrary to the federal APA, the 1946 and 1961 versions of the MSAPA did not exempt guidance from notice-and-comment requirements. This was because the definition of "rule" in both versions was broad and included policy and interpretive statements.[85] The position changed in the 1981 version of the MSAPA, which carved out an exemption from notice-and-comment for state interpretive statements but only if the agency lacked legislative rulemaking authority;[86] this exemption was criticized as "misdirected"[87] and "decidedly stingy."[88]

The 1961 version of the MSAPA was adopted in large part by over half of the states. However, approximately thirty states and the District of Columbia (e.g., Alabama, Colorado, Georgia, Michigan, Wyoming) created statutory or judicial exemptions from notice-and-comment. No exemption existed in about twelve states.[89] California stood out for its procedural requirements for guidance documents that included notice-and-comment, an oral hearing on request, an obligation for the agency to respond to every comment, and mandatory scrutiny by the Office of Administrative Law.[90] These strict requirements ended up producing counterproductive effects as the increased costs and delays resulted in agencies not adopting any legislative or non-legislative rules, skirting, or ignoring the law.[91] By contrast, the 1988 Washington Administrative Procedure Act was praised as "the best approach to the guidance document problem yet enacted in any American jurisdiction."[92] Under the Washington Act, a person "may petition an agency requesting the conversion of interpretive and policy statements into rules" and within sixty days the agency "shall either deny the petition in writing, stating its reasons for the denial, or initiate rule-making proceedings."[93]

State experimentation with the earlier MSAPAs regarding guidance documents gave rise to a new approach in the 2010 MSAPA,[94] which now excludes guidance documents from its revised definition of "rule." Section 102(14) defines "guidance document" as "a record of general applicability developed by an agency which lacks the force of law but states the agency's current approach to, or interpretation of, law, or describes how and when the agency will exercise discretionary functions." Section 311 details the procedural requirements for guidance documents. These documents must be published on the agency's website and be made available to the public[95] but are now exempted from the notice-and-comment requirements of the MSAPA. Notably, "an agency that proposes to rely on a guidance document to the detriment of a person in any administrative proceeding shall afford the person an adequate opportunity to contest the legality or wisdom of a position taken in the document."[96] In addition, a person may petition an agency to adopt a rule in place of a guidance document or to revise or repeal a guidance document.[97] In the latter case, the agency shall within a certain period (the MSAPA suggests sixty days): (1) revise or repeal the guidance document; (2) initiate a proceeding to consider a revision or repeal; or (3) deny the petition in a record and state its reasons for the denial.[98]

Section 311 has been favorably received by commentators because it offers a novel solution to the concern that guidance may operate as *de facto* binding even if it has not been issued following notice-and-comment.[99] To address this risk at the federal level, courts have reclassified guidance documents as legislative rules and invalidated guidance as having been issued without following the federal APA notice-and-comment requirements.[100] However, this judicial technique comes with doctrinal uncertainty and invalidates guidance documents, thus denying the benefits of consistency, predictability, and cost savings associated with them.[101] By contrast, the 2010 MSAPA "offers a completely different and ingenious solution" which does not rely on courts reclassifying and invalidating the guidance. Instead, the focus is on agency action that must comply with procedural obligations, which, while not following the notice-and-comment model, allow for participation by affected parties to contest the legality or wisdom of the guidance.[102] Determining what is an adequate opportunity for a party to contest a policy statement within an agency will be context specific.[103] An agency may issue rules to define what constitutes a meaningful opportunity to challenge the legality or wisdom of a particular guidance document, which will be judicially reviewable.[104] In other words, the agency has the primary responsibility of taking "the first crack at determining what procedural avenues add up to a fair opportunity to make one's case" with courts exercising oversight.[105] Section 311 empowers states and agencies to experiment with various procedural mechanisms that offer the well-established benefits of guidance while also ensuring transparency and participation. The experiments that prove successful can then spread to other states and to federal agencies.[106]

The example of guidance documents offers helpful insights into the feedback loop between the center and the periphery. The 2010 MSAPA text was inspired by federal initiatives, notably ACUS Recommendations ("downloading"), but also drew on state experience and legislative initiatives.[107] However, while it was the center that prompted the periphery to endorse innovative procedural frameworks for guidance documents, it is the periphery that is better placed to innovate through the explicit statutory incorporation of these requirements, using the flexibility allowed in section 311 of the 2010 MSAPA. This flexibility and the importance of experimentation align with the latest ACUS recommendations and final reports on guidance. The latter highlighted that "experimenting agency-by-agency allows for more learning and cabins the consequences of failure" and concluded that decisions about procedural requirements for guidance should normally be made "document by document, or, at most, agency by agency."[108] Enlisting state agencies in this process through the vehicle of the MSAPA expands the loci of experimentation beyond federal agencies. Indeed, states can be learning sites not only in terms of formalizing diverse agency practices but also as cautionary tales about how inflexible procedural requirements may be too burdensome to be efficient and thus ultimately undermine the goals of administrative democracy. Lessons from successes and failures at the state level can then be added to the repository of institutional knowledge into which federal agencies and legal reformers can tap ("uploading").

The US case sheds light on the feedback loops between the center and the periphery. In practice, the interface between the federal and state levels has mostly taken the form of "downloading." However, from a normative perspective, there is scope for "uploading," with states acting as laboratories for administrative procedure that can inform federal agency practice and future reform. A similar story can be observed in the European Union.

The European Union[109]

The EU's Managed Decentralization Model: "Downloading" Procedural Mandates

Feedback loops between the center (EU) and the periphery (member states) operate within the EU's system of regulatory federalism or managed decentralization. One of the earliest and most illustrative examples comes from the public utilities sector, notably electronic communications. Beginning in the 1980s, the EU[110] began to liberalize the telecommunications sector through managed decentralization. Substantive regulatory frameworks were put in place at the EU level with national authorities tasked with implementing these centrally mandated frameworks. In the telecommunications sector, the first generation of EU rules were mostly substantive; they focused on opening up the markets in the member states, homogenizing substantive law, and promoting the creation of an internal market. The development and inclusion of procedural mandates in the EU regulatory framework was incremental and much slower.

The watershed moment came in 2002 with the introduction of the second-generation regulatory package. Article 6 of the Framework Directive (Directive 2002/21/EC) stated that:

> Member States shall ensure that where national regulatory authorities intend to take measures in accordance with this Directive or the Specific Directives which have a significant impact on the relevant market, *they give interested parties the opportunity to comment on the draft measure within a reasonable period.* National regulatory authorities shall publish their national consultation procedures. Member States shall ensure the establishment of a single information point through which all current consultations can be accessed. *The results of the consultation procedure shall be made publicly available* by the national regulatory authority,

> except in the case of confidential information in accordance with Community and national law on business confidentiality.[111]

This public consultation mandate survived subsequent reforms of the EU regulatory framework in 2009 and 2018.[112] The novel provisions of the 2002 Framework Directive and their implementation by the Member States initiated a new period of national procedural reform with long-term implications for the nature of governance. The EU mandates established avenues for public participation that had not previously been open or formalized in most Member States. Elsewhere I have detailed the impact of these novel participatory processes for the democratic accountability of administrative policy-making in Member States.[113] For the purposes of this chapter, two features are key.

First, as a matter of positive law, binding EU legislation for the first time *mandated* a "notice-and-comment"-like procedure. Member states transposed or "downloaded" the EU framework, including the public consultation requirement, often copying almost verbatim the language of Article 6 of the Framework Directive. Therefore, in contrast to the US, the influence from the center to the periphery in the EU context was direct; it took the form of minimum procedural mandates.

The second key feature is that the EU framework introduced only baseline procedural mandates, i.e., obligations to give interested parties the opportunity to comment on draft measures within a reasonable period, to publish their national consultation procedures, to establish a single information point for all current consultations, and to make the results of the consultation procedure publicly available, subject to business confidentiality. These minimum requirements for public consultation processes—the "EU floor"—permitted Member States the flexibility to expand the scope of administrative democracy processes and/or implement alternatives, as long as they do not fall below this floor. This second feature introduces the idea of "uploading" novel processes onto the EU level.

Closing the Circuit: "Uploading" Innovative Administrative Procedures

The mandate to establish a minimum of accountability mechanisms for national regulatory authorities means that Member States were empowered (or even invited) to enact additional measures building on the "EU floor." From this perspective, apart from multiplying entry points for the public into national regulatory processes across the EU, the EU decentralized regulatory system enlisted twenty-eight (now twenty-seven) national regulatory agencies in experimenting with consultation procedures. This diversity and experimentation could give rise to innovative procedural mechanisms which could then feed back into, or be "uploaded" onto, the EU level, for example through revisions to the 2002 Framework Directive. As a descriptive matter, this has not happened. As noted previously, subsequent reforms of the EU regulatory framework in 2009 and 2018 did not significantly revise the public consultation mandate in the original 2002 Framework Directive.

However, as a normative matter, Member States may operate as repositories of useful knowledge on administrative governance that can inform future legislative or soft law reform at the EU level. Elsewhere I have documented that the regulators in France, Greece, and the United Kingdom all built on the EU's baseline procedural requirements.[114] For instance, all three agencies would often publish syntheses that grouped together and summarized the responses to public consultations. The publication of such overviews at the end of the public consultation exercises provided useful insights into the authorities' decision-making processes and strengthened the justification of administrative policy-making in the absence of a general reason-giving requirement.

Another practice, consistent with the ideal of reasoned administration, is the use of multiple (commonly two) rounds of consultation. The telecommunications regulators in both France and the UK on several occasions, usually involving significant issues, resorted to iterated consultations. The first phase would generally invite public input on broader questions or initial thoughts of the agencies, while the final stage pertained more narrowly to the draft measure itself. A related deliberation-enhancing method, which was common until 2001 in the UK, entailed a "comment-on-comments" exercise, whereby the agency would set aside a formal 14-day period for respondents to comment on the views expressed by others during the first consultation round. Besides these methods, national regulators experimented with other tools to provide information and solicit feedback from the public, such as workshops and online chat sessions.

The member states have also been sites of institutional experimentation and innovation. Prior to Brexit, the UK showcased one such example with the position of the "consultation champion," an agency official in charge of ensuring that the regulator followed its own guidelines and reached out to broad range of people and organizations interested in its decisions.

These examples of Member State institutional and procedural creativity were in many cases stimulated by EU baseline procedural requirements. They illustrate how regulatory federalism can be leveraged to enhance administrative democracy.

Canada

Canada also illustrates how leveraging federalism may promote administrative democracy. However, Canada differs from the previous two cases in one significant respect. There is no "downloading" component because Canada lacks a general notice-and-comment process at the federal level. Indeed, Canada only recognizes limited rights for citizens to participate in federal administrative policy-making.

First, as a general common-law rule, procedural fairness, which entails participatory rights, does not apply to administrative decisions of a "legislative and general" nature.[115] This jurisprudence dates back to 1980, when the Supreme Court of Canada in a unanimous decision refused to impose procedural requirements on policy decisions by Cabinet.[116] The Court emphasized that where the executive "has been assigned a function performable in the past by the Legislature itself" and where "the subject-matter is not an individual concern or a right unique to the petitioner," the courts may not impose any procedural requirements.[117] Indeed, the Court noted, even if a court had this authority, it would be "unwise and impractical" to convert "past practice [of consultation] into rigid, invariable administrative procedures."[118] One critical assessment of the decision noted "the persistent refusal on the part of the courts to impose procedural obligations on administrative decision makers exercising powers of a 'legislative nature,' absent statutory indication to that effect."[119] In 1994, the Federal Court of Appeal reaffirmed that it cannot impose a "public consultation process on the Minister when no such thing has been contemplated by the legislation."[120]

However, under section 35 of the Constitution Act, 1982, in certain circumstances courts have recognized a constitutional requirement for the Canadian state to consult and accommodate Indigenous Peoples in decisions that affect them.[121] The scope of the duty to consult exists along a spectrum and is determined by a preliminary assessment of the strength of the Aboriginal rights claim and the seriousness of the potential adverse effects on these rights.[122] Where there is a strong *prima facie* case and the right and potential infringement is of high significance to the Indigenous Peoples, "deep consultation" may be required. This consultation "may entail formal participation in the decision-making process, and provision of written reasons to show that the [Indigenous Peoples'] concerns were considered and to reveal the impact they had on the decision."[123] The Supreme Court has also held that the duty to consult is not confined to a government exercise of statutory powers that may adversely affect Aboriginal rights, but also covers "strategic, higher level decisions."[124]

Second, in addition to the lack of a common-law duty to consult in the administrative policy-making process, there is also no general statutory obligation for participatory mechanisms at the federal level. Only individual federal statutes include public consultation requirements in specific policy domains.[125] There are also Cabinet documents that direct federal departments and agencies to carry out public consultations. The most recent *Cabinet Directive on Regulation* provides that departments and agencies are "responsible for identifying stakeholders impacted by regulations, including Indigenous peoples, and meaningfully consulting and engaging with them" throughout the regulatory life cycle.[126] Under the same Directive, regulatory proposals are pre-published in the Canada Gazette and normally go through a 30-day comment period.[127] However, these are non-statutory directives and thus not legally binding *per se*, in contrast with the federal and state APAs in the United States. Despite the lack of a statutory mandate, over 3,500 federal public consultations have taken place since 2002. Nevertheless, there are limitations to how these exercises have been conducted. For example, reports summarizing their results and thus allowing citizens and stakeholders to monitor the outcome and impact of these consultations were available for only 19% of the public consultations.[128]

By contrast, more extensive, statutory requirements exist for public participation in administrative policy-making at the provincial level. Although the vast majority are sector-specific,[129] Quebec's Regulations Act stands out.[130] Section 8 of the Act provides that "every proposed regulation shall be published in the *Gazette officielle du Québec*." Section 10 stipulates that every such regulation "shall be accompanied with a notice stating, in particular, the period within which no proposed regulation may be made or submitted for approval but within which interested persons may transmit their comments to a person designated in the notice." Therefore, the Quebec statute provides for a general notice-and-comment procedure that applies to every proposed regulation.[131] This Act is the only example in Canada of a binding statutory general requirement for public participation in administrative rulemaking. The unique nature of this legislation turns the spotlight on the absence of such binding general mandates in other provinces and at the national level and highlights the potential of such a general statutory mandate being "uploaded" onto the center.

The lack of a federal statutory mandate for public consultation in the administrative policy-making process has been criticized by others.[132] The existence of sector-specific mandates for public participation at both the federal and provincial levels creates an institutional repository of relevant experience that may facilitate the eventual transition to a general federal mandate. In this process, the Quebec Regulations Act can play a significant role as it provides concrete empirical support for the idea of a general participatory mandate. Therefore, in Canada the absence of "downloading" from the center to the periphery brings to the fore the normative and institutional importance of "uploading," especially when provinces offer concrete examples of administrative democracy.

Conclusion

The three case studies discussed here illustrate how administrative democracy can be enhanced through synergies between national and subnational entities in federal systems. Each case study sheds light on different aspects of the feedback loop between federal and state administrative processes. This is, of course, not the complete picture. More empirical work is required on the causal directions of influence between the center and the periphery. At the same time, the scheme proposed in this chapter may have broader applications that include not only federal and subnational agencies but also administrative bodies at the local government level.[133] Finally, different normative accounts of the two main analytical building blocks in this chapter, namely, administrative democracy and federalism, may result in different perspectives on the forms that this federal–state interface should take. Regardless of our normative starting points, Susan Rose-Ackerman's invitation to take administrative democracy and federalism seriously and her influential contributions to both of these areas of research will remain important, especially as we confront ever-increasing challenges to the administrative state and democracy in the years ahead.

Notes

1 See e.g. Susan Rose-Ackerman, *Democracy and Executive Power: Policymaking Accountability in the US, the UK, Germany, and France* (Yale University Press, 2021) [Rose-Ackerman, *Democracy and Executive Power*]; Susan Rose-Ackerman, "Citizens and Technocrats: An Essay on Trust, Public Participation and Government Legitimacy" in Susan Rose-Ackerman, Peter Lindseth & Blake Emerson, eds, *Comparative Administrative Law*, 2nd ed (Edward Elgar, 2017) 251; Susan Rose-Ackerman, Stefanie Egidy & James Fowkes, *Due Process of Lawmaking* (Cambridge University Press, 2015); Susan Rose-Ackerman, *From Elections to Democracy: Building Accountable Government in Hungary and Poland* (Cambridge University Press, 2005) [Rose-Ackerman, *From Elections to Democracy*]; Susan Rose-Ackerman, *Controlling Environmental Policy: The Limits of Public Law in Germany and the United States* (Yale University Press, 1995) [Rose-Ackerman, *Controlling Environmental Policy*].

2 Rose-Ackerman, *Controlling Environmental Policy*, *supra* note 1.

3 Rose-Ackerman, *From Elections to Democracy*, *supra* note 1.

4 Rose-Ackerman, *Democracy and Executive Power*, *supra* note 1 at 4.

5 See e.g. Susan Rose-Ackerman, "Risk Taking and Reelection: Does Federalism Promote Innovation?" (1980) 9 Journal of Legal Studies 593 [Rose-Ackerman, "Risk Taking and Reelection"]; Susan Rose-Ackerman, "Does Federalism Matter? Political Choice in a Federal Republic" (1981) 89 Journal of Political Economy 152; Susan Rose-Ackerman, "Cooperative Federalism and Co-Optation" (1983) 92 Yale LJ 1344; Susan Rose-Ackerman, "Environmental Policy and Federal Structure: A Comparison of the United States and Germany" (1994) 47:5 Vand L Rev 1587; Jonathan Rodden & Susan Rose-Ackerman, "Does Federalism Preserve Markets" (1997) 83:7 Va L Rev 1521.

6 On the well-established nature of these arguments, see Heather K. Gerken, "Foreword: Federalism All the Way Down" (2010) 124 Harv L Rev 4 at 6; Barry Friedman, "Valuing Federalism" (1997) 82 Minn L Rev 317 at 317–18.

7 Nestor Davidson, "Cooperative Localism: Federal–Local Collaboration in an Era of State Sovereignty" (2007) 93 Va L Rev 959 at 1007.

8 *New State Ice Co v Liebmann*, 285 US 262 (1932) at 311 (Brandeis, J., dissenting).

9 Rose-Ackerman, "Risk Taking and Reelection," *supra* note 5 at 593.

10 A literature search on Hein Online and Westlaw turned up 173 citing sources and a similar search on Google Scholar showed 491 citing sources.

11 Brian Galle & Joseph Leahy, "Laboratories of Democracy? Policy Innovation in Decentralized Governments" (2009) 58 Emory LJ 1333 at 1397.

12 I use quotation marks on the term, because the "federal" features of the EU have been the topic of extensive discussions. I discuss the use of the term federalism in the section "Delineating the Scope of Federal–State Interactions in the Context of Administrative Democracy" below.

13 Mark Bovens, "Analysing and Assessing Accountability: A Conceptual Framework" (2007) 13 Eur LJ 447 at 457.

14 For a more detailed discussion, see Athanasios Psygkas, "Accountability," in Peter Cane et al., eds, *The Oxford Handbook of Comparative Administrative Law* (Oxford University Press, 2020) 443 at 448–49.

15 See Athanasios Psygkas, *From the "Democratic Deficit" to a "Democratic Surplus": Constructing Administrative Democracy in Europe* (Oxford University Press, 2017) at 17–20 [Psygkas, *From the "Democratic Deficit"*]; Rose-Ackerman, *Democracy and Executive Power*, *supra* note 1 at 168–75.

16 Herman Bakvis & Douglas Brown, "Policy Coordination in Federal Systems: Comparing Intergovernmental Processes and Outcomes in Canada and the United States" (2010) 40 Publius: The Journal of Federalism 484 at 487. Germany is the archetype of administrative federalism, see Nathalie Behnke & Sabine Kropp, "Administrative Federalism" in Sabine Kuhlmann et al., eds, *Public Administration in Germany* (Palgrave Macmillan, 2021) 35.

17 Bakvis & Brown, *supra* note 16 at 487.

18 See R. Daniel Kelemen, *The Rules of Federalism: Institutions and Regulatory Politics in the EU and Beyond* (Harvard University Press, 2004) at 8–9.

19 Gillian E. Metzger, "Administrative Law as the New Federalism" (2008) 57 Duke LJ 2023 at 2025 [Metzger, "Administrative Law"].

20 Paul Craig, *EU Administrative Law*, 2nd ed (Oxford University Press, 2012) at 73–75.

21 Damien Geradin & Nicolas Petit, "The Development of Agencies at EU and National Levels: Conceptual Analysis and Proposals for Reform" (2004) 01/04 Jean Monnet Working Paper at 1, 16.

22 Bakvis & Brown, *supra* note 16 at 488 (noting that "on a continuum depicting the range of jurisdictional to administrative possibilities, the Canadian example can be placed close to the jurisdictional end while the German case can be placed on the opposite pole and the American case somewhere in between").

23 Joseph F. Zimmerman, *Congressional Preemption: Regulatory Federalism* (SUNY Press, 2005) at 187, 189.

24 See Bruce Ryder, "The Demise and Rise of the Classical Paradigm in Canadian Federalism: Promoting Autonomy for the Provinces and First Nations" (1991) 36 McGill LJ 309; Wade K. Wright, "Federalism(s) in the Supreme Court of Canada During the McLachlin Years" (2018) 86 SCLR (2d) 207.

25 See Miriam Seifter, "States, Agencies, and Legitimacy" (2014) 67 Vand L Rev 443 at 451–52 (noting that this literature has "arisen from twin perceptions: (1) that many federalism-affecting decisions are being made by agencies, and (2) that administrative law potentially provides important tools for protecting federalism values"); David S Rubenstein, "Administrative Federalism as Separation of Powers" (2015) 72 Wash & Lee L Rev 171 (referring to academic proposals aiming to "enhance states' participatory role in [federal] administrative processes [or] to protect state autonomy through adjustments to the Supreme Court's preemption doctrine" at 174); Gillian E. Metzger, "Federalism under Obama" (2011) 53 Wm & Mary L Rev 567 (noting that "[c]ritical decisions about the actual scope of state powers and autonomy will be made not in Congress or in the courts, but in the halls of [federal] agencies" at 570).

26 Brian Galle & Mark Seidenfeld, "Administrative Law's Federalism: Preemption, Delegation, and Agencies at the Edge of Federal Power" (2008) 57 Duke LJ 1933.

27 For this approach, see Metzger, "Administrative Law," *supra* note 19 at 2027–28 (concluding that "administrative law has important federalism-reinforcing features").

28 Abbe R. Gluck, "What is Federalism in Healthcare for" (2018) 70:6 Stan L Rev 1689; Matthew B. Lawrence, "Fiscal Waivers and State 'Innovation' in Health Care" (2021) 62:5 Wm & Mary L Rev 1477; Kristin Madison, "Building a Better

Laboratory: The Federal Role in Promoting Health System Experimentation" (2014) 41:4 Pepp L Rev 765.

29 Daniel L. Millimet, "Environmental Federalism: A Survey of the Empirical Literature" (2014) 64:4 Case W Res L Rev 1669.

30 Rachel F. Moran, "The Politics of Discretion: Federal Intervention in Bilingual Education" (1988) 76:6 Cal L Rev 1249.

31 Michael C. Dorf & Charles F. Sabel, "A Constitution of Democratic Experimentalism" (1998) 98:2 Colum L Rev 267.

32 Rose-Ackerman, "Risk Taking and Reelection," *supra* note 5 at 596–606.

33 Galle & Leahy, *supra* note 11 at 1374–75.

34 *Ibid* at 1386. For a similar account outlining various reasons for innovation, see David Lazer, "Regulatory Capitalism as a Networked Order: The International System as an Informational Network" (2005) 598 Ann Am Acad Pol & Soc Sci 52 at 61.

35 See Galle & Leahy, *supra* note 11 at 1367 ("low innovation costs, high costs of exit, and the ability to hedge risk all should contribute to innovation"). This idea is developed further in the context of EU administrative governance in Psygkas, *From the "Democratic Deficit," supra* note 15 at 62–63.

36 Rose-Ackerman, Egidy & Fowkes, *supra* note 1 at 80.

37 Mariano-Florentino Cuéllar, "Rethinking Regulatory Democracy" (2005) 57 Admin L Rev 411 at 421 n 37.

38 See Arthur Earl Bonfield, "State Law in the Teaching of Administrative Law: A Critical Analysis of the Status Quo" (1982) 61 Tex L Rev 95 (arguing that examining state administrative law "would stimulate important insights into the administrative process that cannot be obtained from federal materials alone [and] provide examples that better illustrate some problems or solutions in that process than do existing federal materials"); Jim Rossi, "Overcoming Parochialism: State Administrative Procedure and Institutional Design" (2001) 53 Admin L Rev 551 (noting that "understood in its comparative institutional context, [state administrative law] provides a powerful way to explain and help understand many key features and details of administrative procedure" at 554).

39 Ron Beal, "Rulemaking: Procedure as it Relates to Substance under the 2010 Model State Administrative Procedure Act" (2011) 20 Widener LJ 741.

40 Arthur Earl Bonfield, "The Federal APA and State Administrative Law" (1986) 72 Va L Rev 297 [Bonfield, "The Federal APA"].

41 The full text of the MSAPA of 1946 is available in (1948) 33:2 Iowa L Rev 372.

42 Albert S. Abel, "The Double Standard in Administrative Procedure Legislation: Model Act and Federal Act" (1948) 33 Iowa L Rev 228 (noting that the ABA cannot, "strictly speaking, be said to have authored either measure but it has inspired both").

43 For detailed historical accounts, see Walter Gellhorn, "The Administrative Procedure Act: The Beginnings" (1986) 72:2 Va L Rev 219; Emily S. Bremer, "The Undemocratic Roots of Agency Rulemaking" (2022) 108 Cornell L Rev 69.

44 E. Blythe Stason, "The Model State Administrative Procedure Act" (1948) 33:2 Iowa L Rev 196; John Gedid, "Administrative Procedure for the Twenty-First Century: An Introduction to the 2010 Model State Administrative Procedure Act" (2012) 44 St. Mary's LJ 241 at 244 [Gedid, "Administrative Procedure"].

45 Blythe Stason, *supra* note 44 at 199.

46 Bonfield, "The Federal APA," *supra* note 40 at 300.

47 *Ibid* at 302–07.

48 Blythe Stason, *supra* note 44 at 199.

49 For this evolution, see Revised Model State Administrative Procedure Act (with prefatory note and comments) (2010), Preface.

50 See Gedid, "Administrative Procedure," *supra* note 44 at 253.

51 But see Jim Rossi, "The 1996 Revised Florida Administrative Procedure Act: A Rulemaking Revolution or Counter-Revolution?" (1997) 49 Admin L Rev 345 (noting that "federal reformers may be able to learn some lessons by examining administrative law reform in our veritable laboratories of democracy, and state reformers might learn from glancing horizontally at their neighbors rather than above" at 369).
52 Bremer, *supra* note 43 at 131–32.
53 *Ibid* at 123–24.
54 Ronald M. Levin, "The Case For (Finally) Fixing the APA's Definition Of 'Rule'" (2004) 56 Admin L Rev 1077 at 1078.
55 *Ibid.*
56 Model State Administrative Procedure Act § 1–102(10) (1981).
57 Brian D Shannon, "The Administrative Procedure and Texas Register Act and ADR: A New Twist for Administrative Procedure in Texas?" (1990) 42 Baylor L Rev 705 at 729.
58 See Administrative Conference of the United States, Recommendation 2017–2, *Negotiated Rulemaking and Other Options for Public Engagement* (June 16, 2017); Jeffrey S. Lubbers, *A Guide to Federal Agency Rulemaking*, 4th ed (American Bar Association, 2006) at 212–17.
59 Shannon, *supra* note 57 at 734–35.
60 Administrative Conference of the United States, Recommendation 82–4, *Procedures for Negotiating Proposed Regulations* (June 18, 1982), which was based on a background report by Philip Harter (Philip Harter, "Negotiating Regulations: A Cure for Malaise" (1982) 71 Geo LJ 1); Administrative Conference of the United States, Recommendation 85–5, *Procedures for Negotiating Proposed Regulations* (December 13, 1985).
61 Negotiated Rulemaking Act of 1990, 5 USC §§ 561–570.
62 Administrative Conference of the United States, Recommendation 2013–4, *Administrative Record in Informal Rulemaking* (July 10, 2013).
63 *Ibid.*
64 Administrative Conference of the United States, Recommendation 74–4, *Preenforcement Judicial Review of Rules of General Applicability* (May 31, 1974).
65 ACUS, Recommendation 2013–4, *supra* note 62.
66 See US, Bill S 1291, Administrative Practice and Regulatory Control Act of 1979, 96th Cong, 1979 cited in Revised Model State Administrative Procedure Act 2010, *supra* note 49, § 302 cmt (Rulemaking Record).
67 MSAPA 1981, § 3–112; MSAPA 2010, § 302.
68 See e.g. Washington Administrative Procedures Act, § 34.05.370, which has included this requirement since 1988 (1988 c 288 § 313).
69 See Ronald M. Levin, "Rulemaking under the 2010 Model State Administrative Procedure Act" (2011) 20 Widener LJ 855 at 873 [Levin, "Model State APA"]; Administrative Conference of the United States, Recommendation 95–4, *Procedures for Noncontroversial and Expedited Rulemaking* (January 15, 1995).
70 *Ibid.* Section 553(b)(B) of the federal APA provides for an exemption from notice-and-comment procedures when the agency "for good cause" finds that these procedures are "impracticable, unnecessary, or contrary to the public interest."
71 Levin, "Model State APA," *supra* note 69 at 874.
72 Nicholas R. Parrillo, "Should the Public Get to Participate Before Federal Agencies Issue Guidance? An Empirical Study" (2019) 71 Admin L Rev 57 at 59 [Parrillo, "Public Participation"].
73 Nicholas R. Parrillo, "Federal Agency Guidance: An Institutional Perspective" (Final Report to the Administrative Conference of the United States, October 12, 2017) [Parrillo, "Federal Agency Guidance"]; Parrillo, "Public Participation,"

supra note 72 at 60 n 6 ("In general parlance, an agency statement is guidance if it is either a 'general statement of policy' (a.k.a., policy statement) or an 'interpretative rule' (a.k.a., interpretive rule) under the Administrative Procedure Act").

74 Parrillo, "Federal Agency Guidance," *supra* note 73 at 7.

75 Peter L. Strauss, "Publication Rules in the Rulemaking Spectrum: Assuring Proper Respect for an Essential Element" (2001) 53 Admin L Rev 803 at 806.

76 Parrillo, "Federal Agency Guidance," *supra* note 73.

77 5 U.S.C. § 553(b)(A).

78 5 U.S.C. § 552(a)(2).

79 Strauss, *supra* note 75 at 806.

80 Administrative Conference of the United States, Recommendation 76–5, *Interpretive Rules of General Applicability and Statements of General Policy* (December 10, 1976).

81 Administrative Conference of the United States, Recommendation 92–2, *Agency Policy Statements* (June 18, 1992); see also Robert A. Anthony, "Interpretive Rules, Policy Statements, Guidances, Manuals, and the Like Should Federal Agencies Use Them to Bind the Public?" (1992) 41 Duke LJ 1311.

82 Administrative Conference of the United States, Recommendation 2017–5, *Agency Guidance through Policy Statements* (December 14, 2017) at para 2.

83 *Ibid* at para 10.

84 Administrative Conference of the United States, Recommendation 2019–1, *Agency Guidance through Interpretive Rules* (June 13, 2019); see also the background final report by Blake Emerson & Ronald M. Levin, "Agency Guidance through Interpretive Rules: Research and Analysis" (28 May 2019) online (pdf): *Administrative Conference of the United States* <https://www.acus.gov/sites/default/files/documents/ACUS%20IR%20final%20report.5.28.2019.pdf>.

85 1946 MSAPA, § 1(2); 1961 MSAPA, § 1(7). See also Michael Asimow, "Guidance Documents in the States: Toward A Safe Harbor" (2002) 54 Admin L Rev 631 at 633 [Asimow, "Safe Harbor"].

86 § 3–109.

87 Michael Asimow, "Nonlegislative Rulemaking and Regulatory Reform" (1985) Duke LJ 381 (asking "Why should agencies be forced to speculate about whether they have delegated power to adopt rules even though they do not wish to use the power?" at 413)

88 Ronald M. Levin, "Rulemaking and the Guidance Exemption" (2018) 70 Admin L Rev 263 at 283 [Levin, "Guidance Exemption"].

89 Asimow, "Safe Harbor," *supra* note 85 at 637–38.

90 Michael Asimow, "California Underground Regulations" (1992) 44 Admin L Rev 43 (concluding that "California rulemaking procedure probably surpasses that of any other state, and far surpasses the federal government, in the number of steps required, the rigor with which the law is enforced, and in breadth of application" at 45).

91 *Ibid* at 56–62.

92 Asimow, "Safe Harbor," *supra* note 85 at 653.

93 Wash. Rev. Code Ann. § 34.05.230 (West).

94 John Gedid, "An Introduction to the 2010 Model State Administrative Procedure Act" (2011) 20 Widener LJ 697 at 698.

95 § 311(e) and (a).

96 § 311(b).

97 § 311(g) and (h).

98 § 311 (h).

99 For a discussion of this critique, see Levin, "Model State APA," *supra* note 69 at 876; Parrillo, "Public Participation," *supra* note 72 at 61.

100 Levin, "Model State APA," *supra* note 69 at 876.

101 *Ibid.*

102 *Ibid* at 877. See also Michael Asimow, "News from the States" (2011) Admin & Reg L News 27 at 28 n 16 (describing this MSAPA provision as "savvy").
103 2010 MSAPA, § 311 cmt (citing ACUS Recommendation 92–2, *supra* note 81).
104 *Ibid.*
105 Levin, "Model State APA," *supra* note 69 at 878.
106 *Ibid* at 884.
107 See Levin, "Guidance Exemption," *supra* note 88 at 283; 2010 MSAPA, § 311 cmt.
108 Parrillo, "Public Participation," *supra* note 72 at 69, 124.
109 This section draws extensively on Psygkas, *From the "Democratic Deficit," supra* note 15, chapters 2, 6.
110 I use the term "European Union" broadly to include what, in part of the period under examination here, was the European Economic Community and then the European Community.
111 Directive 2002/21/EC of the European Parliament and of the Council of 7 March 2002 on a common regulatory framework for electronic communications networks and services (Framework Directive), OJ L 108/33, 24 April 2002 (emphasis added).
112 See Directive 2009/140/EC, Article 1 (Amendments to Directive 2002/21/EC (Framework Directive)); Directive (EU) 2018/1972 establishing the European Electronic Communications Code, Article 23 (Consultation and transparency mechanism).
113 Psygkas, *From the "Democratic Deficit," supra* note 15, chapters 2–5 (discussing the implementation of this public consultation mandate in France, Greece, and the UK against the backdrop of these countries' public law history, administrative traditions, and state–society relations, and drawing on a compilation of more than 1,000 public consultations and some 8,000 consultation responses).
114 *Ibid* at 307–08.
115 *Cardinal v Director of Kent Institution* [1985] 2 SCR 643 at para 14; *Knight v Indian Head School Division No 19* [1990] 1 SCR 653; Kate Glover Berger, "Fair Processes for Just Outcomes: The Principles and Practices of Procedural Fairness" in Colleen M. Flood & Paul Daly, eds, *Administrative Law in Context*, 4th ed (Emond, 2022) 177 at 201; Mary Liston, "Expanding the Parameters of Participatory Public Law: A Democratic Right to Public Participation and the State's Duty of Public Consultation" (2017) 63:2 McGill LJ 375.
116 *Canada (Attorney General) v Inuit Tapirisat of Canada* [1980] 2 SCR 735.
117 *Ibid* at 758.
118 *Ibid* at 755.
119 Geneviève Cartier, "Procedural Fairness in Legislative Functions: The End of Judicial Abstinence" (2003) 53:3 UTLJ 217 at 218–19.
120 *Canadian Association of Regulated Importers v Canada (Attorney General)* [1994] 2 FC 247.
121 *R v Sparrow*, [1990] 1 SCR 107; *Tsilhqot'in Nation v British Columbia*, 2014 SCC 44; *Haida Nation v British Columbia (Minister of Forests)*, 2004 SCC 73 [*Haida Nation*]; Kate Glover Berger, "The Duty of The Administrative State to Consult Indigenous Peoples" in Colleen M. Flood & Paul Daly, eds, *Administrative Law in Context*, 4th ed (Emond, 2022) 233–46.
122 *Haida Nation*, *supra* note 121 at para 39.
123 *Ibid* at para 44.
124 *Rio Tinto Alcan Inc v Carrier Sekani Tribal Council*, 2010 SCC 43 at para 44.
125 See e.g. Broadcasting Act, SC 1991, c 11, ss 10(3) and 18; Telecommunications Act, SC 1993, c 38, s 69; Pest Control Products Act, SC 2002, c 28, s 28.
126 *Cabinet Directive on Regulation* (2018), BT22–212/2018E-PDF at para 4.1.1.
127 *Ibid* at para 5.4.1.

128 Own elaboration from data available on "Consulting with Canadians" (last visited April 2021), online: *Government of Canada* <https://www.canada.ca/en/government/system/consultations/consultingcanadians.html>.
129 See e.g. in Ontario, Securities Act, RSO 1990, c S.5, s 143.2(4) (as amended in 1994) and Retirement Homes Act, 2010, SO 2010, c 11, s 122; in Alberta, Municipal Government Act, RSA 2000, c M-26; in British Columbia, Community Charter, SBC 2003, c 26. See also Andrew Green, "Delegation and Consultation: How the Administrative State Functions and the Importance of Rules" in Colleen M. Flood & Lorne Sossin, eds, *Administrative Law in Context*, 4th ed (Emond, 2022) 103 at 116–17.
130 RSQ 1986, c 22.
131 Section 12 provides for exceptions when "the urgency of the situation requires it" or when "the proposed regulation is designed to establish, amend or repeal norms of a fiscal nature."
132 Alice Woolley, "Legitimating Public Policy" (2008) 58:2 UTLJ 153. *Cf* Edward Clark, "Procedural Fairness and Citizen Control: Addressing the Legitimacy Deficit in the Canadian Administrative State" (SJD thesis, University of Toronto Faculty of Law, 2017) [unpublished] at 224 (arguing for "a skeletal framework of statute law with flexible common law elaboration").
133 See e.g. Nestor M. Davidson, "Localist Administrative Law" (2017) 126 Yale LJ 564. This approach aligns with Heather Gerken's invitation to push federalism "all the way down" (Gerken, *supra* note 6).

10 From Election to Autocracy

Can Strategic Decentralization Bring Us Back?

Maciej Kisilowski

The relationship between decentralization, democracy, human rights, and equality is a complicated one. Decentralization is often championed as a path to a more accountable and, indeed, more deeply democratic government. It has been explicitly heralded as a tool of democratic resistance against right-wing populism (Katz and Nowak 2017). In the US, left-leaning states try to take the lead in combating global warming, and they vow vigorously to protect their citizens from the so-called "right to bear arms." Most recently, these states have vowed to shield those who can get pregnant from the dystopian laws of some Republican-controlled states; laws aimed at subjugating them to involuntary servitude centered around government-patrolled pregnancies. My own work with the *Social Contract Incubator*—a pro-decentralization group of scholars in Poland (Kisilowski and Przybylski 2019; Kisilowski 2020a; Kisilowski and Wojciuk 2023)—is part of the same initiatives supported by "decentralization optimists."

To some extent, our optimism is a reaction to authoritarian strategies. If decentralization were *not* an effective constraint on authoritarian ambitions, then why would so many twenty-first century autocrats—from Vladimir Putin to Viktor Orbán and Jarosław Kaczyński—attack and weaken regional and local governments as one of their main strategies of choice?

However, especially in the United States, the history of decentralization has a darker side (Simeon 2006). For much of the Republic's history, "states' rights" were an excuse for allowing shocking human rights abuses, including slavery and segregation. The recent decision of the US Supreme Court in *Dobbs v. Jackson Women's Health Organization* (2022) offers a stark reminder of this darker decentralization tradition. In the majority opinion, Samuel Alito heralded his ruling overturning the constitutional right to abortion as a triumph of decentralized democracy: returning the abortion question to the states and their voters.

To be sure, it is easy to see the incoherence of Alito's position. Espousing states' rights does not prevent the right-wing court from also centralizing favorite *Republican* policies, including unfettered access to guns. Nor do they prevent right-wing operatives from plotting the centralization of abortion prohibitions, either through a federal statute or—following the example of

DOI: 10.4324/9781003416036-10

Poland's so-called Constitutional Tribunal—through granting constitutional rights to a fetus, or perhaps even an embryo. Yet the fact that decentralization arguments are used to back such a wide variety of political and moral projects highlights the need for a better theory to understand the true stakes involved in future decentralization efforts. Such a Decentralization Calculus would compare the benefits and costs of a decentralized political system with a realistic centralized alternative.

"Realistic" is the essential word here. In Polish debates around the *Social Contract Incubator*, decentralization's left-leaning opponents compare its risks with a stylized alternative of a centralized country safely controlled by progressive political forces. This is sadly unrealistic in a country that, for more than a quarter of its modern post-communist history, has been governed by one of Europe's most oppressive right-wing regimes. But the "center is ours" fantasy influences democratic thinking in the US and other Western countries.

The first section, on privilege versus equality, seeks to dispel these myths by offering a more honest understanding of the nature of political competition in many of today's closely divided democracies. The second section discusses the risks of Constitutional and Authoritarian Backlash that emerge as a result of well-intentioned efforts to centralize key human rights and equality protections. Next, the essay outlines the consequences of those risks for pro-equality voters in closely divided societies, focusing particularly on the limited choice those voters have in free and democratic elections (the phenomenon dubbed in Kisilowska (2010) as "Choiceless Democracy"). Then, two sections outline the conditions under which decentralization can enhance democracy, human rights, and equality in response to the dynamic discussed earlier. The remainder of the chapter briefly discusses further considerations that should be part of the final version of the Decentralization Calculus. The conclusion calls for more strategic flexibility from the Pro-Equality Camp that would involve conditions-based openness to both the centralized imposition of these policies and, if needed, a decentralized settlement with equality's opponents.

Privilege vs. Equality

The question of whether human beings should be equal or if they should be ordered in a hierarchical system of oppression and unearned privilege is the central, continuing conflict of political life. Constitutional and human rights do not, as a matter of political reality, sit above the messiness of ordinary politics. On the contrary, they remain at the very center of that politics.

Part of our problem in grasping this reality is the sanitized language we use to describe the key axes of our political conflict. We talk about "racial conservatives" (Ackerman 2015, 6), when a more accurate word would be "racists." "Traditional gender roles" (Balkin 1999, 2305) can more aptly be called "misogyny." "Climate skeptics" should perhaps be treated less as the disciples of Burke and more as "climate killers" (Dickinson 2010) who condemn today's children, especially non-white children (Sealy-Huggins 2018) and future generations to near-certain death or misery.

The sanitization is not far from condescension. The very image of our "conservative" compatriots merely clinging to how things were in the past creates a false vision of a misinformed—or to use the famous expression of Jonathan Gruber—"stupid" electorate who, like a scared child, are simply afraid of the inevitable "progress" they barely understand (DelReal 2014).

The recent successes of ambitious right-wing projects on both side of the Atlantic should force us to take our right-wing compatriots seriously. In my research with Anna Wojciuk (Kisilowski and Wojciuk 2022a), we propose to do this by replacing the increasingly misleading tactics-oriented terms "progressives" and "conservatives" with a characterization that would capture the ultimate objectives of the two major sides of the political debate in most of our democracies. On the one side, we have *the Pro-Privilege* Camp: parties, and a large group of voters consistently supporting them, who prefer a society built on racial, gender, religious, national (Kochenov 2019), and, increasingly, generational hierarchies of unearned advantage. On the other side, we have parties and voters committed to far-reaching *equality* between human beings. Neither side is remotely consistent in its beliefs, nor does it always practice what it preaches. But understanding the fundamental objectives of both sides helps one take an honest view of available constitutional solutions.

The proposed terminological convention would match the ways in which we discuss respective interest groups in purely economic political conflicts (Rose-Ackerman 1992). For example, we have no problem admitting that many affluent voters and their allies will always want the rich to be taxed less and, in particular, will want to protect the unearned privilege of their children by endowing them with un- or lightly taxed inheritances (Piketty and Goldhammer 2020). We do not narrate democratic history as a grand arc in which the pro-rich camp wants lower marginal tax rates merely because of some misguided attachment to how things were in the past. We do not expect them to ever acquiesce to a high-tax regime by permanently setting their self-interest aside. We do not conceptualize it as the problem of an "old, waning generation" and expect that the push for wealth inequality will end when the Boomers die out. Most informed political analysts would expect the economic right to be a political force a hundred years from now, just as it is today.

If we adopt a similar framework when discussing non-economic rights, and associated sources of privilege, we can realize that in many, if not most, modern democracies, pro-privilege voters consistently constitute a large enough segment of the electorate that, regardless of the voting system, ostracizing them or otherwise excluding them from the political process would make normal electoral competition impossible. In Poland, after the initial decade when attitudes toward post-communist politicians clouded the picture, the only viable alternative to the center-left coalition became the right-wing, racist, anti-European, bigoted PiS party (Kisilowski 2019). In France, a leader of the far-right National Rally was the presidential contender in the runoff vote in three out of five electoral cycles over the last two decades. Calling a party that routinely puts its leader into the presidential runoff "extremist" seems to be a misnomer, at least as far as the "extremes" of the actual political spectrum are concerned. In the US, the Republican Party, increasingly dependent on an energized right wing, was in power for the majority of the twenty-first century's first two decades.

Constitutional Opportunity

The traditional response to threats against basic human and civic equality is constitutionalization: enshrining essential human rights in difficult-to-change constitutions and international agreements, such as the European Convention on Human Rights. This is a fine strategy, but the story told to justify it is rather disingenuous. That story often starts with the assumption that the main purpose of having rights is to protect citizens against abuses and overreaches of the government. The threat is on the supply side of the political market, to use the language of political economy. If that were the case, it would generally be good news. All citizens should be wary of a tyrannical government. That assumption paves the way to an optimistic notion of a constitutional moment: a staged process in which citizens come together to expand their rights.

Under the story outlined in the previous section, however, that picture becomes considerably grimmer. Yes, power corrupts. But an equally important, if not *the* most important reason why members of oppressed and disadvantaged groups need rights is to protect them *from their fellow citizens*, specifically those belonging to the Pro-Privilege Camp. The threat is decidedly demand-sided. Under this story, government and its coercive powers of "mobili[zing] fiscal and human resources in a compulsory fashion" (Lindseth 2016, 696) are mainly a tool through which pro-privilege voters oppress their fellow citizens to maintain racial, gender, religious, national, and generational hierarchies. In fact, right-wing politicians—agents of the pro-privilege voters—are sometimes demonstrably hesitant to fully implement the oppressive wishes of the electorate.

All of this should deeply affect our thinking about constitutional change. There is no coming together. Constitutionalization or internationalization through a multilateral human rights regime is merely a tactic used by one side of the grand equality–privilege struggle to stack the deck against the other side. As Kisilowski (2020a) explains, constitutional change is not often accomplished through inclusive multi-stage "moments" but rather through exclusionary opportunities. A largely random set of circumstances gives one side a temporary upper hand: the other side bungled its term in office or faced unfavorable macroeconomic conditions. One side had the fortune of a charismatic presidential candidate. In the US, a Supreme Court Justice dies when our side controls the presidency and the Senate. The moment such an opportunity arises, our side uses constitutional levers to lock in favored policies and make it difficult for the other side to change them.

In the late twentieth century, the pro-equality side was, generally, luckier than the Pro-Privilege Camp as far as constitutional opportunities are concerned. Hence, it was rational for the pro-equality side to come up with a number of elaborate theories aimed at dissuading the Pro-Privilege Camp from striking back. Rights were declared inviolable "trumps" in the political process (Dworkin 1977). Broad-based social "ratification" of pro-equality constitutional changes were asserted (Ackerman 1998). When social support became demonstrably less broad and unequivocal, the pro-equality side began to call for respect for the doctrine of stare decisis (in the American context; see Schauer 2018), or for constraints on EU members' behavior in the Hungarian and Polish context (Scheppele, Kochenov, and Grabowska-Moroz 2021).

Constitutional and Authoritarian Backlash

For those who value equality, building up institutional walls around pro-equality policies is commendable. But high walls can trigger backlash—indeed, two types of backlash.

The first is Constitutional Backlash. The Pro-Privilege Camp may finally receive some luck and gain an opportunity to change the constitution. The moment that happens, all the tools that the pro-equality lawyers created to guard constitutionalized rights will be employed in the process of guarding constitutionalized oppression. The enemy took the castle surrounded by the high walls you built. You are now on the outside. Good luck! That, arguably, is America after *Dobbs v. Jackson Women's Health Organization* (2022), *West Virginia v. Environmental Protection Agency* (2022), or New York State Rifle & Pistol Association, Inc. v. Bruen (2022). That is also Poland after the right-wing takeover of the Constitutional Tribunal (Kisilowski 2015).

But, perhaps, we are taking ourselves—the legal scholars—too seriously. Maybe the walls erected by scholars and their beautiful theories of *stare decisis* or constitutional moments are not so impenetrable after all (Brenner and Spaeth 1995). Constitutional Opportunity may primarily be a *political* opportunity. Once it arrives, for either side, proper theories will be found or created.

If so, then a much more serious danger arises. For we may be trading a Constitutional Backlash for an authoritarian one. If it is impossible *really* to protect the fruits of Constitutional Opportunity through universally respected norms, then sooner or later, someone will decide that it makes no sense for us to keep the democratic system at all. If rights, or privileges, are so crucial to us, and if the other side will surely undermine your constitutional achievements on that central dimension, then perhaps it's better to use your governing power, while you still have it, to fundamentally hamper the chances of the other side to compete electorally. That discrepancy between the formal ability to stand in elections and the actual ability to unseat the ruling party is the hallmark of modern electoral authoritarianism (Morse 2012).

Choiceless Democracy

In principle, there is nothing that prevents the Pro-Equality Camp from becoming interested in the authoritarian solution. After all, under the story presented here, democracy is not really a particularly tempting system. For, in essence, it is a system in which we allow the pro-privilege voters freely to vie for political power and use it to oppress. As mentioned above, given the large number of pro-privilege compatriots, it is mathematically impossible in most democracies to create a competitive electoral system without them being the core of one side of the political spectrum.

In view of this unmistakable reality, my own strong democratic preference, despite the full understanding of the stakes involved, may simply be evidence of my privilege. As a white, cis-gender, heterosexual, able-bodied man, and as a person too old to suffer the worst impact of global warming, I suffer little when the Pro-Privilege Camp comes to power. This chapter would certainly have been more persuasive if written by a Polish transgender individual or a person of color in their teens, for whom four more years of the rule of Jarosław Kaczyński and his acolytes constitutes a mortal threat.

But, being aware of my privilege, let me offer a substantive argument for democracy, even under the bleak scenario I have sketched: Eastern Europe pro-equality dictatorships—called "the dictatorships of the proletariat." But sometimes immediately and sometimes after a while, they ceased to be very pro-equality. The very mechanism that prevented others from freely seeking political power created new structures of privilege (Djilas 1957). In the end, Pinochet's generals in Chile looked very much like Jaruzelski's in Poland or Xi Jinping's in China.

But we do not need to go as far as General Jaruzelski to understand the accountability problems that stem from the lack of electoral competition. In many countries, the sad consequence of the strength of pro-privilege political parties has been that, for all practical purposes, pro-equality voters lose their ability to *choose* their democratic representatives. Although details differ depending on the specific electoral system, in many countries, once a voter eliminates politicians who espouse racist, misogynist, homophobic, transphobic, global warming denialist, or otherwise bigoted views, they are left with only one politician/party/coalition to vote for. More worrisome from the perspective of Adam Przeworski's classic definition of democracy as "the system in which parties lose the election" (Przeworski 1991): if those designated pro-equality parties are in power, there is no morally acceptable way for pro-equality voters to punish them for bad performance or corruption—as the only way to sack them is to vote for a pro-privilege challenger (a morally unacceptable choice). Pro-equality voters begin to experience a Choiceless Democracy (Kisilowska 2010).

That sense of choicelessness was prevalent in Poland in 2011 and 2015. Any vote signaling displeasure with the increasingly inefficient government of the Civic Platform liberal party was, in practice, a vote for the bigoted PiS.

A similar problem affected pro-equality French voters during the 2002 and 2022 runoff presidential elections. Given President Biden's intention to run in 2024, it will also be a dilemma for the American Pro-Equality Camp.

Can Decentralization Help?

For a pro-equality voter living in a society closely divided across the privilege–equality dimension, prospects for both democracy and broad equality of rights and opportunities are grim. Our best case is the Choiceless Democracy of continuously supporting the pro-equality party or bloc—regardless of their honesty or effectiveness. Even a single electoral defeat threatens Constitutional Backlash—a radical rollback of basic rights. Under not too demanding conditions, that rollback may be accompanied by an Authoritarian Backlash, making each election potentially the last (at least as far as the "free and fair" ballots are concerned).

Decentralization, often perceived as a solution most suited for so-called "plural" societies divided along "objective" (Lijphart 1977) lines of "linguistic, ethnic, religious, or cultural conflict" (Choudhry 2008), can contribute to solving the dystopian vicious cycle of the equality–privilege political divide. If pro-privilege and pro-equality sentiments are concentrated in geographically distinct areas, it may be possible to create many states, regions, or lands in which rights would be electorally safe. In most democracies, this would especially be the case in city-states (Barber 2013; Katz and Nowak 2017). The citizens of the city-state of Vienna have not voted for a pro-privilege majority in the City Council (which also serves as the Landtag) for the last 100 years.[1]

In many countries, including Poland and the United States, this geographical split runs deeper than the urban–rural divide: in the US, pro-equality politicians tend to be elected in the coastal areas, while, with notable exceptions, much of the Midwest, the Rocky Mountain states, and the South vote for solidly pro-privilege parties. In Poland, politicians committed to human rights consistently do better in the Northwestern part of the country, while the pro-privilege politicians dominate the South-East (Kisilowski 2020a). The ideal would be to create not only safely, but *overwhelmingly* pro-equality states: governance units in which the pro-privilege sentiment is so rare that a competitive electoral system can function within the Pro-Equality Camp. Those states would be able to achieve a situation where democracy and human rights are "the only game in town" (Przeworski 1991). Governmental accountability is ensured by electoral competition *within* a pro-equality consensus. Some US states come close to that ideal. In Vermont, the governorship alternates between Democratic and Republicans candidates, but the latter, by and large, support basic human rights (see "Scott Decries 'Racist Response' to BIPOC Vaccine Eligibility," 2021).

Unfortunately, decentralization is also likely to create a number of strongly, or even overwhelmingly, pro-privilege states. This may be for both historical and cultural reasons that would make state borders not fully malleable. More important, though, is the simple fact that pro-privilege citizens are unlikely to be satisfied with a constitutional arrangement purposefully stack against them. This leads us to the core of our dilemma: the main mechanism through which decentralization can contribute to democratic stability is by giving geographically concentrated pro-privilege citizens at least some of what they want.

The sooner we substitute our romantic rhetoric about decentralization as a superb form of dividing powers (Amar 1991; Wildavsky 1998), a guarantor of efficient economic policy,[2] or a laboratory of governance innovation[3] with the blunt assessment just offered, the sooner we will be able to honestly evaluate the consequences of using decentralization in politically divided societies. Yes, separation of power, experimentation, and other benefits of multi-level governance may have a positive impact if designed right. But at the core, we are talking about a power-sharing settlement with pro-privilege compatriots. To dissuade the Pro-Privilege Camp from the allure of constitutional or Authoritarian Backlash at the center, they must have a stake in the new, decentralized system.

Decentralization Calculus: The First Take

This leads me to the main objective of this chapter—an explicit elaboration of the democratic and human rights tradeoffs involved in any decentralization proposal. For, as should be clear from the preceding discussion, in societies with a large minority of consistently pro-privilege voters, stable democracy (i.e., a competitive electoral system) combined with absolute protection of human rights and equality is not an attainable objective. Both the centralized and the decentralized strategies involve serious risks to both.

On the one hand, centralization of the pro-equality agenda has the immediate effect of universal near-term protection of human rights across the entire country. That protection will not be perfect. In pro-privilege areas, enforcement of national constitutional mandates will have to be partly carried out by local pro-privilege officials. The resistance strategies of conservative states in the US in response to the centralized human right of access to abortion is a good example. The enforcement problem is not merely a consequence of the federal nature of the American Republic, as a very similar "stalling" behavior of local state officials could be observed in unitary, politically centralized Poland. Until 2020, the abortion of deformed fetuses was legal across the country. However, the strong regional sentiments of doctors and other officials meant that the procedure was not actually available in the ultra-conservative Podkarpackie region (Nowicka 2019).

The costs of political centralization are the two types of pro-privilege backlash discussed earlier. In response to any move to centralize rights, the pro-privilege side can use their next Constitutional Opportunity to constitutionalize oppression, or—in the extreme—do away with the governance system of free and fair elections. Furthermore, because basic rights, or even democracy itself, are at stake in every national election, this locks pro-equality voters into a de facto one-party system of Choiceless Democracy; to save democracy and rights they need to continue voting for one pro-equality party. It is, fundamentally, because of these costs that the alternative of decentralization should be considered. That alternative offers some distinct advantages. The pro-equality states will offer long-lasting, expanded protection of rights and a possibility of robust democratic competition among pro-equality politicians. Protecting rights is not only important for human dignity, but it also makes communities better. At least some pro-equality states can shine as powerful examples of the concrete impact of liberal values on individual and collective well-being.

The discrepancy between failing pro-privilege states and successful pro-equality states can trigger what Hirschman (1970) famously called "exit": residents of pro-privilege states voting with their feet. Because mobility within countries is generally higher than internationally, citizens affected by the oppressive policies of the pro-privilege states will have an easier time resettling in the pro-equality states of the same country than emigrating to a different country. Ultimately, high levels of emigration from pro-privilege states will lower these states' economic and, eventually, political power.

Against all those benefits, we should acknowledge a grave cost of decentralization: it will create an opportunity to form highly and long-lasting oppressive democratic governments in some states. We can hope that the incentives for extreme oppression will diminish once the winner-takes-all national competition ends. Governments of safely conservative states, such as German Bavaria, pursue relatively moderate internal policies as polarization is a much less winning strategy (Milosch 2006). However, the extreme racist policies of American Southern states before the centralized effort to impose racial equality offer a chilling counterexample.

The Cost of Struggle

Three additions must be made to the basic calculus just outlined. The first one is the social, political, and economic cost of the pro-equality/pro-privilege struggle at the national level in a centralized country. This cost is independent of the risks that the struggle will turn disastrous for the Pro-Equality Camp (either through the Constitutional or Authoritarian Backlash of the pro-privilege side).

Even successful struggles for equality and rights can be extremely costly. In the American Civil War, the centralization of the abolition of slavery—a horrendous violation of the most basic human rights—came at a cost of more than 600,000 wartime casualties—2% of the US population of the time. Although it seems obvious that the price was worth paying given the intense Southern oppression of Black people, most pro-equality Americans would also agree that not all forms of regional oppression warrant an armed response from the federal government. In response to the decision in Dobbs v. Jackson Women's Health Organization (2022), numerous pro-privilege states moved swiftly to enact oppressive policies. In return, a number of proposals for an assertive response from the central government were advanced, including declaring a public health emergency (Editorial 2022) and offering abortion access on federal lands (Cohen, Donley, and Rebouché 2022). The pro-equality Biden administration rejected those proposals, pointing to the potential for escalation in the struggle between the presidency, controlled by the Pro-Equality Camp, and the pro-privilege states (Sullivan 2022). This and other examples of subdued reactions are proof that, despite our "we'll fight like hell" rhetoric, the Pro-Equality Camp routinely trades regionalized oppression for national stability.

Even short of armed conflict, the continuous winner-takes-all struggle over fundamental constitutional issues imposes a heavy social, political, and economic toll on countries polarized along the equality-privilege fault lines. Although much of the literature on political polarization portrays the problem as in some ways artificially created by manipulative politicians (McCarty 2019; but see Klein 2020; Chua 2018), in fact, the emotional and other stakes involved are fundamentally genuine. In societies divided across the equality–privilege dimension, the other side of the political spectrum *truly* constitutes an existential threat to their opponents' basic values and interests. In a centralized system, the winning strategy for the other side is to impose its values on the entirety of the country and weaken the chances of the opposition to reverse those changes.

I do not forget, however, that I write from a position of considerable privilege. In my endeavors in the *Social Contract Incubator*, which includes scholars from all sides of the Polish political spectrum, I have worked alongside right-wing public intellectuals. They have treated me with respect and kindness, sometimes greater than that which I have experienced from liberal intellectuals. Beyond being an atheist in an overwhelmingly Catholic country, I am not, however, a member of any of the groups that Poland's pro-privilege politics targets: the demonized trans or homosexual people, the non-white refugees brutally pushed back and left to die in freezing temperature by Polish border guards, the women subjected to unspeakable suffering because of Poland's barbaric abortion laws. For members of those oppressed groups, enthusing about a national community with their oppressors may not be viewed charitably.

Personally, however, I cannot deny that I do see value in preserving a sense of cohesive community among Polish citizens. One way to bridge the privileged and the underprivileged perspective may be through the prism of objective interests. Even in closely divided societies, citizens do agree on a lot of things. In the early 2000s, Przeworski (2003) used the example of Poles trying to avoid foreign aggression as an example of a valence issue. Three decades later, foreign and defense policies, increasingly, are subsumed in a vortex of total political war between opposing groups (Kisilowski 2022; Kisilowski and

Wojciuk 2022b). Polish history shows that internal warfare and division leads to the collapse of the state, followed by foreign occupation. And what we can surely agree on is that even underprivileged Poles would fare better under even the most pro-privilege Polish regional administration than under the rule of Vladimir Putin.

Decentralization and Multilateral Regimes

This brings us to the second important qualifier to the initial Decentralization Calculus sketched above: in countries that belong to international, value-driven regimes, such as the European Convention on Human Rights (ECHR), NATO, or the European Union, those regimes will have an asymmetrical impact on, respectively, centralized and decentralized systems.

Those multilateral regimes have become the favorite subject of criticism by pro-privilege politicians. The EU's defense of human rights and democracy has caused intense ire from pro-privilege politicians from Hungary and Poland to Italy, France, and the United Kingdom. The ECHR has been in the crosshairs of the right-wing camp in Russia, Turkey, and the UK, while the US commitment to NATO—a value-driven multilateral regime—was the favorite target of Donald Trump. The Pro-Privilege Camp is perfectly rational here. With varying effectiveness (Ekiert, Kubik, and Vachudova 2007; Kisilowski 2020b), those regimes enforce policies favored by the Pro-Equality Camp. Plainly, they limit how much oppression a pro-privilege government can enact.

And here comes the decentralization asymmetry: international organizations and agreements are entered into or withdrawn from at the central level. If the contentious issues of equality and privilege are decided mostly at the central level, pro-privilege politicians have every incentive to make their country's withdrawal from multilateral human rights regimes an agenda item at their next Constitutional Opportunity. That is precisely what happened with Brexit and with Russia's 2022 withdrawal from the Council of Europe. These are important milestones in the constitutional transformations of those respective countries: transformations aimed squarely at the systematic weakening of equality and human rights.

The more that contentious equality issues are devolved in a society closely divided along the privilege–equality dimension, the less likely would membership in a multilateral, value-driven regime become part of the national conversation. The membership in such a regime would limit the ability of pro-privilege regions to enact the worst forms of oppression. But, since membership in those organizations is not decided at the regional level, regional politicians would be able to plausibly argue that they cannot do anything about lifting those constraints.

At the same time, strong pro-equality regions would have formal or informal powers to prevent another Brexit from happening, even when pro-privilege politicians win at the national level. The possible tools are either formal participation of the regions in national legislative decision-making, through an upper house similar to the German Bundesrat, and/or becoming powerful voices in a national conversation over membership in those organizations.

Part of my optimism here is based on the realization that pro-privilege politicians are, in fact, rarely as radical as they claim and that they are often pushed by the radicalism of their voters. Plausible deniability stemming from the complexity of multi-level governance can be all they need to make their voters grudgingly acquiesce to the multilateral pro-equality constraints on the regional rule.

Obfuscation

The final variable that must be added to our Decentralization Calculus stems from the frequent lack of logical consistency and clarity in our ideological preferences. Late Professor Michael E. Levine wrote about "obfuscation" in implementing public policies (Levine and Forrence 1990). Cass Sunstein claimed that vague laws can allow "incompletely theorized agreements" between politicians espousing different values (Sunstein 1994). Anne-Marie Slaughter proposed a vision of a "disaggregated democracy," under which people do not have a single political identity but "define different parts of themselves by differentiating themselves from others in multiple contexts" (Slaughter 2002, 1072). All these points highlight inconsistence, doubt and, indeed, cowardice as important features of our political life.

Both ideological camps can interpret these inconsistencies as supporting their respective visions of good government and good society. On one hand, inconsistencies displayed by the pro-privilege citizens can be viewed as a hopeful sign that fundamental moral instincts push everybody in the pro-equality direction. White Americans are shocked by the brutal murder of George Floyd, a Black man killed by the excessive force used by a white policeman. Polish conservatives seemed to be genuinely moved by the death of Izabela, a hairdresser from Pszczyna, Silesia, who died from sepsis after being denied an abortion (Wanat and Martuscelli 2021).

Alas, on the other hand, the Pro-Privilege Camp can point to mirroring narratives and concomitant cases (or stylized cases) that supposedly show that, when push comes to shove, we all cling to traditional hierarchies. The perennial story of post-abortion guilt, especially if experienced by liberal, feminist women, is an example here. In Poland, the right beamed with elation when the news broke that General Jaruzelski—an avowed atheist and the last leader of communist Poland—received Catholic rites shortly before his death in 2014 (Bunderson 2014).

An alternative explanation of these mirroring cases is that we are all to some extent afraid of the radical, especially the violent and irreversible consequences of our moral convictions. Although philosophers thrive in uncovering the logical implications of our ordinary moral intuitions, normal people often eschew bringing their abstract, political views to their logical conclusion.

As was already suggested, in the context of multilateral regimes, decentralization can exploit the twilight zone between proclaimed political views and their radical applications. On the one hand, the sense of ownership and control over one's region brings self-confidence and a sense of safety to the Pro-Privilege Camp that will decrease the incentive to excessively "prove themselves" or "hold the line" against the pro-equality onslaught. On the other hand, detachment from the national, winner-take-all contests with the Pro-Equality Camp creates fewer incentives to bring their views to their extreme logical conclusions.

In overwhelmingly conservative German or Austrian states, such as Bavaria or Carinthia, the pro-privilege majority marks their territory with symbolic violence, especially when it comes to omnipresent and state-sanctioned displays of official (and exclusionary) religious identity. However, neither state has sunk to the degree of oppression in centralized countries run by pro-privilege authoritarians, such as Poland or Hungary.

Decentralization Calculus: The Final Version

A proper appreciation of the costs of the centralized, winner-takes-all political struggle over equality of rights and opportunities in closely divided societies, of the asymmetrical impact of international human rights regimes on centralized and decentralized countries, as well as the tendency of elites and voters to obfuscate the practical implications of their ideological commitments, all modify our original Decentralization Calculus in the same direction: by making the decentralized solution relatively more attractive as compared to the centralized one.

The centralized solution offers a national equality standard in the near term, but at a high cost. A pro-privilege Constitutional Backlash can eviscerate the equality gains for the entire nation, while an Authoritarian Backlash can lock in this new oppression for a very long time. Indeed, the stakes here may be larger than what history teaches. It is still unclear if mass digital surveillance technology and the omnipresence of social media have fundamentally constrained the ability of the people to overthrow an authoritarian regime. Examples from Hong Kong to Venezuela are disconcerting. Perhaps the new surveillance tools are, in domestic politics, the equivalent of nuclear weapons in international relations: a technological breakthrough that fundamentally limited the possibility of forced change. If that is the case, then the risk of an Authoritarian Backlash may need to be taken much more seriously. Whilst, in the twentieth century, collective memory and prevailing narratives focused on the *process of losing* democracy, the twenty-first century may mark the era when we will have to come to terms with the virtual *impossibility of regaining* a lost democracy.

On the decentralized side, we see a clear, and terrifying, potential for enthusiastic oppression in pro-privilege states, which will, however, be mitigated by multilateral human rights regimes (when available) and an increased ability of pro-privilege elites, unburdened from the constant tit-for-tat with the Pro-Equality Camp, to obfuscate and avoid the most extreme consequences of their ideological outlook.

Conclusion: Dismay and Hope in Closely Divided Societies

Finding a stable constitutional settlement with compatriots who reject basic principles of equality and human rights is a tortured reality. Those few democratic societies that do not need to face this reality should appreciate how lucky they are. For the rest of us, it is important to introduce more realism about what can be achieved within a democratic system. This chapter has tried to outline the key tradeoffs. It can inform real-life constitutional designers who should fill the categories indicated with nation-specific and case-specific data. What rights are at stake? Whom do the pro-privilege voters want to oppress and how severely? What is the status quo? In Poland, a valid response to the pro-equality critics of the *Social Contract Incubator* is that, as long as Poland stays in the European human rights system, even the most pro-privilege regions cannot impose more suffering on women and minorities than the current authoritarian government is doing at the national level. If a country is still a democracy with basic human rights enforced, what is the realistic chance that a pro-privilege Constitutional Opportunity could materialize in the foreseeable future? How big is the authoritarian risk? What are the social, economic, and geopolitical risks of the continuous all-out political war at the center?

Susan Rose-Ackerman (2005) was one of the lone voices highlighting the deep institutional weaknesses of the supposed democratic frontrunners of the day in Eastern Europe: Hungary and Poland. History has proven her right. Since 2010, backsliding in both countries became the "leading indicator" for a global wave of authoritarian populism engulfing democracies from Brazil, the Philippines, and Turkey to Italy, France, the UK, and the United States.

But the last two decades saw some more hopeful stories as well. Australia—a country characterized by deep urban–rural and regional divides like those in Poland and the United States—never centralized abortion rights. Yet, through a mixture of legislative and judicial action, the procedure has gradually been legalized in all the country's nine states. The resulting hodge-podge is far from perfect (de Costa et al. 2015), but the trend is decidedly away from the worst excesses of misogyny. Ireland—a small country the size of an average American state or Polish voivodeship or region—went through a remarkable centralized change of heart on key equality topics including immigration, abortion, and same-sex marriage and progressed on those issues through centralized constitutional and legislative changes (McWilliams 2018).

Both centralized imposition and decentralized settlement have a role to play in the pro-equality strategy. But each should be employed based on a realistic assessment of the political strength of reformers and a full appreciation of the direct and indirect consequences of both our actions and the likely responses of political adversaries. As in any close fight, dogmatic attachment to one strategy is never the best approach. As Rose-Ackerman argued in a different context: "Self-interested behavior is a fact of life. People who recognize this are neither liberal nor conservative. They are realists. . . . Procedures for managing conflict are central to the design of social institutions" (Rose-Ackerman 1992, 187).

Notes

1 In fact, between 1918 and the abolishment of the popularly elected city government by the Austro-fascist government in 1934, the city was colloquially known as "The Red Vienna" for its social-democratic, highly progressive city government (see e.g. McFarland, Spitaler, and Zechner 2020). Social democrats returned to power after the fall of the Nazi regime in 1945.
2 For the thorough critique of the concept of a market-preserving federalism see Rodden and Rose-Ackerman (1997).
3 For a critique of this see Rose-Ackerman (1980).

References

Ackerman, Bruce A. 1998. *We the People: Transformations*. Cambridge, Mass.: Belknap Press of Harvard University Press.
—. 2015. *We the People: The Civil Rights Revolution*. Cambridge, Mass.: Belknap Press of Harvard University Press.
Amar, Akhil Reed. 1991. "Some New World Lessons for the Old World." *The University of Chicago Law Review* 58 (2): 483–510.
Balkin, Jack M. 1999. "Free Speech and Hostile Environments." *Columbia Law Review*: 2295–2320.
Barber, Benjamin R. 2013. *If Mayors Ruled the World: Dysfunctional Nations, Rising Cities*. New Haven: Yale University Press.
Brenner, Saul, and Harold J. Spaeth. 1995. *Stare Indecisis: The Alteration of Precedent on the Supreme Court, 1946–1992*. New York: Cambridge University Press.
Bunderson, Carl. 2014. "Polish Communist's Reconciliation with Church Hailed as Joyous." *Catholic News Agency*, Jun. 18, 2014. https://www.catholicnewsagency.com/news/29878/polish-communists-reconciliation-with-church-hailed-as-joyous.
Choudhry, Sujit. 2008. *Constitutional Design for Divided Societies: Integration or Accommodation?* Oxford; New York: Oxford University Press.
Chua, Amy. 2018. *Political Tribes: Group Instinct and the Fate of Nations*. New York: Penguin.
Cohen, David S, Greer Donley, and Rachel Rebouché. 2022. "The New Abortion Battleground." *Available at SSRN 4032931*.
de Costa, Caroline, Heather Douglas, Julie Hamblin, Philippa Ramsay, and Mandy Shircore. 2015. "Abortion Law Across Australia—A Review of Nine Jurisdictions." *Australian and New Zealand Journal of Obstetrics and Gynaecology* 55 (2): 105–111.
DelReal, Jose A. 2014, "Obamacare Consultant under Fire for 'Stupidity of the American Voter' Comments," *Washington Post*, Nov. 11, 2014.
Dickinson, Tim. 2010. "You Idiots: Meet the Planet's Worst Enemies." *The Rolling* Stone, Jan. 21, 2010.
Djilas, Milovan. 1957. *The New Class: An Analysis of the Communist System*. New York: Praeger.
Dobbs v. Jackson Women's Health Organization. 2022.
Dworkin, Ronald. 1977. *Taking Rights Seriously*. London: Duckworth.

Editorial. 2022. "It's Time to Declare a Public Health Emergency for Abortion." *The Los Angeles Times*, Jul. 13, 2022.

Ekiert, Grzegorz, Jan Kubik, and Milada Anna Vachudova. 2007. "Democracy in the Post-Communist World: An Unending Quest?" *East European Politics and Societies* 21 (1): 7–30.

Hirschman, Albert O. 1970. *Exit, Voice, and Loyalty: Responses to Decline in Firms, Organizations, and States*. Cambridge, Mass.: Harvard University Press.

Katz, Bruce, and Jeremy Nowak. 2017. *The New Localism: How Cities Can Thrive in the Age of Populism*. Washington, DC: Brookings Institution Press.

Kisilowska, Izabela. 2010. "Choiceless Democracy: Policy-making in Extraordinary Situations." Doctoral dissertation, University of Cambridge, Department of Politics.

Kisilowski, Maciej. 2015. "Poland's democracy is crumbling." *Politico*, Dec. 24, 2015. http://www.politico.eu/article/polands-court-international-help-democracy-reform-rights-rule-of-law/.

—. 2019. "From Refuge to Trap: Formalist Misadventures of Poland's Post-Socialist Legal Profession." *International Journal of the Legal Profession* 26 (2–3): 321–334.

—. 2020a. "Constitutional Strategy for a Polarized Society: Learning from Poland's Post-revolutionary Misfortunes." In *Revolutionary Constitutionalism: Law, Legitimacy, Power* edited by Richard Albert. Oxford: Hart Publishing.

—. 2020b. "The Forgotten Values: How Europe's Bet on the Rule of Law Backfired." *Sept. 24* (blog), *BRIDGE Blog*.

—. 2022. "The West Won't Solve the Ukraine Crisis by Making Deals with Autocrats." *Los Angeles Times*, Mar. 23, 2022. https://www.latimes.com/opinion/story/2022-03-23/russia-ukraine-nato-poland-turkey-authoritarian.

Kisilowski, Maciej, and Wojciech Przybylski. 2019. "Democratic Lessons from the EU." *Project Syndicate*, May 14, 2019. https://www.project-syndicate.org/commentary/poland-democratic-deficit-european-union-by-maciej-kisilowski-and-wojciech-przybylski-2019–05.

Kisilowski, Maciej, and Anna Wojciuk. 2022a. "Rational Rebellion against Reason: The Logic of Conservative Authoritarianism." *Manuscript, under review*.

—. 2022b. "Ukraine's Lessons for NATO's Eastern Flank." *Project Syndicate*, Feb. 25. https://www.project-syndicate.org/commentary/ukraine-lessons-for-nato-eastern-flank-by-maciej-kisilowski-and-anna-wojciuk-2022–02.

—. 2023. "The Authoritarian Hangover." *Project Syndicate*, May 9, 2023. https://www.project-syndicate.org/commentary/poland-democratic-deficit-european-union-by-maciej-kisilowski-and-wojciech-przybylski-2019–05.

Klein, Ezra. 2020. *Why We're Polarized*. London: Profile Books.

Kochenov, Dimitry. 2019. *Citizenship*. Cambridge, Mass.: MIT Press.

Levine, Michael E., and Jennifer L. Forrence. 1990. "Regulatory Capture, Public Interest, and The Public Agenda: Toward a Synthesis." *Journal of Law, Economics, and Organization* 6 (Special Issue): 167.

Lijphart, Arend. 1977. *Democracy in Plural Societies: A Comparative Exploration*. New Haven: Yale University Press.

Lindseth, Peter L. 2016. "The Perils of 'as if' European Constitutionalism." *European Law Journal* 22 (5): 696–718.

McCarty, Nolan M. 2019. *Polarization: What Everyone Needs to Know*. New York: Oxford University Press.

McFarland, Robert B., Georg Spitaler, and Ingo Zechner. 2020. *The Red Vienna Sourcebook. Studies in German Literature, Linguistics, and Culture*. Rochester: Camden House.

McWilliams, David. 2018. *Renaissance Nation*. Dublin: Gill Books.

Milosch, Mark S. 2006. *Modernizing Bavaria: The Politics of Franz Josef Strauss and the CSU, 1949–1969*. Vol. 15. *Monographs in German History*. New York: Berghahn Books.

Morse, Yonatan L. 2012. "The Era of Electoral Authoritarianism." *World Politics* 64 (1): 161–198.

New York State Rifle & Pistol Association, Inc. v. Bruen. 2022.

Nowicka, Kinga. 2019. "Odmowa Dostępu do Legalnej Aborcji Jest Torturą [Denying Abortion Access is Torture]." *Glamour*, Aug. 29, 2019.

Piketty, Thomas, and Arthur Goldhammer. 2020. *Capital and Ideology*. Cambridge, Mass.: Harvard University Press.

Przeworski, Adam. 1991. *Democracy and the Market, Political and Economic Reforms in Eastern Europe and Latin America*. Cambridge: Cambridge University Press.

—. 2003. *States and Markets: A Primer in Political Economy*. Cambridgte: Cambridge University Press.

Rodden, Jonathan, and Susan Rose-Ackerman. 1997. "The Allocation of Government Authority: Does Federalism Preserve Markets?" *Virginia Law Review* 83 (7): 1521.

Rose-Ackerman, Susan. 1980. "Risk Taking and Reelection: Does Federalism Promote Innovation?" *The Journal of Legal Studies* 9 (3): 593–616.

—. 1992. *Rethinking the Progressive Agenda: The Reform of the American Regulatory State*. New York: The Free Press.

—. 2005. *From Elections to Democracy. Building Accountable Government in Hungary and Poland*. Cambridge: Cambridge University Press.

Schauer, Frederick. 2018. "Stare Decisis—Rhetoric and Reality in the Supreme Court." *Sup. Ct. Rev.* 2018: 121.

Scheppele, Kim Lane, Dimitry Vladimirovich Kochenov, and Barbara Grabowska-Moroz. 2021. "EU Values are Law, After All: Enforcing EU Values through Systemic Infringement Actions by the European Commission and the Member States of the European Union." *Yearbook of European law* 39: 3–121.

"Scott Decries 'Racist Response' to BIPOC Vaccine Eligibility." 2021. *The Associated Press*, Apr. 6, 2021.

Sealy-Huggins, Leon. 2018. "The Climate Crisis Is a Racist Crisis: Structural Racism, Inequality and Climate Change." In *The Fire Now: Anti-Racist Scholarship in Times of Explicit Racial Violence*, edited by Azeezat Johnson, Remi Joseph-Salisbury, and Beth Kamunge, xix, 284 pages. London: Zed Books.

Simeon, Richard. 2006. "Federalism and Social Justice: Thinking Through the Tangle." In *Territory, Democracy and Justice: Regionalism and Federalism in Western Democracies*, edited by Scott L. Greer, xiv, 302 pages. New York: Palgrave Macmillan.

Slaughter, Anne-Marie. 2002. "Global Government Networks, Global Information Agencies, and Disaggregated Democracy." *Michigan Journal of International Law* 24: 1041.

Sullivan, Kate. 2022. "White House Press Secretary Says Using Federal Lands for Abortion Services Would Have 'Dangerous Ramifications'." *CNN.com*, Jun. 28, 2022.

Sunstein, Cass R. 1994. "Incompletely Theorized Agreements." *Harvard Law Review* 108 (3): 1733.

Wanat, Zosia, and Carlo Martuscelli. 2021. "Pregnant Woman's Death Renews Abortion Ban Controversy in Poland." *Politico*, Nov. 2, 2021.

West Virginia v. Environmental Protection Agency. 2022.

Wildavsky, Aaron B. 1998. *Federalism & Political Culture*. New Brunswick: Transaction Publishers.

11 Judicial Review of the Executive in Hyper-Presidential Regimes

Edgar Andrés Melgar and Susan Rose-Ackerman

In the global south, presidentialism is pervasive and entrenched. Both as a matter of law and practice, presidents wield significant policymaking powers, often exceeding the ability of fractured and inert legislatures to enact policy changes through legislation. Although the concentration of power in a single figure may limit the instability caused by divided government, without effective procedural safeguards, such power can open the door to governance by presidential fiat. This threat looms heavily over countries that have recently begun to make the transition from an authoritarian regime or where democratic institutions remain weak. In the absence of a strong legislature, responsibility for policing the executive falls on the judicial branch. But, in many countries, the judiciary has been historically unwilling or unable to rein in the power of presidents, owing to a lack of authority, political independence, or even technical competence. Thus, empowering the courts effectively to assist the public in holding the executive accountable for its decisions will require significant changes. In this essay, we briefly summarize Latin American attempts to strengthen the ability of the courts, and through them, the public, to demand reasoned decision-making from the executive.[1] These reforms create opportunities, but also pose challenges. We conclude by urging judicial reform as part of any broad agenda for building effective policymaking capacity in democracies.

Presidential systems take different forms, operating under varying constitutional arrangements. Separation-of-powers presidentialism in the United States, for instance, is distinguishable from the strong presidentialism of France or Turkey, and the "hyper-presidentialism" that pervades in Latin America and elsewhere. Furthermore, strong presidential regimes do not necessarily neuter the ability of other branches of government—the legislature and the courts—or other political actors to rein in the unfettered power of an executive. There are, in other words, many different forms of presidentialism.[2]

Nonetheless, a common feature of modern presidentialism is an expanded role for the president in exercising policymaking discretion, that is, choosing one policy alternative over another without having to secure specific legislative (or, for that matter, popular) assent. Those choices can be very specific, such as the decision to allocate scarce resources to one project over another or to

DOI: 10.4324/9781003416036-11

site a facility in a specific location, or broad and general, like the adoption of one regulatory framework over another. Presidents may, for instance, carry out general policies through regulations, norms of general application with the force of law, based on authority delegated by the legislature, inherent executive authority, or explicit constitutional powers that do not require a statutory delegation.

The ability of presidents to enact policies with the force of law has become a critical asset for modern presidents. Contemporary governance requires complex and technical policymaking that realistically cannot be achieved through legislative text alone. Uniformity and fair notice to the public, in turn, means that piecemeal, case-by-case policymaking will not suffice; broad policymaking can only be achieved through regulations. Modern welfare states, built on the protection of social and economic rights or other entitlements, rely on the ability of the public administration to competently distribute services and impose costs following fair and equitable procedures.[3] Emergencies, including COVID-19, have shown that the ability of presidents to adopt appropriate discretionary policies can prove critical in effectively responding to dynamic crises.

Moreover, as presidents assert direct authority over policymaking, boundaries between the president and the executive—that is, the bureaucracy that operates agencies and the rest of the public administration—are blurred. Presidents, increasingly, take credit for policymaking, even in the most technical fields of the public administration, and they can be held directly accountable for an administration's policy failings.[4]

Broad presidential control over the executive offers key advantages for effective public governance. Presidential supervision can be executed through different mechanisms, including removal or censure of officials, promulgation of broad directives or guidelines that aim to guide an administrative agency's policymaking, direct assumption of an agency's regulatory or policymaking decisions, or the enactment of regulations or policies independent of any agency.[5] These mechanisms ensure that administrative agencies only enact policies that have received the assent of the single top elected official in the executive branch.[6] And, in countries that have historically been plagued by corruption or malfeasance, particularly at lower levels in the bureaucracy, presidential control could be a safeguard against policymaking influenced by a single subordinate official's biases or interests. Accordingly, advocates of presidential administration argue that direct presidential control ensures the democratic legitimacy of policymaking by administrative agencies.[7]

Yet, a president's broad policymaking discretion also raises significant challenges, especially about the democratic legitimacy of decision-making processes. Without clear safeguards, policymaking discretion can quickly creep toward unaccountable unilateralism, allowing presidents to adopt a given policy choice without having to consult interested parties or offer a reasoned explanation. Particularly in countries with weak democratic institutions, where courts are unable or unwilling to effectively enforce judicial review, policymaking discretion can morph into authoritarianism or even kleptocracy.[8] Without effective limits, the public can be left without any clear means of expressing objections or qualified support for a proposed policy action until after a president or the executive has chosen one alternative over another. The ballot box offers a final opportunity to express frustration at a president's policy priorities. But an institutional design that focuses on elections as the sole source of political legitimacy takes a narrow, plebiscitary, view of democracy, and one that overlooks the importance of process over outcomes.[9] Such a view of democracy, in turn, is particularly dangerous in countries where some part of the citizenry is vocally opposed to democratic electoral transitions, or in countries that have otherwise struggled to build trust in the fairness and transparency of government institutions.

In the United States, judicial review and administrative law has evolved into the primary safeguard against executive overreach in policymaking. Congress itself can impose limits by narrowing the scope of delegated rulemaking powers or by limiting a president's ability to intervene directly in an agency's rulemaking processes. But, it needs to do so in the text of the original stature because the Supreme Court has held that legislative vetoes of administrative rules are unconstitutional.[10] Hence, Congress rarely, if ever, interferes with or obstructs an agency's policy decisions. Instead, courts play an active role in limiting agency discretion. The Administrative Procedure Act ("APA") establishes judicially enforceable procedural safeguards that ensure that binding regulations are adopted only after notice and public comment.[11] And the APA's requirement that instructs the courts to strike down agencies' arbitrary and capricious actions has been understood to imply that agencies must provide a reasoned and transparent explanation for their actions.[12] Courts also regularly enjoin agency decisions that fail to follow proper procedures.[13] Moreover, although courts have historically deferred to agencies' interpretations of technical statutes, under controversial principles, such as the major questions doctrine, courts in the United States are adopting an assertive and broad view of their role in reviewing the substance of executive action.[14]

Judicial review, anchored in administrative law, may provide a suitable check on executive power where, as in the United States, there is a well-settled practice of respect for separation of powers. Our focus, instead, is on jurisdictions where presidents hold outsized power, whether as a matter of law or practice, relative to other branches of government. Drawing on our 2022 article, we reference Latin American cases, but the phenomenon has a global scope.[15] These hyper-presidential regimes present a particular challenge for the institutional design of public administration. We accept, as a fixed point of departure, that certain countries have chosen constitutional structures that afford their presidents oversized powers, relative to the judiciary and, in particular, the legislature. With that in mind, we ask what, if any, should be the proper role of courts in regulating executive policymaking discretion.

Under existing administrative law in hyper-presidential regimes, judicial review is unlikely to provide an effective check on executive policymaking. Many countries with such regimes have adopted laws designed to guard against violations of rights in specific, individual agency decisions, such as the distribution of licenses.[16] Unlike the APA, administrative law in most countries with hyper-presidential regimes does not have specific procedural requirements that govern the executive's policy decision-making. That choice may be a conscious desire to insulate executive power, consistent with a constitutional design favoring presidential control. Or it may reflect the traditional reluctance of civil law regimes to concentrate judicial review over executive actions in administrative tribunals with limited jurisdiction.[17]

Nonetheless, examination of the Latin American cases shows that most hyper-presidential regimes are evolving to recognize a need for judicial review over executive policymaking. We have identified mechanisms that have emerged as vehicles to allow courts (and by extension, the public) to check executive policymaking. These innovations allow courts and, indeed, the public in hyper-presidential regimes to begin to demand that the executive account for its policy choices by offering a transparent and reasoned explanation or by requiring consultations with communities and individuals likely affected by a given policy choice. In some jurisdictions with hyper-presidential regimes, courts, relying on these mechanisms, have been willing to enjoin executive action, notwithstanding their historical reluctance to constrain executive power.

In limiting executive policymaking discretion, courts have been driven primarily by a concern with ensuring that decision-making processes are consistent with democratic values, both by informing the public of evolving policy choices, and by ensuring the public an opportunity to comment or intervene before a final choice is made.[18] Faced with an underlying constitutional structure that favors the executive, however, courts in hyper-presidential regimes have been reluctant to significantly constrain executive power, and presidents continue to have broad latitude to exercise lawmaking powers.[19] On the one hand, courts have been reluctant to impose one policy choice over another, and they have regularly deferred to agencies' expertise over highly technical matters. On the other hand, even though statutory reforms to administrative laws have begun to introduce notice-and-comment-like procedures for agency rulemaking, concerned or affected members of the public have no clear right to seek judicial enforcement of these provisions. Given the structure of hyper-presidential regimes, it is unlikely that courts will ever have the willingness or the statutory power to eliminate the ability of presidents to act unilaterally. Nonetheless, an emerging trend recognizes that courts can play an important role in placing democratic guardrails on executive discretion, even in countries that have been historically reluctant to allow courts to constrain presidential power.

Courts, thus, are increasingly a key site for policing irrational or arbitrary decision-making. As such, courts have also become a vital tool for ensuring transparency and reasonableness in administrative decision-making in general.[20] This trend suggests that judicial reform should be viewed as an integral part of building a state's capacity for effective policymaking. Institutional reform within the executive, through tools like civil service reform or anti-corruption legislation, has been traditionally viewed as the primary mechanism for strengthening and ensuring rational policymaking.[21] Such reforms are clearly important, but in hyper-presidential regimes, where much final decision-making authority resides with presidents themselves, reform of the bureaucracy alone will not be enough. Instead, in light of the increasingly broad role of the judiciary, strengthening the capacity of courts to review agency decisions that implement public policies will become essential for ensuring rational, accountable, and transparent decision-making.

This chapter proceeds in three sections. We first introduce hyper-presidential administration, connecting theories of hyper-presidentialism, developed in political science, with models of presidential administration, primarily discussed in legal scholarship. The second section describes the traditional limits on judicial review over executive actions in countries with hyper-presidential regimes, where administrative law has traditionally been defined in narrow terms. The next section identifies legal innovations, both within administrative law and without, which have strengthened the ability of courts to review executive decision-making directly. Looking forward, the conclusion identifies some challenges and discusses the importance of capacity-building in the judiciary itself.

Hyper-Presidential Administration

Our focus on hyper-presidentialism builds on the work of political scientists, especially the seminal work of Juan Linz, who characterized many governments in Latin America as hyper-presidential.[22] For Linz, presidential systems are plagued by "the problem of dual legitimacy," where, as a structural and abstract matter, "no democratic principle exists to resolve disputes between the executive and the legislature about which of the two actually represents the will of the people."[23] Hyper-presidential systems have resolved the problem of dual legitimacy by favoring presidents over legislatures, granting the executive significant policymaking powers and limiting legislative supervision of the public administration.[24] Under this view, elections alone offer presidents a sufficient democratic mandate to carry out extensive policy actions, and victorious presidential candidates should not have to explain their choices or seek additional consent for their actions.[25]

An implicit feature of hyper-presidentialism, albeit often overlooked, is skepticism towards courts as checks on executive power. One way to resolve the "problem of dual legitimacy," in a classical tri-partite system of separation of powers, would be to empower courts to resolve disputes between the executive and the legislature over effective implementation of the "will of the people." In hyper-presidential regimes, however, courts are viewed as either illegitimate or ineffective arbitrators. Illegitimate, because judicial review raises the specter of counter-majoritarian rule, in countries where the legacy of authoritarian regimes or rule by the fiat of *juntas* continues to loom. Ineffective, because courts may be viewed as weak or corrupt. They also lack the bureaucratic capacity to carry out structural reforms themselves that could enhance the public legitimacy of executive policymaking processes. And, of course, once presidents gain extensive powers through a hyper-presidential regime, they can exercise those powers in ways that curtail the independence and legitimacy of the courts.

Hyper-presidentialism has traditionally been associated with Latin America because many presidents in that region have significant policymaking discretion. As heads of state, heads of government, and chief executives of the civil service, presidents control the public administration, appoint and remove cabinet officers, assume legislative powers in times of emergency, and enact binding regulations.[26] Commentators have argued that these powers amount to "executive lawmaking" and represent a distinctive feature of Latin American constitutionalism.[27] But while the term "hyper-presidentialism" was initially coined to characterize the specific form of presidentialism that emerged in Latin America during the wave of democratization that followed the end of military rule in the 1980s,[28] it can also be aptly used to describe presidential regimes elsewhere, including the Philippines and Turkey.[29] Unsurprisingly, a common feature across countries with hyper-presidential regimes is a legacy of military rule, often fueling, paradoxically, both toleration and fear of strong executives.

But hyper-presidentialism and authoritarianism are distinguishable. Hyper-presidentialism continues to recognize the ballot box as the ultimate source of legitimacy. The gravest threat to democratic stability posed by hyper-presidentialism is not a coup or another permanent usurpation of powers but, rather, creeping, if legally legitimate, expansion and concentrations of power. As Nancy Bermeo has pointed out, contemporary democratic backsliding is less likely to involve radical disruptions to institutions, such as coups, but instead operates via creeping, and potentially even lawful, abuse of statutory or delegated powers.[30] The absence of strong procedural safeguards to constrain the scope of executive discretion not only weakens the democratic legitimacy of policymaking, but also opens a backdoor to democratic backsliding by allowing presidents with autocratic inclinations to test the limits of their policymaking power. And, it is precisely in these grey zones, at the outer edges of legality, where courts could, ideally, intervene to clarify the boundaries between legitimate use of delegated powers and illegitimate aggrandizement.

Chief executives in hyper-presidential regimes typically have three key powers. First, presidents have broad control over the public administration, including the power to appoint and remove cabinet officers and to direct them to implement the president's specific policy agendas.[31] Second, during states of exception or other extreme circumstances, presidents have the power to issue decree-laws, that is, executive orders with a status equal to legislation that do not immediately require parliamentary assent.[32] Third, presidents hold broad powers to issue regulations.[33] We focus primarily on executive regulations, as the site where, in the course of their non-emergency, day-to-day operations, presidents can exercise expansive powers with few procedural protections or judicial oversight, in ways that can have an impact on large swaths of the public. Because they are enacted pursuant to a statutory or constitutional delegation of powers, without clear safeguards, regulations offer executives in hyper-presidential regimes an opportunity for gradually expanding and entrenching their power.

In particular, presidents may be more tempted to abuse rulemaking if they have broad constitutional powers, rather than narrower and more clearly defined statutory mandates. In Latin America, for example, constitutions grant presidents the power to issue regulations with the force of law. Doctrinally, regulations are classified into three main categories: (1) implementing regulations; (2) autonomous regulations; and (3) delegated regulations. In addition, presidents can issue sub-regulatory norms, such as technical standards, or informal guidance documents. We focus on the first two types of regulations, as the most common and the best examples of sites where limited oversight can lead to creeping assertions of added power.

Implementing regulations allow the executive to give effect to legislation and, where necessary, to fill technical gaps.[34] Their primary function is to clarify, specify, facilitate, and complement the law, or to fill in details that were omitted explicitly from the law but are contemplated by the law's context and purpose.[35] Implementing regulations make statutory provisions operative that, because of their generality, cannot otherwise be applied to individuals.[36] In some cases, a statute may explicitly call on the executive to issue implementing regulations.[37] In others, the need for implementing regulations may be implicit in the broader statutory framework.[38] These regulations are a ubiquitous form of executive policymaking and could be subject to specific legislative constraints.

Autonomous regulations, in contrast, lack a clear legislative mandate.[39] They do not depend on a single law, although sometimes they may intersect with and complement existing laws. They are also called organizational regulations because they primarily codify an agency's rules of internal organization.[40] Occasionally, autonomous regulations have external binding effects on the public at large. Those regulations, also known as constitutional regulations, appear in one of two contexts. First, the constitutional text may explicitly authorize certain regulations, even in the absence of a predicate statute, for example, by granting a president the power to "regulate" a specific sector of the economy.[41] Second, regulations may be necessary to give effect to a constitutionally protected right, where the legislature has otherwise failed to enact an implementing statute but a constitutional protection cannot be abandoned.[42] Although these regulations may be necessary for ensuring the efficient operation of the executive branch, or for giving effect to constitutional provisions, they can also raise questions of democratic illegitimacy because they can be insulated from legislative or public deliberation.

Much more problematic, however, is the absence of clear procedural safeguards that might demand that presidents enact regulations not only within the scope of legality but also through processes that require reasoned and participatory decision-making. Hyper-presidential administration is defined by the executive's broad policymaking powers, combined with the absence of procedural safeguards that might constrain a president's arbitrary decision-making power. Most countries with hyper-presidential systems have viewed administrative law as primarily concerned with organizing the public administration and resolving disputes between individual private actors and the state. Administrative law in such jurisdictions has historically been inclined to uphold, rather than resist, executive power, borrowing from French public law's notions of public service and public power, and its resistance to judicial review.

In these legal systems, administrative law developed largely to establish the procedures employed by specialized administrative courts to adjudicate challenges to executive actions. Disputes heard in these courts were, almost exclusively, individual challenges to an administrative agency's ruling involving decisions such as the award of a license. Administrative law was not concerned with an agency's policymaking procedure unless individual rights or vested interests were clearly affected.[43] Individuals might claim that an agency had infringed on their due process rights, but only insofar as an arbitrary outcome had led to a deprivation of rights or interests, not because the decision-making process itself was unlawful. The role of the courts, at least as far as administrative law was concerned, was not to limit or to check the executive's broad policymaking powers but to protect individual rights in particular disputes.

Judicial Review and Legality

Nonetheless, in hyper-presidential regimes, courts can seek to ensure that the executive adheres to basic principles of legality. In carrying out this function, courts have focused on policing against actions that exceed statutory authority, rather than ensuring an appropriate decision-making process. Unsurprisingly, however, in hyper-presidential regimes, where the constitutional cards are generally stacked in the executive's favor, courts have primarily focused on holding the legislature accountable for effective or ineffective legislative drafting, rather than on limiting the scope of executive power. Constitutions in hyper-presidential systems may include a non-delegation clause, restricting the legislature's ability to delegate its powers to the executive.[44] And while courts have been unwilling to directly address the scope of those constitutional provisions, principles of non-delegation have animated judicial review over the legality of executive regulations.

In checking the executive's rulemaking powers, courts have primarily invoked two doctrines: statutory supremacy and reserve of law.[45] Both seek to ensure that executive regulations, particularly those that implement legislative policies, remain subordinate to statutes issued through traditional lawmaking processes.[46] Statutory supremacy requires that regulations abide by the hierarchy of norms set out in the constitution, demanding that regulations do not directly contradict hierarchically superior statutes but, rather, complement existing statutes.[47] The reserve-of-law doctrine places three additional limits on a president's rulemaking authority.[48] First, under reserve of law, certain areas of policymaking, traditionally those that involve fundamental rights, can only be regulated through legislation.[49] In other words, legislation has primary authority or "reserve" over that particular policy area. Second, statutes that delegate rulemaking authority must set specific limits to the scope of implementing regulations, and the legislature cannot delegate open-ended legislative power to presidents over matters that the constitution specifically entrusts to the legislature.[50] Third, if a given issue is subject to reserve of law, executive regulations cannot contradict or otherwise infringe the statutory framework.[51]

This traditional framework, then, constrains the ability of courts to restrict presidential abuses of power. The scope of judicial review is limited to ensuring that statutes are properly drafted, on the one hand, and that the executive operates within constraints set by the legislature, on the other. Such narrow review leaves presidents with extensive discretion to act in ways that, while legal, may be unreasonable.

Judicial Review and Constitutional Rights

Constitutional reforms, in contrast, have significantly expanded the ability of courts to review executive actions for consistency with protected rights, including the right to a clean environment. Although classic administrative law allowed courts to protect the due process rights of individuals affected by a discrete agency action, today, under constitutional law principles, courts can review broad policies for inconsistency with protected rights. Thus, citing the protection of constitutional rights, judicial review has gone beyond supervising the legality of executive actions, to ensure that policies satisfy certain substantive thresholds. Notably, because certain protected rights are deemed to include a procedural component, courts can enforce rights in a way that requires policies concerning certain matters, such as the environment, be adopted in ways that satisfy specific procedural safeguards. Although not directly framed as a procedural check on presidential power, in protecting the procedural components of constitutional rights, courts, in effect, can intervene more directly in an executive's decision-making process.

Consider, for example, the right to a clean environment, recognized by several countries with Latin American hyper-presidential regimes as a relatively new constitutional innovation. That right is individual and collective, protecting individuals and the community at large from excessive environmental degradation, and includes substantive and procedural prongs. At a substantive level, the right to the environment prohibits state action that would unreasonably increase environmental degradation, for example, because it ignores less-polluting alternatives.[52] At a procedural level, the right to a clean and balanced environment has been interpreted to include a procedural component that requires state actors to carry out environmental impact assessments and engage in consultations with potentially affected communities before adapting a particular policy.[53] Such safeguards are designed to ensure reasoned decision-making and public accountability. They require agencies to consider relevant factors, including a policy's potential detrimental effects that might only be revealed by an impact assessment and to engage in more participatory decision-making.

In Latin America, the rights of indigenous communities operate as a similar check. Likely acknowledging the historical marginalization of sizable indigenous communities in these countries, constitutions throughout the region have evolved to recognize indigenous peoples as a protected group entitled to specific rights. As a baseline, these rights include recognition and preservation of the distinctive identity of indigenous communities.[54] At the same time, however, through constitutional provisions or legislation, courts in the region have recognized that, as part of their right to recognition, indigenous communities are entitled to prior consultation before state actors adopt policies that would have a direct detrimental impact on their welfare.[55] As with the procedural prong of the right to the environment, the right to indigenous consultation operates collaterally as a procedural safeguard, requiring that government agencies take specific steps before adopting a particular policy choice.

Constitutional rights, thus, have emerged as a new constraint on executive discretion. Particularly surprising is the extent to which courts, even in hyper-presidential regimes, have been willing to enjoin agency actions where there is a clear violation of the substantive or procedural prongs of the right to the environment or the rights of indigenous communities.[56] In such cases, courts appear to be stepping out of their traditional reluctance to place specific constraints on the executive itself. Importantly, however, these checks have been imposed only in specific areas of law that appear to raise particular procedural concerns. As such, they do not provide courts with the opening to review executive policymaking broadly in a trans-substantive uniform manner.

Procedural Safeguards with Limited Judicial Review

Despite their general reluctance to constrain the executive's policymaking discretion, countries with hyper-presidential regimes have begun to adopt statutes that require greater transparency from decision-makers or that otherwise indicate that agencies should follow particular procedures when engaging in rulemaking. Two important steps include public information access laws and, in a few jurisdictions, new administrative procedure laws that incorporate requirements similar to U.S. notice-and-comment processes. These changes may reflect growing popular demands for accountability, as well as other types of external pressures to implement accountable regulatory practices. When incorporating these regulatory good practices into domestic law, however, countries with hyper-presidential regimes have been reluctant to extend judicial review too broadly. On the one hand, public information laws typically allow courts to examine, albeit to a limited degree, an agency's refusal to grant access to certain information. On the other, reforms to administrative laws tend to create new procedural safeguards that have no clear mechanism for judicial enforcement. The effectiveness of these reforms, thus, may ultimately depend on the willingness of legislatures in hyper-presidential regimes to shed some of their traditional reluctance to constrain the executive and to grant greater authority to the judiciary.

Public information access laws have broadly expanded the right of the public to become informed of the executive's decision-making processes.[57] As a general rule, these laws require agencies either affirmatively and periodically to disclose certain information,[58] such as any proposed regulations, or to make internal information accessible to the public upon request.[59] An agency may deny a request only if the information is deemed confidential or reserved.[60] Because any member of the public can submit information requests, information access laws can increase transparency and have, in fact, assisted journalists in uncovering corruption within the executive, even in several hyper-presidential countries.[61] But in hyper-presidential systems, public information laws typically include provisions that allow presidents to exempt certain information from disclosure by deeming it "reserved."[62] Such designations are, typically, subject to judicial review, but because presidents may rely on sensitive categories, such as "national security," to designate information as reserved, courts are reluctant to review and reconsider the executive's judgment.[63]

Some countries with hyper-presidential regimes have reformed their administrative procedure laws to adopt new regulatory practices, including regulatory impact assessments and, in a few instances, notice-and-comment procedures. Regulatory impact assessments, such as environmental impact assessments, may require agencies seriously to weigh the costs and benefits of a proposed regulation, to consider alternatives, and to engage in public consultation when evaluating an anticipated action.[64] The results of such proceedings, however, are not binding, and the president has discretion to accept or reject a regulatory impact assessment's finding.[65] A few countries have also begun to incorporate rulemaking processes that largely mirror the notice-and-comment procedures required by the U.S. APA. Even countries with hyper-presidential regimes have traditionally required agencies to provide the public some form of notice of proposed and, certainly, adopted regulations.[66] The innovation, rather, lies in new requirements that agencies must open their proposed regulations to public comment.[67] Such an approach has the potential to change the way an agency engages with the public: from one in which the executive is responsible only for informing the public of a final decision, to one in which the executive seeks to engage the public throughout its decision-making process. In other words, even in a hyper-presidential regime, executives have something to learn from the public. As far as we can tell, no country with a hyper-presidential regime has made notice-and-comment requirements or any other similar procedural innovation subject to judicial review. Thus, the extent to which an agency will seriously take public input into account when engaging in policymaking continues to depend from beginning to end on the president.

Conclusions

Procedural reforms are important in fostering greater transparency and public engagement in executive policymaking in any polity, but it remains to be seen whether they can improve the public accountability of hyper-presidential administrations without clearer enforcement mechanisms, such as expanded judicial review. In countries whose constitutional structures favor the executive, fostering external checks on an agency's decision-making processes may well require broader structural reforms that recognize not only public demands for reasoned and participatory decision-making, but also include an effective role for courts in balancing the interests of the public and the power of the executive.

Although our focus here and in our published article on Latin America is on presidential democracies other than the United States, recent developments in U.S. public law are relevant to the issues that we raise. Under the *Chevron* doctrine, dating from 1984, the U.S. federal courts defer to government agencies' "reasonable" statutory interpretations when they implement regulatory statutes through binding rules.[68] That case dealt with the substance of an Environmental Protection Agency (EPA) rule implementing a portion of the Clean Air Act. The nature and sufficiency of the administrative process were not at stake, but, rather, the question of whether the rule was consistent with the legislative history and the language of the statute delegating implementation to the EPA. Presently, the *Chevron* doctrine is under challenge in the federal courts on substantive grounds.[69] But the experience of hyper-presidential regimes suggests that participatory decision-making processes, like those enshrined in the APA, may alone be a reason to afford agencies some discretion.

The Supreme Court has recently examined the adequacy of administrative procedures, in spite of the limits imposed by *Vermont Yankee*.[70] An important example is the 2020 decision in Department of Homeland Security v. Regents of the University of California, a case challenging the attempted rescission of the Deferred Action for Childhood Arrivals (DACA) program.[71] The Court acknowledged that the executive had the authority to terminate the program, created via a memorandum from a cabinet secretary, but it held that the repeal process was inadequate because the administration did not consider the reliance interests of the beneficiaries.

Overall, both the U.S. judiciary and the courts in hyper-presidential systems face two related issues. First, should they seek to encourage procedural practices that incorporate input from the public? And, second, should the judiciary encourage or require the executive to justify its regulatory actions to the public in a transparent manner?

Notes

1 More coverage of the Latin American cases can be found in Susan Rose-Ackerman & Edgar Andrés Melgar, *Hyper-Presidential Administration: Executive Policymaking in Latin America*, 64 Arizona Law Review 1097 (2022).
2 The seminal critique of presidential systems is Juan J. Linz, *The Perils of Presidentialism*, 1 J. Democracy 51 (1990). *See also*, Robert Elgie, *Varieties of Presidentialism & Leadership Outcomes*, 145 Daedalus 57 (2016); Carlos Pereira & Marcus André Melo, *The Surprising Success of Multiparty Presidentialism*, 23 J. Democracy 156 (2012).
3 This claim is an underlying theme of Susan Rose-Ackerman, Democracy and Executive Power: Policymaking Accountability in the U.S., the U.K., Germany, and France 2 (2021).
4 Elena Kagan, *Presidential Administration*, 114 Harv. L. Rev. 2245, 2302 (2001).
5 *See, e.g.*, Robert Percival, *Presidential Management of the Administrative State: The Not-So Unitary Executive*, 51 Duke L.J. 963 (2001); Cass Sunstein & Adrian Vermule, *The President's Statutory Authority over Independent Agencies*, 109 Geo. L.J. 637, 657–659 (2021).
6 Kagan, *supra* note 4, 2251–2252 (2001).
7 *Id.* at 2331–2332.
8 For a general discussion of the link between corruption and the weakness of government institutions *see* Susan Rose-Ackerman & Bonnie Palifka, Corruption and Government: Causes, Consequences, and Reform (2d ed. 2016).
9 Rose-Ackerman, *supra* note 3, at 19.
10 *INS v. Chadha*, 462 U.S.919 (1983). *See also id.* at 80–89.
An attempt to get around *Chadha* is the Congressional Review Act, 5 U.S.C. §§801–808 that allows Congress to pass a bill repealing a regulation within a fixed time period. Because the president must sign the bill into law, it has only been used during transition periods when both the incoming president and Congress wish to cancel a regulation promulgated near the end of the former president's term.
11 5 U.S.C. § 551–559.
12 *See Motor Vehicle Mfrs. Ass'n v. State Farm*, 463 U.S. 29 (1983).
13 *See, e.g.*, *Dep't of Homeland Sec. v. Regents of the Univ. of Calif.*, 140 S. Ct. 1891 (2020).
14 *See, generally*, *West Virginia v. Envt'l Protection Agency*, 2022 WL 2347278 (2022); *Biden v. Nebraska*, 600 U.S. ___ (slip op) (2023).
15 *See* Rose-Ackerman & Melgar, *supra* note 1 and *generally* Presidentialism and Democracy in Latin America (Scott Mainwaring & Matthew Shugart eds., 1997).
16 Michael Asimow, *Five Models of Administrative Adjudication*, 63 Am. J. Comp. L. 3 (2015); Allan Brewer-Carías, Principios del Procedimiento Administrativo en América Latina 35, 66–67 (2020); Allan Brewer-Carías, *La regulación del procedimiento administrativo en América Latina con ocasión de la primera década de la Ley de Procedimiento Administrativo General del Perú*, 67 Derecho PCUP 47 (2011).
17 *See, e.g.*, Ricardo Perlingero, *A Historical Perspective on Administrative Jurisdiction in Latin America: Continental European Tradition Versus U.S. Influence*, 5 Brit. J. on Am. Legal Stud. 241 (2016). In many European jurisdictions a separate set of tribunals, distinct from the ordinary courts, adjudicates disputes that arise in public law. *See* the cases of French and Germany discussed in Rose-Ackerman, *supra* note 3.
18 *See, generally*, Jerry Mashaw, Reasoned Administration and Democratic Legitimacy: How Administrative Law Supports Democratic Government 163–179 (2018); Blake Emerson, The Public's Law: Origins and Architecture of Progressive Democracy 12–18 (2019).

19 Diana Kapiszewski & Katja Newman, *Judicialization of Politics*, *in* Oxford Handbook on Constitutional Law in Latin America 430 (Conrado Hübner Mendes, Roberto Gargarella & Sebastián Giudi eds., 2022); Rogério B. Arantes, *Constitutionalism, the Expansion of Justice, and the Judicialization of Politics in Brazil*, *in* The Judicialization of Politics in Latin America: Studies of the Americas 231 (2005).

20 Eduardo Jordao & Susan Rose-Ackerman, *Judicial Review of Executive Policymaking in Advanced Democracies: Beyond Rights Review*, 66 Admin. L. Rev. 1 (2014); Benjamin Eidelson, *Reasoned Explanation and Political Accountability in the Roberts Court*, 130 Yale L.J. 1748 (2021).

21 *See, generally*, Moisés Naim, *Latin America: The Second Stage of Reform*, 5 J. Democracy 32 (1994); Inter-American Development Bank, Serving Citizens: A Decade of Civil Service Reforms in Latin America (2004–2013) (2014).

22 Linz, *supra* note 2 at 54–55.

23 *Id.* at 62–64.

24 José Antonio Cheibub, Zachary Elkins & Tom Ginsburg, *Still the Land of Presidentialism? Executives and the Latin American Constitutionalism*, *in* New Constitutionalism in Latin America: Promises and Practices 73, 85–94 (Detlef Nolte & Almut Schilling-Vacaflor eds. 2012).

25 This view is critiqued in Guillermo O'Donnell, *Delegative Democracy*, 5 J. Democracy 55, 56 (1994).

26 For overviews, *see* José Antonio Cheibub, Zachery Elkins & Tom Ginsburg, *Latin American Presidentialism in Comparative and Historical Perspective*, 89 Tex. L. Rev. 1707 (2011); Marcelo Alegre & Nahuel Maisley, *Presidentialism and Hyper-Presidentialism in Latin America*, *in* Oxford Handbook of Constitutional Law in Latin America 381 (Conrado Hübner Mendes, Roberto Gargaraella & Sebastián Guidi eds., 2022).

27 Cheibub, Elkins & Ginsburg, *supra* note 26, at 1709.

28 *See* Carlos Santiago Nino, Fundamentos de Derecho Constitucional 504–531 (1992) (defining hyper-presidentialism); Alegre & Maisley, *supra* note 26, at 382.

29 For discussions of hyper-presidentialism elsewhere, *see* Susan Rose-Ackerman, Diane A. Desierto & Natalia Volosin, *Hyper-Presidentialism: Separation of Powers without Checks and Balances in Argentina and the Philippines*, 29 Berkeley J. Int'l L. 246 (2011); Şule Özsoy Boyunsuz, *The AKP's Proposal for a "Turkish Type of Presidentialism" in Comparative Context*, 17 Turkish Stud. 68 (2016); H. Kwasi Prempeh, *Presidential Power in Comparative Perspective: The Puzzling Persistence of the Imperial Presidency in Post-Authoritarian Africa*, 35 Hastings Const. L.Q. 761 (2008).

30 Nancy Bermeo, *On Democratic Backsliding*, 27 J. Democracy 5 (2016).

31 Constitución Política de Colombia [C.P.], art. 115 (Colom.). *See also* Constitución Política de los Estados Unidos Mexicanos, CP, art. 80, DOF 05-02-1917, últimas reformas DOF 28-05-2021; C.F. art. 76; Arts. 87, 99(1) Constitución Nacional [Const. Nac.] (Arg.); Constitución Política del Peru art. 110; Constitución de la República del Ecuador art. 141; Constitución Política de la República de Guatemala art. 182; Constitución Política de la República de Honduras art. 245.

32 Constitución Política de los Estados Unidos Mexicanos, CP, art. 29, DOF 05-02-1917, últimas reformas DOF 28-05-2021; Constituição Federal [C.F.] [Constitution], art. 136 (Braz.); C.F. art. 137 (Braz.); C.P. arts. 212–215 (Colom.); Arts. 22, 61, 99(16) Const. Nac. (Arg.); Constitución Política del Peru art. 137; Constitución de la República del Ecuador art. 164; Constitución Política de la República de Guatemala arts. 138, 183(f); Constitución de la República de El Salvador art. 29; Constitución Política de la República de Honduras arts. 187, 245(7); Constitución de la República Dominicana arts. 128(1)(g), 262–266.

33 Constitución Política de los Estados Unidos Mexicanos, CP, art. 89(I), DOF 05–02–1917, últimas reformas DOF 28–05–2021; C.F. art. 84(IV) (Braz.); C.P. art. 189(11) (Colom.); Art. 99(2), Const. Nac. (Arg.); Constitución Política del Peru art. 118(8); Constitución de la República del Ecuador art. 147(13); Constitución Política del Estado arts. 172(8), 175(I)(5) (Bol.); Constitución Política de la República de Guatemala art. 183(e); Constitución de la República de El Salvador art. 168(14); Constitución Política de la República de Honduras art. 245(11); Constitución de la República Dominicana art. 128(1)(b).

34 Corte Suprema de Justicia de la Nación [CSJN] [National Supreme Court], 12/02/1993, "Cocchia, Jorge Daniel c. Estado Nacional y Otro s/ acción de amparo," Fallos (1993–316–2647) (Arg.). *See also* Gabino Fraga, Derecho Administrativo (25th ed. 1986), at ¶ 81; José Roldán Xopa, Derecho Administrativo 123–124 (2008); Andrés Serra Rojas, Derecho Administrativo 198–199 (1982); Justen Filho, Curso de Direito Administrativo § IV.8.2 (5th ed. 2010); Hely Lopes Meirelles, Direito Administrativo Brasileiro § 4.1.2 (32d ed. 2006); Julio Rendón Cano, Manual de Derecho Administrativo 119–120 (2018); Francisco Ortega Polanco, Derecho Administrativo 131 (2017); Jorge Mario Castillo González, Derecho Administrativo: Teoría General y Procesal 71 (2011).

35 Corte Suprema de Justicia—Sala de lo Constitucional [C.S.J.-S.C.] [Supreme Court-Constitutional Chamber], 29 abr. 2013, 56–2010, Inconstitucionalidad, § IV.1.A(a) (El Sal.).

36 C.S.J.-S.C., 11 ene. 2013, 41–2005, Inconstitucionalidad, § III.3.C(b) (El Sal.).

37 *See, e.g.*, Decreto No. 330: Ley de Protección y Promoción del Bienestar de Animales Domésticos, art. 38, D.O. No. 82, Tomo No. 411, 4 mayo 2016 (El Sal.).

38 Some countries authorize the president to "execute the laws," by issuing regulations. *See* Constitución Política de los Estados Unidos Mexicanos, CP, art. 89(I), DOF 05–02–1917, últimas reformas DOF 28–05–2021; Constitución Política de la República de Guatemala art. 183(e); Constitución de la República de El Salvador art. 168(8). Other countries have explicitly granted presidents the power to issue "necessary" regulations. *See* Constitución Política de la República de Honduras art. 245(11); Constitución de la República Dominicana art. 128(1)(B); C.P. art. 189(11) (Colom.); Constitución de la República del Ecuador art. 147(13); Constitución Política del Peru art. 104; Art. 99(2), Const. Nac. (Arg.); C.F. art. 84(4) (Braz.).

39 C.S.J-S.C., 29 abr. 2013, 56–2010, Inconstitucionalidad, § IV.1.A(a) (El Sal.).

40 *See* Fraga, *supra* note 34, at 82; Roldán Xopa, *supra* note 34, at 124–27; Serra Rojas, *supra* note 34, at 209–12; Rendón Cano, *supra* note 34, at 120; Castillo González, *supra* note 34, at 71.

41 Corte de Constitucionalidad [C.C.] [Constitutional Court], 24 nov. 2011, Exp. 1072–2011, Amparo en Única Instancia, § IV (Guat.).

42 C.C., 12 ene. 2016, Exp. 411–2014, Apelación de Sentencia de Amparo, § I (Guat.).

43 Ricardo Perlingero, *A Historical Perspective on Administrative Jurisdiction in Latin America: European Tradition Versus British Influence*, 5 Br. J. Am. Leg. Stud. 241, 245 (2016).

44 Constitución Política de los Estados Unidos Mexicanos, CP, art. 49, DOF 05–02–1917, últimas reformas DOF 28–05–2021; Art. 76, Const. Nac. (Arg.); Constitución de la República de El Salvador arts. 86–87; Constitución de la República Dominicana art. 4; Constitución Política de República de Costa Rica art. 9.

45 *See, e.g.*, Facultad Reglamentaria del Presidente de la República. Principios que la rigen, II Sala de la SCJN, SJFG, Novena Época, Tomo IX, abr. 1999, Tesis 2a./J. 29/99, página 70 (Mex.).

46 *See, e.g.*, Facultad Reglamentaria del Poder Ejecutivo Federal. Sus principios y limitaciones, Pleno de la SCJN, SJFG, Novena Época, Tomo XXX, ago. 2009, Tesis P./J. 79/2009, página 1067 (Mex.).

47 *See, e.g.*, Facultad Reglamentaria del Presidente de la República. Principios que la rigen, I Sala de la SCJN, SJFG, Novena Época, Tomo XVII, sept. 2007, Tesis 1a./J. 122/2007, página 122 (Mex.). *See also* Fraga, *supra* note 34, at ¶ 80, 107; Roldán Xopa, *supra* note 34, at 91–93, 112–113; Serra Rojas, *supra* note 34, at 172–173; Justen Filho, *supra* note 34, at § IV.9.2; Rendón Cano, *supra* note 42, at 122; Castillo González, *supra* note 34, at 66.

48 Corte Constitucional [C.C.] [Constitutional Court], 6 septiembre 2010, Sentencia C-704/10, Mag. Pon. Calle Correa, § VI-5 (Colom.), *citing* C.C., 5 julio 2001, Sentencia C-710/01, Mag. Pon, Códroba Triviño, §§ V.1–7 (Colom.).

49 *See* Comercio Exterior, Impuestos a. La disposición contemplada en el artículo 107 del Reglamento de la Ley Aduanera vigente en 1995, de no exentar a los tripulantes de los medios de transporte internacional del pago de aquellos por la entrada o salida del territorio nacional de su equipaje, no viola los principios de primacia y reserva de ley qu limitan la facultad reglamentaria, II Sala de la SCJN, SJFG, Novena Época, Tomo IV, jul. 1996, Tesis 2a. LV/96, página 206 (Mex.). *See also* Roldán Xopa, *supra* note 34, at 89, 94–96, 113–116 (2008); Fraga, *supra* note 34, at 80; Justen Filho, *supra* note 34, at § IV.9.1; Rendón Cano, *supra* note 34, at 122–124; Castillo González, *supra* note 34, at 66.

50 C.C., 26 septiembre 2007, Sentencia C-782/07, Mag. Pon. Araújo Rentería, § VI-4–4 (Colom.).

51 C.C., 5 diciembre 2005, Sentencia C-1262/05, Mag. Pon. Sierra Porto, § VI.47–48 (Colom.).

52 Derechos a la Salud y a un Medio Ambiente Sano para el Desarrollo y Bienestar. Acciones que debe realizar el Estado Mexicano para su salvaguarda y para ajustarse a los estándares internacionales, en materia de medidas de restricción a la circulación de vehículos por la aparición de contingencias ambientales, TCC, GSJF, Décima Época, Libro 42, Tomo III, mayo 2017, Tesis I.3o.A.1 CS (10a), página 1907 (Mex.).

53 C.C., 23 octubre 2015, Sentencia T-660/15, Mag. Pon. Pretelt Chaljub, § 2.4.1 (Colom.); Participación y Consulta Pública. El Estado debe garantizar este derecho en proyectos o actividades que puedan causar una afectación al medio ambiente, II Sala de la SCJN, GSJF, Décima Época, Libro 78, Tomo I, sept. 2020, Tesis 2a. XVI/2020 (10a), página 631 (Mex.).

54 C.F. art. 251 (Braz.); Constitución Política de los Estados Unidos Mexicanos, CP, art. 2(A), DOF 05–02–1917, últimas reformas DOF 28–05–2021; Constitución Política del Peru art. 89.

55 Art. 75(17), Const. Nac. (Arg.); Constitución Política del Estado art. 30(II)(15) (Bol.); Constitución Política de los Estados Unidos Mexicanos, CP, art. 2(B)(IX), DOF 05–02–1917, últimas reformas DOF 28–05–2021; C.P. art. 330, Párrafo (Colom.).

56 Sentencia No. 273–19-JP/22, *Consulta previa en la comundiad A'I Cofán de Sinangoe*, Caso No. 273–19-JP, Juez Ponnte Karla Andrade Quevedo, 27 jan. 2022 (Ecuador). C.C., Exp. 1072–2011, Amparo en Única Instancia, 24 nov. 2011, consid. III, (Guat.). *See also* C.C., 3 febrero 1997, Sentencia SU-39/97, Mag. Pon. Barrera Carbonell, 3.3 (Colom.).

57 *See, e.g.*, Ley 27.275: Derecho de Acceso a la Información Pública [LAIP], B.O. No. 33472, 29 sept. 2016 (Arg.); Lei no. 12.527, Regla o acesso a informações [LAIP], de 18 de novembro de 2011, D.O.U. 18.11.2001 (Braz.), Decreto No. 7.724, Ley 1712, por Medio de la Cual se Crea la Ley de Transparencia y del Derecho de Acceso a la Información Pública Nacional y se Dictan Otras Disposiciones [LTDAIP], D.O. No. 49.084, 6 mar. 2014 (Colom.); Ley No. 24: Ley Orgánica de Transparencia y Acceso a la Información Pública [LOTAIP], Registro Oficial Suplemento 337 del 18 mayo 2004 (Ecuador); Decreto No. 534: Ley de Acceso a la Información Pública [LAIP], D.O. No. 70, Tomo No. 391, 8 abr. 2011 (El Sal.); Decreto No. 57–2008: Ley de Acceso a la Información Pública [LAIP], D.O.

No. 45, 22 oct. 2008 (Guat.); Decreto Legislativo No. 170–2006: Ley de Transparencia y Acceso a la Información Pública [LTAIP], D.O. 30 dic. 2006 (Hond.); Ley Federal de Transparencia y Acceso a la Información Pública [LFTAIP] DOF 09–05–2016, última reforma 20–05–2021 (Mex.); Ley No. 27806: Ley de Transparencia y Acceso a la Información Pública [LTAIP], 2 ago. 2002 (Peru).

58 LTAIP, art. 13 (Hond.); LAIP, art. 10 (El Sal.); LTDAIP, arts. 9, 11(a) (Colom.); LOTAIP, art. 7 (Ecuador); LTAIP, arts. 5(1)–(2), 22 (Peru); LAIP, art. 32 (Arg.)

59 LFTAIP, arts. 1, 11 (Mex.); LAIP, art. 6 (Guat.); LTAIP, arts. 3(A), 34(a)–(b) (Hond.); LAIP, arts. 7, 8 (El Sal.); LTDAIP, art. 5(a)–(b), 5(e) (Colom.); LOTAIP, arts. 1, 3(a), 5(c), 5(e) (Ecuador); LAIP, arts. 1(I)–(II), 2 (Braz.).

60 LAIP, art. 24 (El Sal.); LTDAIP, arts. 6(c), 18 (Colom.); LOTAIP, art. 6 (Ecuador); LTAIP, art. 15B(1)–(5) (Peru); LTAIP, art. 17(1)–(3), 17(5)–(6) (Hond.); LAIP, art. 19(a)–(g) (El Sal.); LOTAIP, art. 17(a) (Ecuador); LTAIP, art. 15A(1)–(2) (Peru); LAIP, art. 31 § 4 (Braz.).

61 *See, e.g.*, Fátima Peña & Jimmy Avelardo, *Sala reprende al IAIP y ordena liberar información de viajes y publicidad de Funes*, El Faro (Sept. 1, 2016) https://elfaro.net/es/201609/el_salvador/19193/Sala-reprende-al-IAIP-y-ordena-liberar-informaci%C3%B3n-de-viajes-y-publicidad-de-Funes.htm [https://perma.cc/W4DP-P6U6].

62 *See, e.g.*, Valeria Guzmán & Nelson Rauda, *Casa Presidencial responde al juez que el Ejército no tiene archivos de El Mozote*, El Faro (Nov. 29, 2019), https://elfaro.net/es/201911/el_salvador/23810/Casa-Presidencial-responde-al-juez-que-el-Ej%C3%A9rcito-no-tiene-archivos-de-El-Mozote.htm [https://perma.cc/N6ES-Y4KY]; Nelson Rauda, *Juez de El Mozote envía inspectores a buscar los archivos que el Ejército niega*, El Faro (June 26, 2020), https://elfaro.net/es/202006/el_salvador/24589/Juez-de-El-Mozote-env%C3%ADa-inspectores-a-buscar-los-archivos-que-el-Ej%C3%A9rcito-niega.htm#:~:text=Impunidad-,

63 LTAIP, art. 18 (Hond.).

64 Ley General de Mejora Regulatoria [LGMR], arts. 1, 3(XV), D.O.F. 20–05–2021 (Mex.); Decreto No. 202: Ley de Mejora Regulatoria [LMR], art. 161, D.O. No. 5, Tomo No. 422, 9 ene. 2019 (El Sal); Lei no. 13.874 [Lei no. 13.874], Institui a Declaração de Direitos de Liberdade Econômica, de 20 de setembro de 2019, art. 5, D.O.U. Edição extra-B (Braz.); Decreto No. 10.411, de 30 de junho de 2020, art. 4, D.O.U. Edição 124, Seção 1, pág. 35 (Braz.).

65 *See, e.g.*, LMR, art. 7 (El Sal.); Decreto 1595, art. 2.2.1.7.5.12 (Colom.).

66 LFPA, art. 4 (Mex.); Ley no. 19.549 de 3 de abril de 1972 del Procedimiento Administrativo [APL], art. 11 (Arg.); LPA, art. 32 (Hond.); CPACA, art. 65 (Colom.).

67 *See, e.g.*, Decreto 2696, por el cual se definen las reglas mínimas para garantizar la divulgación y la participación en las acutaciones de las Comisiones de Regulación, art. 11.5, D.O. No. 45651, 25 ago. 2004 (Colom.); LPD, art. 55 (Colom.); Lei no. 13.848, art. 10 (Braz.); LPA, art. 162(3) (El Sal.); LPA, art. 31(3) (Dom. Rep.).

68 Chevron v. NRDC, 467 U.S. 837 (1984).

69 *See* Loper Bright v. Raimundo, No. 21–5166 (U.S. Nov. 15, 2022).

70 Vermont Yankee Nuclear Power Corp. v. NRDC, 435 U. S. 519 (1978).

71 Department of Homeland Security v. Regents of the University of California, 140 S. Ct. 1891 (2020).

12 Equal versus Efficient Security against Crime

Differences and Unintended Consequences

*Hans-Bernd Schäfer**

We argue that public police forces in constitutional, rule-of-law states often do not aim to mimic a well-functioning market for security by reducing losses from crime to an efficient level. On the contrary, the policy aim of crime fighting by public police forces—especially against violent crimes—has moved towards ensuring equal security for all residents. This view gained influence especially from the writings of constitutional law scholars. They argue that providing equal security against crimes derives from human rights. The resources of police allocated to deter and solve crimes should lead to an equal security of residents in all police districts of a state, independent of their willingness to pay for the reduction of crimes. Ideally, police budgets and forces should be allocated such that any resident in a state has an equal probability of becoming the victim of a crime. The consequences of equal security policy can deviate substantially from those of tort law, which tries to minimize the sum of damages, prevention costs, and other costs of accidents. The policy aim of equal security against crime has gained acceptance not only among constitutional law scholars, who derive it from an interpretation of pre-existing constitutional rights. It is included in the Bill of Rights of the European Union (Art. 6), and it influences practical police strategy.

We analyze equal security and how it deviates from efficient security. A move from efficient to equal security causes unintended consequences. An equal security policy, almost necessarily, fails to reduce the number of crimes to the lowest possible level, given total police resources. We also show that an equal security policy implies crime clearance and punishment rates that differ across police districts and communities and might lead to discrimination against minorities. More equality among all potential crime victims in a society is likely to cause more inequality among suspects and offenders and more discrimination against minorities and immigrants. This adverse effect results from the equal security aim itself and is not dependent on racism or a taste for discrimination among the police forces. Intentional discrimination against suspects is sufficient but not necessary for severe discrimination.

The chapter is organized as follows. We show that the market failure rationale of public police finds little support in public law scholarship and legal history. We then present the main arguments made by constitutional lawyers,

DOI: 10.4324/9781003416036-12

who regard security against crime as a fundamental constitutional right or a goal of the state. This implies that police forces should be organized to support this policy. We then point to several potential unintended consequences of equal security, and analyze in some detail to show that equal security cannot be effective. It cannot minimize the number of crimes in a state, given the total budget for the police. We also show, that, under reasonable assumptions, equal security causes indirect discrimination against offenders from minorities or immigrant groups. Their punishment rates might end up being much higher than the punishment rates for the majority population and higher than under a policy of efficient security.

Efficient Loss Reduction from Crimes versus Equal Protection against Crimes

The Public Good Argument

Police services are a standard example of a public good, which the state must provide to prevent undersupply due to the missing demand from free riders, thus leading to market failure. Correcting a market failure leads public authorities and agencies to finance public good with state money and to mimic a well-functioning market.[1]

In much of the law and economics literature crime control follows the same rationale as the regulation of an industry. In his theory of crime, Richard Posner asserts "that the substantive doctrines of the criminal law, as of the common law in general, can be given an economic meaning and can indeed be shown to promote efficiency."[2] Posner writes that similar arguments were already raised by the 18th century scholars Cesare Beccaria and Jeremy Bentham. He argues that criminal justice is an extension of tort law because many criminals are judgment-proof, cannot pay damages, and must therefore be incentivized by other means, including public enforcement and incarceration. Gary Becker expressed similar views.[3] In his theory, crimes are forbidden inefficient acts, in which illegal, involuntary, and often violent transactions occur, unlike in markets or in relations. Crime control, including policing, then follow the same rationale as economic regulation or tort law. Following this rationale police should reduce losses from crimes to a level, which equalizes marginal gains from crime reduction and marginal costs of crime control.

The Equal Security Concept in Constitutional Law and in Politics

Despite its merits, the public good theory of state police as an answer to a market failure invites critique. The literature on the history of the police shows that a publicly funded police force is a relatively recent development and closely related to the growing scope of police tasks under the modern concept of the rule of law with a state monopoly for the legitimate use of violence. Until well into the 19th century, police in England and, before, in the colonial English states in North America were mainly privately organized and financed.[4] It seems from this literature that the public good theory, asserting the necessity of a public criminal police, is as debatable as the public good theory for the existence of public lighthouses, which Ronald Coase criticized in a well-known paper.[5]

Equal security for all as the mission of public police is now widely and internationally accepted not only among constitutional lawyers, but among practitioners and in the political arena as well.

In a debate that started 40–50 years ago, constitutional law scholars in different countries have argued that equal security for all residents in a state is either a fundamental human right or a state objective, which derives from human rights. They developed a new theory of security against crimes and the mission of criminal police, which deviates from the traditional law and order concept. The traditional theory focuses on the functioning of the state and its organs. It does not relate security against crime to basic human rights, equal for all citizens for all residents of a state. It implies ample discretion for police forces and politics to define their policy aims.

In Germany, in an influential essay Josef Isensee (1983) articulated "the basic right to security"[6] as a constitutional right, even though such a right is not explicitly part of the German constitution. The author derived it as a corollary of other basic rights. These are human dignity (Art. 1 GG, Germany's basic law), the general freedom of action, the inviolability of life and body (Art. 2 GG), and the equality before the law (Art. 3). This line of argument provided a new perspective for looking at security against crimes.

In traditional constitutional legal doctrine, fundamental constitutional rights were, of course, important for all activities of the criminal police, but only insofar as crime clearance or deterrence activities cut into basic rights of suspects and citizens. This relates especially to restrictions on the secrecy of correspondence, mail and telecommunications, and the inviolability of the home and the dignity of suspects. These rights and their interpretation by Supreme Courts constrain the actions of the police force and protect citizens against an encroaching use of state force and violence. They led to numerous court decisions prohibiting police action, regulating police methods, and, in countries with judicial review, to the removal of sub-constitutional norms regulating police if they violated fundamental rights. The security of residents becomes itself a human right, whose violation might trigger legal action and influence court decisions.

The new interpretation of the German constitution by Isensee (1983) led to further, mostly affirmative, writings and elaboration. Gerhard Robbers (1987) proposes "Security as human right."[7] Christoph Gusy (1982, 1996) demands equal security.[8] Jutta Limbach (2002), former president of the German Constitutional Court, supports such views with some caveats.[9] In a survey paper Oliver Lepsius (2004) concludes that the rationale of crime fighting is "not a state duty," but results from "an equal right to security."[10] There seems to be a broad consensus among German constitutional lawyers that the policy goal of "equal security" derives from the national constitution. Different views exist, however, on whether equal security is a subjective fundamental right, which opens the door to the courtroom for every resident, or whether it is a duty of the state and not a direct right. Limbach (2002) supports the latter view:

> This responsibility (of equal security) is preferably directed at the legislature. It cannot be interpreted in the sense of a direct right of intervention against third parties. . . . Instead of a fundamental right to security, it is therefore more correct to speak of a state duty of maintaining equal security.[11]

A constitutional state duty does not grant individuals the right to bring an action against an alleged violation of the objective. This does make it relevant, for instance, for court decisions in disputes between state organs like parliament and government.

The legal discussion on the right to equal security is not confined to Germany. It is part of a worldwide legal discussion, from which we present some examples of authors who published in English.

In the USA, Lawrence Rosenthal (2003) derives a policy aim of equal security from the 14th amendment and argues that:

> The Equal Protection Clause is not limited to securing equality with respect to particular civil rights. Criminal law affords protection as well. . . . Indeed, the most obvious type of "protection" that the government provides under the law is the protection against lawbreakers offered by the criminal justice system.[12]

For Australia, Dan. A. Lewis and Greta W. Salem (2016) explicitly reject the market-mimicking rationale for police forces and argue that "Providing effective equal protection (against crimes) . . . is a constitutional norm."[13] This text leaves open whether the authors regard it as a direct right or as a state duty. Also regarding Australia, Colleen Lewis and Jennifer Wood (2006) advocate a rethinking of the market-mimicking rationale of public security regulation and favor protecting equal access to human rights and justice instead (p.233).[14] For Brazil Laura Chinchilla (2003) argues that equal security is "a constitutional norm in Brazil."[15] In Israel, Alon Harel and Gideon Parchmovosky (1999) demand equalization of individuals' vulnerability to crime as the rationale of crime fighting.[16] This does not necessarily imply equal security as a direct right. It can also mean a state duty of equal security which derives from constitutional principles.

This debate influenced the interpretation of constitutional bills of rights. The emergence of a right to security in Europe is part of an international legal development, which regards human rights not only as defensive rights against an encroaching state but also as protective rights that require state action in favor of the protected.

This author is not aware of any state in which a constitutional "right to security" exists in the text of the constitution. It is therefore noteworthy that this right is explicitly part of the Charter of Fundamental Rights of the European Union. "Everyone has the right to liberty and security of person" (Art. 6). As fundamental rights are conceptually equal rights this is an explicit codification of equal security as a right. The EU Charter was proclaimed in the year 2000. It became part of the Treaty of Lisbon in December 2007. The European parliament voted for it with a majority of 525:112 and the European Council with a supermajority representing the governments of more than 65 percent of the citizens of the EU. It was then ratified by all parliaments of EU member states. In Ireland ratification even required a referendum. After these procedures the Charter entered into force on 1 December 2009.[17] In the EU a right to equal security enjoys a higher legitimacy than by the reinterpretation of existing constitutional texts by a constitutional or a supreme court of a nation state.

The aim of providing equal security has reached the level of politics and practical police work. The UN Security Council (2004) urged "promotion of . . . equal security . . . for all inhabitants of Kosovo."[18] The Fundamental Rights Survey of the EU (2021) regards "personal security and safety (as) key issues in ensuring human rights."[19] In the coalition agreement of the grand coalition between Christian Democrats and Social Democrats (2018) in Germany one can read: "We do not want zones of unequal security in Germany."[20] A similar text is included in the German coalition agreement of 2021 between Social Democrats, the Green Party and the Free Democratic Party, which demands "freedom, security, and the rule of law for all people in Germany" and thus places security in a row of fundamental rights. [21]

Observed public police activity and the scholarly debate on the mission of criminal police among constitutional lawyers are not in line with an economic theory of public police, which maintains that it corrects the public good market failure and mimics a competitive market. Public police ideally achieves equal state protection of those human rights for which all citizens have an identical endowment, such as life or bodily integrity. It does not achieve an efficient reduction of the losses, including non-monetary and psychic damages. Ideally, everybody should have the same high perception of security. Fear of crime should not have a chilling effect on the daily life or on the exercise of political rights, such as the right to assemble in public places. This is important for individual freedom and necessary for a free and equal use of rights in a democratic society.[22] Public police services should therefore be understood as enforcers of fundamental and equal human rights and not as a public organization for the correction of a market failure.

The measure of equality for a market-driven private police force or a market-mimicking public police force is the marginal loss reduction from crime of a marginal dollar spent on crime prevention across all police districts and all crime categories. The measure of equality for the public police is an equal security level for all residents. The state provision of security, therefore, differs categorically from economic regulation, which corrects market failure and tries to establish or mimic workable markets, as in antitrust law, regulation of capital markets, natural monopolies, networks or in tort law.

The above discussion among constitutional lawyers was sparked by several developments. A wave of terrorism starting in the 1970s, in Germany especially by the Baader Meinhof gang, called for better protection of potential victims. The increase in hate crimes against minorities led to similar considerations. An important line of argument was discomfort with the idea that the level of protection against violent crimes should be based on the potential victims' willingness to pay. An armed robbery causes pain not only from the lost property but also from the chilling effect of the assault and the feeling of being unsecure, wherever it occurs. However, the value of lost property and the willingness to pay for the avoidance of psychic pain and its chilling effects differ in different districts. It is then reasonable to reduce the pain from crime equally for all residents rather than to equalize marginal police costs and marginal willingness to pay for the avoidance of losses and pain.

Inconsistencies of the Equal Security Approach

The "equal security for all" mission of the public police, however, is not without inconsistencies. "Equal security" can violate other important principles of justice and public policy:

(1) Effectiveness. The marginal spending for police should have the same effect on crime reduction in every police district. Effectiveness guarantees that the total number of crimes in a state is minimized with a given police budget. An equal security police does not meet this criterion except accidentally
(2) Non-discrimination. Police activities against offenders should be non-discriminatory with respect to gender, ethnicity, or religion. We show that this criterion is violated even if no taste for discrimination among police forces exists and that indirect or statistical discrimination arises as a corollary of the equal security policy. Also, not necessarily but under plausible assumptions, an equal security police policy causes more statistical discrimination among suspects and offenders than an efficiency-oriented police.
(3) Balance between rights. As we will show, discrimination disappears under an equal security policy if the police budget becomes extremely high. To achieve this the balance between the right to equal security and other human rights might be affected.

Public police, who try to establish equal security for all, are likely to violate one or more of these principles. Consider an easy illustrative case. Assume that a municipality has two police districts with the same number of residents, a low-income district with a high crime rate (hot spot) and a high-income district that would have half of this crime rate if no police existed. Assume, for the sake of argument, that in the low-income district all offenders are people of color and in the high-income district they are all white. This implies that without any police a third of all crimes are committed by whites. Then equal security across districts requires the police to concentrate in the hot-spot area until crime rates are the same in both districts. As long as the budget of the police is so low that equal security requires all police officers to be deployed in the high crime district, all convicted criminals will be people of color and none will be white. One will find only people of color in prisons and no whites even though whites now commit more than 1/3 of all crimes, because some crime is deterred in the hot spot by police enforcement. This violates (2) because all arrested and convicted criminals are people of color. If one wants to avoid this by dividing the small police budget evenly in each district, this grossly violates (1) and the principle of equal security for all residents. If the police budget is increased to such a high level that the police can substantially reduce crimes in both districts and avoid intolerable racial discrimination against offenders of color, discrimination disappears. This might violate the balance between rights.

Lower Effectiveness of Crime Fighting under Equal Security

This section uses graphs to illustrate the difference between an equal security policy and a policy that aims to minimize general crime levels.[23] The following considerations are driven by the fact that police forces and police budgets must be allocated across police districts where the tendency to crime and the losses from crimes differ. In police districts with a large quota of immigrants, the number of violent crimes can be—*ceteris paribus*—relatively high if the immigrants are younger than others, because most violent crimes are committed by young people between 12 and 34 years.[24] To guarantee an equal level of security everywhere police forces must be concentrated in immigrant districts. Some police districts usually in poor neighborhoods are hot spots with a concentration of drug trafficking, racketeering, and related violent crimes. Other districts might be neighborhoods of minorities, who suffer from hate crimes. Equal security requires that their official buildings, such as schools, meeting rooms, or religious buildings, must be specially protected. Some police districts might have many public places that need special protection that might otherwise fall under the control of violent groups. Some police districts might differ only in terms of the income and wealth of their residents but be homogeneous otherwise. In that case, equal security requires the same police budget across such districts even though the willingness to pay for crime reduction differs. Efficient security would, on the contrary, require the concentration of police forces in the rich districts because the residents' willingness to pay for security is relatively high.

Assumptions for Analysis

Throughout the following analysis we assume, for convenience, that two types of police districts with the following characteristics exist within the state.

- All police districts have the same number of residents. This allows us to express the level of security in each district in terms of the number of crimes in the district.
- A crime is a representative crime, for instance "armed robbery." All other crimes are weighted with a factor whose value is between 0 and 1 if the crime is less severe than the representative crime and bigger than 1 otherwise. We assume that this aggregation problem can be solved. Otherwise "equal security" would not be a reasonable concept.
- There exist two types of police districts with high and low crime respectively. In a high-crime district, crime numbers are higher than in the low crime district given the same police expenditures in each district.
- A police district is either a high- or a low-income district. The monetary and non-monetary losses from any individual crime are higher in the high-income district than in the low-income district. Consequently, the per resident willingness to pay for reducing losses from crime are higher in the high-income district than in the low-income district, other things being equal.
- N is the number of offences. Assume for convenience that one offender commits one crime, Therefore, N is also the number of offenders.
- The following notations will be used. N_1: number of representative crimes in the low-crime district. N_2: number of representative crimes in the high-crime district. N_1^{max}: maximal number of representative crimes in the low-crime district if no police exists. N_2^{max}: maximal number of representative crimes in the high-crime district if no police exists. $N_1^{max} < N_2^{max}$; x_1, x_2 are police expenditures in the low- and in the high-crime district; b is the total police budget. We assume that only two police districts exist: one low-crime district and one high-crime district. In that case the police budget is: $b = x_1 + x_2$.
- Assumptions about the crime functions in the two different police districts {1,2}, which are widely used in the literature, are:

$$N_1 = N_1(x_1) \geq 0;\; N_1(0) = N_1^{max} > 0;\; N_1'(x_1) < 0;\; N_1''(x_1) > 0;$$
$$N_1'(0) = -\infty;\; N_1(x_1) \to 0 \; if \; x_1 \to \infty.$$
$$N_2 = N_2(x_2) \geq 0;\; N_2(0) = N_2^{max} > 0;\; N_2'(x_2) < 0;\; N_2''(x_2) > 0$$
$$N_2'(0) = -\infty;\; N_2(x_2) \to 0 \; if \; x_2 \to \infty.$$

- Assumptions about the low- and the high-crime sectors are:

  $N_2^{max} > N_1^{max}$ and more general $N_2 > N_1$ if $x_1 = x_2$.

Equal Security Cannot Minimize Crimes

In Figure 12.1 the vertical axis represents the number of crimes weighted with the severity of crimes in the two police districts (N_1, N_2), the low-crime district 1 and the high-crime district 2. The crime numbers N_1 and N_2 are functions of police expenditures (x_1, x_2) in districts 1 and 2, which are shown on the horizontal axis. In both districts there is a maximal number of crimes if the police budget is 0, that is N_1^{max} and N_2^{max} with $N_1^{max} < N_2^{max}$.

This might be for the simple reason that immigrants are on the average younger than the members of the majority population. Violent crimes concentrate among young people, mostly males.[25] There exist deeper reasons why immigrants or ethnic minorities, if they are not integrated and suffer from racist or ethnic discrimination and rejection by the majority, might have a higher crime rate than others. (Arrow 1971, Chaudhuri and Sethi 2008).[26] These causes are not part of this study.

Suppose the government's goal is to achieve equal security across the districts with a given police budget (b), which is the result of a democratic decision. The budget is distributed between the two districts so that the (weighted) number of crimes in each district is equal, that is: $N_1 = N_2 = N_e$. In Figure 12.1, the equal number of crimes across districts is achieved by police expenditures x_1^e and x_2^e in district 1 and 2. The reader can see that an infinitely large number of budgets exist that fulfill this requirement. Every horizontal line leading from a point on the vertical axis to a point on the lower curve and from there to a point on the higher curve determines a particular level of equal security, the related necessary police expenditures in the two districts, and the necessary total police budget.

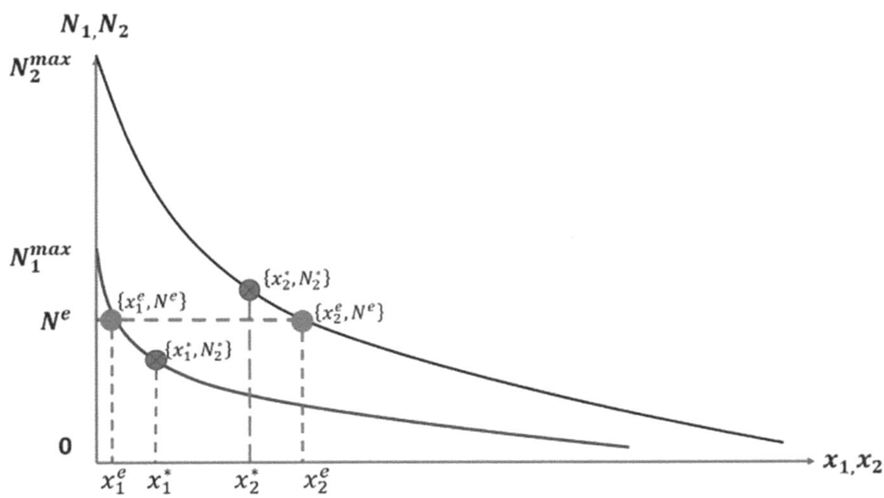

Figure 12.1 Equal and effective security with the same total police budget.

Under equal security and a given budget (b) the total (weighted) crime numbers are $N_1 + N_2 = 2N_e$. N_e is the equal number of crimes in police districts, given the total police budget. With two districts the total number of crimes is then $2N_e$. We now ask whether this is also the lowest total crime number achievable with this budget. To compare the effects of equal security with those of crime minimizing security it is necessary to choose the level of equal security for comparison that can be achieved with a police budget (b). For a budget of (b) there exist optimal values for police expenditures in district 1 and 2, which derive from the optimization problem:

Minimize $N = N_1(x_1) + N_2(x_2)$ subject to $x_1 + x_2 = b$

This yields x_1^*, *and* x_2^* and N_{min}, the lowest overall crime number that can be achieved with the budget (b). This is the point where the slopes of N_1 and N_2 are equal so that marginal increase in spending in each district has the same marginal impact on crime levels. In Figure 12.1 one can see that there exists an allocation of this police budget $\{x_1^e, x_2^e\}$, which leads to equal security, namely with police expenditures of

$x_1^* + x_2^* = x_1^e + x_2^e = b$ but with
$x_1^e \neq x_1^*$ and $x_2^e \neq x_2^*$.

Under some crime functions this inequality between crime minimizing police expenditures and crime equalizing police expenditures does not exist. Equal and effective security, which minimizes the number of all crimes can be the same. But this is purely accidental and of no practical or theoretical relevance. The general result is that equal security cannot minimize the total weighted number of crimes in a state, given the police budget. This is an unintended effect of equal security. It implies that $N_1^* + N_2^* < 2N_e$, if the total police budget is the same in both cases.[27]

An equal security policy often makes potential crime victims with low incomes more secure than under efficient security and vice versa, as it weighs the severity of crimes not by the willingness to pay for crime reduction but with another weight. However, the tradeoff between equal and effective security persists, regardless of whether the policy goal is either efficient security or—alternatively—equal security, which weighs the severity of crimes differently. To illustrate: assume that the only crime is armed robbery and that an equal security policy gives equal weight to every armed robbery (disregarding the different willingness to pay for crime reduction in high- and low-income districts). Then—with a given police budget—the equal security policy fails to reduce the total number of armed robberies to its lowest achievable level.

A redistributive effect in favor of low-income groups is a typical but not necessary effect of the equal security policy. On the contrary, it is possible that equal security requires police expenditures in the high-income sector, which are even higher than the willingness to pay of the members of a rich but ethnically or religiously different community, for instance if those fear murderous attacks. This example shows that "equal security" derives its essential justification not from considerations of distributive justice for the potential victims. It flows from fundamental equal human rights, which exist regardless of income differentials and can sometimes work in favor of an affluent part of the population, if public police expenditures, which reflect their willingness to pay for crime avoidance, would still leave them more vulnerable than others. Again, the tradeoff between equal security and effective security persists.

All in all, there exists a persistent tradeoff between equal security and effective general security. If this difference becomes too high a rights-based equal security concept might have to give way to a budget allocation that leads to moderately unequal security across different police districts and thus achieves a higher level of general security.

Statistical Discrimination of Offenders

Indirect Discrimination

This section argues that tensions can exist between the goals of equal security and non-discrimination, even if they are defended in similar terms. For analytical clarity, we rule out racist, sexist, or similar causes for discrimination among the police and—to paraphrase Gary Becker—assume that nobody in the police force has "a taste for discrimination." All police forces adhere loyally to the policy of efficient or equal security. We show that even under this ideal and unrealistic assumption severe indirect discrimination can still arise. We show that a police force, which tries to achieve equal security, might lead to a crime clearance and punishment rate for offenders from the minority that is higher than the punishment rate of offenders in the majority population.

The concept of indirect or statistical discrimination describes discrimination that occurs without any intent to discriminate. The legal status of this form of discrimination differs across countries. We leave it open under what conditions indirect discrimination might be of direct legal relevance and when it is only an unwanted adverse effect without legal consequences. The concept of statistical or indirect discrimination is in line with the EU antidiscrimination directive, which differentiates between direct discrimination, following from discriminatory intent and indirect discrimination.

> Indirect discrimination shall be taken to occur where an apparently neutral provision, criterion, or practice would put persons of a racial or ethnic origin at a particular disadvantage compared with other persons, unless that provision, criterion, or practice is objectively justified by a legitimate aim and the means of achieving that aim are appropriate and necessary.[28]

This Council Directive acknowledges the possibility that a legitimate state policy can have indirect discriminatory consequences that are not per se illegal but are constrained by the proportionality principle of public and constitutional law.

Equal Security as a Cause for Indirect Discrimination

For further analysis, we assume again that two types of residents live in a state, members of the majority and minority population. In the following analysis we assume for analytical clarity that higher propensities to crime exist among ethnic minorities and immigrants in comparison to the rest of the population and that police forces have no intent to discriminate.

An indirect discrimination emerges, however, if the number of crime clearance and punishment cases as a percentage of all offences is higher among minorities than among the rest of the population and if this is an unintended consequence of a policy. The punishment rate (r) in a police district is the number of cleared and punished cases divided by the number of crimes. Statistical discrimination occurs, if the crime clearance rate in the high-crime police district with the minority population is relatively high, that is if $r_2 > r_1$.

A measure of discrimination (D) is: $D = (r_2 - r_1)$.

The punishment rate is a number between 0 and 1. We assume that it is 0 if no police exists.

Without police the number of crimes in police district 1 is $N_1 = N_1^{max}$, that is, the maximal number of crimes. The number of punished offences is zero, and the crime clearance and punishment rates are also zero. The same applies for the high-crime district 2, if $N_2 = N_2^{max}$. Consequently, under this condition no discrimination can occur. The punishment rate increases with more police forces in a district. It approaches 1, if police force and expenditures in a district increase above all limits. Then, the crime numbers become very low and approach zero because the huge police forces can clear almost every case. In both districts, if such a large police force is deployed crime clearance rates in both districts again become equal and approach a maximal value of 1, or not much below 1. Between the two extreme cases the crime clearance rate increases continuously with lower numbers of crimes, which are caused by more police expenditures which directly deter crime (boots on the ground) and more crime clearing detective work. Figure 12.2 illustrates this.

The lower part of Figure 12.2 represents numbers of crimes as a function of police expenditures as in Figure 12.1 but rotated 90 degrees to the right. The police expenditures in district 1, the low-crime district, and district 2, the high-crime district, determine the number of crimes N_1 and N_2 in the two districts. The vertical axis represents the punishment rate in the two districts. Without police, we assume that the crime clearance and punishment rates are zero. Starting from the maximum number of crimes, every further reduction of crime numbers in both districts by an equal number requires a more than proportional increase of police expenditures. Lower numbers of crime caused by police expenditures are associated with more detectives per crime and a lower number of crimes, and consequently with higher crime clearance and

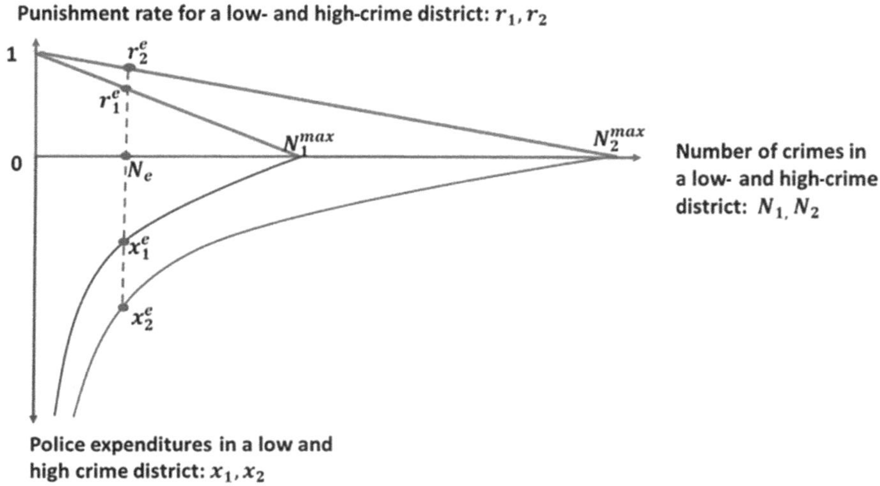

Figure 12.2 The relation between police expenditures, crime rates, and punishment rates under equal security.

punishment rates. They rise from 0 at the maximal crime level and approach 1, when police expenditures rise above all limits as is shown on the vertical axis in the upper part of Figure 12.2.

Equal security results from an equal number of crimes in both districts, as by assumption different districts have the same number of residents. The realization of equal security requires a political decision on the total police budget. The police department must then decide how the total budget is distributed between the two districts to reach equal security. Many equal security levels are therefore possible, depending on the size of the budget. Notice that under the assumptions imposed on the crime functions for each equal security level the police expenditures in the high-crime sector must be higher than in the low-crime sector regardless of the size of the budget.

Given our assumptions for each level of equal security, the crime clearance and punishment rate in the high-crime district must be higher than in the low crime district because more police forces including detectives are deployed in the high-crime district than in the low-crime district. Therefore, under all levels of equal security, discrimination occurs provided the minorities live in the high-crime sector. It decreases, however, with more police deployed in both sectors. No discrimination of offenders occurs both with a police budget and a crime clearance rate of 0, and with a crime clearance rate that approaches 1 in both districts, that is, the police budget and police expenditures in both sectors rise beyond all limits. In both cases, indirect discrimination is eliminated but both cases are empirically and normatively irrelevant.

In Figure 12.2 we picked one of the potential equal security levels to show the related values of police expenditures and punishment rates. Political decision-makers decide on a police budget (b) which must be allocated to the two districts. To achieve equal security in both districts the amount of x_1^e flows to the low-crime district 1 and the higher amount of x_2^e to the high-crime district. This causes an equal number of crimes in both districts (Ne). As police forces are concentrated in district 2 this leads to a punishment rate, which under our assumptions is higher in the high-crime district than in the low-crime district, $r_1^e < r_2^e$. As by assumption the high-crime district is populated by minorities, it also leads to discrimination of offenders, suspects, and other affected residents among the minority. Therefore, equal security causes discrimination without discriminatory intent. This is a general result because discrimination ceases to exist only if either no police and no punishment of offenders exists or if the police budget becomes excessively high, which increases the crime clearance and punishment rate in both districts to a level close to 1.

Assume now that the total police budget increases gradually from 0 to higher levels. This first leads to punishment only in the high-crime district. This is necessary because the policy aim of equal security requires the total budget to flow to the high-crime sector as long as the crime numbers there remain higher than in the low-crime district without any police. In that case the level of discrimination is $r_2 - r_1 = r_2 - 0 = r_2$ with an ever-rising punishment as well as discrimination rate in the high-crime district 2. Discrimination as a consequence of a higher police budget, which must be spent exclusively in the high-crime district, reaches a peak value when the level of crime in the high-crime district reaches the maximal level of crime in the low-crime district (without police forces deployed there). Then crime rates are the same in both districts. The reader can easily imagine why this implies a peak value of discrimination. All punished offenders and all people in prison must then be from the minority, and no criminal from the low-crime sector is punished even though the number of crimes in the low-crime district is the same as the number of crimes in the high-crime district. This outcome is an unintended consequence of equal security with a low budget. Only with a higher budget than at this peak value are police forces deployed in both districts and increase in both districts with an increased budget. Discrimination decreases and tends to disappear when the police budget increases beyond all levels.

How does this result compare to efficient security? Under our assumptions for the crime functions, an optimal amount of expenditure, crime numbers, and punishment rates can be calculated for each district. Efficient police expenditures are strictly positive in both districts. Also, efficient security policy does not concentrate police expenditures in the same way in the high-crime districts as under the equal policy aim. Therefore, under efficient security, indirect discrimination should be lower than under equal security if the equal security budget equals total police expenditures under efficient security. This result is aggravated if the low-crime district is also the high-income district and the high-crime district is the low-income district. Then, efficient security discriminates less against suspects from the high-crime district. This comes, however, at the expense of unequal security and a low level of security for the residents of the high-crime district. With a large police budget and high police expenditures in each district this unintended consequence of the equal security policy disappears; however, it is at the potential cost of an unreasonably high police budget.

In Figure 12.3 the reader can see how discrimination values change as a result of the police budget size. Remember that we define discrimination formally as difference in clearance rates or $D = r_2 - r_1$.

The horizontal axis in Figure 12.3 represents the potential values of the total police budget under the equal security policy. The vertical axis represents the resulting values of discrimination in the high-crime district $(r_2 - r_1)$. In the interval from 0 to A the whole police budget must be spent in the high-crime district because crime rates there are higher than crime rates without police forces in the low-crime district. In that range the level of discrimination is $r_2 - r_1 = r_2$ because no crimes are cleared in the low-crime district. Punishment rates and discrimination rates increase with decreasing marginal returns. The police budget at point A is the lowest budget which achieves equal security. At this point the level of discrimination reaches a peak. This is necessary because the budget 0–A is the highest police budget that must flow exclusively into the high-crime sector. If the budget rises beyond A, additional police expenditures must go to both districts to achieve equal security. Punishment rates become positive in both districts. With an ever-increasing police budget the expenditures in both sectors increase, which leads to a reduction of the difference between r_2 and r_1 (the discrimination level). Discrimination approaches zero if the police budget rises beyond all limits, as this implies that police forces in both districts also rise beyond all limits.

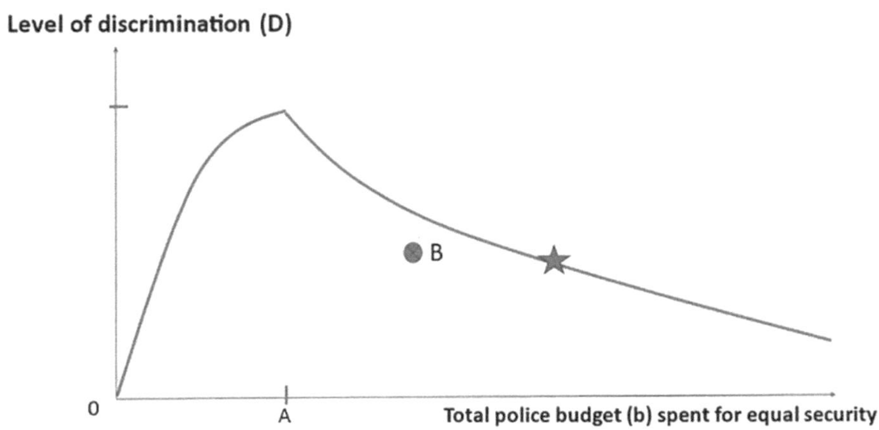

Figure 12.3 Level of discrimination in the high-crime district under equal security as a function of total police expenditures.

Let point B represent an arbitrary discrimination level and the total police expenditures under efficient security. We assume that this point is lower than the peak discrimination value under equal security because efficient crime fighting by the police causes strictly positive values of r_2 and r_1. Also, if the low-crime district is also the high-income district, the willingness-to-pay for crime fighting is higher for the reduction of a representative crime than in the low-income district. High discrimination levels of immigrants and minorities are then less plausible under efficient security than under equal security.

However, under the equal security aim there exists a high threshold budget size, which makes discrimination smaller under equal security than any potential level of discrimination under efficient security. The star in Figure 12.3 symbolizes the budget under which equal security leads to the same discrimination level as efficient security. A higher budget than this would guarantee that equal security leads to lower discrimination levels of suspects among minorities than efficient security. In other words: if the police budget is high enough, equal security can always lead to less discrimination than efficient security. This budget might, however, be unreasonably high because it leads to tax increases and/or reductions of other government services like education or healthcare.

To sum up: with a low overall police budget, statistical discrimination under an equal security policy can be so high that it cannot be tolerated because it violates the proportionality principle or the constitutional equality principle. Our analysis shows that equality for potential victims from crime can cause discriminatory inequality among offenders, suspects, and others who fall into the net of the police. Increasing the police budget can reduce the statistical discrimination to a tolerable level and/or to a level which is lower than under efficient security. But this budget might be so high and might cut so much into government revenue that other important political aims must be neglected.

Further Considerations

- We assumed that the crime level is unilaterally determined by the level of public police expenditures. This is a simplification. In fact, any reduction of the police force in a police district will increase private security investments in houses, offices, shops and for the protection of movables as well as the demand for private security services. With decreasing public police expenditures in a district, crime numbers will not increase in the way assumed here but will be lower because of higher private security expenses. Ram Singh and this author have dealt with this and other problems elsewhere.[29] This might affect the overall result somewhat. The equal security policy based on human rights will lead to less policing in rich districts and to more policing in high-crime areas and in low-income districts.
- Throughout this paper we assume that there are no spillover effects of police deployments from one district to another. Police expenditures in the one district only determine crime rates only in that district. If, however, police expenditures in one district increase and remain the same in all other districts

or if they are redistributed from one district to another, the result can be crime diversion. If one takes this into account equal security is still achievable, but it requires a more complex decision-making process, which includes the analysis of the actions and reactions of offenders in different districts.

Conclusion

Traditionally, legal scholars did not relate the policy goal of public policing to a fundamental human right. Human rights played an important role in crime fighting only insofar as the defensive, subjective rights of citizens against the state ought to limit police power and prevent state encroachment on private life. Beginning about 40 years ago, the legal debate in constitutional law changed worldwide through claims that security against crimes, especially against violent crimes, itself was a constitutional right that implied equal security for all residents. Equal security is an equal probability for all residents in a state of becoming a crime victim. This debate is international and has led to a new interpretation of constitutions and existing bills of rights. Equal security as a right is derived from human rights to life, health, property, and equal treatment. It seems now that among constitutional law scholars, equal security for all residents of a state is the prevailing opinion about the policy aim of the public crime fighting police. A human right to security against crimes is an explicit part of the Charter of Fundamental Rights of the European Union (Art. 6). In Germany and other member states of the European Union equal security against crimes has become a bipartisan political aim for the crime fighting police forces.

Without questioning this rationale, we show that the equal security aim leads to unintended consequences. It necessarily reduces the effectiveness of crime fighting insofar as it does not—given the size of the total police budget—reduce total crime numbers in a state to the lowest possible level. Also, indirect discrimination against offenders and suspects from minorities can result from police work both with a market-mimicking police and with an equal security police, but it is likely to be higher under equal security. Indirect discrimination is discrimination without intent, which can follow from pursuing a legitimate policy goal. Criminal police work leads to indirect discrimination if crime clearance and punishment rates differ and are higher among minorities or immigrants than among other offenders. Our analysis shows that this type of discrimination does not necessarily occur, but it is likely relatively high under the goal of equal security in comparison with the goal of efficient loss reduction from crime. Following the equal security goal can cause statistical discrimination to become excessively high if the overall police budget is small and most police forces must then be concentrated in crime areas and "hot spots," which are often the residential areas of immigrants and ethnic minorities. In that case an enormous difference of crime clearance and punishment rates in different police districts and an enormous level of indirect discrimination results as an unintended consequence of equal security.

***

I dedicate this chapter to Susan Rose-Ackerman, who helped me throughout my academic carrier to better understand law and economics. Susan often visited the doctoral program at the University of Hamburg and gave lectures and tutorials for doctoral students. She contributed over the years to the success of the newly founded Institute of Law and Economics and to my own scholarly endeavors, including my co-authored textbook on the economic analysis of civil law, whose last edition was published in 2022.

Notes

* The author thanks Ram Singh, Stefan Magen, Hans-Peter Bull, Michael Fehling, and Hermann Pünder for help and valuable comments.

1 K. Morrell and B. Bradford (2019). *Policing and Public Management* (London: Routledge,), ch. 2.

2 R. Posner (1985). An Economic Theory of the Criminal Law. *Columbia Law Review* 85(6): 1193–1231, at 1195.

3 Becker and Foucault on Crime and Punishment, A Conversation with Gary Becker, François Ewald, and Bernard Harcourt, The Second Session, The University of Chicago—May 15, 2013. Becker defends efficiency as the overarching rationale of crime fighting. http://www.law.uchicago.edu/Lawecon/index.html

4 "By the eighteenth and nineteenth centuries in Britain and America, volunteer groups using private funding complemented, supplemented, or supplanted the mandatory systems of community protection. In Britain, felons associations posted rewards to apprehend criminals, assisted their members in prosecuting criminals, and sometimes hired private patrols. Victims hired private thief takers to retrieve stolen property. In colonial America, Boston established a night watch in 1636, and watchmen became commonplace throughout the colonies. 'Crime control administered by a centralized government did not exist, and responsibility for protection was thrust upon the people themselves.'" M. Rhead Enion (2009). Constitutional Limits on Private Policing and the State's Allocation of Force. *Duke Law Journal* 59: 519–53, at 533.

5 R. H. Coase (1974). The Lighthouse in Economics. *Journal of Law & Economics* 17(2): 357–76.

6 J. Isensee (1983). *Das Grundrecht auf Sicherheit, Zu den Schutzpflichten des freiheitlichen Verfassungsstaates* (The fundamental right to security, On the duties of protection of the liberal constitutional state) (Berlin: Walter de Gruyter).

7 G. Robbers (1987). *Sicherheit als Menschenrecht, Aspekte der Geschichte, Begründung und Wirkung einer Grundrechtsfunktion* (Security as a human right, Aspects of the history, justification, and effect of a basic right) (Baden-Baden: Nomos).

8 C. Gusy (1996). Rechtsgüterschutz als Staatsaufgabe—Verfassungsfragen der Staatsaufgabe Sicherheit (The protection of rights as a policy aim of the state). *Die Öffentliche Verwaltung*, 573.

9 J. Limbach (2002). *Ist die kollektive Sicherheit der Feind der individuellen Freiheit?* (Is collective security an enemy of Freedom?) Cologne: Carl Heymanns Verlag.

10 O. Lepsius (2004). Liberty, Security, and Terrorism: The Legal Position in *Germany. German Law Review* 5(05): 435–60.

11 J. Limbach (2002). *Ist die kollektive Sicherheit der Feind der individuellen Freiheit?* (Is collective security an enemy of Freedom?) op. cit., footnote 9.

12 L. Rosenthal (2003). Policing and Equal Protection. *Yale Law & Policy Review* 21: 53–103. Available at https://ssrn.com/abstract=926356.

13 D. A. Lewis and G. W. Salem (2016). *Incivility and the Production of a Social Problem.* New Jersey: Transaction Publishers, ch. 8.

14 C. Lewis and J. Wood (2006). The Governance of Policing and Security Provision, in: J. Fleming and J. Wood (Eds.) *Fighting Crimes Together, The Challenge of Policing and Security Networks*. Sydney: UNSW Press, p. 234. (The authors advocate a rethinking on the market-mimicking rationale of public regulation as protecting equal access to human rights and justice (p. 233), pp. 218–45.)

15 L. Chinchilla (2003). Police Community Partnerships in Brazil, in: H. Frühling, J. S. Tulchin, and H. A. Golding (Eds.) *Crime and Violence in Latin America, Citizen Security and the State*. Baltimore: The Johns Hopkins University Press, p. 194; on equal security services, pp. 153–78.

16 A. Harel and G. Parchmovoski argue that fair protection against crime "imparts a duty on the state to equalize individuals' vulnerability to crime." This would imply more police efforts or higher punishment of crimes for those who are particularly vulnerable, like crimes related to race, gender, religion, and sexual orientation. A. Harel and G. Parchmovoski (1999). On Hate and Equality. *Yale Law Journal* 109: 507–39.

17 Huang, Chen-Yu (2014). The UK and the Ratification of the Treaty of Lisbon—A Liberal Intergovernmentalist Analysis. *EurAmerica*.

18 UN Security Council, Press Release, SC 8082, April 30, 2004.

19 Fundamental rights survey | European Union Agency for Fundamental Rights (europa.eu).

20 Koalitionsvertrag zwischen CDU, CSU und SPD, 19. Legislaturperiode, 2018, at p. 126. (Coalition agreement between parties forming the federal government in Germany 2018). A board decision of the Christian Democratic Party in Germany of January 2017 reads: „Jeder Mensch hat ein Recht auf Sicherheit. Nur wer sicher ist, kann in Freiheit leben." (Every individual has a right to security. Only those who are safe can live in freedom.)

21 Koalitionsvertrag 2021–2025 zwischen der sozialdemokratischen Partei Deutschlands (SPD), Bündnis 90/ Die Grünen und den Freuen Demokraten (FDP), p. 81.

22 H.-B. Schäfer and M. Fehling (2021). Privatization of the Police, in: A. Dorfman and A. Harel (Eds.) *Cambridge Handbook of Privatization*. Cambridge: Cambridge University Press, pp. 206–29.

23 H.-B. Schäfer and Ram Singh (2023). Equal versus Efficient Security and Its Paradoxes, unpublished paper, available upon request.

24 Statista (2021). Prevalence rate of violent crime, by age U.S. 2019 | Statista.

25 Statista (2021). See note 24.

26 Kenneth Arrow (1971). The Theory of Discrimination. Industrial relations section. Working paper no. 30A. Princeton University. S. Chaudhuri and R. Sethi (2008). Statistical Discrimination with Peer Effects: Can Integration Eliminate Negative Stereotypes? *The Review of Economic Studies* 75: 579–96.

27 For a rigorous proof of this proposition, which relies on even milder assumptions on the crime functions than in this paper, see H.-B. Schäfer and Ram Singh (2023), op. cit., see note 23.

28 Council Directive 2000/43/EC, Art. 2.2(b).

29 H.-B. Schäfer and M. Fehling (2021) Privatization of the Police, in: A. Dorfman and A. Harel (Eds.) *Cambridge Handbook of Privatization*. Cambridge: Cambridge University Press, pp. 206–29.

13 Administration and Democracy

Peter L. Lindseth

It has been an honor of my scholarly career to be a collaborator, co-author, and co-editor with Susan Rose-Ackerman. For this reason, I am grateful for the opportunity to contribute some final reflections to this volume—one of two emerging out of the conference in her honor at Yale Law School in August 2022.

Over the past three decades, Susan has been a forceful advocate for a set of normative commitments on the possibilities of making "democratic values operational in modern states where hierarchy and expertise cannot be avoided."[1] This is indeed a core challenge of administrative law, comparative or otherwise. In facing this challenge, Susan has been tireless in advancing the cause of judicially enforced procedural rights as an instrument of democratization in the administrative space.

Democracy, of course, is an "essentially contested concept,"[2] whose substantive content and institutional realization is subject to significant debate and variation across time and place. One might understand Susan's emphasis on the democratic potential of administrative procedure, in effect, as an effort to respond to one of the core "broken promises" of traditional electoral democracy identified by Norberto Bobbio in the 1980s.[3] I am referring to the incapacities of centralized democratic sovereignty (as represented by the elected assembly or chief executive) in the face of plural power centers and the triumph of neo-corporatist interest representation over political representation. Among those who hope to realize democracy within the confines of administrative governance, alternative technologies beyond the elected assembly or elected chief executives—typically transparency, participation, and reasoned decision-making within the administrative sphere itself—have a crucial role to play, as Susan's work repeatedly emphasizes. Procedural rights of this type in effect seek to replace what Bobbio called the "centripetal" ideal of democracy—in which "the many" become "one" via an elected assembly or chief executive—by accepting instead the "centrifugal" nature of society as a polyarchy with multiple power centers.[4]

The precise relationship between classical (electoral) and novel (administrative) forms of democracy, however, remains difficult to discern in many systems. It has been a core task of Susan's work to tease this relationship out,

DOI: 10.4324/9781003416036-13

both descriptively and normatively, in a comparative sense. Modern systems of administrative governance must of course rely on forms of transparency, participation, and reasoned decision-making, often enforced through judicial review. Nonetheless, these mechanisms have generally not displaced traditional forms of hierarchical oversight and control by political actors, whether legislative or executive. What this non-displacement suggests, I would argue, is that, even as normative and regulatory power has diffused into a complex system of administrative governance, elected political representatives must play a crucial role in legitimizing conduct of the administrative sphere. These representatives continue to serve, through various means of oversight and steering, as conduits through which the democratic and constitutional legitimacy of the new forms of administrative governance can be mediated in a historically recognizable, if still evolving, sense.[5]

The effort at reconstructing the meaning of democracy in modern administrative governance is, as Susan's work very clearly shows, also necessitated by the rise of technocracy—the rule by experts—or at least by the pervasiveness of technocratic values as a competing source of legitimation. The felt need for heightened transparency, participation, and reasoned decision-making is a testament to the ever-increasing power of (purported) expertise both within and beyond the state. It is also a response to the challenge of "maintaining the connection" to traditional modes of political control in a classic sense, despite the diffusion of power to experts.[6]

In this regard, as many of the contributions to this volume show, administrative law has become an important site of contestation and renegotiation in this process of rethinking democracy in an era of technocracy and administrative governance. Perhaps the most prominent example is the well-known struggle to make a workable distinction between *politics* and *policy*, a distinction that can be said to underpin both legislative delegations as well as the constitutionalized demarcations that exist in certain systems between the realms of legislation and regulation.[7] In a similar vein, one can look to the distinction between *policy* and *law*, which can be said to underpin doctrines of judicial deference to administrative determinations. The emergence of these distinctions can be understood, at least in part, as a vindication of technocratic values in the face of countervailing demands for political or judicial control of the administrative process.

These distinctions can also be seen, however, as a way of warding off juristocracy, or rule by judges. Indeed, one of the very interesting phenomena in modern administrative governance is the extent to which all actors in the system, judges perhaps above all, have internalized at least some measure of respect for the prerogatives of both scientific expertise and democratic politics as essential to defining the proper contours of external legal control of administrative action. This is especially evident in what has become known as "process review" in which judges scrutinize the process by which administrative decisions are made without purporting to substitute a judicial judgment on the merits of the decision itself. This internalization, of course, has not been absolute, particularly as concerns over proportionality and human rights have intensified over the last quarter century. Judges retain, *in extremis*, a sense of law's ultimate supremacy—the "rule of law" in the most generic sense, even as that phrase may have a more specific meaning in some systems compared with others.

In enforcing law's ultimate supremacy (even if only episodically, given the nature of administrative litigation), judges are often motivated by the classic ideal of rendering justice in the particular case. Nonetheless, concerns over the systemic consequences of particularized decisions are generally never far from the surface. Invoking a higher-law norm to protect a litigant from unlawfully or unreasonably exercised public power can almost always be justified as a means of promoting systemic legitimacy. In these instances, the litigant successfully enlists the aid of a judge to vindicate that party's particular interest over that of the public (or "general") interest putatively represented by the administrative actor exercising authority delegated from the legislature.

Beyond doing justice in the individual case, my own view is that judges should strive to mediate the legitimacy of administrative governance *in conjunction* with the political branches. That is, they should work to achieve a reconciliation between, on the one hand, the inevitability of technocracy and juristocracy in administrative governance and, on the other, our deeply held commitments, inherited from the past, to democratic self-government through the mechanisms of political representation, whether legislative or executive. Out of such a reconciliation, one hopes, courts can strive to make their own contribution to a durable constitutional settlement for administrative governance over the long term.

With these general considerations in mind, let me turn to a discussion of a selection of the contributions to this volume, focusing on those that, to my mind, most clearly address Susan's central concern about the nature (and fate) of democracy in an age of administrative governance. I structure this discussion around several interrelated themes that I see these selected contributions raising.

The threshold theme is the relationship of democracy, administration, and constitutional structure, understood along two different dimensions. The first—considered immediately below—relates to the diffusion of governing power between a purported center and periphery (decentralization, federalism, and supranationalism). The second—considered in the next subsection—relates to the diffusion of power within the center of governance itself, i.e., separation of power among various "branches" (legislative, executive, and judicial) and their relationship to the administrative sphere and hence to the realization of democracy however defined.

Maciej Kisilowski's contribution, "From Elections to Autocracy," explores the potential of political decentralization in Poland. Although not centrally concerned with administrative governance, the chapter is a healthy reminder of certain *sine qua non* that make democracy possible, whether electoral, administrative, or otherwise. Foundationally, democracy requires a reasonably coherent political community—a *demos*—within which it is possible for the majority to rule over the minority without that rule being experienced as rule by an "other." The Polish *demos*, however, is currently fractured between two broad camps whose divisions threaten the stability and legitimacy of majority rule at the center. Kisilowski chooses to call these camps "Pro-Privilege" and "Pro-Equality" but one could just as easily call them authoritarian populists and liberal-democratic pluralists. The problem is that, over the last three decades, governments of all stripes have exploited the current system to excessively concentrate power, exacerbate political fractures, and thus undermine Poland's democracy. This sort of winner-take-all politics has made it increasingly difficult for Poles to maintain a sense of shared democratic identity constitutionally embodied in the unitary Polish state.

Given more general commitments to a unitary state in Polish political culture, a form of federalism is out of the question. The problem is that federalism presupposes a divided sovereignty among two levels of strongly legitimated constitutional governance, representing two levels of federated *demoi* interacting with each other. For that reason, the project of the Social Contract Incubator (IUS) in Poland, which Kisilowski co-leads, posits instead a form of strategic decentralization to diffuse the tensions that currently beset the Polish *demos*. (In the interest of full disclosure, I have been an advisor to that project and thus am generally supportive of its aims.) What I want to stress here, however, is the linkage of decentralization to administrative governance; indeed, I would argue that there is an intimate linkage between the two. Political decentralization will raise the comfort level of Poles in various regions precisely because the policy agenda of decentralized electoral majorities will be implemented by administrative actors with whom the local population can more closely identify.

Akis Psygkas's chapter, "Administrative Democracy and Federalism," also seeks to tackle the question of administrative governance and constitutional structure, but this time from the perspective of federalism *tout court*. Psygkas expertly surveys the literature on both federalism and administrative democracy—two domains in which Susan's work has been of decisive importance—to construct what he calls "an ideal type of federal–state interaction that can lead to the development of effective administrative democracy." By the latter, he means—very much in the vein of Susan's work—"the direct relations between administrative agencies and citizens and emphasizes public input in the policy-making process."

There can be no doubt that such direct input is a good thing for a variety of reasons, not least that it makes administrative policy-making better and more responsive, while also reducing the information costs of political oversight and monitoring by elected representatives. But whether non-hierarchical, bottom-up forms of participation, transparency, and reason-giving in the administrative sphere are, socio-politically speaking, experienced as a form of "democracy"—and hence properly labelled as such—is a topic I want to bracket for the moment.

What I wish to focus on instead is Psygkas's conception of federalism. He uses the term so broadly as to encompass all manner of decentralized and multi-level forms of governance, regardless of the actual locus of democratic and constitutional legitimacy in particular systems. With such a broad definition, it is entirely fair for Psygkas to characterize the US, Canada, and the EU as variants of federalism. However, that stratagem elides a crucial difference whose ultimate relevance cannot be ignored. Certainly all three can no doubt benefit from the sort of "feedback loops," "downloading," and "uploading" that are the central features of Psygkas's ideal model of interaction between multiple levels of governance. However, whereas the multi-level governance in the US and Canada can fairly be described as federal (in the sense of multi-level *demoi* interacting with each other through strongly legitimated and autonomously constitutional levels of governance), that is simply not the case in the EU.

No doubt many strongly pro-Europeans wish that it were so—indeed, this view is especially strong among EU lawyers, judges, and law professors, who love to describe the EU "as if" it were a robustly democratic and constitutional level of governance in its own right.[8] But despite that discourse, Europeans have consistently refused to grant the EU the ultimate *sine qua non* of genuine constitutionalism: the autonomous capacity to mobilize resources in a legitimate and compulsory fashion. The EU has instead remained, despite some constitutional-rhetorical window dressing, a highly technocratic and juristocratic (i.e., "administrative") type of governance.

This lack of autonomous democratic and constitutional legitimacy at the EU level has deeply shaped the way in which the system of European integration operates in practice. **Joana Mendes**, in her chapter "Law and Monetary Policy," discusses a notorious example: the dysfunctional character of the EU's Economic and Monetary Union (EMU). Three decades ago, the EU made a fundamental choice to build the EMU, albeit with an "asymmetric" structure. Monetary policy would be supranationalized but economic and related fiscal policies would remain national, subject only to "coordination" at the EU level. This asymmetric structure—as well as the difficult (if not impossible) boundary issues it creates—derives directly from the lack of autonomous democratic and constitutional legitimacy at the EU level. Given the broad acceptance (at least until recently) of the purportedly technocratic character of monetary policy, the Member States could delegate power over such questions to a similarly technocratic, but still supranational, European Central Bank (ECB). But given that economic and related fiscal policies need to be addressed by institutions possessing robust democratic and constitutional legitimacy (something the EU lacks in its own right), power over those questions was necessarily retained in national parliaments and executives—the only place where such legitimacy actually exists in the European system.

Much of the legal and political bickering in the EU of the last fifteen years of crisis (and indeed longer) has revolved around the constraints that this asymmetric structure/legitimacy imposes. Mendes focuses on one important domain in which this bickering has been salient: in the ECB's adoption of unconventional monetary instruments to address the eurozone crisis, as well as in their spill-over effects into (national) economic policy domains. EMU asymmetry meant, over the course of the crisis decade, that the ECB's purportedly technocratic monetary interventions became (economically speaking) the only game in town, as the saying goes. The ECB was compelled to take on a central role at various stages of the crisis because only it had the tools to intervene at scale, supported by the requisite legitimacy, in this case, technocratic. The EU itself lacked, however, any similar power and legitimacy in the economic or fiscal domains.

The boundary issues between monetary and economic policy led to legal challenges as to whether and to what extent courts could or should force the ECB, as a technocratic actor, to explain and justify the economic policy spill-over effects of its crisis-driven monetary interventions. The Court of Justice of the European Union (CJEU) approached the question as one of technocratic expertise demanding near total deference to the ECB. Accountability, if any, belonged to EU-level politics, as lame as that might appear to be in this context (the so-called "monetary dialogue" between the ECB and the European Parliament, the EU's sole directly elected body). The German Federal Constitutional Court (FCC), by contrast, viewed the matter more from an administrative law perspective, in which a court could enforce the procedural requirements of the principle of proportionality as the basis for a type of process review. The FCC found that, unless the ECB could provide clearer evidence of rational deliberation and reason-giving to justify its encroachments on national economic policy domains, the Court would need to find that the ECB's actions fell outside the scope of its delegated technocratic authority.

The FCC ultimately backed down from its aggressive stance after a relatively perfunctory additional proportionality assessment (provided not by the ECB but by the Bundesbank). Nonetheless, Mendes finds "untapped potential" in the FCC's process-oriented proportionality approach as a means of bringing the unchallenged expertise of central banking within the scope of more traditional administrative law accountability. Rather than see process review here as a route to some kind of "administrative democracy," she sees it as a means of reducing information costs to elected political actors elsewhere, a position that I would generally endorse. But that "elsewhere," in her view, should be the European Parliament and an improved "monetary dialogue" with the ECB. She favors this, perhaps, because a "one-stop shopping" accountability mechanism in the European Parliament is functionally less cumbersome than forcing the ECB to justify itself before all the national parliaments of the Member States, which, in principle, are the proper fora for discussing economic and related fiscal policies. However, she also explicitly declines to characterize a reinforced role of the European Parliament here as a step toward EU "democratization," thus admirably avoiding an "as if" constitutional discourse to justify her proposed approach.

The second dimension of the relationship of democracy, administration, and constitutional structure in this volume involves separation of powers. It is a truism that, in a liberal-democratic system, administrative governance has a great deal of difficulty sustaining itself without maintaining some kind of legitimating connection to the *trias politica*—legislative, executive, and judicial—at least in some historically or culturally recognizable sense. But the nature of that legitimating connection is not fixed or static. Although there may be an irreducible minimum of power that must be maintained by each—given, as Peter Strauss eloquently put it many years ago, "the paradigmatic function which [each] alone is empowered to serve"[9]—beyond that minimum there is a good deal of variation in how the democratic and constitutional legitimacy may be mediated through the three branches (or indeed possibly through more than three branches).[10] In other words, we must recognize that the very idea of separation of powers, particularly in relation to administrative governance, is historically and culturally contingent.[11]

Matthias Rossbach's contribution assesses "The Creation of the Modern American Civil Service and the (Constitutional) Limits of German Influence." As Rossbach shows, American civil service reform at its inception in the final quarter of the nineteenth century operated at the intersection of both US constitutional requirements as well as purported European (and particularly German) influences. Consequently, this history provides an interesting point of entry into the dynamic and evolving nature of presidential power vis-à-vis subordinate administrative personnel in the US federal context. In response to recent agenda-driven critiques by Philip Hamburger,[12] Rossbach cogently demonstrates that the US system of a competitive and professional civil service was not a "departure from [US] constitutional law on executive personnel since the founding, nor did it lead to a German-style career civil service in the United States. The present American personnel system is the product of a specifically American development." The system as established in the later nineteenth century sought, in particular, to respect the demands of both the Appointments Clause and traditional understandings of presidential removal power. Both those dimensions continued to evolve over the course of the twentieth century. As a consequence, they have faced considerable pressure recently, whether before the Roberts Court or under the Trump Administration, often influenced by those same agenda-driven critiques.

To Rossbach this political contestation is evidence of the peculiar nature of the American competitive civil service. In the US, the civil service depends not merely on law but also on politics, and, more specifically, on the legitimacy of administrative autonomy from presidential oversight and control. Rossbach concludes: "The courts give an important framework. But the final answer to the crucial question of where to draw the line [between autonomy and control inevitably falls to] the political process." This stands in sharp contrast to the autonomy of the career civil service in Germany, which is built on "an explicit constitutional guarantee" that places it "beyond ordinary politics."

Stefanie Egidy's discussion of "Administrative Resilience" in times of crisis might seem inflected by a similarly German sensibility concerning the value of reinforcing administrative autonomy. That sensibility brings to mind competing legal-cultural caricatures of the administrative actor (variously a Hegelian *pouvoir neutre* existing above social divisions, or a Weberian/rational technocrat bearing the authority of the general-interest state, versus a mere bureaucrat who is the product of interest-group politics, susceptible to capture, and thus in need of constraint). The latter caricature certainly has motivated those in the US who want to "drain the swamp" in Washington or more politely (but still quite radically) "deconstruct the administrative state." But the same political currents, in their more scholarly form, also point to the purported infiltration of German ideas into US governance as paving the way for the construction of the administrative state in the first place.[13]

For those who see modern administrative governance as a great achievement and a triumph of liberal democracy (and I certainly count myself among that group), the idea of reinforcing administrative resilience in the face of such pressures is obviously attractive. Certainly, one would hope that the commitment to the rule of law and due process, for example, would give administrative actors the backbone to resist the erratic demands of populist possessors of executive power who might otherwise trample those values. These momentary possessors of executive power should not have the right to disregard the substance of existing legislation or regulation or the constraints of procedural requirements in order to realize populist aims that only they purportedly embody. In such circumstances, administrative resilience has a clear purpose and value. Moreover, one would hope that the judiciary would be an ally in enforcing more enduring legislative, regulatory, or procedural commitments—although that is becoming increasingly uncertain in many systems.

I worry, however, that by focusing on the question of administrative resilience, we distract ourselves from the more pressing task at hand: *winning in electoral politics* so that anti-democratic forces cannot gain the power to run roughshod over the administrative sphere in the first place. Without political backing, the administrative sphere is simply unable to mobilize the resources necessary for maintaining its resilience, no matter how necessary that project may be. The normative or institutional guardrails that Egidy identifies as essential to resilience will be of diminishing effectiveness without political allies to mobilize the needed human and fiscal resources in a legitimate and compulsory manner. This mobilization capacity is what distinguishes democratic and constitutional from merely administrative power.[14] We must never lose sight of the fact that winning in the game of electoral politics—thus keeping the legislative, executive, and even judicial branches anchored in the liberal-democratic and pluralist project—is essential to the success of any program of reinforcing administrative resilience.

Edgar Andrés Melgar & Susan Rose-Ackerman consider whether "Judicial Review of the Executive in Hyper-Presidential Regimes" could act as a check on the authoritarian tendencies of such regimes. However, the ability of the judiciary to play that role also depends, one would think, on liberal-democrats winning and maintaining political power. But, instead of a frontal attack on hyper-presidentialism through the political process, Melgar & Rose-Ackerman advocate for a more subtle strategy of asking judges to build on existing trends to transform the meaning of legality and the protection of rights, thus developing more process-oriented forms of judicial review of executive action. Courts need to take on a greater role in enforcing process constraints to encourage rational deliberation, reason-giving, and thereby checking tendencies toward unilateralism or worse, creeping authoritarianism or kleptocracy. They suggest that this may be the only strategy possible "in countries where some part of the citizenry is vocally opposed to democratic electoral transitions, or in countries that have otherwise struggled to build trust in the fairness and transparency of government institutions."

In this context of democratic weakness or even absence, such a move by judges would certainly not be unprecedented in the history of the emergence of modern administrative law. It brings to mind the famous observation of Léon Aucoc, a French *conseillier d'Etat* under the Second Empire. Aucoc argued that, in the absence of robust political legitimation in other forms, external legal control of administrative action should serve as a kind of "safety-valve which should always remain open."[15] There is much truth in this statement. Restated in the modern terms of principal–agent theory, judicial review should serve as a kind of "fire alarm," in which litigants enlist the aid of a judge to adjudicate whether the executive or administrative agent has acted unlawfully or unreasonably.[16] How aggressively the judge undertakes this role will necessarily have a bearing on, but also be informed by, the dominant understandings of the proper balance of power between general and particular interests (including human rights), as well as between democracy (politics), technocracy (expertise), and juristocracy (law) in the system.[17]

Nearly all the contributions considered so far have implicated, at least implicitly, the final theme I would like to consider in these reflections: the legitimating function of administrative law within the framework of liberal-democratic constitutionalism.

The contribution of **Jud Mathews & Joshua Spannaus**, on "The Lawfulness of Public Law in Germany and the Unites States," takes direct aim at this topic. The argument comes in the form of a response to the recent agenda-driven critiques of Philip Hamburger that German administrative law—and, by purported historical lineage, American administrative law—is somehow so lawless as to be beyond legal or even political control.[18]

One is tempted simply to dismiss Hamburger's accusation as absurd on its face. But the claim has gained traction in right-wing circles in the US, so Mathews & Spannaus do the necessary work of counter-acting the caricatures and baseless assertions (just as others have done in challenging Hamburger's distortions of both the English and US administrative law traditions).[19] As Mathews & Spannaus point out, Hamburger builds his attacks on a set of stipulative definitions that are designed to lead the unwary reader toward the seeming inexorable conclusion that somehow German law, and again, by derivation, American administrative law, are "unlawful." But as Mathews & Spannaus exhaustively demonstrate, German administrative law is "fully lawful in every sense that matters": "it provides robust and effective protection of individuals' interests plus conceptual machinery that facilitates the clear legal analysis of administrative law issues. . . . Germany [thus] demonstrates in exemplary fashion how administrative power can be effectively domesticated by law."

Moreover, that law is designed specifically to reinforce political control (and hence democratic legitimation) over administrative action: "A key concept in German public law is the chain of legitimation (*Legitimationskette*), whereby all exercises of state power are traceable back, through an unbroken chain, to electoral choices made by the people." Susan, of course, famously criticized German administrative law three decades ago for its excessive reliance on this purported chain of legitimation and its failure to adopt US-style transparency, participation, and reason-giving obligations to make up for its inadequacies.[20] Mathews & Spannaus argue that subsequent developments have done much to address Susan's concerns, even if these features have not been adopted generally. But Mathews & Spannaus also credit Susan for identifying "what for German administrative law is an uncomfortable truth: administrators as a practical matter enjoy substantial policymaking latitude when they decide how to apply statutes in the form of regulations."

Focusing on the other major progenitor of the continental European tradition in administrative law—France—**Thomas Perroud** critiques what he sees as "The Neoliberal Turn of Contemporary French Administrative Law." Perroud discerns a recent, disturbing deviation from the classical French administrative law tradition, "characterized by the desire to ensure the preeminence of representative democracy." As Perroud puts it: "Judges were formerly to ensure the preeminence of statutory law; today, in contrast, they are incrementally increasing the possibilities for neutralizing it." Perroud sees this antidemocratic tendency operating hand in hand with the infiltration of what he calls "neoliberal" ideas into French administrative law, which have the effect of emptying French administrative law of its traditional substance and balance.

Perroud acknowledges that many of the changes he decries, in fact, flow from acts of the French parliament itself over many decades, which would seem in tension with his claim that the French administrative courts are resisting rather than accommodating legislative demands. Moreover, when he examines decisions of the Council of State that have blurred many of the traditional boundaries between public and private, he downplays the role of European Union law as the impetus for these changes. Similarly, when Perroud laments the declining supremacy of parliamentary legislation in French public law, both constitutional and administrative, much of the impetus is again European.[21] The importance of the European influence would seem to temper the claim that French administrative judges are an independent variable driving change rather than reacting to changes taking place elsewhere.

That said, Perroud is on firmer ground when he focuses more squarely on jurisprudential developments—for example, limitations on associational standing to challenge the legality of administrative action. Additionally, his critiques of privatized dispute resolution or the blurring of regulatory and white-collar criminal law (as well as the role that seemingly captured independent agencies play in the regulation of the public financial markets or competition law), fit his neoliberal framing better. These developments suggest a hollowing out of the traditional republican state, something linked to the rise of "compliance" as a blurred domain of legal and regulatory enforcement.[22] But the rise of compliance incorporates a deeper irony: regulatory demands persist even as the enforcement capacities of the state decline, which, in turn, has led to a shift of personnel (and cost) to the private sphere in the form of well-staffed corporate compliance departments.

The evolving character of the regulatory state is also, in effect, the subject of the final contribution I want to consider here: **Blake Emerson**'s chapter, provocatively titled "What's Democratic about Administration?" Focusing on American administrative law at the federal level, Emerson notes how faith in administrative procedure as a mechanism of democratic legitimation—the project at the heart of Susan's work in comparative administrative—now seems to be waning in the face of attacks not just on administrative governance but on liberal democracy itself. And yet, Emerson remains hopeful. He argues that, even as critics may identify "weak spots . . ., they abandon the project of participatory administration too quickly." Rather, that project will continue to exist "[b]ut its form and content need to adapt in response to the inhospitable institutional landscape."

Emerson's adaptation strategy is to recast administrative agencies not as makers of regulatory "policy"—a function to which the increasingly conservative judiciary shows itself increasingly hostile—but as defenders of "collective rights" (such as, to "healthy and safe living and workplace conditions, fair and stable marketplaces, the maintenance of the physical and institutional infrastructure," and so on). This is an attractive proposition. Aside from its weightier normative valence, the concept of collective rights has grounding in the common law and lends itself to direct advocacy in the public sphere. Although Emerson does not argue this directly, the common law grounding suggests a license for administrative actors to speak beyond the confines of strict statutory authorization (an interesting proposition, but one that would no doubt encounter resistance in certain quarters). But he also points out that agencies, qua executive "departments," are specifically contemplated in the constitution and, as constitutional actors and are authorized to take part (via the Opinions Clause) in "collaborative processes of consultation and justification in the execution of law."

All this strikes me as an intriguing but perhaps ultimately tenuous basis for agencies to insert themselves into the public sphere as collective rights advocates. When Emerson turns to the forms of agency action to promote these rights, the initial promise of the argument gets even more deflated. Out goes notice-and-comment rulemaking and in comes . . . guidance documents, enforcement actions, interim final rules, and procedural rules? This strikes me as less a strategy to engage in robust public advocacy and more a retreat to regulation by obscure and less participatory means (at least in the broadest sense). Undoubtedly this strategy responds "to the inhospitable institutional landscape," but it is hard to see how it is an adaptation of the "form and content" of participatory administration in the sense that Emerson suggests.

In closing, I would like to consider one final point implicitly raised by Emerson, one that illuminates an important dimension of the relationship of administration to democracy. It touches once again on the capacity to mobilize human and fiscal resources in a legitimate and compulsory fashion, a point I also made above.[23]

In discussing the major questions doctrine in the US, Emerson cites a case that applied the doctrine to invalidate a mask-or-vaccinate mandate on large businesses, which had been adopted by the Occupational Safety and Health Administration (OSHA) as a response to the Covid-19 pandemic. The Court found that OSHA exceeded its statutory authority by adopting the mandate as an "occupational" safety and health standard; the Court instead saw it as a general public health measure over which OSHA did not have authority.[24] For all the reasons Emerson suggests, one might question the application of MQD here. But one should also remember the companion case, decided the same day. There, the Court found that the Secretary of the Department of Health and Human Services (HHS) acted *within* the scope of his authority to adopt a similar rule in the hospital sector, under HHS's statutory power to impose conditions on the receipt of Medicaid and Medicare funds that "the Secretary finds necessary in the interest of the health and safety of individuals who are furnished services."[25]

A crucial difference in the second case is not just the relatively greater clarity of the statutory authorization in a matter of "vast economic and political significance" (the standard MQD trigger). It is also that the authorization to impose conditions on the receipt of funds was *incident to Congress's spending power* (in short, its power of legitimate compulsory mobilization of resources). This is the very essence of democratic and constitutional authority, which inures to the benefit of the administrative agency but which the agency does not possess on its own. Only the elected legislature has the mobilization power that gives this essential lifeblood to the regulatory regime. But when the regulation operates as a condition on this sort of democratic mobilization capacity, its constitutional basis (and regulatory traction) is that much greater.

This, then, brings us to the final point: no matter how much we value participation, transparency, and reason-giving as a potential source of democratic legitimacy in the administrative sphere, it will never be sufficient to give the agency an autonomous capacity to mobilize these resources. For that, the administration necessarily depends on the elected legislature, either directly or indirectly, because that is where the needed democratic and constitutional legitimacy resides in the most robust sense. Any legitimation derived from administrative procedures will therefore be, from a democratic standpoint, supplemental at best—important, no doubt, but still supplemental.

Notes

1 Susan Rose-Ackerman, *Controlling Environmental Policy: The Limits of Public Law in Germany and the United States* (Yale University Press 1995) 1.
2 WB Gallie, 'Essentially Contested Concepts' (1956) 56 Proceedings of the Aristotelian Society 167. The general reflections in this sub-section draw from Peter L Lindseth, 'Judicial Review in Administrative Governance: A Theoretical Framework for Comparative Analysis' in Jurgen CA Poorter, Ernst Hirsch Ballin, and Saskia Lavrijssen (eds), *Judicial Review of Administrative Discretion in the Administrative State* (Springer 2019).
3 See generally Norberto Bobbio, *The Future of Democracy: A Defence of the Rules of the Game* (University of Minnesota Press 1987).
4 Ibid 28.
5 See Peter L Lindseth, 'The Paradox of Parliamentary Supremacy: Delegation, Democracy, and Dictatorship in Germany and France, 1920s–1950s' (2004) 113 Yale Law Journal 1341, 1414–15. See also Peter L Lindseth, *Power and Legitimacy: Reconciling Europe and the Nation-State* (Oxford University Press 2010).
6 Peter L Strauss, 'Formal and Functional Approaches to Separation-of-Powers Questions—A Foolish Inconsistency?' (1987) 72 Cornell Law Review 488, 493.
7 Articles 34 and 37 of the French Constitution of 1958 is the classic example of such a textual demarcation. However, this demarcation has a judicial counterpart, in judge-made doctrines that seek to specify certain "reserved domains" (*Vorbehalt des Gesetzes*, *riserva di legge*) in which the legislature must define the controlling norms itself, as a protection against a return to dictatorship through legislative abdication. See generally Lindseth, 'The Paradox of Parliamentary Supremacy' (n 5).
8 Peter L Lindseth, 'The Perils of "As If" European Constitutionalism' (2016) 22 European Law Journal 696.
9 Strauss (n 6) 493.
10 See generally Bruce A Ackerman, 'Good-Bye Montesquieu' in Susan Rose-Ackerman and Peter L Lindseth (eds), *Comparative Administrative Law* (Edward Elgar 2010).
11 Just to name some famous models from the North Atlantic world, one could define it in terms of Westminster-style parliamentarism, US-style presidentialism, or French-style *dualité de juridictions*, as well as many variants in between and beyond.
12 See, e.g., Philip Hamburger, *Is Administrative Law Unlawful?* (University of Chicago Press 2014).
13 Again, see ibid.
14 Lindseth, 'Perils of "As If" European Constitutionalism' (n 8).
15 Quoted in Pierre Lampué, 'Le développement historique du recours pour excès de pouvoir depuis ses origines jusqu'au début du XXe siècle' [1954] Revue internationale des sciences administratives 359, 380.
16 The initial development of the concept of 'fire alarms,' together with that of 'police patrols,' trace to Mathew D McCubbins and Thomas Schwartz, 'Congressional Oversight Overlooked: Police Patrols versus Fire Alarms' (1984) 28 American Journal of Political Science 165. For an application of this concept in a comparative analysis of judicial review of administrative action, see, e.g., Tom Ginsburg, 'Administrative Law and Judicial Control of Agents in Authoritarian Regimes' in Tom Ginsburg and Tamir Moustafa (eds), *Rule by Law: The Politics of Courts in Authoritarian Regimes* (Cambridge University Press 2008) 63.

17 For further discussion, see Lindseth, 'Judicial Review in Administrative Governance: A Theoretical Framework for Comparative Analysis' (n 2).
18 Hamburger (n 12).
19 See, e.g., Paul P Craig, 'The Legitimacy of US Administrative Law and the Foundations of English Administrative Law: Setting the Historical Record Straight' (30 June 2016) <https://papers.ssrn.com/abstract=2802784> accessed September 10, 2023; Adrian Vermeule, '"No" Review of Philip Hamburger, "Is Administrative Law Unlawful?"' (2015) 93 Texas Law Review 1547.
20 Rose-Ackerman (n 1).
21 Nor does he discuss the complex and subtle ways that both administrative and constitutional judges have advanced jurisprudential formulae that permit resistance to claims of European primacy. For an overview, see Peter L Lindseth, 'Primacy vs Supremacy: Comments on John Bell and François Lichère, Contemporary French Administrative Law (CUP 2022)' (*British Association of Comparative Law*, May 18, 2023) <https://british-association-comparative-law.org/2023/05/18/primacy-vs-supremacy-comments-on-john-bell-and-francois-lichere-contemporary-french-administrative-law-cup-2022-by-p-lindseth/> accessed September 11, 2023.
22 See, e.g., Antoine Vauchez and Pierre France, *The Neoliberal Republic: Corporate Lawyers, Statecraft, and the Making of Public-Private France* (Cornell University Press 2021).
23 See n 14 above and accompanying text.
24 Nat'l Fed'n of Indep. Bus. v. DOL, 142 S. Ct. 661 (2022).
25 Biden v. Missouri, 142 S. Ct. 647, 652 (2022), quoting 42 U. S. C. §1395x(e)(9).

Index

Note: for figures, the number span appears in *italics*.